The New York Times

EASY CROSSWORD PUZZLE OMNIBUS VOLUME 13

THE NEW YORK TIMES EASY CROSSWORD PUZZLE OMNIBUS VOLUME 13.
Copyright © 2018 by The New York Times Company. All rights reserved.
Printed in the United States of America. For information, address St. Martin's Press,
175 Fifth Avenue, New York, NY 10010.

www.stmartins.com

All of the puzzles that appear in this work were originally published in
The New York Times from January 10, 2005, to April 12, 2005, or from March 1, 2016,
to February 27, 2018. Copyright © 2005, 2016, 2017, 2018 by The New York Times Company.
All rights reserved. Reprinted by permission.

ISBN 978-1-250-19819-8

Our books may be purchased in bulk for promotional, educational, or business use.
Please contact your local bookseller or the Macmillan Corporate
and Premium Sales Department at 1-800-221-7945, extension 5442, or
by email at MacmillanSpecialMarkets@macmillan.com.

First Edition: September 2018

10 9 8 7 6 5 4 3 2 1

The New York Times

EASY CROSSWORD PUZZLE OMNIBUS VOLUME 13
200 Solvable Puzzles from the Pages of *The New York Times*

Edited by Will Shortz

ST. MARTIN'S GRIFFIN ✠ NEW YORK

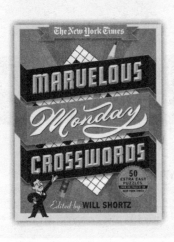

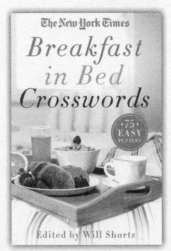

ACROSS

1 "Put a tiger in your tank" brand
5 One watching very, very closely
9 Egyptian vipers
13 Theater ticket price factor
14 Bread spread
15 Like the Parthenon
16 Tri and tri again?
17 Ooze
18 Fine Cremona violin
19 2000–03 Disney Channel series with Shia LaBeouf
22 Pink Floyd's "The Dark Side of the Moon" and "The Wall"
23 Pigeon's perch
24 High-stress hosp. area
25 Follower of wye
26 Daredevil who survived more than 400 bone fractures
31 Not socially acceptable
35 Dawn goddess
36 Advil competitor
37 Oil-producing matter in shale
39 User names on Twitter
41 Each and ___
42 Extension for the White House website
43 Number two: Abbr.
44 Place to buy a Slurpee
48 Like most Twizzlers
49 Accept, as losses
50 "Eek!"
55 Watergate monogram
56 1950 Bette Davis film hinting at something found 15 times in this puzzle
59 Chat up at a bar, say
61 Missing, militarily
62 W.W. II British gun
63 56-Down opener
64 Some shortening
65 ___ Health magazine
66 Throws in
67 Affirmations to captains
68 Art Deco designer of the 1920s and '30s

DOWN

1 Merman of song and stage
2 Forty-niner's tool
3 Birds-and-the-bees class
4 Sumatran swinger, informally
5 Chris Rock, for the 2016 Oscars
6 Sailor's heading
7 Plantation pests
8 Fraction of a ruble
9 Fjord vis-à-vis an ocean
10 Things that are rising globally, according to scientists
11 Personal annoyances
12 Super G needs
15 "What a ___!"
20 "Get it?"
21 Certain rosary counter
25 Nintendo video game princess
27 Shape of some shirt necks
28 It's been a long time
29 Sir ___ McKellen (Gandalf portrayer)
30 For fear that
31 Luau music makers, for short
32 "Forget I said that"
33 Stopped
34 Hollowed out, as an apple
38 Ob-___
39 Kind of lane for carpoolers
40 "___ Maria"
42 Quick vacation
45 Prey for a barracuda
46 Syllables delivered with fingers in the ears
47 Greenwich Village sch.
51 Response to "Who's there?"
52 Flying Pan
53 High jump or 4 × 100-meter relay
54 Brains
55 Cousin of an ostrich
56 Year, in Uruguay
57 Snoozer
58 Bygone G.M. car, appropriately enough
60 Surgery sites, briefly

by Freddie Cheng

2

ACROSS

1 Exterior
6 Acronym on an online help page
9 Treat cruelly
14 Toy company that gave us Frisbee and Slip 'N Slide
15 Sch. in Tempe
16 Type of composition that Bach is noted for
17 They're taken in punishment, so to speak
18 *Hairstyle popularized by Jennifer Aniston's character on "Friends"
20 Omar who portrayed Dr. Zhivago
22 Happy as a __
23 In a cheerful and pleasant manner
26 Write permanently
30 Mysterious sightings that hover
32 Compete (for)
33 The __ Kid (Willie Mays)
35 Tennis match units
36 A low one is good in baseball, in brief
37 Words written by a teacher on a failed test, perhaps
38 Nelson Mandela's org.
39 What the answers to the four starred clues are
42 Fellows
43 So not cool
45 Tell a whopper
46 Mom's mom
47 Tremors
49 Female sheep
50 Does stage work
51 "Oh, one more thing . . ."
52 Set of info about sets of info
55 Opposite of quiet
57 Little blue cartoon characters whose adversary is named Gargamel
60 *Boots brand big in grunge fashion
65 Shatter

66 Sharper than 90°
67 Trivial gripe
68 Jouster's weapon
69 "War and Peace" famously has more than 1,200
70 Crafty
71 Thrill

DOWN

1 Avian hooters
2 "Forget it!"
3 *Hand-held "pets" with digital faces
4 Catherine the Great, for one
5 Bagful on a pitcher's mound
6 Obese
7 Baseball bat wood
8 Stop, as an uprising
9 Many miles off
10 Ohio State student
11 "Blech!"
12 "A Boy Named __" (1969 song)
13 Fish that is long and thin
19 Fish that are flat and wide
21 TV's "Hawaii __"
24 Puts on TV
25 Printed handout
27 *Dance associated with a #1 Los del Rio hit
28 Sidewalk material
29 "Laughing" animals
30 Patriotic Olympics chant
31 Herb sometimes called "sweet anise"

34 Donkey
39 2100, in civilian time
40 Onetime big name in Japanese electronics
41 Monopoly cards
44 Quarantine
46 Word before gas or disaster
48 Obscene material
53 Perfect places
54 Mosey along
56 Metals from lodes
58 Fiction's opposite
59 __-Ball (arcade game)
60 Fist bump
61 __ Victor
62 Make a face for the camera
63 Zero, in a soccer score
64 Very messy room

by Damon Gulczynski

ACROSS

1 Unable to escape
8 Double helix parts
15 Cuckoo, from the Yiddish
16 Hard work
17 Something to check if the lights go out
18 Tree whose berries flavor gin
19 Memorable hurricane of 2011
20 Disneyland locale, briefly
21 Rebellious Turner
22 Lay out plates, silverware, napkins, etc.
28 Princess in "Frozen"
30 __ shark
31 Cabbage for miso soup?
32 Where Samsung is headquartered
34 Cut out (for)
37 "Anatomy of a Murder" director
40 The Taj Mahal, for one
41 Mrs. Eisenhower
42 One of the five W's
43 Poetic measure
44 Step on a ladder
48 Quick-cooking cut of meat
53 An eagle beats it
54 Fracking material
55 Major artery
57 Placate
60 Wrap "worn" by 17-, 22-, 37- and 48-Across?
62 Cafeteria worker's wear
63 Opening on the side of a vest
64 Toads and kangaroos
65 Sci-fi weapon

DOWN

1 "Nothing's broken!"
2 __ network (term in anatomy and artificial intelligence)
3 Building, inventory, cash on hand, etc.
4 Now's partner
5 Unsophisticated sorts
6 Previously
7 __ Romana
8 Virgin Island that's 60% national park
9 Armistice
10 Stampeded toward
11 Walled Spanish city
12 40 winks
13 Game cube
14 Camera inits.
20 No-win chess outcome
23 Marry a cutie on the q.t., maybe
24 Get the show on the road
25 Tiny memory unit
26 Wolfish look
27 Crusty bread slice
29 Sparkling wine region
33 Word found in "time on end," appropriately
34 "The Lion King" lion
35 Prefix with brow
36 Disney bigwig Bob
37 "Fancy seeing you here!"
38 Video game film
39 Broadway auntie
40 Certain bachelor, in personal ads
43 Archipelago parts
45 Pull from the ground
46 Christmas, in Italy
47 Gadget for Parmesan
49 Seize unlawfully
50 __ of Fife (Macduff's title)
51 Like a beaver
52 Destiny
56 Adolph in New York Times history
57 "That feels amazing!"
58 __ Tomé and Príncipe
59 Drink hot chocolate, maybe
60 Like the Beatles, in 1960s lingo
61 Bookmarked thing

by David Steinberg

4

ACROSS

1. "Away with you!"
5. Snide
10. Skier's lift
14. "Nah!"
15. Hawaiian hi
16. Southwest tribe
17. Cheese in spinach pies
18. "Wilbur, get in the game!"
20. "Elijah, press your clothes!"
22. Woman who lent her name to a business-locating "list"
23. Philosopher Immanuel
24. 2005–08 position held by Barack Obama: Abbr.
26. Employees at the Times or Post, for short
27. Wuss
30. Fought head to head, like bighorns
32. End of a univ. email address
33. "Eric, give some to us!"
38. McEntire at the Grand Ole Opry
40. Manage to avoid
41. Glutton's desire
42. "Sally, keep up the fight!"
45. Become the champ
46. Introduction
47. Possessed
49. Ginger __
51. Reverse of NNW
52. Clown's name
54. Potato treat for Hanukkah
56. "Larry, shoot!"
60. "Emma, do that sexy dance!"
63. The "B" of Roy G. Biv
64. Chevy that's now called the Sonic
65. Slow, in music
66. Arm or leg
67. A.L. division for the Yankees
68. "Omigosh!"
69. Talks one's head off

DOWN

1. One practicing a mystical form of Islam
2. Sonny's old singing partner
3. Chevy, e.g.
4. "That was so nice of you!"
5. Rooster destined for dinner
6. Apportion
7. Amphibian that doesn't really cause warts
8. "Frailty, __ name is woman!": Hamlet
9. Deviate erratically from a course
10. Slender
11. Mired
12. Crop-destroying insect
13. Bat mitzvahs and baptisms
19. Totaled, as a bill
21. House Committee on __ and Means
24. Velvety leather
25. Merman in old musicals
27. Novak Djokovic, for one
28. Notion
29. Easy-to-overlook details
30. Boston pro on ice
31. Victim of a bark beetle barrage
34. Considers carefully, as advice
35. Title role for Michael Caine or Jude Law
36. Lake on Ohio's northern border
37. Tear apart
39. Chowed down
43. Cut with an intense light
44. Nod off
48. Unsteady
49. Organisms that cause red tide
50. Tadpole or caterpillar
52. Spree
53. Things to "Twist, Lick, Dunk" in a game app
55. Tie that's hard to untie
56. Decision point in a road
57. Largest pelvic bones
58. Posterior
59. Socialites having a ball
61. Furtive
62. Mai __ (bar order)

by Lynn Lempel

5

ACROSS

1 Tori who sang "Cornflake Girl"
5 Inspiring part of the body?
9 Shot the bull
14 Handed-down tales
15 Bibliographic abbr.
16 As a friend, in France
17 Nut from Hawaii
19 Certain nonviolent protest
20 Elements' various forms
22 Wanna-___ (copycats)
23 Have on
24 Ottoman bigwig
28 Tapioca or taro root
31 "Eternally nameless" Chinese concept
34 Places where knots are tied
36 ___ chi
37 "The Magic Mountain" novelist Thomas
38 Places to do figure eights
41 One preparing for a coming flood
42 Sports org. with a five-ring logo
43 Rudely interrupt, as a comedian
44 "Cheers" bartender
45 Like mud, in an idiom
47 Under siege
48 Lacking adornment
50 Mil. mail center
52 Three main 20-Across . . . with examples included in 38-Across and 11- and 26-Down
59 Parts of combination locks
60 Bursting with joy
61 Leading the pack
62 Middle's middle?
63 Sell
64 Like much chili
65 Greased auto part
66 Just manages, with "out"

DOWN

1 Help for the poor
2 Ring around a castle
3 Toothed whale
4 Ticket specification
5 Alternative to buy
6 Nth degree
7 Babe in the woods
8 Early rock genre for David Bowie
9 Court entertainer
10 ___ Bath (prank call name)
11 Large containers often found atop buildings
12 Abu Dhabi dignitary
13 Loud noise
18 Go down the gangplank
21 Just free of the sea bottom
24 Annoying sorts
25 Giant in lightweight metals
26 Some Mississippi River traffic
27 This-and-that dish
29 City on the Erie Canal
30 The U.N.'s ___ Ki-moon
32 Site for a parolee tracking device
33 Get-go
35 Went by sloop, say
37 Computer alternatives to touchpads
39 "Piggy"
40 Bring to 212° again
45 Fried chicken option
46 Welch of "Myra Breckinridge"
49 Divvy up
51 A vital sign
52 It's 1 for 90°
53 Mother of Helen of Troy
54 Alpine goat
55 Run-down tavern
56 Show one's nerdy side, with "out"
57 Youngest Brontë
58 Yardsticks: Abbr.
59 Qty. at a bakery

by Gordon Johnson

6

ACROSS

1 Psychedelic drug
4 Davenport
8 Messy
14 Not their
15 Billiards game
16 Knuckle rub
17 #1 success
19 Two of them don't make a right
20 Author Zola
21 Jean ___, old-time French pirate with a base in New Orleans
23 Lady of Lima
25 Likeliest time for a traffic jam
28 Fury
29 Santa's little helper
31 Hi-___ graphics
32 G.I. entertainers
33 Banks of "America's Next Top Model"
35 Baseball hit that doesn't go far
37 English class assignment
39 Rubbish pile
42 "Goodbye, mon ami!"
45 Luge, e.g.
46 "Be on the lookout" messages, for short
50 Score in baseball
51 Baking meas.
53 No longer in the game: Abbr.
55 Deserter of a sinking ship
56 It's at the end of the line
59 Dawning period
61 Beer can opener
63 "That's enough out of you!"
64 Criticized angrily, with "out"
66 Top-secret . . . or a hint to 17-, 25-, 39- and 56-Across (AND 66-Across!)
68 Not filled, as a part
69 Not fat
70 Grp. that meets after school
71 Nevertheless
72 Not fooled by
73 Oscar- and Grammy-winning singer Smith

DOWN

1 Goes bonkers
2 Suitable for warm weather
3 Sink-side rack
4 Ball, geometrically
5 "That's amazing!"
6 Wrap for leftover food
7 Place for a bride and groom
8 Foolhardy
9 Body of water between Denmark and Scotland
10 A candy lover has a sweet one
11 Like granite and basalt
12 Like, in slang
13 "I agree"
18 ___-mo
22 Advance, as a cause
24 Jessica of "Sin City"
26 ___ Today
27 Cowboy Rogers
30 Hard-to-please sort
34 Consumed
36 Org. in which Ducks play with pucks
38 Relaxing getaway
40 Cold-blooded
41 Garden with forbidden fruit
42 Relative of "Bowwow!"
43 Busted boozer's offense, for short
44 Where "no one can hear you scream," per "Alien"
47 Union agreements, informally?
48 Coffee shop employee
49 Action star Jason
52 Did some business with
54 Electronic music genre
57 What "to err is"
58 Artist Frida
60 "Do ___ Diddy Diddy" (1964 #1 hit)
62 Good, in Guatemala
64 Regret
65 Part of S.A.S.E.: Abbr.
67 Used a davenport

by Michael Hawkins

ACROSS

1 Fail big-time
5 To any degree
10 Cash caches, briefly
14 "Garfield" drooler
15 Artoo-___
16 Pan handler
17 ___ Raton, Fla.
18 Clear, in a way
19 Once-popular roadside chain, familiarly
20 Losing some love handles, say
22 "Yes sir" overseas
24 Manhattan neighborhood next to SoHo
26 ___ bear
30 Maxim magazine's intended audience
31 Arouse, as curiosity
36 French female friend
37 The "common" sort is said to be not so common
39 Yawn-provoking
40 Walmart competitor
42 Fiji competitor
44 Where scrubs are worn, for short
45 "Mazel ___!"
47 Floor coat
48 Bosox great Carl, familiarly
49 They're never away
52 Pet lovers' org.
55 Precollege exams
56 Car radio button
60 Tiniest bit
62 Commercial ending with Water
63 Botanist's specialty
64 One way of ordering things, like all the consonants in rows three, six and nine
67 Unexpected hit
68 Just as good
69 Sister fast-food chain of Carl's Jr.
70 Browning's "How Do I Love Thee?" and others

DOWN

1 Common clown name
2 Consume too much of, in brief
3 Sheet rock?
4 Rosary part
5 Puff ___
6 Golf reservation
7 Org. shifted to the Dept. of Justice in 2003
8 Eases
9 Sudoku solver's need
10 Arthritis symptom
11 SpongeBob or Scooby-Doo
12 Self-confidence, slangily
13 Hershey toffee bar
21 "Give ___ rest!"
23 Easy mark
25 Title rat of a 1972 film
26 Bruce Lee's role in TV's "The Green Hornet"
27 Longtime Sudanese president ___ al-Bashir
28 Puts on TV
29 One of six for an insect
32 Fingers, as a perp
33 Where ships get loaded
34 Bone below the elbow
35 Part of QE2: Abbr.
37 Defeat soundly
38 Red-coated cheeses
41 D.D.E.'s charge in W.W. II
43 Timber feller
46 Sunset prayer service
47 New York's ___ Glen State Park
49 Discussed, with "out"
50 Trot or canter
51 California's ___ Sea
52 Cut drastically, as prices
53 Big name in windows
54 Lark
57 Wavy-patterned fabric
58 Concern for a fall gardener
59 Thick locks
61 3M product
63 Be a toady
65 Stinger
66 Workplace for some veterinarians

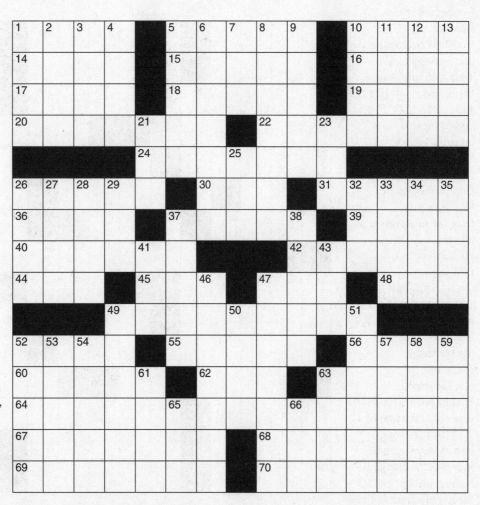

by Don Gagliardo and Zhouqin Burnikel

ACROSS

1 Bills and coins
5 Light punishment on wrists
10 Sumptuously furnished
14 Pear-shaped stringed instrument
15 Hebrew school reading
16 Throw a chip in the pot
17 Bump on the neck
19 Letter-shaped girder
20 Like monkeys and 59-Downs
21 Key with no sharps or flats
23 What angry bees do
24 Issue that's too dangerous to touch
27 Charged particle
28 Quickly
30 Connected to the Internet
31 Constant complainer
33 State-of-the-__
34 Tennis champ Agassi
35 Winsome . . . or like the ends of 17-, 24-, 51- and 58-Across, to a punster?
39 Steeple
42 Sloe __ fizz
43 Completely gratify
47 Having a gun
48 Like the numerals I, V, X and L
50 Highest setting, informally
51 Grand pooh-bah
53 100-meter dash or shot put
55 Itzhak Perlman's instrument
56 Come out
57 Huckleberry __
58 Hand-blown wine bottle that's also the title of a 1968 Beatles song
61 Favorable margin
62 Increase the energy of
63 Scored 100 on
64 Sleep indicators in the comics
65 Many a middle schooler
66 Young fellows

DOWN

1 Like rock music from the 1950s–'70s, now
2 Tax fraud investigator
3 Something a long-distance runner needs
4 Encircle
5 __ Lee of Marvel Comics
6 Cut (off)
7 Painter/poet Jean __
8 Gourmet's heightened sense
9 Curly's replacement in the Three Stooges
10 "Sunflowers" and "Water Lilies"
11 In a plane or train
12 Opposite of a bench player
13 His counterpart
18 Multigenerational tale
22 Early caucusgoer
24 Aesop character who lost a race
25 Shape of a stop sign
26 Appreciative poem
29 Easy-to-chew food
32 Nitty-gritty
36 One of two on a bike
37 Capital of Peru
38 Any port __ storm
39 Used a bench
40 Bring home the bacon, so to speak
41 Encroach (on)
44 "Sweet land of liberty," in song
45 Did a stylized ballroom dance
46 Widens
48 Was almost out of supplies
49 "Finding __" (2003 Pixar film)
52 When one sees stars
54 Open to bribery
56 Channel that describes itself as "The worldwide leader in sports"
57 Hat with a tassel
59 Jungle swinger
60 Begin litigation

by Gary Cee

ACROSS

1 Volleyball actions between bumps and spikes
5 Name on an orange-and-white truck
10 "Hey, buddy!"
14 "What ___" (1996 Sublime hit)
15 Some chip dip
16 Ceremony
17 What red markers may indicate on 59-Acrosses
19 Altar exchange
20 Even (with)
21 Cat in a record store
23 To date
24 Musician Reed or Rawls
26 Tripoli's land
27 Musical name after Tori or before Lee
29 Ancestor of the harmonica
31 Supporter
32 Top-shelf
33 1960s Egyptian president
37 "___ My Children"
38 Some links holes . . . with a hint to the circled letters
40 ___-Magnon
41 Capital of Saudi Arabia
43 Capital of Norway
44 Big export of Saudi Arabia and Norway
45 Lithe
47 When summer officially starts
48 Like a disciplinarian's talk
51 Luau instrument, informally
52 Symbol of power, with "the"
53 Like some lights
55 Scored, as on a 59-Across
58 "Out of Africa" author Dinesen
59 18 holes, often
62 Suffix with disk
63 Indian ___
64 Pipeline problem

65 Animal that's sometimes frozen in the headlights
66 Like a chimney sweep
67 Nobel winner Wiesel

DOWN

1 Missile ___
2 Op-ed columnist Timothy
3 "Act quickly! This offer will end very soon!"
4 Supporting stalks
5 Country in a classic Beatles title
6 Overhead expense?
7 Pub order
8 Exhausts
9 Z's position
10 Outhouses
11 Obsolescent designation in the music business
12 Expressionless
13 Girl's name that's a benefit in reverse?
18 Sup
22 Texas home of the Sun Bowl
24 Early filmmaker Fritz
25 It just took this before "I fell so hard in love with you," in a 1960s hit
27 Way off
28 Burkina Faso neighbor
29 Some stuffed bears
30 Hearth
32 Doing sums
34 Rascal
35 "___ go bragh!"

36 Something cast
39 Salinger title girl
42 Morning TV weatherman
46 Gas brand with an arrow in its logo
47 "Always on Time" rapper
48 Recoiled (from)
49 Flavor
50 Thrill
52 World leader with a distinctive jacket
54 Divas have big ones
55 Sch. overlooking Harlem
56 Morales of "La Bamba"
57 Hockey feint
60 Many an August birth
61 What beef marbling is

by Peter A. Collins

ACROSS

1 Republican grp.
4 Owns up to
10 That guy
13 "Cat __ Hot Tin Roof"
14 Billionaire Aristotle
15 Point of no return?
16 Lunar New Year in Vietnam
17 Actor who portrayed Newman on "Seinfeld"
19 Be behind
21 "Honest!"
22 Obvious indication
26 Fascinated by
27 Explore, as the Internet
28 Mortarboard attachment
31 Glock, e.g.
34 It may keep cafeteria food warm
38 In time past
39 Red or yellow card issuer
41 Channel for Anderson Cooper
42 Neither's partner
43 Billiards variant
46 Prefix with intestinal
48 "Come on, no cheating"
50 Went in haste
51 Commotion
54 Ushers' offerings
57 Native of Akron or Cleveland
60 Dante's "La Vita __" ("The New Life")
61 Rural area . . . or what can be found in each set of circled letters?
64 Spoiled
67 "Able was I __ I saw Elba"
68 Notable products of Persia
69 Poem "to" somebody or something
70 Thumbs-up response
71 Helping after seconds
72 Heed the coxswain

DOWN

1 Understood
2 Result of dividing any nonzero number by itself
3 James whose novels have sold more than 300 million copies
4 Diarist Nin
5 Naturally illuminated
6 Yahoo alternative
7 Suffix with expert
8 Kind of torch on "Survivor"
9 ID thieves' targets
10 Actress Uta
11 Apple messaging software
12 The first "M" in MGM
14 Man __
18 Volunteer's response
20 Flat floater
22 Channel with hearings
23 Mario's video game brother
24 Exasperated cry
25 Tiny div. of a minute
29 Serenaded
30 One of three active volcanoes in Italy
32 "Kill __ killed"
33 Thumb (through)
35 Like 1947's Taft-Hartley Act
36 Edible mushroom
37 Herders' sticks
40 Commotion
44 Kindle download
45 Rap's __ Kim
47 Prison weapon
49 __ and raved
51 Maguire of Hollywood
52 Midway alternative
53 Does some kitchen prep work
55 Mongolian tents
56 All students at Eton
58 A debit card is linked to one: Abbr.
59 "The Daily Show" host Trevor
62 Mentalist Geller
63 "Wait Wait . . . Don't Tell Me!" airer
65 Commotion
66 It might get your feet wet

by David Kwong

ACROSS

1 Like the best kind of vacation
5 Look over
8 Olympian's achievement
13 First James Bond film
14 Crew chief
15 "You think I won't try that?!"
16 Pagoda placement consideration, often
18 Reddish-brown
19 Climate features of equatorial countries
21 What a mute button affects
24 Radon regulators, in brief
25 ___ Tin Tin
26 Savior, in popular parlance
30 Release
32 Fluffy trio?
33 Big name in bandages and hardware
34 Baked or stoned
35 Prognostication tool
40 First female Nobelist, 1903
42 LinkedIn profile, e.g.
43 Band-___
46 Onetime center of Los Angeles
47 Clumps of sugar on a stick
50 Kind of school
51 Anaheim nine, on scoreboards
53 Loosen, as a knot
54 Cards #53 and #54 in a deck . . . or a hint to the answers to 19-, 26-, 35- and 47-Across
59 Home of the National Gallery of Canada
60 Partied like it was 1999
64 Pete who co-wrote "If I Had a Hammer"
65 Home of the Burning Man festival: Abbr.
66 Rim
67 Broke off

68 James Bond, e.g.
69 Speckled steed

DOWN

1 JPEG alternative
2 "___ we done here?"
3 It might have a bed icon on a highway sign
4 Doesn't give one's full effort
5 Reverberate
6 B.Y.O.B. part
7 Freeway sign
8 It last erupted in 1984
9 Once, once
10 Cactus, for one
11 Explorer Vespucci
12 Turndown to the suggestion "We should . . ."

15 Sound that can prevent sleeping at night
17 Loafer, e.g.
20 Itsy-bitsy
21 Knock the socks off
22 TV band above channel 13, in brief
23 Damaged the reputation of
27 Dines on
28 Mo. when the Supreme Court reconvenes
29 Two-time Grammy winner Bryson
31 Photo blowup: Abbr.
36 Inlet
37 Like old newspaper clippings
38 D.M.V. issuance: Abbr.

39 ___ choy
40 Write music
41 Like leftovers
44 Dictator Amin
45 Bottleful at a salon
47 Rule Gandhi opposed
48 Terse
49 R.S.V.P.
52 Many miles away
55 Road hazard?
56 Dominates, informally
57 Stay good
58 Go green?
61 Engagement-ending words
62 Airport alternative to JFK
63 ___ of iniquity

by Dan Schoenholz

ACROSS

1 *With 9-Across, loose-fitting bottoms
6 Mini-albums, briefly
9 *See 1-Across
14 Hate
15 Prefix with liberal or conservative
16 Legend automaker
17 Incline
18 Grade of wine
19 Who thought of "The Thinker"
20 ___ Sabe (the Lone Ranger, to Tonto)
21 Tedious task
23 Ready for picking
24 *Where you can hear a pin drop
27 Kind of tip, in baseball
28 Emulates Jay Z
29 Small recipe amt.
32 Unfiltered and unpasteurized brew
34 Grp. holding after-school events
37 Island ring
39 Guacamole or salsa
40 Soft-serve ice cream shape
42 Sounded like a cow
43 Corroded
44 Up to the point that
45 Versailles and others
47 Vacationers to Vail may carry them
49 Wed. follower
50 Run up ___ (owe)
51 Maidenform product
53 Keeps for oneself . . . or features of the answers to all the starred clues
57 Snitch (on)
60 Features of biology classes
62 "Kiss me, I'm ___" (T-shirt slogan)
63 Jay who preceded Jimmy Fallon
64 Hideous
65 "Won't you let me?"
66 The "O's" of Cheerios
67 Deeply regretted
68 "Oh, shucks!"
69 Poetic paeans

DOWN

1 Poe's "The ___ of Amontillado"
2 Having what it takes
3 Diamond shape
4 Magically vanish
5 It might be found in a deposit
6 Stuffed tortillas
7 Evita of "Evita"
8 Reaction from a sore loser
9 4, maybe, on a golf hole
10 Nuts from oaks
11 Skin flick
12 Stumble
13 Rational
21 One of 77 in this puzzle
22 Carrier to the Holy Land
25 Quadrennial soccer event
26 Hairy Halloween rentals
29 Drive (down)
30 Athenian colonnade
31 *Where you might be behind the eight ball
33 Illuminated
34 *Falafel holder
35 Pre-calc course
36 "___ fair in love and war"
38 Wife of Jacob
41 Lady hoopsters' org.
46 Beethoven's Symphony No. 3
48 ___ Lee Gifford (morning TV host)
51 Image of a speeding car, maybe
52 Prego competitor
54 Stick in one's ___
55 Double-decker checker
56 Villa d'___
58 Get into a poker game, say
59 Something to do to a salad or coin
61 Hip-hop's ___ tha Kyd
63 Place to go in Britain?

by Ron Toth and Zhouqin Burnikel

13

ACROSS

1 Playwright Fugard
6 Airline to Stockholm
9 Narnia nabob
14 SeaWorld attraction
15 Legendary boy king
16 Belt holder
17 Fast-food kitchen fixture
18 A retirement party might toast the end of one
19 Jon of "Two and a Half Men"
20 Anthem preposition
21 Heartthrob Zac
23 Kind of admiral
24 Dancer and Prancer
26 Drill attachment with teeth
28 Like a fully initiated Mafia member
29 Like good soil
31 Place for a chaise longue
32 Culinarian who cries "Bam!"
34 Bunker fill
36 Eastern path
37 Tip, as a hat
39 Brief admission of responsibility
41 "The Racer's Edge"
44 Sandwich with toothpicks
46 Look for truffles as a pig might
50 Faux
52 National alternative
54 Relative of "Smash!"
55 Most twisted, as humor
57 Common deli order . . . or a literal occurrence five times in this puzzle
59 "Shoot!"
60 53-Down product
61 Always, poetically
62 Say something bleep-worthy
63 Bran source
64 ___ of Strength (Festivus rite)
66 Firearm, slangily
67 Actress Long
68 "Is there no ___ this?"

69 Longest continental range in the world
70 Director Lee
71 Either of the twin child stars of "Full House"

DOWN

1 "In my opinion . . ."
2 Time to which you "spring forward" in daylight saving
3 Tractor-drawn fall activity
4 Kipling's "Follow Me ___"
5 Brought in
6 Non-mono, say
7 Night lights
8 "South Park" boy
9 Capital of Ghana
10 Sharp
11 Wager
12 Another name for "My Country, 'Tis of Thee"
13 "All Things Considered" network
22 Didn't land, as a joke
25 Dorkmeister
26 Pattern of symptoms
27 Fight-ending letters
30 ___ tai
33 Quadrennial games org.
35 One worshiped in Rome
38 Suffix with pocket
40 In the dumps
41 Opposite NNE
42 Add haphazardly
43 Give careful attention
45 Kingdom on the Persian Gulf
47 Clothes, slangily
48 Complete outfit for a newborn
49 Poet/essayist who wrote "To be great is to be misunderstood"
51 Threaten
53 Kenmore alternative
56 Tender spots
58 "___ ed Euridice" (Gluck opera)
60 Spanish lady
62 Where one might hear oohs and aahs
65 Blowup: Abbr.

by Alan Derkazarian

ACROSS

1 Smooth-talking
5 "___ and Punishment"
10 Number in a quartet
14 Capital of Italia
15 Fable writer
16 "___ Karenina"
17 Send ___ errand
18 *1938 Horse of the Year
20 Relax
22 Artificial jewelry
23 Unsophisticated sort
24 See 45-Across
26 Actress/singer Pia
29 Mensch
32 Praise highly
33 Scarlett O'Hara, for one
34 "___ the land of the free . . ."
36 Window base
37 Moolah . . . or the makeup of the ends of the answers to the starred clues
38 Lion's locks
39 Bathwater tester
40 "The Lorax" author
41 About 39 inches, in England
42 Onetime rival of Facebook
44 Untrustworthy sort
45 With 24-Across, body of water that's in four African countries
46 Condé ___ (magazine company)
47 Watering spot in the desert
50 KEY USED FOR THIS CLUE
54 *Hunk
57 Like most businesses between 9 to 5
58 There's no place like it
59 Orchard
60 Prefix with dynamic
61 Roman god of love
62 Idiot, in Canadian lingo
63 Source of linseed oil

DOWN

1 Grasp, in slang
2 Actress Anderson who was once married to 21-Down
3 Popular desktop computer
4 *Provide funds for
5 Yellow-skinned melon
6 Athlete/model Gabrielle
7 Dinesen who wrote "Out of Africa"
8 Flash ___ (faddish assembly)
9 Prefix with -dermis
10 Building front
11 Burden
12 Corporate division
13 Put on a scale from 1 to 10, say
19 Garden shovel
21 Actor Reynolds who was once married to 2-Down
24 Pepsi and RC
25 "Please ___" (operator's request)
26 Verve
27 Universal truth
28 Longtime name in Chicago politics
29 V fliers
30 Farm animals that butt
31 Romance or science fiction
33 Actor Willis
35 Fishing line holder
37 A toucan has a colorful one
38 *"Bat Out of Hell" singer
40 Jerk
41 Pigsty
43 Mini-burger
44 Original judge on "The People's Court"
46 Trustingly innocent
47 Employee protection org.
48 Part of a molecule
49 Heavyweight wrestling
50 Corp. money managers
51 German auto make
52 Michael of "Arrested Development"
53 Kentucky's Fort ___
55 "Yuck!"
56 To's partner

by Janice Luttrell

ACROSS

1 Practice boxing
5 Dr. who's done 19-Down for Dr Pepper
8 Tree houses?
13 Auricle's site
15 Produced, as coins
16 Breadwinner
17 Kitchen covers
18 Former House leader Nancy
19 "The Fox and the Crow" storyteller
20 Cheerleader's cheer
21 2011 World Series champs, informally
24 Office V.I.P.
27 Pageant winners' wear
29 Alternative to Enterprise
30 Call letters?
33 Tizzy
34 Navy student, informally
35 Be rough with, in a way
36 Warning appropriate for this puzzle?
38 90° turn
39 Moon of Mars
41 Tombstone lawman
42 Father's study: Abbr.
43 Go ___ for (defend)
44 Agreed
46 Circus performer with a ball
47 Veil material
48 Jodie Foster and Meryl Streep, collegiately
52 Reason to use a visor
54 Opera's Tebaldi
56 Name repeatedly sung in Rossini's "Largo al factotum"
58 One of the "E's" in E.E.C.
60 Stranded due to frigid weather
61 Shoal
62 Anatomical pouch
63 Christmas ___
64 Some savings, for short

DOWN

1 Too sentimental
2 Food processor setting
3 Bikini, for one
4 Not take it anymore
5 Names in someone's honor
6 Girl's name that's a homophone for a boy's name
7 Make a goof
8 Barely beats
9 Attired, as a judge
10 "Buy" or "sell" directive at a specified price
11 Start of a countdown
12 1960s protest grp.
14 Sue Grafton's "___ for Ricochet"
15 Fannie ___ (securities)
19 Commercials
22 Locality
23 Unfair treatment
25 Arena entrance feature
26 George ___, longtime maestro of the Cleveland Orchestra
28 "___ the Sheriff" (1974 #1 hit)
29 Land animal whose closest living relatives include whales
30 Data in a daily planner: Abbr.
31 North America's largest alpine lake
32 Double, in baseball lingo
34 Certain homicide, in police lingo
37 Something that may be trimmed or rigged
40 "Oh! Susanna" and others
44 Take to court
45 Obi-Wan ___
47 High-tech 1982 Disney movie
49 Tennessee senator ___ Alexander
50 Turner autobiography
51 Fires
53 Rossini's "Largo al factotum," e.g.
55 Not continue
56 Lie a little
57 Hosp. locale
58 Suffix with Japan
59 Cleveland cager, for short

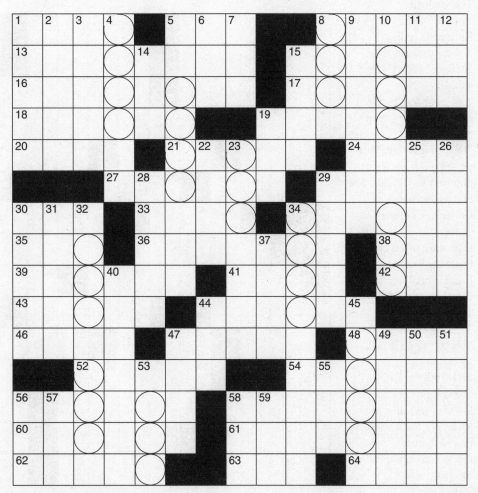

by David J. Kahn

ACROSS

1 Go out with __
6 Toy with a tail
10 "Get __ writing"
14 "Vive __!" (old French cry)
15 Score after deuce
16 U2 lead singer
17 Walter who created Woody Woodpecker
18 64-, 65- and 66-Across, in this puzzle
20 Heavy vehicle that smooths a road surface
22 Time in history
23 Ernie of the P.G.A.
24 Antipoverty agcy.
25 Goof up
26 Samurai sash
27 __ Trueheart, Dick Tracy's love
29 The year 2051
31 Rotisserie rod
32 TV series with "NY," "Miami" and "Cyber" spinoffs
34 Thoroughfare in the name of Springsteen's band
37 "Don't mess with" him, per an old song lyric . . . or a hint to 18-, 20-, 55- and 58-Across
39 College or company starter
40 Big name in ice cream
41 Putter or 9-iron
42 Promotional hoopla
44 Court legend Arthur
48 Thornton Wilder's "__ Town"
49 "I love," to a Latin lover
51 Sixteenths of lbs.
53 Dress (up)
54 K-O connector
55 Means of fortunetelling
58 Audio feature that comes standard on cars
60 Provoked
61 Gloomy

62 Card with the headings "Appetizers," "Entrees" and "Desserts"
63 Overly anxious
64 Rotating car part
65 Mumbai titles
66 Proverbial waste maker

DOWN

1 Completely ready
2 John, Paul, George or Ringo
3 James of "Gunsmoke"
4 The "N" of N.B.
5 Thingamabob
6 Explosion sound
7 TV's discontinued "American __"
8 Big name in golf balls
9 Exit's opposite
10 "Let's Build a Smarter Planet" co.
11 Ripped the wrapping off
12 Circling the earth, say
13 "Oh, hang on a minute!"
19 Former Bruin Bobby
21 Jog the memory of
28 Use elbow grease
30 Apprehensive
31 "Ciao!"
33 One of the seven "deadly" things
35 Pluck, as an eyebrow
36 Crimson, e.g.
37 Heavy-hearted
38 Witness
39 Discombobulate
41 Piña __ (fruity drink)
43 Permeable
45 Beach building supports
46 "I kid you not!"
47 Easter dip
49 Mo. before May
50 Sirs' partners
52 Politico Palin
56 5×5 crossword, e.g.
57 Actress Merrill
59 Field fare for a G.I.

by Betty Keller

ACROSS

1 Medieval drudges
6 Word before shot or season
9 Imbecile
13 Gives a heads-up
15 Protection provided by military planes
17 Watch in astonishment
18 Scandal surrounding copy editors' proofreading marks?
19 Scandal involving Tesla C.E.O. Musk?
21 Completely fine
22 Some hosp. tests
23 Facilitate
25 Storyteller Wilhelm or Jakob
28 Scandal affecting iPhone owners?
33 ___ Canyon Park (running spot in the Hollywood Hills)
35 Restaurant dip for bread
36 Do the breaststroke, say
37 N.Y.C. subway inits.
38 "Hamilton," e.g.
41 Sleeve filler
42 Title on "Downton Abbey"
44 TV-watching room
45 Rink game
47 Scandal in the aftermath of a tsunami?
50 Removes, as a layer
51 Small, brown songbird
52 "Toodles!"
54 Words of sympathy
57 Scandal that implicates a detective?
61 Scandal depicted in "Avatar"?
64 "Amen to that!"
65 Popular strength-training program
66 Be a pilot
67 Warmonger
68 Shirt for a workout
69 Come after

DOWN

1 Wise one
2 Its inaugural flight was in 1948
3 Pickup that gets picked up, perhaps
4 Ally who's not completely an ally
5 Aggressive manager for a child star
6 Lose vibrancy
7 Bit of fiction
8 Address you can't enter into a GPS
9 Angled golf holes
10 Shape of the president's office
11 Jared of "Dallas Buyers Club"
12 Long hike
14 Doe's mate
16 Desist
20 Decidedly not-lax grp. at LAX
23 Filmdom's "The Bible," e.g.
24 Deity to 1.5+ billion
25 "Good ___!"
26 Nonurban
27 Course that might be labeled "101"
29 North, south, east or west
30 Up from bed
31 Ready for bed
32 TV's "Oscars"
34 Wink accompanier
39 Actor Bean, whose first name looks like it rhymes with his last, but doesn't
40 Frequent theme for Adele
43 Not having much chance of failure
46 "Much to my ___ . . ."
48 Bottom-of-the-barrel stuff
49 Hellenic "H"
53 Former Sanyo competitor
54 Ruler division
55 ___ mia (Italian term of endearment)
56 Declare assuredly
57 Head of the French department?
58 Ones helping a public prosecutor, for short
59 Ballerina's wear
60 Olympics sword
62 Back on board
63 Suit accessory

by Finn Vigeland

18

ACROSS

1 Coke rival
6 Popular hairstyle in the 1960s
10 "No ifs, ___ . . ."
14 Birdlike
15 Next year's jr.
16 Wife of Jacob
17 Electric car maker
18 8:00–11:00 p.m., TV-wise
20 Anticipate
22 Actress Strahovski of "Dexter" and "Chuck"
23 ABAB in a poem, e.g.
27 Tax form ID
28 Superiors of sarges
29 Wildcat with tufted ears
31 "So gross!"
32 D-E-A-D dead
35 Harmonizes, informally
39 Large or extra-large
41 Copycat's comment . . . or, phonetically, a hint to this puzzle's theme
43 Émile of the Dreyfus Affair
44 Mattress brand
46 "Thanks," in Deutschland
48 Letter between sigma and upsilon
49 Roman marketplaces
51 Breaks off a romantic relationship
53 Lawyers' org.
56 Greeting to a returning soldier, maybe
59 V.I.P.
61 Coffee shop lure
62 What a finger-pointer "plays"
64 Robbery at a police station, e.g.
68 Abbr. in a footnote
69 Prefix with -logical
70 Roast host
71 Many millennia
72 Those, in Mexico
73 One side of a Faustian bargain

DOWN

1 Butter serving
2 Night before a holiday
3 Detectives, for short
4 Deli meat
5 Seven days from now
6 Savory jelly
7 ". . . and so on and so ___"
8 Sch. in Troy, N.Y.
9 "Good heavens!"
10 Choir voice
11 Dresden denials
12 Curses
13 Luster
19 Odds' opposite
21 Indian state known for its tea and silk
23 Like non-oyster months
24 Comic Mandel
25 "Holy moly!"
26 John who sang "Philadelphia Freedom"
30 End run of the alphabet
33 Power a bike
34 Tony winner Hagen
36 "On the contrary!"
37 Demand by right
38 Pan-frying instruction
40 Santa's little helper
42 Vermont skiing destination
45 "Ouch, that hurts!"
47 All the people attacking you
50 Jackson who was on five World Series-winning teams in the 1970s
52 Cosmic order, in Buddhism
53 Hoffman of 1960s radicalism
54 "The Hobbit" hero Baggins
55 Once more
57 One of many Hitchcock appearances in his own films
58 Sandwich cookies now sold by Mondelez
60 Iraq war concerns, for short
63 Commercials
65 Halloween mo.
66 Teachers' org.
67 Tokyo currency

by Paula Gamache

ACROSS

1 Laid up
5 Toward a boat's wake
10 Kindergarten lesson
14 Big name in denim
15 Equestrian, e.g.
16 Lummox
17 Wax makers
18 Dough
19 Political columnist Klein
20 How the Great Emancipator got around?
23 Controversially patented thing
24 Source of a common allergy
25 How the star of the Indiana Jones films got around?
31 Leveled
32 See 41-Across
33 "Leave!"
35 Give proper attribution
36 Embroidery loop
38 "Hey, __" (casual greeting)
39 Gobbled up
40 Mother of Helen
41 With 32-Across, place to snorkel
42 How a Seattle Mariner great got around?
46 "Sure"
47 __ empty stomach
48 How Queen's former frontman got around?
56 Word before window or end
57 Its capital is Oranjestad
58 List-ending abbr.
59 __ buco
60 City near Avignon
61 All the __
62 Underworld river
63 Something a composer composes
64 Bogus

DOWN

1 Actress Jessica
2 Channel that airs "Sherlock," with "the"
3 __ since
4 Clash (with)
5 Giorgio of fashion
6 Wetlands and tundra, e.g.
7 Kerfuffles
8 Cut down
9 Something to keep track of?
10 One of the Furies
11 Buffoon
12 Permanent thing?
13 "South Park" boy
21 What's rounded up in a roundup
22 "__ said!"
25 Where Toussaint L'Ouverture led a revolt
26 Coyolxauhqui worshiper
27 Penguin predators
28 Prefix with realism
29 Howard __, "The Fountainhead" protagonist
30 Home of the world's tallest building, completed in 2009
31 Panasonic competitor
34 __ Avivian
36 Xerxes' people
37 Swear words?
38 They might bar bargoers
40 Emulated Pinocchio
41 Peter the Great, for one
43 Longtime Oreo competitor
44 Like the mood in a losing locker room
45 Agita
48 Big dos
49 Staff break?
50 Like one-star puzzles
51 "South Park" boy
52 __ wrestler
53 Salt flats location
54 Music of Mumbai
55 Proto-matter of the universe

by John Westwig

20

ACROSS

1 Protein-rich bean
5 Prices
10 Nursery school, informally
14 "Wait __!" ("Hold on!")
15 "Tiny Bubbles" singer
16 "Arsenic and Old __"
17 Article of tropical apparel . . . whose start is a state nickname for the state indicated by the circled squares
19 Arthur who was king of the court?
20 Julie __, portrayer of Claire on "Modern Family"
21 Go from one social gathering to another
23 Facebook __ (collection of posts)
26 Sought legal redress
27 Catchphrase shouted in "Jerry Maguire" . . . whose start is a state nickname for the state indicated by the circled squares
33 1/24 of a day
34 Designer's degree, for short
35 Samsung Galaxy, e.g.
36 Naval leader: Abbr.
37 Secretariat's mother, for one . . . whose start is a state nickname for the state indicated by the circled squares
40 Boise's state: Abbr.
41 Officer below a captain, slangily
43 Punk rock subgenre
44 A-1 tennis server
45 Emergency worker . . . whose start is a state nickname for the state indicated by the circled squares
49 __ Lee, creator of Spider-Man
50 Secretariat's father, for one
51 Succession
55 Dressed to the __
59 Detective's lead
60 Biblical idol . . . whose start is a state nickname for the state indicated by the circled squares

63 Landed
64 Peeved
65 Excursion
66 Seized vehicle, informally
67 Superbright colors
68 Whole lot

DOWN

1 Discontinued Swedish car
2 Norwegian capital
3 "Ouch!"
4 Want badly
5 Conservative investments, briefly
6 La-la lead-in
7 Little scissor cut
8 Beat handily
9 "You can say that again!"
10 Moldable kids' stuff
11 Impulsive
12 Returned call?
13 Not go bad
18 All over again
22 Arizona home of the nation's largest public university
24 Madame Bovary
25 Stand up to
27 "Me, too!"
28 Funny business
29 Domesticates
30 Feature of a neat drink
31 What can follow week or rear
32 2016, e.g.
33 50%
37 Davis of "What Ever Happened to Baby Jane?"
38 Volume enhancers
39 Cheer (for)
42 Give, as a passport or parking ticket

44 Druggies, e.g.
46 Welcomed, as the new 32-Down
47 "We want more!," at a concert
48 Sam for whom Georgia Tech's School of International Affairs is named
51 Surgery memento
52 Palindromic fashion magazine
53 Witticism
54 Nevada city
56 Pusher buster
57 Kazan who directed "On the Waterfront"
58 Law force in 1960–'70s TV's "Ironside"
61 Lair
62 Paper cutters, briefly?

by Dan Schoenholz

21

ACROSS

1 Some rote learning
5 Cutup
10 Not ___ many words
14 "You make me laugh"
15 Sponsorship
16 Oracle
17 Bosnian, e.g.
18 Longtime Orioles manager in the Baseball Hall of Fame
20 El-overseeing org.
21 TV Guide chart, for short
22 "Buenos ___!"
23 Co-author of the Federalist Papers
25 Fathers, to tots
27 More foolish
28 Big name in skateboarding
31 "Dude!"
32 9-3 automaker
33 Covert org.
34 "The Broken Tower" poet
38 "Annie" characters
41 Alsace assents
42 Havens
46 Boy genius of old teen fiction
49 Team esteem
50 Relative of a blintz
51 Best Picture of 2014 . . . or what 18-, 23-, 28-, 34-, 46- and 56-Across each is?
52 Parts of small intestines
53 Famed synthesizer
55 Genre first included in the Rock and Roll Hall of Fame in 2007
56 "Network" Oscar winner
58 ___ Minor
60 Like fine wines and cheeses
61 Put into office
62 Appearance
63 Mouthfuls of chewing gum
64 Poking around in other people's business
65 Lead-in to masochism

DOWN

1 Sounds of comprehension
2 One set in a "Romeo and Juliet" production
3 Georgia county of which 4-Down is the seat
4 Oldest city in Georgia
5 "Veni, vidi, vici" speaker
6 Like a faulty pipe
7 Shrek, e.g.
8 Word repeated before "West" in a film and 1960s TV series
9 Its capital is Sydney: Abbr.
10 Book after Song of Solomon
11 Many a resident on Lake Tahoe
12 Vacillates
13 Boston Bruin great
19 Turning point?
23 Brown or Rice
24 Actress Malone of "The Hunger Games"
26 Cousin of reggae
28 Implied but not stated
29 Sculls
30 Magic and Wizards org.
32 Double ___ Oreos
35 Reine's husband
36 Former queen of Jordan
37 Catchers of some waves
38 And everything else, for short
39 Former dictator of Panama
40 Refined
43 Biblical city of Palestine
44 Passed, as time
45 Jack Reed or Harry Reid: Abbr.
47 Barrels along
48 Have on
49 Powerful
51 Lawn game
53 Minderbinder of "Catch-22"
54 Cash register compartment
56 Manhandle
57 Swamp
59 Enero begins it

by David Kwong

ACROSS

1 Picking out of a lineup, informally
6 Magazine with a "Person of the Year"
10 Former "Meet the Press" host Marvin
14 Craze
15 Freshly
16 French lady friend
17 Reason for a cast
19 Spanish newborn
20 Period after dark, in poetry
21 Fifth-century pope known as "the Great"
22 Impressionist Claude
23 Ugandan tyrant Idi __
25 Piece of sports equipment that's spiked
28 Grand __ National Park
30 Pie __ mode
31 Insect with a stinger
32 Cozies keep them hot
36 Cutlass or 88, informally
37 Family gathering place
39 Leopard's marking
41 Starts liking
42 Skillet, e.g.
43 It's thinner as you go up
44 City-related
48 Device with a snooze button
53 Idiot
54 "I agree"
55 Emmy winner Perlman
57 Call of Duty: Black __ (video game)
58 Hermes' mother
59 "Ready to go!" . . . or a description of 17-, 25-, 37- and 48-Across?
62 Tesla co-founder Musk
63 Opera part
64 Tin or titanium
65 Scouting groups
66 Something rising in a gentrifying neighborhood
67 Choice plane seating

DOWN

1 "Man, what a day!"
2 Comment after "You think I'm chicken?"
3 Part of a prank, say
4 Suffix with peace or neat
5 Certain Scotsman
6 Off-limits
7 How foods are often fried
8 All Supreme Court justices until 1981
9 Ram's mate
10 Meat on a skewer
11 Willing to go along
12 Defamed in print
13 Small VWs
18 Home to Vegas: Abbr.
22 R&B singer with the hit "It's All About Me"
24 Cry in a game of tag
26 Foamy coffee order
27 "__ Dream" (63-Across from "Lohengrin")
29 Former All-Star closer Robb
33 Shenanigan
34 Gem whose authenticity can be checked by rubbing it against the teeth
35 Mork's birthplace, on TV
36 Prayer starter
37 Gift to a nonprofit
38 A/C measure, for short
39 Sent millions of emails, say
40 Brew with a rhyming name
43 __, amas, amat
45 Raises
46 Take to a higher court
47 Snuggle
49 Speckled horses
50 Utah's Sen. Hatch
51 Have an affair
52 Mauna __ (Hawaiian peak)
56 __ mater
59 Card game that can go on and on
60 Before, to a bard
61 Gift given while saying "Aloha!"

by Sam Buchbinder

ACROSS

1 Thing on a string
5 Listening device?
9 __ bag
14 One of several on a big rig
15 Poet Teasdale
16 Brother of Prometheus
17 *Especially memorable, as a day
19 Burner holder
20 Garbage transporters
21 *Campground amenity
23 Beings, in Bretagne
25 A dress line
26 Pictionary company
29 It's carbonated
33 *Feature of a carpenter's level
36 Valley with many cabs?
37 Last: Abbr.
38 Naval base builders
41 [Damn, this is annoying!]
42 Gamboling spots
44 *Beef alternative in many countries
46 Gamblers use them
49 Low-end
50 Obsolescent mobile device, briefly
51 186,000 miles/second, for light
53 *Basic china color
57 Courage
61 Hit musical set in Buenos Aires
62 "Don't wait for me to proceed" . . . or what either part of the answer to each starred clue can do?
64 Arrest
65 Writer Sarah __ Jewett
66 Eugene O'Neill's "__ Christie"
67 Dummy Mortimer
68 Breather
69 Quaint affirmative

DOWN

1 Criminals may be behind them
2 Corner office type
3 Designer Gucci
4 Big name in retirement community development
5 Suffix with human
6 Company that invented newsreels
7 They can be crushed for a pie crust
8 It may be thrown at a corkboard
9 Ruined, as dreams
10 __ Empire (land of Suleiman the Magnificent)
11 What fireflies do
12 Handed over
13 River to the North Sea
18 Stage when an animal is in heat
22 HBO rival
24 Spa amenity
26 Fisherman's takes
27 Alvin of American dance
28 Mex. misses
29 Oracle
30 Website parts
31 O of the magazine world
32 Part of G.O.P.
34 Dismissive cries
35 Wall St. debt deal
39 Villa d'__
40 A Williams sister
43 Heavenly gatekeeper
45 Seized the opportunity
47 One of eight English kings
48 __-jongg
51 Mall tenant
52 Drudges
53 Hospital capacity
54 Kiln
55 Dark time, in ads
56 Prince of opera
58 Actor Auberjonois
59 Some shuttles
60 Dutch export
63 Part of a soccer goal

by Paula Gamache

24

ACROSS

1. __ browns (breakfast order)
5. Golf target
9. Where "they tried to make me go," in an Amy Winehouse hit
14. Red Muppet on "Sesame Street"
15. Last word of grace
16. Wear away, as soil
17. Defeat decisively
18. __ Payne, One Direction heartthrob
19. Turn on one foot, in basketball
20. One being laughed at
23. "A Nightmare on __ Street"
24. "Help!," at sea
25. Cheese-loving pest
28. Where Mom or Dad sits at dinner
33. "__ sells" (advertising maxim)
34. Take to the skies
35. Not walk completely upright
36. Mama's mate
38. Org. co-founded by W. E. B. Du Bois
41. When doubled, a Hawaiian fish
42. Each and __
44. Place after win and place
46. Totally cool
47. Locale
51. Building blaster, for short
52. R&B's __ Hill
53. Cub Scout unit
54. Where it's calmest in a hurricane
61. Part of a bicycle or loom
63. An hour before office closing time, maybe
64. Cookie in cookies-and-cream ice cream
65. Actress Berry
66. Brink
67. Space race competitor, for short
68. Clothesline alternative
69. Word that follows steel, open or pigeon
70. Boring way to learn

DOWN

1. Oregano, for one
2. Baseball's Felipe
3. Filth
4. Good drink for a sore throat
5. First or last quarter in the lunar cycle
6. Exclude
7. Jacob's wife
8. Catch in a net
9. Shares on Facebook, maybe
10. "The Phantom of the Opera" lead role
11. Futuristic mode of transportation in the "Back to the Future" films
12. Big fuss
13. Wager
21. Early automaker Ransom E. __
22. "Average" guy
26. Greetings in Honolulu
27. Lukewarm
28. What's beyond the Pearly Gates
29. As predicted
30. Flight watchdog org.
31. Get rid of
32. Cash dispenser, briefly
33. Exhausted
37. Animal house?
39. Guerrilla Guevara
40. Like some doughnuts and wigs
43. One calling from a Swiss mountaintop
45. Troubles
48. Questlove's hairdo, for short
49. Nursery rhyme seat
50. Doing concerts here and there
55. Connecticut Ivy
56. Kind of list
57. Ginormous
58. Approximately
59. Slumber
60. "Encore!"
61. Prof's degree
62. Corn unit

by Ori Brian

ACROSS

1 Frat party staples
5 Wrote a four-star review
10 Open a smidge
14 TV's "__ Betty"
15 Singer Turner's memoir
16 Doughnut feature
17 It can be left 10-Across
18 "Open" things for a call-in show
20 Not recommended
22 Resort near Venice
23 Get rid of
24 "__ bet?"
26 "Huh?"
28 Scare word
30 __ buco (veal dish)
32 China's Chou En-__
33 End in __ (not be resolved)
35 Places for shawls
40 Canyon vantage points
41 Phony
42 O.T. book before Daniel
43 Coal and natural gas
45 Like bratty comments
46 Reverse of SSW
47 Rebuke to a traitor
49 Unusual
50 Petite dress specification
54 Absorb, as gravy
56 "Il était __ fois" ("Once upon a time": Fr.)
57 Kids' guessing game
59 Some vintage photos
62 Syrup comes from them
65 Suddenly lose patience
66 Competitor of Pedigree
67 Totally wipe out
68 Poet Pound
69 Blood worry
70 Safari sighting, for short
71 Bugle tune . . . or what one does to 1-, 18-, 35-, 43- and 62-Across

DOWN

1 African antelope with curvy horns
2 Dr. __ Spengler, "Ghostbusters" role
3 Luminescent larvae
4 Origin of much 2015–16 emigration
5 Gets redder, say
6 N.C.A.A. part: Abbr.
7 Baroque stringed instrument
8 __ Del Mar, "Brokeback Mountain" role
9 Icarus' father, in myth
10 Hawaiian yellowfin tuna
11 Biblical prophet who had a whale of a time?
12 Vega of "Spy Kids"
13 Put back to 0, say
19 True-blue
21 Forecast eagerly awaited by schoolkids
25 N.C.A.A. part: Abbr.
27 Make broader
28 Roseanne of "Roseanne"
29 Slobbering cartoon character
31 "Well, I'll be!"
34 In unison
36 Ejects from office
37 "South Pacific" co-star
38 Comic Foxx
39 Timetable, informally
41 William __, Pilgrim Father
44 Loosen, as neckwear
45 Apartment building V.I.P., for short
48 Throw at
50 Poison oak cousin
51 Entirely
52 One of Groucho's brothers
53 Show on which Dr. Phil became famous, familiarly
55 Surprise win
58 Himalayan mystery
60 __ The Magazine (bimonthly with 35+ million readers)
61 Massage spots
63 Parking area
64 German article

by Jonathan Gersch

26

ACROSS

1 Funny Groucho or Harpo
5 Lover of Tristan, in legend
11 Place with R.V. hookups
14 Swear
15 GoDaddy purchase
16 90° bend
17 Tropical drinks often served with umbrellas
19 ___ Period (time in Japanese history)
20 Lustful deity of myth
21 Rooster's mate
22 Store sign during business hours
23 Spicy ballroom activity?
27 Communication for the deaf, in brief
30 Try to win, as a lover
31 Baseball Hall-of-Famer Mel
32 Finishing eighth out of eight, say
35 Strain the body too much
38 Stupefy
39 Baby horses
41 Nipple
42 Rococo and Postmodernism
44 Application to highways before a winter storm
46 Take to court
47 Actress Thurman
48 Zodiac lion
49 "The Hitchhiker's Guide to the Galaxy" author
55 Boleyn, Brontë or Bancroft
56 Prof helpers
57 Earl or baron
61 2012 #1 album for Taylor Swift
62 Common first course . . . or what's literally contained in 17-, 23-, 32-, 44- and 49-Across?
65 Maker of the Optima and Sorento
66 "Hey!," from someone who's hiding
67 Wander
68 Foxy
69 Butcher's implement
70 The Ugly Duckling, actually

DOWN

1 Rand McNally items
2 Big name in running shoes
3 $2,000 for Boardwalk, with a hotel
4 Penetrating looks?
5 Declaration made with a raised right hand
6 Note between fa and la
7 Warren Buffet, the Oracle of ___
8 Stowed on board
9 Singer Ross with the Supremes
10 Coast Guard rank: Abbr.
11 Stay authentic, colloquially
12 Of yore
13 See 18-Down
18 With 13-Down, move at a snail's place
22 Groups of eight
24 Hangs around and does nothing
25 Just all right
26 Thanksgiving's mo.
27 Does sums
28 Bench or chair
29 Relaxing time after church, say
33 Downpour
34 Paver's supply
35 Target of a decade-long manhunt, informally
36 Over hill and ___
37 Germany's ___ von Bismarck
40 Eardrum-busting
43 Squirmy fish
45 Curses
49 Opposite of whites, laundrywise
50 Longtime NBC newsman Roger
51 Do penance (for)
52 An Obama girl
53 Thing in the plus column
54 Goes way, way up
58 Erupt
59 What a volcano erupts
60 Biblical garden
62 Dickens's Tiny ___
63 Long, long time
64 Showtime's serial killer protagonist, familiarly

by David Woolf

ACROSS

1 "Gotta run!"
6 Cretan peak: Abbr.
11 Home of George W. Bush's library, for short
14 Potty-mouthed
15 Rowed
16 ___ and feather
17 Bruce Springsteen's group
19 Sheepskin boot name
20 Jazz combo, often
21 Advantage
22 Vodka brand
26 Offensive football lineup
30 Makes happy
32 Longtime New York Times film critic
33 Adele song with the lyric "I must have called a thousand times"
34 Letters associated with a rainbow flag
35 Phrase on the back of a buck
41 Move, in real-estate lingo
42 Subject of discussion
44 Gourd-shaped rattles
48 Respectful term for a conductor
50 Cole Porter classic from "Can-Can"
52 Earring shape
53 "___ here!"
54 Folkie Phil
56 Top-left button on most keyboards
57 Surprise ending, as in "The Gift of the Magi"
64 11-Down that made "King Kong"
65 Picture book character lost in a crowd
66 "Oh no!"
67 Frodo's best friend
68 Fishline material
69 Children's song refrain found at the starts of 17-, 26-, 35-, 50- and 57-Across

DOWN

1 ___ Palace (Elsa's hideout in "Frozen")
2 "___ Doubtfire"
3 Publicly 34-Across
4 New Deal prez
5 Pedicure targets
6 Recurring musical ideas
7 No-no
8 Glass of "This American Life"
9 Lion's hide-out
10 Stir in
11 Where to find a soundstage
12 Housefly larva
13 Subject heading for an important email
18 Buffalo's county
21 "Yadda, yadda, yadda"
22 Globe shape: Abbr.
23 "Red Balloon" painter Paul
24 App with restaurant reviews
25 Informal pronoun
27 Prego alternative
28 Unruly crowds
29 Quick on the uptake
31 Reporter's contact
34 Corp. takeover
36 Gather what's been sown
37 Ingrid Bergman's "Casablanca" role
38 Snack
39 "What've you been ___?"
40 Joan of art
43 Bobby : U.K. :: ___ : U.S.
44 Scrooge types
45 U.S. state closest to the International Date Line
46 "My Big Fat Greek Wedding" or "When Harry Met Sally . . ."
47 "___ Maria"
48 One-millionth of a meter
49 Like a barbecue pit
51 Last movement of a sonata
55 Eye irritation
57 Part of B.Y.O.B.
58 Cushion material for some horse-drawn rides
59 Building wing
60 Rival of Xbox
61 "I Like ___" (old campaign slogan)
62 Due × tre
63 Chinese menu general

by Sarah Keller

ACROSS

1 Common lunchbox sandwich, for short
4 Florida home to Busch Gardens
9 Equally distant
14 Prevaricate
15 Wears, as clothing
16 Serviceable
17 Outcome
19 Ankle bones
20 From east of the Urals
21 Indication that someone's home at night, say
23 Chicago exchange, briefly
26 Found's opposite
27 The first "A" in N.C.A.A.: Abbr.
30 Bird on a weather vane
33 "Wanna ___?"
36 Midday
38 Six-time N.B.A. champion Steve
39 How kids are grouped in school
40 Damage
41 Texas A&M student
42 Alan who played Hawkeye
43 Return to a former state
45 "Go team!"
46 Roman goddess of wisdom
47 "N.Y. State of Mind" rapper
48 John Kasich's state
50 Capital of Norway
52 Stair rail
56 Voices above tenors
60 Money sometimes said to be "filthy"
61 Like 17-, 36- and 43-Across as well as 11- and 29-Down
64 Not this or that
65 Not reacting
66 Room that needs a serious cleanup
67 Merchandise
68 Australian "bear"
69 Chi-town team

DOWN

1 ___ bargain
2 Trash receptacles
3 User of the Force
4 "What gall!"
5 Batteries in TV remotes
6 The Spartans of the N.C.A.A.
7 Voting place
8 ___-aging cream
9 Stephen King or Ellery Queen
10 Rebounds and field goal average
11 Started
12 Too
13 Free ___ (total control)
18 Symbol of Aries
22 Secluded valley
24 ___ v. Wade
25 Scam artists
27 Being litigated
28 Choreographer Tharp
29 Top dog
31 Dry, white Italian wine
32 Matador
34 Writer Jong
35 Odysseys
37 N.Y.C. airport code
38 C.I.A. : U.S. :: ___ : Soviet Union
41 Maiden who raced Hippomenes, in myth
43 Uproar
44 Mobile accommodations, for short
46 Scrooges
49 Put on the payroll
51 Long in the tooth
52 Modern journal
53 Volvo or Volt
54 ___ the Red
55 City at the foot of the Sierra Nevada
57 Itar-___ news agency
58 "I'm ___ you!"
59 River to Hades
62 Traffic-stopping org.
63 It might be bookmarked

by Mary Lou Guizzo

29

ACROSS

1 Shapes of bacilli bacteria
5 Snug
10 North-of-the-border station
14 State that voted Republican by the highest percentage (73%) in the 2012 presidential election
15 River to the Rhône
16 Sporty car feature
17, 18 & 19 Classic song that starts "'Mid pleasures and palaces though we may roam"
20 Company shakeup, for short
22 Hero war pilot
23 Suit coat feature
24 Popular setting for 17-/18-/19-Across
27 Hagen of stage and screen
29 Fanatic
30 GPS suggestion: Abbr.
31 Was down with
34 Swinger's target at a party
36 Yale, affectionately
38 Façade feature
40 Small flycatchers
41 Korean performer with a monster 2012 international hit
42 Jeanne d'Arc, e.g.: Abbr.
44 1974–75 pigskin org.
45 Pastoral poem
47 With 53- and 56-Across, certain abode
49 Certain military hazards, for short
52 Evening, in ads
53 See 47-Across
54 Q*__ (1980s arcade game)
55 Homer Simpson cry
56 See 47-Across
57 "__ Rosenkavalier"
58 Bygone Ugandan despot
61 Oxide in rubies and sapphires
64 Harvesting machines
65 Possession of property
66 What initials on something may signify
67 Where femurs are located

DOWN

1 Germany's __ Valley
2 Indian tribe that lent its name to a county in Nebraska
3 Classical exemplars of steadfast friendship
4 Hite of "The Hite Report"
5 Modern prefix with gender
6 Comedian Patton __
7 Little rodents, jocularly
8 Having one's business mentioned in a news article, e.g.
9 Up to now
10 Patriot Allen
11 Avert more serious losses
12 Four or five, say
13 German-based G.M. subsidiary
21 How George Harrison's guitar "weeps"
23 Hide out
25 Like many exhausts
26 "Looking at it a different way," in texts
27 Something a scanner scans, in brief
28 20–20, e.g.
32 Stein filler
33 Insult, informally
35 Dairy __
37 "Clear!" procedure, for short
39 Actor Kutcher and others
40 Watches intently
43 Pants, in slang
45 Former Indian P.M. Gandhi
46 Semiconductor devices
47 Improper attire at a fancy restaurant
48 Hole in one's shoe
50 Make sopping wet
51 Humane Society pickups
59 Hairy primate
60 Not-so-hairy primates
62 Durham sch.
63 __ tai (drink)

by Peter A. Collins

ACROSS

1 Spike on a cowboy boot
5 Tweak, as text
9 What ran away with the spoon, in "Hey Diddle Diddle"
13 As well
14 Some passport stamps
16 Ferber who wrote "Giant"
17 Leave one's vehicle in a traffic lane, say
19 Cautionary words for a buyer
20 Larch or birch
21 "___ the only one?"
22 President William Howard ___
23 Four Corners-area tribesman
24 Iconic U.S. cabinetmaker of the early 1800s
28 Italian luxury carmaker
30 Jefferson Davis's govt.
31 ___ Andreas Fault
32 Approximately
33 Academic record, in brief
35 Plunders
37 Physical expression of victory
41 Instant decaf brand
44 High point of a European ski trip?
45 Simplicity
49 "Gattaca" actress Thurman
50 Kibbutz locale: Abbr.
53 Spoon or spatula
55 Spinal cord cell needed for muscle contraction
58 Query
59 Song for a diva
60 PC connecting device
61 Loser in a momentous 2000 Supreme Court case
63 Grabbed
64 Engage in some horseplay . . . or a hint to the words spelled out in the circles
68 Letter in an Anglo-Saxon script
69 Swing wildly, as one's arms
70 Devious maneuver
71 The "A" in N.B.A.: Abbr.
72 Suffix with luncheon or kitchen
73 Withered

DOWN

1 Melancholy
2 Conspiracy member
3 Loan sharks
4 Justice's garment
5 She loses paradise in "Paradise Lost"
6 Quick swim
7 "I, Robot" writer Asimov
8 Airport landing area
9 Sudden ___ (overtime format)
10 "Sounds about right"
11 Regard dismissively
12 Hurries up
15 Animal pelts
18 "___ and the Swan" (Yeats poem)
23 Otherworldly craft, for short
25 Prod
26 Playful bites
27 Coconut's place
29 Scissors topper, in a game
34 ___ snail's pace
36 Available for business
38 Rapunzel's bounty
39 Hazy image
40 Until
41 Large Indonesian island
42 Romantically inclined
43 Slovakia and Slovenia
46 Generally
47 "Yes sir!," south of the border
48 Large deer
51 Tobacco that's inhaled
52 Repair, as a shoe bottom
54 One practicing the "E" of STEM subjects: Abbr.
56 Like an old wooden bucket of song
57 W.W. II German vessel
62 Klutz's cry
65 Soused
66 Ginger ___
67 Easter egg embellisher

by Lynn Lempel

ACROSS

1 Baseball slugger's datum
6 Duchess of Cambridge, to friends
10 Like a cashmere sweater
14 Much of a maze
15 The People's King of Norway
16 Athletic footwear brand since 1979
17 Dangerous virus strain named for its original outbreak location
19 Galoot
20 Token opening
21 Barcelonan bravo
22 N.J. city at the west end of the George Washington Bridge
23 Mexican revolutionary
27 Comfy shoe
28 Engage in a brawl
29 Cut up into small cubes
32 Traveler's stopover
33 Fey or Turner
34 Santa __, Calif.
35 "Legends of the Fall" director, informally
39 'Neath's opposite
40 Indian flatbreads
42 Jeff Bezos, for Amazon
43 Young partner?
45 Caesar salad ingredient
47 Big fish __ small pond
48 Sensual areas
53 Grasslike perennial
54 Nanki-__ of "The Mikado"
55 Feeling upon winning the lottery
57 Fish story
58 "Not too hard now" . . . or a homophonic hint to 17-, 23-, 35- and 48-Across
61 You are, in Yucatán
62 Old home of the Mets and the Jets
63 Liquid-Plumr competitor
64 Sound before passing a note in class
65 Super Bowl XLIX champs, to their fans
66 Krupp ironworks city

DOWN

1 Amazes
2 Periodic __
3 Boutonniere part
4 Never-surpassed
5 Org. with a 3-1-1 rule for carry-on liquids
6 Eucalyptus-eating marsupial
7 Many a "Guardians of the Galaxy" character
8 Sticky cigarette stuff
9 Garden of Eden dweller
10 Seawater evaporation site
11 Part of the menstrual cycle
12 Makes small adjustments to
13 Dismantle
18 Geological period suffix
22 Obsolescent means of sending a document
24 Mineral vein
25 Marriott competitor
26 Mineral contained in oysters
29 Move taught by a choreographer
30 Overdue, as rent
31 Makes out
32 __ Jima
36 Big name in rodent control
37 Greek philosopher of paradox fame
38 Casino game
41 Propose
44 Madison Square Garden team
46 Capital of Texas?
47 Preppy clothing line
49 Surprising victory
50 Forage beans
51 Many "Frozen"-inspired Halloween costumes
52 What the Left Bank is a bank of
56 Harrow and Radley rival
58 Clairvoyant letters
59 Epiphany word
60 Ceremonious verse

by Tracy Gray

32

ACROSS

1 Wonderment
4 Movie house
10 Prejudice
14 With 37-Down, Al Capp cartoon
15 He "cometh" in an O'Neill play
16 Home to the Colosseum
17 Frodo's portrayer in "The Lord of the Rings"
19 Wister or Wilson
20 Queen of the Nile, informally
21 Three, in Tuscany
22 Prop for a magician
23 Battered appliance?
28 Exchanged vows at the altar
30 Tiny bit
34 Dined
35 Radner of the original "S.N.L." cast
38 Conductor Solti
39 Big stinger
41 Items found at the ends of 17-, 23-, 53- and 64-Across
43 ___ bag (party handout)
44 Tire mark
46 Submarine detector
48 Sgt. or cpl.
49 Offshore structure for Shell or ExxonMobil
51 Comes out of hiding
53 Kylo Ren's portrayer in "Star Wars: The Force Awakens"
56 Auctioneer's cry when dropping the hammer
59 Sheep sound
60 Hammer's target
63 Bangkok native
64 Iced tea garnish
68 Uses a riflescope
69 Brought to mind
70 Very long time
71 Part of a hangman drawing
72 Taste and touch
73 A.M.A. members

DOWN

1 One of the Baldwin brothers
2 Document that says "I hereby bequeath . . ."
3 Nobel Peace Prize winner who survived the Holocaust
4 Org. based in Langley, Va.
5 I, in Germany
6 Like emails with still-bolded headings
7 Overact
8 New Zealand natives
9 Scientist Celsius of the Celsius scale
10 Treats named for their color
11 Where the presidential primary season kicks off
12 Cry to a preacher
13 Transmit
18 Family name in "The Grapes of Wrath"
24 ___ Newton
25 Bank account protector, for short
26 Lounges
27 Texter's "Wow!"
28 Took care of
29 ___ 2600 (early game console)
31 Changed from A to B, as a credit rating
32 "Lord, we bless this food . . . ," e.g.
33 Breakfast items that come frozen
36 Batman and Robin are a "dynamic" one
37 See 14-Across
40 Seventh heaven
42 People of Lapland
45 "Look what you ___!"
47 Gun, as an engine
50 Seven things on a Nathaniel Hawthorne house
52 Philosopher Descartes
54 Irish novelist ___ Binchy
55 Matt who was nominated for an Oscar for "The Martian"
56 One of seven in the Big Dipper
57 Cleveland's state
58 Genie holder
61 Frankenstein's assistant
62 Eye or camera part
65 Approves
66 Maiden name indicator
67 Dict. entries

by Jason Mueller

ACROSS

1 Bakery attraction
6 Mate
9 Muslim holy site
14 Source of supposed extraordinary health benefits
16 Shades of blue
17 They need signatures
18 Paavo __, 1920s Olympic gold medalist
19 Designer Oscar de la __
20 Justice who died in 2016
21 James Bond, e.g.: Abbr.
24 Big part of a ship's rigging
26 Easily damaged
28 Sacker of ancient Rome
29 __-pitch
32 Spanish soccer star Sergio __
33 Of mind, body and spirit
35 Basic rhyme scheme
36 "Scram!"
38 Fast time?
39 Where Reagan was born
41 Jessica with two Oscars
42 Poor grade
43 Gobble up
44 Said quickly and angrily
46 Makes amends for
48 Nordic airline
49 Reconfigures, as a book to a screenplay
52 "Enough, Enrico!"
54 Well-founded
55 Band frontman, often
59 Feminist author Jong
60 God-awful
61 Brazen
62 Correspondent's afterthoughts, briefly
63 L'eggs shade

DOWN

1 Deadly Egyptian slitherer
2 Kick oneself for
3 Go (for)
4 Israel's fourth prime minister
5 Apollo's twin sister
6 Baby's footwear
7 "Brooklyn" actress Saoirse __
8 Some E.R. cases
9 "Moon River" composer
10 50–50
11 Ringlet
12 Victoria's Secret buy, informally
13 Where the 27-Down is
15 Biggest determinant of a school grade, often
20 __ Ste. Marie
21 Terror-stricken
22 1940s pinup Betty
23 Steaming Mexican treat
25 "Scram!"
27 Desert that ancient traders crossed
29 Shorthand takers
30 __ franca (common tongue)
31 Some jazz groups
33 Syllables from Santa
34 Blind part
36 Melodramatic shows
37 Queens's __ Field
40 Overnight
41 Denouement
44 Way up or way down
45 Linguine sauce
46 Heroic tales
47 Borders
49 D.C.'s New York and Pennsylvania
50 Five-time Olympian Torres
51 Father-and-daughter boxing family
53 Met solo
55 __ year (precollege experience)
56 Promising letters?
57 Have dinner
58 Market for Jap. shares

by Julie Bérubé

34

ACROSS

1 Spanish red wine
6 Taters
11 Insult, slangily
14 Actor Ed who voiced Carl Fredricksen in "Up"
15 Tim __, N.F.L. player known for kneeling in prayer
16 Environmental prefix
17 1940s–'50s Dodgers great who lent support to Jackie Robinson
19 Moving day vehicle
20 Prefix with vision or market
21 Teri __, Best Supporting Actress nominee for "Tootsie"
22 "Dallas" family name
24 Bread unit
26 Australian gem export
27 Comedian who hosted the 2014 Oscars
33 Egypt's capital
34 Sent back to a lower court
36 "The Addams Family" cousin
37 Tot's three-wheeler
39 I, to a psychologist
40 Admonishment for public displays of affection
43 Verbally spar
45 Actress with the classic line "You had me at hello"
48 Tatters
49 News anchor Lester
50 "__ español?"
52 __ Spring (2010s movement)
54 Impact sound in the comics
58 Wed. follower
59 Carefree existences . . . or, punnily, what 17-, 27- and 45-Across have
62 Shout before "You're it!"
63 "The Faerie Queene" woman whose name means "peace"
64 Gossip, from the Yiddish
65 "Mister Rogers' Neighborhood" airer
66 Ohio city where Goodyear is headquartered
67 Cry when accepting a challenge

DOWN

1 In awe
2 "Aha!"
3 First-year law student
4 Dealer in diamonds
5 "All bets __ off"
6 Attack from a low-flying plane
7 Jury member
8 Lyft competitor
9 Uno + uno
10 Popeye's son
11 Hors d'oeuvre often topped with paprika
12 Words of confidence
13 Spotify selection
18 "Yipe!"
23 Alert
25 Musician Yoko
26 "This one's __"
27 Vaping need, informally
28 "Catch you on the flip side"
29 Ones eschewing trash cans
30 Dirty coating
31 Cartoon shriek
32 "Speaking of which . . . ," for example
35 Active person
37 Pedicurists work on them
38 The New Yorker cartoonist Chast
41 __-retentive
42 Crown, scepter, etc.
43 Leather punch
44 Share with one's followers, in a way
46 From the capital of Tibet
47 Timber wolf
50 URL starter
51 "Moby-Dick" captain
52 State definitively
53 Cabinet member who once appeared beside her impersonator on "S.N.L."
55 Prince in "Frozen"
56 Regarding
57 Not nice
60 Bother
61 "This might be of interest . . . ," for short

by Kevan Choset

ACROSS

1 World of Warcraft enthusiast, e.g.
6 Enemy org. in many a spy thriller
9 North Carolina fort
14 Prefix with transmitter
15 Meadow
16 Mathematician whose name sounds like a ship
17 City in SE France
18 Architectural add-on
19 Airline whose main hub is in Atlanta
20 "__ 'em!"
21 Not slippery at all, as a winter road
24 Grp. holding quadrennial competitions
25 Sneaky laugh
27 Not gendered, as a noun
29 Spider's class
32 Begged
35 Mens __ (guilty mind)
36 Cloud in space
40 Neuter, as a stallion
41 Sophia of "Marriage Italian Style"
43 Designer Cassini
44 Japanese martial art that emphasizes not injuring the attacker
46 Night before
47 Melville's second novel
48 Things spiders leave
51 Actress Angela of "American Horror Story"
54 Antarctic volcano named for a place in the underworld
58 Child-care expert LeShan
59 Moniker for German chancellor Konrad Adenauer
62 The "e" of i.e.
63 Volunteer's phrase
65 Rumble in the Jungle participant
66 Conductor Georg whose name consists of two musical notes
68 Niece's counterpart, in French
69 Blue on an electoral map: Abbr.
70 Ancient Greek physician
71 Open the door for
72 Psyche part
73 Scraping (by)

DOWN

1 Grind, as the teeth
2 Eagle's residence
3 Soil enricher
4 Poet's "before"
5 More optimistic
6 Swiss-German artist Paul
7 Murray __-Mann, Physics Nobelist who coined the term "quark"
8 Whalebone
9 Night stand locale
10 __ the day
11 1980s TV's "Kate & __"
12 Board, as a plane
13 Blessing before a meal
22 Spider of children's literature
23 Spider's web-producing organ
26 Staked a claim
28 Last car
30 One who might have a corner office, for short
31 Decidedly nonfeminist women's group
32 Links org.
33 Use for flowers in Hawaii
34 Antlered beast
37 City where Einstein was born
38 Obama, astrologically
39 In days of yore
42 Mrs. Perón
45 Went extinct
49 Charles Schwab rival
50 Source of the "K" in Kmart
51 Organism
52 Freud contemporary Alfred
53 Healing ointment
55 Casus __ (cause of war)
56 Hwy. through Minnesota, Wisconsin and Michigan
57 Police setup
60 Words after break or shake
61 Long way to go?
64 "No kidding!"
67 Sturdy tree

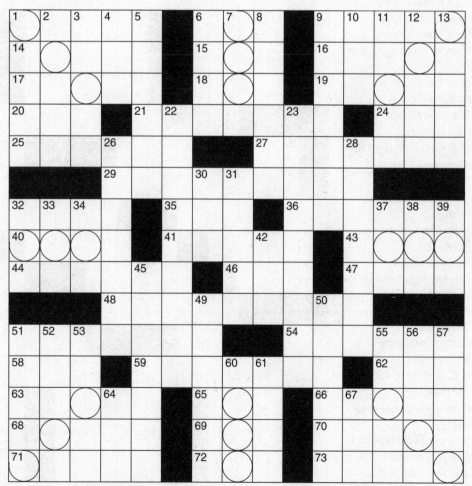

by Alex Vratsanos

ACROSS

1 Sam who directed "Spider-Man"
6 Greek "Z"
10 __ of Fame
14 Revved engine sound
15 Privy to
16 Annual theater award
17 Campaign trail
18 When repeated, a Stooge's laugh
19 What can be a real drag?
20 Longtime F.B.I. chief
23 German author who wrote "Faust"
25 Demeanors
26 Van for moving day, maybe
30 Zodiac divisions
31 Herman who ran for the 2012 Republican nomination
32 Back talk
35 They're exchanged at the altar
36 Drug used to treat Parkinson's
38 See 2-Down
39 Crossed (out)
40 Street likely to have the most stoplights
41 Watch that "takes a licking and keeps on ticking"
42 Male characteristic
45 Perplexed
48 Skybox locales
49 Holiday suggested by the starts of 20-, 26-, 36- and 42-Across, literally
53 Threesome
54 Guthrie who sang at Woodstock
55 N.B.A. Hall-of-Famer Thomas
59 Caesar's accusation to Brutus
60 Russia's Nicholas I or II
61 1/16 of a pound
62 The first "R" of R&R
63 Keystone __ of early film
64 Clucked in disapproval

DOWN

1 Traveling homes, for short
2 With 38-Across, 1920s–'30s design style
3 Payment-to-come-later note
4 Much-ridiculed pants for women
5 Instigation
6 "Oh, snap!" elicitor
7 Writer/singer of an Elvish song for "The Lord of the Rings"
8 With 23-Down, leader of a sightseers' group
9 Symbol of life in ancient Egypt
10 Necessity for deep-frying
11 On top of
12 Make an analogy with, with "to"
13 Satyrs' looks
21 FedEx competitor
22 Arabian Peninsula sultanate
23 See 8-Down
24 "This is terrible!"
27 Low-priced, in brand names
28 Short snooze
29 __ Maria (coffee liqueur)
30 Highest roll of a die
32 Helpful theorem, in math
33 Slushy drinks with a polar bear mascot
34 Curse
36 "Well, __-di-dah!"
37 Boardroom V.I.P.: Abbr.
38 Greek god of wine
40 Exam for future docs
41 "The Waste Land" poet
42 Ump's cry at home
43 College students' declarations
44 Sch. in Tulsa, Okla.
45 Pursuing
46 Rich dessert
47 Spades, hearts, diamonds and clubs
50 Cabbie
51 Rice-shaped pasta
52 Kerfuffle
56 Newspaper coverage, informally
57 Expert
58 "If only __ listened . . ."

by Jill Denny and Jeff Chen

ACROSS

1 Jazz legend __ James
5 Like the path of a high basketball shot
11 "One no-trump," e.g.
14 Indian bread
15 Funnyman Carl
16 Hawaiian instrument, for short
17 Retroactively, at law
19 Animation frame
20 "I __ every word I said"
21 Email chuckle
22 Outspoken
24 Football units: Abbr.
25 Poetic preposition
27 Lady in Spenser's "The Faerie Queene"
29 Red giants
33 Women, impolitely
36 Drink often served with a lemon wedge
37 City between Tempe and Apache Junction
38 "The __ on you!" (classic gag line)
39 @@@
40 Went letter by letter, British-style
41 Impolite
42 Late boxing great
43 Long-winged seabird
44 How Ivan the Terrible ruled
47 __ Court (district in London)
48 Rank above maj.
49 Passenger-screening org.
52 Maureen of "Miracle on 34th Street"
54 Bit of apparel with a ring neck
56 Copy changes
58 Joe
59 Pirate's guide that's hinted at phonetically by the starts of 17-, 29- and 44-Across
62 Roman "I"
63 Magic Johnson's real first name
64 Stuff of legends
65 Yule beverage
66 Music mixes at a nightclub
67 Pirate's interjection

DOWN

1 Spartans, to the Athenians
2 Imposed a levy on
3 __ bar
4 Shortly
5 Paintings
6 Involuntary action
7 "So long, Sofia!"
8 Leans
9 Amount after all is said and done
10 Abase oneself
11 Pirate
12 Store with a "Self Serve" furniture warehouse
13 Big name in PCs
18 Places
23 Risky way for a car to be running
26 B&O and Pennsylvania: Abbr.
28 Food label stat
29 Finish a hole between a birdie and a bogey
30 Room under a roof
31 What may be pictured on a 59-Across
32 The "N" in NASA: Abbr.
33 Robert __, longest-serving senator in U.S. history (51 years)
34 Dissolute man
35 Pirate, informally
39 Top celebs
40 One end of an eBay transaction
42 Home of the Brave?: Abbr.
43 Oslo Accords grp.
45 Spoke on the stump
46 Does really well on a test
49 East __ (nation since 2002)
50 __ Report (political document of 1998)
51 According to
52 Portent
53 Science fiction award
55 Place for an icicle
57 Hip-hop trio __ Soul
60 British rule in India
61 Little __

by Jules Markey

38

ACROSS

1 Jab with a knife
5 One of the a's in Nascar: Abbr.
9 "Well, golly!"
14 What Jack and Jill went up
15 Bygone dagger
16 Middays
17 Sitar piece
18 Heated argument
20 Stretches in history
21 "Either you do it __ will!"
22 Shoe ties
23 Take while no one's looking, say
26 __ Buddhist
27 Relative of ltd.
28 Some special f/x
31 Iconic action figure
34 Material in a fire starter set
37 "Unto us __ is given": Isaiah
38 Tree with papery bark
39 Not quite circular
40 Have a midday meal
42 Stockholm native
43 CBS symbol
44 Ernie who won the 2012 British Open
45 Response to a punch in the gut
46 Exhibits a superhuman ability
52 Beetle Bailey's superior
54 2 + 1 in italiano
55 Arrived
56 1937 Laurel and Hardy romp in the frontier
58 London subway, with "the"
59 Mountain ridge
60 Swear
61 Newspaper piece with a viewpoint
62 Argon and xenon
63 Alien: Prefix
64 "Stop" lights

DOWN

1 Shakespeare's "The Taming of the __"
2 Pageant sparkler
3 Like some pond growths
4 Detonation area
5 In a faint
6 Wolf (down)
7 Feature of a font
8 Opposite of paleo-
9 Doing sentry duty
10 Illegal liquor, informally
11 What's seen in "Saw"
12 Termini
13 Twisty road curve
19 Recoil slightly, as from an oncoming punch
24 10-pointer in Scrabble
25 Halloween costume with a pointy black hat
28 Shore recess
29 Prod
30 Not working
31 Entrance to a field
32 "By Jove!"
33 Ha-ha elicitor
34 Capital of Belarus
35 Rainbow's shape
36 Pizazz . . . or what 18-, 23-, 46- and 56-Across each has?
38 Bit of ammo
41 "Twenty Thousand __ Under the Sea"
42 Boar's mate
45 Boxing combo
46 Corresponded with
47 Rock's Perry or Tyler
48 "Ender's Game" author __ Scott Card
49 Stocking shade
50 Implant
51 Clarinets and such
52 Fleetwood Mac hit
53 Assents to the captain
56 What dogs' tails do
57 Sealing __

by Freddie Cheng

ACROSS

1 Canadian beer ___ Blue
7 Tolkien creatures
11 ___-Man (pint-size superhero in a 2015 film)
14 Distinguished N.F.L.er
15 Antioxidant berry
16 "The Tell-Tale Heart" writer
17 Take a tumble
19 Chicken ___ (kid's ailment)
20 Winter hazard on the autobahn
21 Charges
22 Solidify, as a friendship
24 Tranquil
26 Jazz composer with an Egyptian-inspired name
27 One given the red-carpet treatment
28 Went on and on
31 Is ready for the summer weather, for short
34 Gambino boss
35 Disco ___ ("The Simpsons" character)
36 Military sch.
37 Cousin of the mambo
38 Statistician's concern
39 Permit
40 Chrome dome
41 Language of Copenhagen, to locals
42 MTV documentary series about everyday people
44 "Good Will Hunting" director Van Sant
45 "___ Hope" (1970s–'80s soap)
46 More obscure
50 Owing (to)
52 "Game of Thrones" actress Chaplin
53 Palindromic houseware brand
54 Small brain, metaphorically
55 Injuries illustrated four times in this puzzle
58 Actress Adams of "American Hustle"
59 A Saarinen

60 Cult film heroine called "Mistress of the Dark"
61 Number between uno and tres
62 Stink to high heaven
63 Laughs or cries, maybe

DOWN

1 Surgical tool
2 Rachel McAdams's character in "The Notebook"
3 Euphoria
4 Modern kind of store
5 Driver's excuse for being late
6 Build muscle
7 Klutzes
8 It released the first 45 r.p.m. records
9 Indian home to Mother Teresa
10 Sound part of business?
11 Is part of the cast of
12 12
13 It might contain an emoji
18 ___ Mar (California racetrack)
23 G.I. grub
25 Broadcast commercial
26 Failed to get involved
28 ___ plume
29 Itinerary data, for short
30 Closing time for many city parks
31 "Stop right there!"
32 Lenovo alternative
33 Times for most college football games
34 Chasms

37 "___ County" (Elizabeth Taylor movie)
38 Lie in the sun
40 Spew nonsense
41 Long-lasting, as goods
43 Body part following black or pink
44 Overly ambitious student, in slang
46 One of the Three Stooges
47 Architectural column style
48 Apply, as pressure
49 Valentine's Day flowers, in Spain
50 Tablet purchased without a prescription?
51 Pixar's "Finding ___"
52 "All right, I'll do it!"
56 Mined metal
57 Eggs in clinics

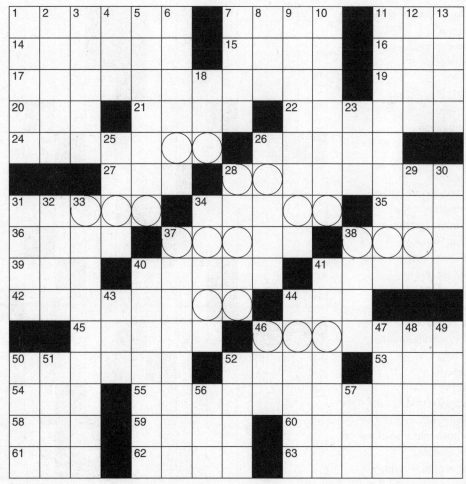

by Samuel A. Donaldson

ACROSS

1 Police vehicle
7 Vessel for slow cooking
14 Baltimore ballplayer
15 Bravery
16 Sailor, informally
17 Harvest festival events
18 Heavy weight
19 Bond girl Shirley
21 Beginning
22 "C'mon, quit it!"
24 Fuel efficiency fig.
25 Mafia bigwig
27 Snicker
29 Workplaces for R.N.s
32 City on the Black Sea
34 Pulitzer-winning writer Maureen
35 Dog, cat or maybe a parrot
36 Professional on a catwalk
37 With it
38 "All Day Strong. All Day Long" sloganeer
40 Glass of public radio
41 Ancient Greek theaters
43 Assessed visually
44 Animation frame
45 Pound repeatedly
47 King toppers
48 Victory symbol with the fingers
49 Take too far
51 __ on a true story
54 Scoundrel
55 TV screen option, in brief
58 O.K.'d
60 Survive
62 Surface to drive on
63 Seinfeld's neighbor whose name is spoken as an epithet
64 Short, quick runs
65 Some playground equipment

DOWN

1 Price
2 Black-and-white cookie
3 One of three at the base of a Steinway
4 North Atlantic fish
5 Succulent flowering plants
6 Yachting competition
7 Make a digital image of
8 Yo-yo or doll
9 Annual celebration when a 12-star flag may be flown
10 Twist, as a wet towel
11 Cushions
12 Pulitzer-winning James
13 Home composed of twigs
17 Large gem in the Smithsonian
20 Body part with a nail
23 Extension from a fire truck
24 Kitten's cry
25 Joke teller
26 Love to bits
28 Use a pogo stick
29 Place for airing an opinion . . . or what five of this puzzle's Down answers contain?
30 "Side by Side by Sondheim," e.g.
31 Stairs
33 Decline, as a ramp
37 __ and haw
39 Pb, to a chemist
42 Word before north or after payment
43 High dice rolls
46 "Uncle Tom's Cabin" girl
48 "La Traviata" composer
50 Extend, as a subscription
51 Taverns
52 Each
53 Argue (with)
54 Janitor's ringful
56 Steep, rugged cliff
57 Paneled rooms, maybe
59 Brewery container
61 Bad record for a motorist, for short

by Jacob Stulberg

ACROSS

1 German export
5 Polish, as text
9 Up
14 Hat part
15 "The kissing disease"
16 Hindu mystic
17 *Car part that works in a similar manner to the human hip
19 Mythical abductee
20 100%, as effort
21 ___ milk
23 "What ___ is new?"
24 Dodge Viper engine
26 Not pro
28 America's most-watched TV series of 2012–13
30 Prudential competitor
33 Crooner ___ King Cole
36 Indian bread
37 *Retaliate
39 Upscale hotel chain
40 Avoirdupois unit
41 Spanish eight
42 *Tenants' protest
44 Membership fees
45 Fuss
46 Spinning, quaintly
47 Kills, as bugs
48 When doubled, a sitcom sign-off
50 Mind-blowing, in modern lingo
52 "Mine!"
54 Golf pencil holder
57 Enmity
61 Event for a Comedy Central special
63 3-2 . . . or what's represented by the answers to this puzzle's starred clues?
65 Place setting?
66 "All ___!" (court exclamation)
67 Letters on some meat packaging
68 "The Godfather" actress Shire
69 Burden
70 Toffee candy bar

DOWN

1 Pop group that broke through at the 1974 Eurovision contest
2 Eurasia's ___ Mountains
3 Pickle variety
4 McDonald's slogan that replaced "Put a Smile On"
5 Ham it up
6 "And how!"
7 Stopovers for wayfarers
8 Dorothy's dog
9 ___ Wednesday
10 Many a comment from Donald Trump
11 *Children's toy that tests dexterity
12 College town in Iowa
13 Fork part
18 Sticks (out)
22 Ruth, for one
25 Word after human or second
27 Highlander's "not"
28 Titled
29 *Cry just before hitting the pool
31 Bert's pal
32 Amuse
34 Ibuprofen targets
35 Boxing decisions
36 "When Harry Met Sally . . ." screenwriter Ephron
37 "You got that right!"
38 Attractive, informally
43 Part of S.F.
47 Multivitamin ingredient
49 Very, to a conductor
51 Loses color
52 "Dagnabbit!"
53 Skosh
55 Spherical locks
56 Reduce to rubble
58 Elon who cofounded Tesla
59 Control+Z computer command
60 Hollywood Walk of Fame symbol
62 ___ Precheck
64 The Tigers of the S.E.C.

by James Mulhern

42

ACROSS

1 "That's hilarious!"
5 Acting groups
10 Flexed, as at the elbow
14 Pitchers' stats
15 Dizzying illusions
16 ___ Ant (cartoon superhero)
17 Harvard rival
18 Disprove
19 Sand hill
20 1899–1901 uprising in China
23 Actress Thurman of "Gattaca"
24 Fictional news director Grant
25 Palindromic term of address
28 Style of "iPhone" or "eBay," typographically
34 Poet Dickinson
35 Banned apple spray
36 Potter's oven
37 Talk smack about
38 Poor passing grade
39 June honoree
40 Ancient Peruvian
42 ___ Mountains (range east of Moscow)
43 Tequila plant
45 "Great!"
47 Rattan furniture maker
48 Connected PC group
49 YouTube video additions of 2007
50 Vacillate
58 Ride to an awards show
59 Overly enthusiastic
60 Muslim pilgrimage
62 Manipulator
63 Negotiated peace
64 "Twist, Lick, Dunk" cookie
65 Stinky
66 Internet troll, maybe
67 Stow on a ship

DOWN

1 With 61-Down, Jimi Hendrix's first single . . . or a hint to the starts of 20-, 28-, 45- and 50-Across
2 Saudi, e.g.
3 Angel's topper
4 Like amoeba reproduction
5 Snake charmer's snake
6 Imitator
7 "50% off" event
8 Chicago daily, familiarly
9 Pittsburgh N.F.L. team
10 What the number 13 brings, supposedly
11 Sewing case
12 Taboo thing
13 Capone's adversaries, informally
21 One of 22 for Jon Stewart
22 1-Across, in textspeak
25 Military first-aid expert
26 Protein acid
27 Dance club with a glittery ball overhead
28 Frank who directed "It's a Wonderful Life"
29 Writer Edgar ___ Poe
30 Claws savagely
31 Actor Quinn
32 One emancipated by emancipation
33 Rear-___ (certain accident)
38 0 degrees, on a compass
41 This, and no play, make Jack a dull boy
43 "For Those About to Rock" band
44 Low-ethanol fuel blend
46 Scrooge outburst
49 Puff ___ (snake)
50 Photo of a speeding car, maybe
51 Bart Simpson's sister
52 Harbinger
53 Scarlett O'Hara's plantation
54 Touch, as two states
55 Naughty's opposite
56 Doctor Zhivago's love
57 Handled tunes at a dance, say
61 See 1-Down

by Kevin Christian

ACROSS

1 Ones whose business is picking up?
5 Yodeling locale
9 Up until now
14 Mideast monarchy
15 "Stop procrastinating!"
16 "From your mouth to God's ears!"
17 *Drink holder near a sofa
19 Discombobulate
20 Think tank output
21 *Listing on a Billboard chart
23 Kit __ bar
25 Braxton with seven Grammys
26 Instant lawn
27 *Carnival cruise, e.g.
31 Dept. of Justice heads
33 Move slowly (along)
34 *Things that stick out conspicuously
40 Foe of Rocky and Bullwinkle
42 Deli delicacy
43 Rainbow __
44 *Craving for desserts
47 "Little" girl in "David Copperfield"
48 __ Four
49 *Tearjerker
51 Fraction of a joule
54 Huckleberry Finn carrier
57 "Not impressed"
58 *Bygone R&B showcase
61 Prancer's partner on Santa's team
65 Stun gun
66 *What good ratings for a new show can lead to
68 Girl's name that phonetically provides the initials to the answers to the asterisked clues
69 Adjust, as guitar strings
70 Pirate's quaff
71 Bird on a birth announcement
72 Dick and Jane's dog
73 Nordstrom rival

DOWN

1 "__ Fan Tutte"
2 Surrounded by
3 Requested
4 *Shoplifter, e.g.
5 Decay-fighting org.
6 Defensive tennis shots
7 Charles Lindbergh, e.g.
8 __ pad
9 *"Don't go anywhere!"
10 "Fancy meeting you here!"
11 Knox and Dix
12 Speed skater __ Ohno
13 Take some new vows
18 Winter Palace autocrat
22 Cookout annoyance
24 "__ a pity"
27 Close kin, for short
28 Sufficient, to a bard
29 Part of a plot
30 Casual Friday shirt
32 *Really safe bets
35 Friend of Pooh
36 Tel. no. add-ons
37 N.Y.C. cultural center
38 Animal in a Wall Street sculpture
39 Irritating subject for an ophthalmologist?
41 *Film words before "Nemesis," "Into Darkness" and "Beyond"
45 Ski lift
46 With 52-Down, Sunday entree
50 "Whip It" rock band
51 __ Park, Colo.
52 See 46-Down
53 Zeal
55 Eschews food
56 Traffic jam
59 Evil look
60 Small Apple offering
62 More, in ads
63 Furry Endor creature
64 Yuletide quaffs
67 Game-match connector

by Bruce Haight

44

ACROSS

1 Guacamole, e.g.
4 Trudge
8 Playful animal on a stream bank
13 Dangers for drug addicts, for short
14 Gordie ___ a.k.a. Mr. Hockey
15 Very rich . . . or drunk
17 Barbies, e.g.
19 Game piece with pips
20 Most hip
22 Wyoming's Grand ___ mountain
23 Dull hurt
25 Land, as a plane
27 Prefix with classical
28 IV units
30 Kanye West's genre
31 Genetic carrier
32 "It's not just me?"
34 The "A" in James A. Garfield
36 Big band trombonist
39 Conical home for a Plains Indian
40 Canada's capital
43 ___-cone
46 Business card info: Abbr.
47 Chowed down
48 Driver of a black-and-white car
49 The highest price
52 Word after pork or karate
53 Rose oil
54 Removed without much effort
57 Newsman Holt
59 Planner's aid . . . or what 17-, 25-, 36- and 49-Across are?
62 What's new, with "the"
63 "Immediately!"
64 "I mean . . . this instant!"
65 Linzer ___ (pastry)
66 Artist Lichtenstein and others
67 Day-___ paint

DOWN

1 "i" completer
2 Words exchanged at a wedding
3 Intimidate, as before a game
4 "Away, fly!"
5 Laze
6 Baby nocturnal birds
7 Artist's base
8 Aged
9 Aim or Crest
10 Domesticated
11 Masthead title
12 Fame
16 Woman's name that means "woman" in Italian
18 Mother of a fawn
21 Certain jet engine
23 Whatever
24 No. 1 in a company
26 Stick : punishment :: ___ : enticement
28 Stop moving
29 Make mandatory
33 Little one
34 Ending with orange or lemon
35 Big Apple opera lover's destination, with "the"
37 Shouts
38 America's Cup sport
41 Try to win, as for romance
42 Pokémon Go, e.g.
43 Conk out, as an engine
44 Skip dinner, say
45 Decides one will
47 Melodic
50 One doing carbon 14 testing
51 Where 2-Downs are exchanged
52 ___-de-sac
55 Attack time in W.W. II
56 "My bad!"
58 Numbered rd.
60 Note between fa and la
61 Requirement for a tango

by Kurt Mengel and Jan-Michele Gianette

ACROSS
1 Reaction to a crack
5 Pickled garnish
10 Briton of old
14 "Uh-huh, sure it is"
15 Fashion cut
16 __ about (approximately)
17 What the beat cop didn't want to be?
19 "Good heavens!"
20 Sheer
21 What the 1920s Yankees didn't want to be?
23 Christopher Robin's creator
25 No friend
26 Sparkling effect
27 Martha's Vineyard alternative
29 Serving goofs in tennis
30 "Wow!"
31 Generally speaking
34 Short albums, for short
35 What the museum curator didn't want to be?
36 Have a bawl
39 Try to answer or estimate
40 Onetime Nintendo rival
41 Harbor high hopes
44 "Good heavens!"
46 Tibetan capital
47 Apple devices run on it
49 V and X, on a sundial
50 What the G.I. didn't want to be?
52 Phone
53 Business letter abbr.
54 What the trial attorney didn't want to be?
58 Mideast money
59 Incoming text ding, e.g.
60 __ ID
61 Chaucer offering
62 Cartoonist Trudeau
63 Pro bono spots, briefly

DOWN
1 Sot's sound
2 Blood-typing letters
3 What the mansion owner didn't want to be?
4 Out for a bite, maybe
5 Worry
6 100%
7 Painter __ di Cosimo
8 Happen next
9 Chill
10 It has a tip for players in the game room
11 Suffering, figuratively
12 Orbiting info relayer
13 Assignations
18 Something a line lacks
22 Makes better
23 Part of F.N.M.A.: Abbr.
24 Denny's alternative
25 Fun gatherings
28 Gay __
29 Rigidly old-fashioned
32 Lou Gehrig's disease, for short
33 Bawls (out)
35 Heard only
36 What the coal company didn't want to be?
37 Tyrannical sort
38 One who can't hit high pitches?
39 Princess in Disney's "Enchanted"
40 Not yet slumbering
41 Queen Victoria's husband
42 "Any Man of Mine" singer Twain
43 French mathematician Blaise
45 Tennis great Smith
47 Sicilia, for one
48 Blender maker
51 Online publication, informally
52 Big name in perfumery
55 Like some mdse. marked "as is"
56 It has arms and waves
57 Commencement participants: Abbr.

by Paula Gamache

46

ACROSS

1 Home of the N.F.L.'s Dolphins
6 iPhone purchases
10 Objects of an Easter hunt
14 Of the city
15 "Shoot!"
16 Squirrel's home
17 *1932 Greta Garbo classic
19 ___ diagram
20 It acquired Lucasfilm in 2012
21 Squirrel away
22 Garfield's favorite food, in the comics
25 Upscale business accommodations
26 Like the accent in "é"
27 Dishonorable
30 Apologize for one's sins
32 007 creator Fleming
33 Pale as a ghost
36 Contend
37 *Winner of 11 1997 Oscars
40 Iowa's ___ College
41 Sister brand of Gillette's Sensor
43 Sportscaster Berman
44 Jewish mysticism
46 Sidewalks line them
49 Easy runs
50 Ear trouble
52 Like the Burj Khalifa among all the buildings in the world
54 Seeing stars
55 Orchestra section next to the cellos
57 City near Provo Peak
58 Long view . . . or what the answer to each starred clue is?
62 Easy win
63 Amoeba's shape
64 "The Tortoise and the Hare" fabulist
65 Editor's "Let it stay"
66 Leading man Grant
67 Temper tantrum throwers

DOWN

1 Root beer container
2 Like the verb "to be": Abbr.
3 Attorneys' org.
4 What a landslide political victory confers
5 Poor
6 God, in the Torah
7 Fancy party spread
8 Flies, to spiders
9 "Weekend Update" show, for short
10 "There you have it!"
11 *1963 Steve McQueen epic, with "The"
12 Rom-com or horror
13 Drops off at the post office
18 QVC alternative
21 Airline's base of operations
22 Immature stage
23 Nail the test
24 *2004 documentary about fast food
25 ___ boom (what a jet may create)
28 *1956 James Dean western
29 Bert's sister in "The Bobbsey Twins"
31 Scrabble rackful
34 What colanders and Swiss cheese both have
35 Brewer's fermenting agent
38 Perch for a golf ball
39 Eschew Uber, say
42 Have a go at
45 Strengthen
47 Get ___ of (throw away)
48 Visit
50 Dump emanations
51 Deck with 78 cards
53 "___ Baba and the 40 Thieves"
55 Bob of TV's "This Old House"
56 Hunchbacked assistant of film
58 TV channel established under a royal charter
59 Springsteen's "Born in the ___"
60 Go beyond ripe
61 Short albums, for short

by Zhouqin Burnikel and Don Gagliardo

ACROSS

1 Computers that are un-PC
5 With 9-Across, an auto ad slogan
9 With 5-Across, quickly
13 Workplace protection agcy.
14 "My Heart Can't Take __ More" (1963 Supremes song)
15 Two cents, so to speak
17 "Pay me later" marker
18 Sly look
19 Salon jobs, for short
20 Casino game that looks like a thou in reverse
21 Grouches
23 Lawyer's org.
24 With 26-Across, 1982 Al Pacino film
26 With 24-Across, 1962 P. G. Wodehouse book
28 Bonkers
30 Horsefeathers
32 Spanish treasure
33 Ottoman bigwigs
36 Colors, as Easter eggs
40 With 42-Across, Frank Sinatra signature song
42 With 40-Across, where Broadway is
44 Hamlet or Ophelia
45 Scanty, in London
47 Prefix with lateral
48 They turn litmus paper red
50 Monk's superior
52 With 55-Across, town crier's cry
55 With 52-Across, Aaron Copland ballet
58 Pipe fitting
59 Equivalent of C natural
61 __ A Sketch
64 Samuel on the Supreme Court
66 Cross inscription
67 Final Four grp.
68 River near the Vatican
69 British prep school
70 Resistance units

71 With 72-Across, noted maximum security prison
72 With 71- and 72-Across, classic Louis Prima tune
73 "__ ME" (phrase written on dirty cars)

DOWN

1 Poke fun at
2 Tennis legend Arthur
3 Neighborhood south of SoHo
4 Skipped, as a dance
5 Bubkes
6 County in Colorado or New Mexico
7 ". . . __ as it is in heaven"
8 Daybreak, to Donne
9 Closes, as a fly
10 Ironically, the last song in "A Chorus Line"
11 She's got her OWN network
12 __ jumbo
16 Old Russian ruler
22 Old German ruler
25 Exmaple for example, for example
27 Former New England Patriot Bruschi whose name is a bear to pronounce?
28 "GoldenEye" spy
29 Vicinity
31 Called
34 What generals keep up their sleevies?
35 Program listings, briefly

37 "Damn right!"
38 "Um . . . sorry!"
39 "Saturday Night Live" sketch
41 687 days, on Mars
43 "I haven't a thing to __!"
46 She had a hit with "Foolish"
49 RoboCop, e.g.
51 "Toodles!"
52 You can pack it
53 __ Island (immigrants' site)
54 Excuse
56 __ the side of caution
57 Mimicking
60 Hurries
62 Skyping needs
63 Dish made of leftovers
65 Word after Big or top

by Andrea Carla Michaels

ACROSS

1 Droop
4 Squished circle
8 What to get an "E" for
14 Drink that's steeped
15 Mama's mate
16 Word before name or voyage
17 Easter Day activities
19 "It's my turn!"
20 Detachable toy blocks
21 "___, meenie . . ."
23 Grain used in making beer
24 Competition in a rodeo ring
29 Personal identity
31 "Trainwreck" star Schumer
32 Trade some punches
33 "Come onstage" stage direction
35 Alternative to "trick" on Halloween
37 "Someone's gonna pay" . . . or a statement about 17-, 24-, 51- and 60-Across?
41 "In God We Trust," for the United States
42 "They're mine now!," informally
43 Openly gay
44 Groovy
47 God, with "the"
51 Legs at KFC
54 ___ of the above
55 Culture: Prefix
56 Garlicky mayo
57 Walk very, very quietly
60 Early home for Lincoln
63 Natural
64 Bangkok native
65 Alex and ___ (jewelry retailer)
66 Takes pleasure in
67 Red-lettered announcement added to a real estate sign
68 Bear's home

DOWN

1 Patron of mariners
2 Sea crossed by the Argonauts
3 Group of geese
4 Numbered musical work
5 What may help you make your move?
6 Likely
7 Intense beam
8 "8 Mile" rapper
9 Genealogist's drawing
10 Like sand vis-à-vis gravel
11 "___ on a Grecian Urn"
12 Latin for "king"
13 Detonation material
18 Place where one is under uncomfortable pressure
22 Time in history
24 Usually toasted sandwiches, for short
25 Not many
26 Brother of Cain
27 Big product of Kentucky
28 Phone no. addition
30 "And that's that"
34 Fix, as an election
36 Bucharest's home
37 Midnight, for one
38 "___, Brute!"
39 Key's partner
40 Mail: Abbr.
41 "The ___ Squad" of TV and film
45 Home to Plato and Aristotle
46 Trash container
48 "That's a shame"
49 Connected to Wi-Fi, say
50 Bring under control
52 "Same here!"
53 Indianapolis footballers
56 Boric ___
57 Score before sudden death
58 Word after Holiday or Days
59 Homemade sandwich, informally
61 "What a surprise!"
62 ___ pal (female bestie)

by Sam Trabucco

ACROSS

1 Sounds from schnauzers
5 Blue Ribbon brewer
10 Mt. Rushmore's state: Abbr.
14 Bisque or gazpacho
15 Quran deity
16 Fit __ tied
17 Guy shouting "Cowabunga!," say
19 Romney's 2012 running mate
20 Rational self, to Freud
21 __ greens
22 Implement for eating 14-Across
24 Pulsate painfully
26 Onetime CBS News anchor
29 Kind of port on a PC
31 Troupe grp.
32 Brother of Shemp and Curly
33 Saver's bank holding: Abbr.
36 Revealing skirt
39 Like a ram or lamb
41 Lacking broad application
44 Thin porridge
45 Sorbets, e.g.
46 Gambler's chances
47 MS. readers at Ms., e.g.
48 Peter out
50 Like rappers Wayne and Kim
52 Rammed from behind
56 Gets lucky with one's car downtown, say
60 Decorate
61 Mex. miss
63 De-squeaker
64 Trebek with all the answers
65 "Star Wars" droid . . . or a phonetic hint to what's found in 17-, 26-, 41- and 52-Across
68 Prefix with -meter or -scope
69 Minuscule
70 Blog update, e.g.
71 Celtic tongue of the British Isles
72 Olympic swords
73 Torah holders

DOWN

1 Liability's opposite
2 Still in draft form
3 Uproar
4 UV blockage no.
5 Lessen, as expenses
6 Birch relative often used in electric guitars
7 Popeye's brawny rival for Olive Oyl
8 Heartsick
9 Hurdles for Ph.D.s
10 Thurmond who left the Senate at age 100
11 "Um . . . excuse me?"
12 Deserted
13 Documentarian Burns
18 Diminishes
23 Ironclad evidence
25 Quite bizarre
27 Tour leader
28 Ownership documents
30 Auto with a black, blue and white logo
33 Wrath
34 One offering test drives
35 Group led by Richard the Lionheart
37 Words before "So sue me!"
38 Big Apple inits.
40 Cello cousin
42 Like 10-Down vis-à-vis any other senator in history
43 Subj. for the foreign-born
49 Like a trait present at birth
51 Tablet since 2010
53 __ Hart, lead role in "Chicago"
54 Lauder with a cosmetics empire
55 Remotely controlled flier
57 Helicopter part
58 Mall stand
59 Job openings
62 Output of Santa's workshop
64 Gorilla
66 Sales worker, briefly
67 Superfund org.

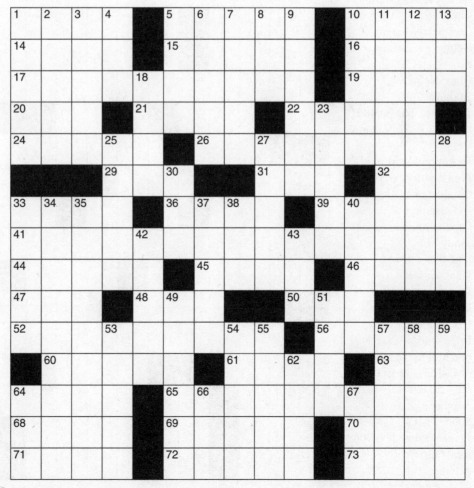

by Lynn Lempel

ACROSS

1 ___ above (better than)
5 Run one's mouth
11 Bit of acne, informally
14 Unhurried run
15 Protective tooth layer
16 Blunder
17 Archfoe
19 Bikini top
20 Previous to, in poetry
21 Say "Please, please, please," say
22 Rep on the street
23 Profanity
27 Official sometimes said to be blind
29 "___-hoo!" ("Hello!")
30 Nostradamus, for one
31 "The Witches" director Nicolas
33 NBC weekend show since '75
35 Completely wrong
39 Golden parachutes, e.g.
42 Peace Nobelist Sakharov
43 Title like "The Santa Clause" or "Knight and Day"
44 Faucet problem
45 Prefix with dexterity
47 Galahad or Lancelot
49 Pas' partners
50 Popular movie theater candy
55 Kite flier's need
56 Plant, as seeds
57 Like the stage after larval
60 QB Manning
61 Influential sorts . . . or a hint to the starts of 17-, 23-, 39- and 50-Across
64 Teacher's ___
65 Sudden runs
66 "___ Enchanted" (2004 rom-com)
67 Attempt
68 Classic cameras
69 Where to drop a coin

DOWN

1 Jessica of "Dark Angel"
2 Hairdo
3 Fully informed, informally
4 Four: Prefix
5 The "p" of m.p.h.
6 In single file
7 Group of experts
8 Last Greek letters
9 Opposite of masc.
10 Travel like Superman
11 Alphabetically last animal in a zoo, usually
12 Clearance rack abbr.
13 Swap
18 Slippery
22 Like pigs' tails and permed hair
24 Samsung competitor
25 Fastidious sort
26 Neuter, as a stud
27 ___ Major
28 Like a well-kept lawn
32 Depardieu of film
34 Pool unit
36 Period of higher-than-average temperatures
37 Charles Lamb's "Essays of ___"
38 Kitchen amts.
40 Office sub
41 Important time at a fraternity or sorority
46 "How tragic"
48 Kelly of morning TV
50 Won the World Series in four games, say
51 Edmonton hockey player
52 Togetherness
53 Terra ___
54 "Put up your ___!"
58 Guthrie who performed at Woodstock
59 Future atty.'s hurdle
61 "Naughty!"
62 Abbr. in a military address
63 Things eds. edit

by Emily Carroll

ACROSS

1 Classic TV show with a celebrity panel
10 Verbally attack
14 Taverns
15 Yo-Yo Ma's instrument
16 Plea that accepts conviction without admitting guilt
17 Picture puzzle
18 Soda brand introduced in 1924
19 Feudal status
21 Philosopher Descartes
24 Musical set in Oz, with "The"
25 "Aaron Burr, ___" ("Hamilton" song with a rhyming title)
28 Like Monopoly deeds that are flipped upside down
32 Starchy substance found in some plant roots
34 Direction
35 Software issues
38 Strong suit?
39 Gift in a relationship that's getting serious, maybe
40 "Network" director Sidney
41 Cat call
42 Saldana of "Star Trek Beyond"
43 Unsteady
44 4, for 19 divided by 5
47 Windows : Microsoft :: ___ : Apple
48 Snooze
49 Some airport postings, for short
51 Flawed
56 Counselor employer
60 Ice cream feature represented four times in this puzzle
61 "False!"
64 Chutney fruit
65 Springing back in disgust
66 Rural carriage
67 Many flower children, these days

DOWN

1 Thomas who wrote "Death in Venice"
2 ___ vera
3 Silicon Valley specialty
4 "Hallelujah!" singers
5 Sweetie
6 Belly
7 Unfailingly
8 Formation with steep cliffs
9 Best guesses: Abbr.
10 The Devil
11 Duchess of ___ (Goya subject)
12 Creature leaving a slime trail
13 Garden watering aid
15 Bond player after Brosnan
20 Influence
22 Sheik's peer
23 Prefix with issue
25 Thailand, before 1939
26 About, on a memo
27 One might start "I heard . . ."
29 11-year old, e.g.
30 Part of L.G.B.T.
31 Toon that flies with his ears
33 Lethargic
36 Hair stiffeners
37 One hell of a river?
39 Garden pond fish
40 Feudal figure
42 ___ Dingbats (font)
43 Soaked
45 Drug kingpin on "The Wire"
46 Separate
50 Skullcap?
51 Schools of thought
52 Sound of an air kiss
53 ___ colada
54 French "to be"
55 Party mix cereal
57 Et ___ (and others)
58 Seven Dwarfs' workplace
59 Mastermind game pieces
62 French "you"
63 Small taste

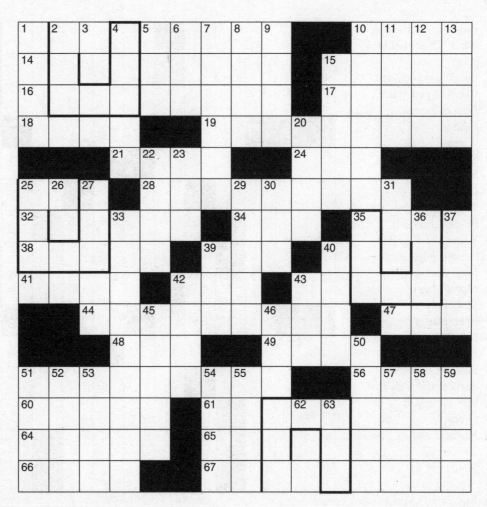

by Joel Fagliano

ACROSS

1 Apple computers
6 Game with a stack of blocks
11 Nevada/Arizona's Hoover __
14 Gold __ flour
15 Sometimes-bad bacteria
16 Political period
17 Famous geyser in 39-Across
19 Good job for an animal-loving ex-G.I.?
20 Gentle discipline for a misbehaving child
21 Hue
22 Style of music north of the Rio Grande
25 Cosmic clouds
27 __ the Terrible
28 Preparer of fast food that's "finger-lickin' good"
31 Catches red-handed
32 Clic Stic pen maker
33 Dish of greens
35 Inhibit
38 "Gross!"
39 Squarest of the 50 states
41 Lab eggs
42 Where the buoys are?
44 British coins
45 Rainy
46 Crew implements
48 Luau necklace
49 Money due in Monopoly
50 Exemplar of masculinity
53 Like Mustangs and Camaros
55 Sore, as 56-Across
56 Parts of the body that may be ripped
59 Greek "r"
60 Historic trading post in 39-Across
64 Note after fa
65 Topic to debate
66 Boy Scouts squad
67 Soil-turning tool
68 1990s fitness fad with infomercials
69 Evil animal in "The Lion King"

DOWN

1 Texter's "I think . . ."
2 Brooks of "Spaceballs"
3 __ Friend (Facebook option)
4 Mideast robe
5 Killed
6 Ballet leap
7 Canyon phenomenon
8 Completely joyless
9 Protein in bread
10 Not feel well
11 Noted rock formation in 39-Across
12 Gladiators' locale
13 Nonglossy finish
18 "Don't worry, nothing's broken"
21 Inner __ (flotation device)
22 Lower leg bone
23 Kick out
24 Skiing mecca in 39-Across
26 Boy Scouts award
29 Edsel or New Coke, notably
30 Animal with a hump
33 Group of gnats
34 Have a fancy meal
36 Wedding or concert
37 In very bad condition
40 CBS spinoff set in SoCal
43 Eggs over __
47 Stuffed Indian pastry
49 Set of religious beads
50 Crocodile's home
51 Allergy season sound
52 One administering shots, maybe
54 Australia's City of Light
57 What's left of a ticket after it's used
58 Queen killed by an asp, familiarly
60 Go on snugly
61 One of the Three Stooges
62 Lithium-__ battery
63 Energy Star org.

by David Steinberg

ACROSS

1 Android purchases
5 Campfire treat
10 Ones coming out
14 Lady of the Haus
15 Forty __ and a mule (post-Civil War allotment)
16 Like only one prime number
17 Flowering plants from Australia
19 End of a movement
20 Director Kazan
21 FICA tax payer
23 Sounds from a happy kitty
26 What hath the gardener wrought?
29 Fake
30 Reason for school cancellation
31 Makes a big stink
32 Region affected by Brexit
34 Sun and Sky org.
36 This puzzle's circled letters, for the words that precede them
42 Bell town in a Longfellow poem
43 Bring under control
44 Buddy who played Jed Clampett in 1960s TV
48 How M.L.B. games are often broadcast
50 Part of a family inheritance
51 Second-greatest period in something's history
53 Subside
54 Invent
55 Contact lens care brand
57 Had too much, briefly
58 Antiquated office duplicate
64 Tear apart
65 __ sprawl
66 Toy with a tail
67 Ticked (off)
68 Train track parts
69 Barbecue side dish

DOWN

1 Patriots' org.
2 Old hand
3 Soft food for babies
4 Family multitasker
5 Bollywood costume
6 Palin was his running mate
7 Tulsa sch. named for an evangelist
8 Gym unit
9 Ruhr Valley city
10 Court order
11 Goolagong of tennis
12 Festoon
13 Some drums
18 Old Third Ave. trains in New York City
22 Ski lodge, often
23 Tiny fraction of a min.
24 "No way!"
25 Steak specification
27 Best-selling author who was a runner-up for Time's 2007 Person of the Year
28 Completely dominates
30 Splinter group
33 Electric keyboard heard on "I Am the Walrus"
35 Admiral who explored the Antarctic
37 Vegas resort with a musical name
38 Considerable salary to pull down
39 Fit for service
40 Dryer screen buildup
41 Old blade
44 Go along with
45 One over an eagle
46 Something a tank top lacks
47 Got around
49 Kind of supplement
52 Come around again
53 Massachusetts' Cape __
56 Stars exist over them
59 Notre Dame's Parseghian
60 Ballpark fig.
61 Tin Man's need
62 Sch. group
63 Tree used in bow-making

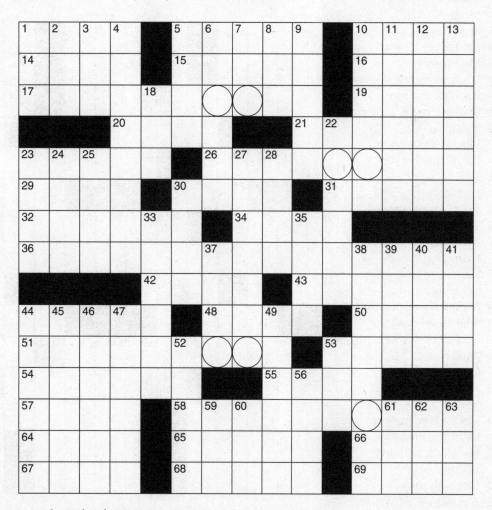

by Roland Huget

ACROSS

1 Apparel
5 Installs, as a lawn
9 Prilosec and Prozac
14 Double-reed woodwind
15 Drive-___ window
16 Bus station
17 Facial sign of sleep deprivation
19 Roof material
20 Decorate, as a cake
21 Actor Don of "Trading Places"
23 Pony up, in poker
24 Like outfits with ruffles and lace
26 Bathe in the buff
28 Symbol of royalty in ancient Egypt
30 Baseball's Slammin' Sammy
31 Sparkling Italian wine
34 Hard to see through
38 Male turkey
41 It has only a few stories
44 Battle of ___ Jima
45 Springsteen's E ___ Band
46 Thing
47 Luau dance
49 Lamb's mother
51 Distress signal producers
56 Board for a séance
60 Telephoned
61 Romanian composer Georges
63 Number of lords a-leaping
64 Break off a relationship
66 Tool for severing a steel cable, maybe
68 "And . . . ___!" (director's cry)
69 Asia's diminishing ___ Sea
70 Moth whose name is Latin for "moon"
71 Not give a definitive answer
72 City with piers
73 America's Cold War foe, for short

DOWN

1 Shoot for the stars
2 Counting devices
3 "I read you," in radio lingo
4 Plead
5 Thorn's site on a rose
6 "I totally agree!"
7 Worthless stuff
8 Japanese food
9 Orthodontist's deg.
10 Pass-the-baton track events
11 Energetically starting one's day
12 Mobster John
13 Descriptive of some bills or hills
18 Celebratory cheers
22 Connected, as a bath to a bedroom
25 Den
27 Yule tune
29 Mailing charge
31 Late, great boxing champ
32 "You reap what you ___"
33 Like some tennis grips
35 The "p" of r.p.m.
36 He's next to Teddy on Mount Rushmore
37 "___ pasa?"
39 Bill with Washington's face
40 "The Wizard of Oz" studio
42 Castaway's spot
43 "Mon ___!"
48 Insistence
50 Dog's bark
51 Scoring high on Rotten Tomatoes
52 Jouster's weapon
53 Open, as a toothpaste tube
54 Prefix with transmitter
55 Celestial cool red giant
57 Couple's answer to "Who's there?"
58 Article of apparel with styles found at the starts of 17-, 26-, 41-, 51- and 66-Across
59 Egypt's Sadat
62 Male foal
65 Jockey purchase, informally
67 It might give you the chills

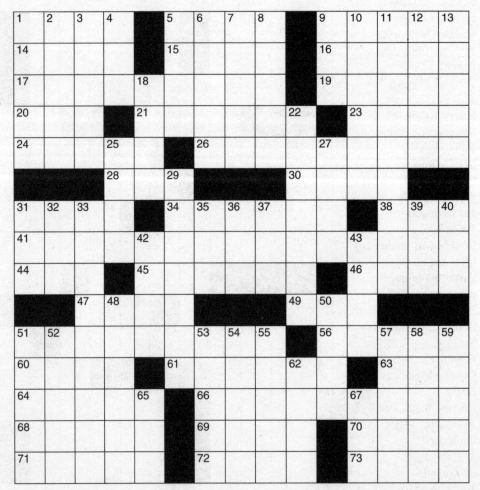

by Tracy Gray

ACROSS

1 Punch bowl dipper
6 Room with a tub, informally
10 Tobacco holder
14 Tool for climbing the Alps
15 Words before "old chap"
16 "What's the big ___?"
17 With 18-Across, phrase of resignation
18 See 17-Across
20 Regarding this matter
22 Second-longest river in Iberia
23 Weeding tool
24 Some E.R. cases
25 Phrase of resignation
28 Land divided by the 38th parallel
30 "Well, lah-di-___!"
31 Smooth-talking
33 Post-blizzard vehicle
36 Maguire who played Spider-Man
40 Phrase of resignation
43 Attacked on all sides
44 Squeal in pain
45 Gait between a walk and a canter
46 Brand at the Daytona 500
48 The "F" of T/F
50 Phrase of resignation
55 Nurtured
58 Developmental rink org.
59 Former attorney general Janet
60 Go hungry
62 Phrase of resignation
65 Literal phrase of resignation
66 VW or BMW
67 Minuscule, informally
68 Adjoining hotel accommodations
69 Flightless South American bird
70 Wizard
71 Envious critic, in modern lingo

DOWN

1 Collectible art print, in brief
2 Was heartsick
3 Hides in the forest?
4 Totally uncool
5 Former celebrity
6 Comedy routine
7 What a phoenix rises from, with "the"
8 Cardio workout regimen
9 Toyota Prius, e.g.
10 Thanksgiving dessert
11 Washington/Montana separator
12 Type of black tea
13 Lightens, as one's load
19 Go in circles
21 Early afternoon hour
26 Big name in Chicago politics
27 Haunted house inhabitants
29 Constantly worry
31 Early 2000s White House inits.
32 It's not the truth
34 "Bravo!"
35 Tom who wrote "The Electric Kool-Aid Acid Test"
37 Achieved results
38 Offshoot of punk
39 "Still . . ."
41 Frolicking mammals
42 Practices boxing
47 Qualifying match, informally
49 Somewhat tardy
50 Only U.N. member whose name comes alphabetically between P and R
51 "Sure thing"
52 Send over the moon
53 Santa ___ racetrack
54 The sixth letter of "garbage," but not the first
56 Paperless party summons
57 Scare off
61 Beautiful water hue
63 Have down ___ science
64 CBS logo

by Timothy Polin

ACROSS

1 Dislike intensely
6 Londoner or Glaswegian, informally
10 Mariner in a whale of a novel?
14 Sergeant's superior, slangily
15 Particular points
16 __ Strauss & Co.
17 Asks Warsaw residents their opinions?
19 Bushy part of a squirrel
20 Modest swimming garment
21 Under __ pretenses
22 Plus
23 Mideast chiefs
25 P.G.A. part: Abbr.
28 1965 Yardbirds hit
31 Wheel's center
34 Describe in greater detail, with "out"
36 Deserves
37 Music producer Brian
38 Up to, informally
39 Increases the number of commercials?
41 Ecologically oriented org.
42 Symbol of slipperiness
43 Hands (out), as money
44 "Tall" stories
46 Monopoly game's B&O and Reading: Abbr.
47 "R-E-S-P-E-C-T" diva Franklin
49 Two steps above cpl.
50 "Close but no __"
52 __-jongg
54 Take care of
56 Body of water between Dublin and Liverpool
61 Cuba or Aruba
62 Peels some fruit?
64 What comes before the storm
65 Sacred image
66 You might be stuck with these when traveling in the Southwest
67 What a lipstick print signifies
68 Man who might tip his cap
69 Church recesses

DOWN

1 Brand for Fido
2 Benefit
3 Ozone problem
4 Crankcase attachments
5 Tree secretion
6 Group of like-minded voters
7 Offering from a casting director
8 Diamonds, slangily
9 "My Country, __ of Thee"
10 Place to say "With this ring, I thee wed"
11 Cures the backs of feet?
12 "We try harder" company
13 Ill humor
18 Mani-__ (salon offering)
21 Of the highest quality
23 Punctuation mark akin to a semicolon
24 Bond girl Adams
25 Photo caption following a major weight loss
26 More like a fox
27 Finds buyers for smartphones?
29 Bette who won a Golden Globe Award for "Gypsy"
30 Plus quality
32 Remove, as a currency from a fixed rate
33 "I am the greatest," e.g.
35 Tried
40 __ the Explorer
45 Waste pile
48 French friends
51 Agenda units
53 Abbreviation on a pound sign?
54 __ as a dog
55 Actor Morales
56 Clothes unwrinkler
57 Apartment dweller's payment
58 Anatomical pouches
59 Art Deco artist
60 Garage sale disclaimer
62 Baby back ribs source
63 Top of a royal flush

by Victor Fleming and Andrea Carla Michaels

57

ACROSS

1 End of "Macbeth" or "Othello"
5 Airer of F.C.C. hearings
10 Something caught in a filter
14 "Downton Abbey" countess
15 "Macbeth" or "Otello"
16 Davenport's home
17 Person between 50 and 59
20 Supermarket checkout lines?
21 RCA introduction of 1977
22 Surfacing for a golf course
23 Pie pan material
24 Sort
25 The Goddess of Pop
27 Vindictiveness
29 Rebuke, with "off"
31 Rights, informally
34 Oblique look
35 Brews, as tea
38 Orators' aids
40 O'Neal's memoir of his N.B.A. rookie year
42 __ Brewster, Cary Grant's role in "Arsenic and Old Lace"
45 Gushes, as from a water fountain
49 Domain
50 Water swirl
52 Workplace fairness agcy.
53 Acknowledge as true
55 Things sometimes seen in banks
58 __ Lanka
59 The Braves of the N.L. East
60 Chicken drumstick
63 Mythical bird
64 Black __ (secret missions)
65 N.H.L. team that became the Colorado Avalanche
69 Frequent follower of "said" in the Bible
70 Vietnam's capital
71 Mistyping remedy
72 1950s British P.M. Anthony __
73 Central Florida metropolis, informally
74 Perfume

DOWN

1 Emulates the O. J. Simpson jury
2 "Men seldom make passes / At girls who wear glasses," e.g.
3 Sparse flow
4 Moving day vehicle
5 Davenport, e.g.
6 Let off from punishment
7 Violin's string tightener
8 Mars, to the Greeks
9 iPod Mini successor
10 Title bestowed on 72-Across
11 Sidney of "Lilies of the Field"
12 Was in store for
13 Miss __, etiquette columnist
18 Channel for TV shoppers
19 15+ minutes of a typical TV hour
26 Lucy or Ricky on "I Love Lucy"
28 Award on a wall
30 Vampire in "The Vampire Chronicles"
32 Waffle introducer?
33 Gels
36 __ Beta Kappa
37 Unchanged
39 Beanie, e.g.
41 Logician's "There you have it"
42 Cousin of a baboon
43 Deep and sonorous, as a voice
44 Filled (with)
46 Reverberate
47 Sink, as one's chances
48 __ kick (swimming technique)
51 Peter of Peter, Paul and Mary
54 Corrida cheer
56 "The Thinker" sculptor
57 Many an ology: Abbr.
61 Reverberate
62 Metaphor for insignificance
66 "__ courage!" (French cry)
67 Donator of Lennon's home to the National Trust
68 Quid pro __

by Stanley Newman

ACROSS

1 Termini
5 Black __ (deadly African snake)
10 "Beat it!"
15 Most important part of a carrot or turnip plant
16 South American range
17 __ Island Red (chicken variety)
18 1995 Hugh Grant/Julianne Moore romantic comedy
20 "The X Factor" judge Cowell
21 __ Arena, home to the Kentucky Wildcats
22 Feel lousy
24 Socially maladroit sort
25 1981 Alan Alda/Carol Burnett comedy
30 "Humbug!"
32 Secluded valley
33 Pinball foul
34 Mine: Fr.
36 &
37 "Medium hamburger and a Coke," e.g.
41 Classic TV game show . . . or what 18-, 25-, 55- and 66-Across are, in a way
46 Cub Scout leader named after a character in "The Jungle Book"
47 Part of a hosp. with oxygen tents
48 Deviant, in slang
49 "On top of that . . ."
52 Innocent sort
54 Soak (up)
55 1984 Molly Ringwald coming-of-age comedy
60 Redwood or dogwood
61 Aunt: Sp.
62 Pub potables
64 Hearing-related
66 1996 Michelle Pfeiffer/ George Clooney romantic comedy
71 Lip shine
72 First president to visit China
73 Unclothed
74 School health class, informally
75 Rear of a ship
76 Long-armed banana lovers

DOWN

1 Suffix with north
2 Detective fiction genre
3 Bite-size Krispy Kreme offering
4 __ Curry, 2015 and '16 N.B.A. M.V.P.
5 China's __ Zedong
6 __ Arbor, Mich.
7 Summer hrs. in Colorado
8 Joy of "The View"
9 Passing a ball to a scorer, e.g.
10 Grads-to-be: Abbr.
11 Football helmet attachment
12 Juliet's love
13 Decorate
14 Gives a darn?
19 Digital video file format
23 Necklace for one in a hula skirt
26 Imperfection
27 Wine: Prefix
28 Bring to naught
29 Surname of the only M.L.B. brother trio to play together in the outfield
30 __ Men ("Who Let the Dogs Out" band)
31 In a frenzy
35 Uncomfortable
38 In one's Sunday best
39 Designer Saarinen
40 Request in an invitation
42 Last Ivy League school alphabetically
43 Actress Merrill
44 Digitize, as a document
45 __ pro quo
50 "Ready, __, go!"
51 They can bring tears to chefs' eyes
53 Custardy dessert
55 Men-only parties
56 "Go me!"
57 Pioneer in photocopying
58 "Zip your lip!"
59 Justice Kagan
63 One-named singer with the 1985 hit "Smooth Operator"
65 Drug for tripping
67 Palindromic file extension
68 In favor of
69 Word with Comfort or Holiday
70 "Absolutely!"

by Zhouqin Burnikel

59

ACROSS

1 — of the Apostles
5 Ending with neo- or proto-
10 Pushing conventional limits
14 Blade in the pen
15 Strip of fabric used for trimming
16 Low ground, poetically
17 Rock's — Inch Nails
18 Habitual customer's order, with "the"
19 Clothes presser
20 Layers of sherry-soaked torte, homemade custard and fruit served chilled in a giant stem glass
23 Dreadlocked ones, informally
24 Comical "Dame"
25 "Kilroy — here"
28 Give off, as vibes
30 Summary
32 —-December romance
35 Ice cream and sponge topped with meringue and placed in a very hot oven for a few minutes
38 Oodles
40 Singer with the site imaginepeace.com
41 Boxer Max
42 Steamed-for-hours, aged-for-months concoction of treacle, brandy, fruit and spices, set afire and served at Christmas
47 Fabric purchase: Abbr.
48 Teacher's plan
49 Uncles, in Acapulco
51 — contact
52 Units of resistance
55 Ham-handed
59 What a chef might call each dessert featured in this puzzle, literally or figuratively
62 Command-Z command
64 Actress Watts
65 Kardashian matriarch

66 Fool
67 Latches (onto)
68 Land of Blarney
69 Ones who are splitsville
70 Lauder of cosmetics
71 "Phooey!"

DOWN

1 Ed of "Up"
2 Set traditionally handed down to an eldest daughter
3 Tiny bell sounds
4 Willowy
5 German kingdom of old
6 Growing luxuriantly
7 Severe and short, as an illness
8 Glass fragment
9 Gates of philanthropy
10 Voldemort-like
11 "Hesitating to mention it, but . . ."
12 Mop & —
13 Itch
21 da-DAH
22 Pass's opposite
26 "— and answered" (courtroom objection)
27 Constellation units
29 Walloped to win the bout, in brief
31 Chew the fat
32 Sugar —
33 Locale for urban trash cans
34 Sam Cooke's first #1 hit
36 Come to a close
37 "I dare you!"
39 Designs with ® symbols: Abbr.
43 Lowdown, in slang
44 Drive mad
45 Salade —
46 Club game
50 Lollipop
53 "Square" things, ideally
54 "Git!"
56 "West Side Story" seamstress
57 Mini, e.g.
58 Positive R.S.V.P.s
60 Error report?
61 J.Lo's daughter with a palindromic name
62 Manipulate
63 Kill, as an idea

by Tracy Bennett

ACROSS

1 Diminishes in intensity
7 Resident of Oman or Yemen
11 Breaks you wish would end?
14 "Sweetheart"
15 Protein-rich vegan staple
16 "Do ___ disturb" (motel sign)
17 *Iron Man's love interest
19 ___ Jima
20 Mean dog sound
21 Hit one out of the park
23 Trim, as a photograph
26 *Intimate chitchat
29 Old-fashioned address organizer
31 Most correspondence nowadays
32 Unsettled feeling
33 Actor McKellen
34 Display
37 Ford Escape or Jeep Cherokee, for short
38 "Shut up already!" . . . or what you can do to the start of the answer to each starred clue
42 Cheer at a fútbol match
43 Goes out with
45 Slip-___
46 Mistreat
48 Disney fawn
50 Diminished in value, as a currency
52 *Annual Thanksgiving Day run
55 Refuse to admit
56 Copper + zinc
57 Came to light
59 "Deadly" offense
60 *Knit headwear that may have a tufted ball at its end
66 Stephen Colbert's Americans for a Better Tomorrow, Tomorrow, e.g.
67 Part of the roof where icicles form
68 ___ Beach, Calif.
69 Admonition in a movie theater
70 Shadowbox
71 Former celebrity

DOWN

1 Concert haul?
2 "Ciao"
3 Swiss mountain
4 Number one position
5 Fair and balanced
6 Mexican shawl
7 Ring-shaped reef
8 Spoil
9 Sternward
10 Complete rubbish
11 *Classic comedy set at the fictional Faber College
12 Carpentry pin
13 Bird on a birth announcement
18 ___ fixe (menu notation)
22 Soul singer Reading
23 Lacking refinement
24 Charming scoundrel
25 *Offer of reconciliation
27 Page (through)
28 All: Prefix
30 Prosecutors, briefly
33 "No ___, ands or buts"
35 Jimmy ___, reporter for the Daily Planet
36 Like overgrown gardens
39 ___ Keith, singer with 20 #1 country hits
40 Gram or dram
41 Indenting computer key
44 Fifth Avenue retailer
47 Perpetual troublemakers
49 Pigsties
50 Nerd
51 Prima ballerina
52 Cookbook amts.
53 Dickens's ___ Heep
54 Indy 500 car
58 Chips and popcorn, in commercialese
61 "Singin' in the Rain" dance style
62 Fertilizable cells
63 Sever
64 Santa ___, Calif.
65 72, for many golf courses

by Timothy Polin

ACROSS

1 Start of a "recuperative" word ladder ending at 73-Across
5 Pres. Jefferson
9 1000 or 2000, but not 0
13 Cookies with a Double Stuf variety
15 Part 2 of the word ladder
16 Singer Fitzgerald
17 Socially unacceptable
18 Cleveland's lake
19 Part 3 of the word ladder
20 Morsel for an aardvark
21 Seeking victory
24 Blue Jays, on scoreboards
25 Switch ups?
26 Place to get outta, in a saying
30 How to avoid becoming 1-Across, so they say
35 60 minuti
36 ___-majesté
37 Wires for thrill-seekers
39 Palindromic band name
41 "Are not!" retort
43 No. on a periodic table
44 Come together
46 ___-ho
48 Quaint lodging
49 Aid for getting 73-Across, so they say
53 Capital of Senegal
55 ___ Lingus
56 General ___ (name on a Chinese menu)
57 Dunk
61 "___ Pinafore"
62 Part 4 of the word ladder
65 Football coach Jim
66 Really bothered
68 Taiwan-based computer maker
69 Part 5 of the word ladder
70 Andrea ___ (ill-fated ship)
71 Alien: Prefix
72 Fr. honorees
73 End of the word ladder

DOWN

1 Hyundai model
2 Attach, as a patch
3 The Fed, for example
4 Keystone ___
5 Fly over sub-Saharan Africa?
6 Trumpeter Al
7 Mélange
8 Slant
9 Answerable with a head nod or shake
10 Inventor Whitney
11 The whole enchilada
12 Subway station sighting
14 Reporters' coups
22 Let loose
23 Tranquil scene
27 "Can we not talk about that!"
28 Ballooned
29 Heading for Marco Polo
31 Church bell sound
32 The Mexica people ruled over them
33 God, in Roma
34 Orbital high points
38 Writer Fleming and others
39 If you drop this you'll trip
40 ___ fide
42 Former telecom giant
45 Hosiery shade
47 Not book-smart
50 Gold standards
51 Service symbolized by a blue-and-white eagle
52 Relating to 51-Down
54 Houston ballplayer
58 German autos
59 Brand of bubbly, familiarly
60 Writer ___ Stanley Gardner
62 Madame Tussaud material
63 Rocks or diamonds
64 Judge Goodman of "Dancing With the Stars"
67 A busy mom might keep a child in this

by Robert Cirillo

ACROSS

1 Makes eyes at
6 Start of four TV drama titles of the 2000s
9 Twisted, as a wet towel
14 Entry in the Rose Parade
15 "Winnie-the-Pooh" baby
16 Course you hardly have to study for
17 Brand of orange or grape soda
18 Misbehaving
20 Unit of work in physics
21 N.F.L. team that plays in Jersey, strangely enough
23 Marquis ___ (French writer)
25 Regarding
26 ___ News (Roger Ailes's former channel)
29 Tool for laying cement
31 Locale for mobile campers
33 ___ jacket (denim top)
34 Pie ___ mode
36 "Miss" of TV's "Dallas"
37 Jazz group
38 "Yo"
39 Caramel-filled candies
40 Server overseer, informally
41 Conan O'Brien's network
42 Romulus or Remus
43 Put (together), as a jigsaw puzzle
45 "Little" folk tale character with lazy friends
47 One of the Kennedys
48 "Stumblin' In" singer Quatro
50 Didn't give a definitive answer
53 Something bid on on "The Price Is Right"
55 Drunk motorist's infraction, for short
56 California's says "Eureka"
59 Sag
61 Speakers' platforms
62 ___ and outs
63 Stares (at)

64 Emmy or Espy
65 Sporty Pontiac
66 Minuscule, informally

DOWN

1 Took care of, mob-style
2 What a sun visor reduces
3 Like some wineglasses and roses
4 Dine
5 Perform an inverted feat
6 Rocky outcropping
7 Alcohol, per its effect at a party
8 Smidgens
9 Lost one's sanity
10 From ___ to riches
11 Military entertainment grp.
12 Sch. on Manhattan's Washington Square Park
13 Gun, in old mob slang
19 Like some verbs: Abbr.
22 Tree whose name sounds like a letter of the alphabet
24 Language of Yemen and Oman
26 Like the contents of this puzzle's circled squares, in a nursery rhyme
27 Hunter of myth
28 Sporty Jaguars
30 "It is the ___, and Juliet is the sun": Romeo
32 Prepared for planting, as a field

33 Actress Foster
35 Cathedral recess
37 Lt.'s superior
44 Twosomes
46 Some A.L. sluggers
49 Stefan ___, influential Austrian writer of the 1920s–'30s
51 Furry "Star Wars" creatures
52 ___ Doodles (snack brand)
53 Kerfuffle
54 In addition
56 Health resort
57 Pull to a pound
58 Nabokov novel
60 Singer Carly ___ Jepsen

by Jacob Stulberg

ACROSS

1 President who ended "don't ask, don't tell"
6 Women's suffrage leader Carrie Chapman __
10 Swanky
14 Fortuneteller's deck
15 "Famous" snack maker
16 Teeny
17 Overboard, to a sailor
19 Maryland athlete, for short
20 Talk back to
21 Actress Skye of "Say Anything . . ."
22 Jazz vocalist Carmen __
23 Data storage devices
25 "Let me take care of that"
29 Function
30 Kathmandu's land
31 Chicken of the Sea product
34 __ team (police unit)
38 Punch in the mouth, slangily
41 Neither good nor bad
42 To whom God said "For dust you are and to dust you will return"
43 Nintendo character who hatches from an egg
44 Prefix with athlete
46 Website that investigates urban legends
47 Bright sort
53 International court site, with "The"
54 Jagged cliff
55 __ fide
59 With 2-Down, star of 2003's "Hulk"
60 Backpack containers where you can find the ends of 17-, 23-, 38- and 47-Across
62 No-longer-fashionable fur
63 Common ingredient in lotions
64 Dance move added to the O.E.D. in 2015
65 Things to hang coats on
66 "What a __!" ("Too bad!")
67 Meanders

DOWN

1 Soul singer Redding
2 See 59-Across
3 The "A" of B.A.
4 __ scale (measure of hardness)
5 Had dinner
6 Rebound on a pool table
7 __ acid (protein builder)
8 Photocopier powder
9 "Naughty!"
10 Is a romancer, old-style
11 Former "S.N.L." comic Cheri, whose last name rhymes with her first
12 Bridle rein, e.g.
13 Promotes, with "up"
18 Weight-loss program
22 Show hosts, in brief
23 Skim or 2%
24 Chinese money
25 Signs, as a contract
26 Jets quarterback Smith
27 Grand work
28 Street vendors selling Mexican food
31 Senator Cruz
32 Made in __
33 Place of service for John McCain, briefly
35 Bit of smoke
36 Aftereffect from working out
37 "__ ends here!" (fighting words)
39 Of the flock
40 Unit of force
45 GPS calculation: Abbr.
46 [Ah, me]
47 Oldest of the Three Stooges
48 __ Antoinette
49 Getting into a gray area?
50 Eyes: Lat.
51 Words after "like it" and "ready"
52 Singer Musgraves who won a 2013 Grammy for Best Country Album
55 Heavyweight champ Riddick
56 Headstrong animals
57 Do 10 crosswords in a row, say, with "out"
58 Questions
60 Once around the track
61 "Oh, before I forget . . . ," in a text

by Sam Buchbinder

ACROSS

1 Numbered things in a hotel hallway
6 Not fully closed, as 1-Across
10 Sicilian volcano
14 Cry to a battlefield medic
15 Pasta sauce "trusted since 1937"
16 "Um, pardon me"
17 Airborne animal with a monstrous name
19 Not medium or well done
20 "Who knows the answer?"
21 Mare's mate
23 Pod fillers
25 Site with the option "Shop by category"
26 Top choice, informally
29 Anonymous John
31 Exclamation when raising one's champagne glass
35 University of Maine town
37 Airborne animal with a monstrous name
39 Zilch
40 12:00
42 Spot for a cat
43 Undersea animal with a monstrous name
45 Lessen
47 Much
48 Remove from a no-parking zone, say
50 High/low cards
51 __-serif font
53 Singer who starred in "Moonstruck"
55 Beret-wearing individualists of the 1950s–'60s
59 U.S. moon-landing program
63 Play's start
64 Undersea animal with a monstrous name
66 "For __ the Bell Tolls"
67 Half: Prefix
68 No longer in the closet, and not by choice
69 Brain or ear part
70 Fearsome dino
71 Must-haves

DOWN

1 Performer inclined to throw tantrums
2 Muscat is its capital
3 "Goodness gracious!"
4 Tear the wrapping off
5 Children's writer R. L. __
6 "__ you kidding me?!"
7 Quick punches
8 Banded rock
9 Relative of a turnip
10 In the beginning stages
11 Bangkok resident
12 Emperor accused of starting the Great Fire of Rome
13 "I'll second that, brother!"
18 Enjoy a book
22 One of the Jacksons
24 "Ditto"
26 Hollywood's Henry or Jane
27 "The Little Mermaid" mermaid
28 Swedish car whose name is Latin for "I roll"
30 German artist Max
32 Insurer with a duck in its commercials
33 Something to write on with chalk
34 Uses a computer keyboard
36 Borrowed, as artwork between museums
38 For one particular purpose, as a committee
41 Subpar performance for a team or musician, say
44 "We've waited long enough"
46 Ornate architectural style
49 "__ the heck"
52 One going down a slippery slope
54 Printer brand
55 Cry like a baby
56 Canyon rebound
57 Very limited range
58 "Ditto"
60 Troubadour's stringed instrument
61 Told untruths
62 10:1 at a racetrack, e.g.
65 Veto

by Patrick Merrell

65

ACROSS

1 Hawaiian greeting
6 Growth on the forest floor
10 Seller of the Söderhamn sofa
14 Like three NASA rovers
15 "This is disastrous!"
16 Lima's home
17 PowerPoint slide with fake data?
20 Hershey bar with toffee
21 Go to the mall
22 "Duty, __, Country" (West Point motto)
23 Fancy affair
25 Pressing business?
26 Sliced serving with ritzy crackers?
31 Restaurant basketful
32 Stir-fry vessel
33 Octagonal sign
37 Everybody
38 Rag covered in dirt?
42 Pal of Piglet and Pooh
43 "Holy moly!"
45 Bill __, the Science Guy
46 Japanese auto import
48 Pep squad member's lament?
52 Cotton fabric
55 Flying circus performer?
56 __ Sam
57 Eatery with sidewalk tables, often
59 Breckinridge of fiction
63 Briefs from Walmart or Target?
66 Biggest city on the Big Island
67 Length × width, for a rectangle
68 Innocent's reply to "Who did this?"
69 Store sign
70 Like morning grass
71 From Zurich, e.g.

DOWN

1 "Woe is me"
2 Stand in the shadows
3 Not fooled by
4 What may keep a Mohawk in place
5 Dog's yap
6 Latte alternatives
7 Lima's home
8 "Oh, __!" ("Good one, girlfriend!")
9 Fa follower
10 Products featuring Siri
11 "The Family Circus" creator Bil
12 Goof
13 Cowboy singer Gene
18 Capri or Man
19 Something a thoughtful person strokes
24 Lead-in for prof. or V.P.
25 Reference page edited by a group
26 Steep rock face
27 Golfer's target
28 Glamour rival
29 It gives a little hoot
30 Rock's __ Fighters
34 "You make a good point"
35 Primordial muck
36 Rain really hard
39 Unknown source, informally
40 School about 40 miles from S.L.C.
41 "God does not play __ with the world": Einstein
44 Ginormous number
47 Cloth made famous by infomercials
49 Appearance
50 When nothing seems to go right
51 Escape (from)
52 A ton, in Tijuana
53 Square
54 Item on many a bathroom floor
57 Successfully treat
58 From square one
60 Supposed sighting in Tibet
61 Aries animals
62 God who sounds like he was mentioned in the preceding clue
64 __ sack
65 E.R. staffers

by Samuel A. Donaldson and Doug Peterson

ACROSS

1 Ten to one, for one
6 "I Am __" (Jenner's reality show on E!)
10 "Madam, I'm __" (palindromic introduction to Eve)
14 Something "walked" on a pirate ship
15 Merry-go-round or roller coaster
16 Nevada's so-called "Biggest Little City in the World"
17 *Serving between appetizer and dessert
19 Puts out, in baseball
20 Dedicated poems
21 Confuse
22 Politically left-leaning
26 Hairstyle with straight-cut bangs
28 Mrs. whose cow supposedly began the Great Chicago Fire
29 Philosopher who tutored Nero
30 __ Claus
31 James of "The Godfather"
32 Germany's von Bismarck
35 Abbr. at the bottom of a letter
36 *It's signaled by a white flag on the racetrack
39 Austin's home: Abbr.
40 Witty Mort
42 Hearts of PCs, for short
43 "Me, Myself & __" (Jim Carrey film)
45 Punch hard
47 Offset, as costs
48 Exchange, as an old piece of equipment for a new one
50 "Aren't I the fortunate one!"
51 Fruit-filled pastries
52 Window frame
53 Prefix with sphere
54 Plan that has no chance of working . . . or the answer to each starred clue?
60 Stay fresh

61 Winter ailments
62 Wet, weatherwise
63 Does wrong
64 Toy block brand
65 "__ Boots Are Made for Walkin'" (1966 Nancy Sinatra hit)

DOWN

1 33⅓, for an LP
2 In the manner of
3 __ chi (martial art)
4 Bed-and-breakfast
5 Shootout site involving the Earp brothers
6 Mean, mean, mean
7 Is broadcast
8 Check-cashing requirements, for short
9 Golf peg
10 Design style of the 1920s and '30s
11 *Reason for jumper cables
12 __-Saxon
13 Putter (along)
18 Anita of jazz
21 Get on in years
22 Finishes with fewer votes
23 Glazer of "Broad City"
24 *Athlete who "rides the pine"
25 Chow down
26 Rings, as church bells
27 Kournikova of tennis
29 Stopped lying?
31 Bill also called a benjamin
33 Brunch time, say
34 Common daisy

37 Free speech advocacy grp.
38 Infographic with wedges
41 Go-with-you-anywhere computers
44 D.C. stadium initials
46 The "L" of L.A.
47 Attic accumulation
48 Vampire hunter's weapon
49 H₂0
50 Rodeo rope
52 Close-fitting
54 Lombardi Trophy org.
55 Stadium cheer
56 Stadium cheer
57 Suit accessory
58 U.S.N. officer: Abbr.
59 Whiskey type

by Damon Gulczynski

ACROSS
1 Plumbing problem
5 Gulf of ___ (arm of the Red Sea)
10 Progeny: Abbr.
14 Flying start?
15 Stock of words, informally
16 Country's McEntire
17 1961–75
19 Asia's disappearing ___ Sea
20 ___ Master's Voice
21 Reprimand to a dog, maybe
23 Prank
26 Cigarette stat
28 Manipulators
29 Public transportation system in the capital of Catalonia
32 Carnival city, casually
33 Time of one's life?
34 I-85 and I-77 to get from Atlanta to Cleveland, e.g.: Abbr.
35 National Historic Landmark in Pearl Harbor
42 Tattoo parlor supply
43 Egg: Prefix
44 Rap's Dr. ___
45 Marvel Comics superhero wielding a nearly indestructible shield
50 Ralph ___ Emerson
51 Wine: Prefix
52 What birds of prey do
53 Clarinet need
55 "___ Little Teapot"
56 Roasted: Fr.
57 What 50-Across is . . . or a clue to 17-, 29-, 35- and 45-Across
63 Belarussian, e.g.
64 Change from "I do" to "I don't"?
65 Illusionist Henning
66 3M product
67 Guess things
68 Additionally

DOWN
1 Cleveland player, for short
2 Hawaiian shirt go-with
3 Bank deposit?
4 "Wuthering Heights" genre
5 Actress Gardner and others
6 Iranian holy city
7 Top fighter pilot
8 Singer Streisand
9 Rhyme scheme in the last verse of a villanelle
10 "The Fast and the Furious" racer
11 More spooky
12 Italian restaurant chain
13 "Safe!" and "You're out!"
18 French city named after the Greek goddess of victory
22 As a result of
23 Start of a magician's cry
24 Commercial alternative to waxing
25 Enterprise counselor
26 Attire for Atticus
27 Tentacled marine creature
30 Sri ___
31 1983 Michael Keaton comedy
36 Obsolescent data storage device
37 En pointe, in ballet
38 ___ Spiegel, co-founder of Snapchat
39 Prefix with -syncratic
40 Gas brand rendered in all capital letters
41 ___ of faith
45 Olive oil alternative
46 Pub fixture
47 What I may stand for?
48 Salinger title girl
49 Neighbor of Tanzania
50 Razzie Award word
54 Key with four sharps: Abbr.
55 Woes
58 Subject for Watson and Crick
59 Grayish-brown
60 The "A" of AIM
61 Followers of lambdas
62 Id's counterpart

by Mary Lou Guizzo

68

ACROSS

1 Molars usually have four of these
6 Prisons
11 Place to enter a PIN
14 First-stringers
15 Final stanza of a ballad
16 Musician Reed
17 Virginia city known for its shipbuilding
19 Dashboard-mounted gadget, for short
20 Mine cart contents
21 Cabbagelike vegetable
22 San ___ (Silicon Valley city)
23 Manuel ___, former dictator of Panama
25 Presided over, as a meeting
28 Flow of narcotics
30 Money in Yemen
33 Lash mark
34 Prefix with -ceratops
36 Not feeling so hot
41 China's ___ Zedong
42 Coffin stand
43 CPR experts
44 Killjoys
49 Really dislikes
50 Shoe material
54 Anything below 7 on the pH scale
55 Norse god of war
56 "As I see it," in texts
57 Inhabitant of Kanga's pouch
58 Breakfast-time TV fare that usually includes the ends of 17-, 28-, 36- and 44-Across
62 Anderson Cooper's channel
63 Best of the best
64 Speak grandiloquently
65 Gridiron gains: Abbr.
66 Kids' building toys
67 Having eaten enough

DOWN

1 Maker of the EOS and PowerShot cameras
2 In ___ (unborn)
3 Waste conduit
4 Drivel
5 One often seen standing just outside a building's entrance
6 Problem after a trans-Atlantic flight
7 Actress Hathaway
8 "___ Gotta Be Me" (Sammy Davis Jr. song)
9 Gentle heat setting
10 Bro's sibling
11 Procedure for solving a mathematical problem
12 Highly classified
13 Ruminated (on)
18 Italian-style sauce brand
22 Skippy rival
24 "___ hands are the devil's playthings"
25 All hands on deck
26 Physically fit
27 Old Spice alternative
29 Pipsqueak
30 ___ and Coke
31 "Be there soon"
32 Humane Society successes
35 Recipient of many checks dated Apr. 15
37 Stats for sluggers
38 Feature of the earth's axis that causes the seasons
39 Gas company selling toy trucks
40 Trial run
45 British ref. work
46 Music from the '50s or '60s, say
47 Bridle strap
48 Argentine dances
49 Mr. ___ of "Pride and Prejudice"
51 Pair of cymbals operated by a foot pedal
52 Overact
53 Used oars
55 Aware of
58 Gibson who directed "The Passion of the Christ"
59 Cheer for a torero
60 Oil-drilling apparatus
61 Spanish Mrs.

by John Guzzetta

ACROSS

1 Common name for a cowboy
6 Winner's cry in a card game
9 Leaky parts of an old tent, often
14 __ nous
15 A, in Asunción
16 Dustup
17 Hidden symbol between the "E" and "x" in the FedEx logo
18 Drug for Timothy Leary
19 End of a lasso
20 Nipple
21 Cloudless
23 Elizabethan stringed instrument
24 Fedora or fez
25 Final part of a relay
27 [their error, not mine]
28 Actor Christian of "Mr. Robot"
30 State-of-the-art electronically
32 Cradled
34 Mata __ (spy)
35 Offer at a pub . . . as suggested by this puzzle's circled squares
40 Cock-a-doodle-doo
41 Dentist's focus
42 Coal-rich German region
44 Like Cheerios cereal
46 "Facilities," informally
47 Suit material
48 Device that keeps a ship's compass level
50 "O Romeo, Romeo!" crier
51 SSW's opposite
52 & 54 Tavern total
55 Lead-in to fix, appropriately
56 Put __ on (limit)
58 __ Picchu, site of ancient Inca ruins
60 Shouts of dissent
61 Bathroom powder
62 Trimmed area around a green
63 "Hey . . . over here!"
64 Once, in olden days
65 Burly
66 Snitches (on)

DOWN

1 Opposites of births
2 "That is SO incredible!"
3 Geological layers
4 Gait faster than a walk
5 Tree with medicinal uses
6 Birds near the shore
7 Detailed blowup on a map
8 Longtime Federer adversary
9 Personal identifier, for short
10 Subj. of interest for the Green Party
11 Move to action
12 Tile adhesive
13 When repeated, cry to an honoree
21 Place for wheeling and dealing?
22 Go over and over again
25 Unwelcome look
26 Big name in bicycle helmets
29 What Wi-Fi can connect you to
31 Yule glitter
33 Highlight in a Zorro movie
34 Modern home entertainment option
35 Sleeper or caboose
36 Soup kitchen offerings
37 Teachers' org.
38 Tuliplike flower whose name means "butterfly" in Spanish
39 Most ready to get started
40 Related linguistically
43 Examination do-overs
45 Arrest
47 Teacher who may get no respect, informally
49 Tibetan holy men
50 Brief excursion
53 Completely focused
54 Biblical pronoun
57 Polling fig.
59 __-Magnon
60 "Wait Wait . . . Don't Tell Me!" airer

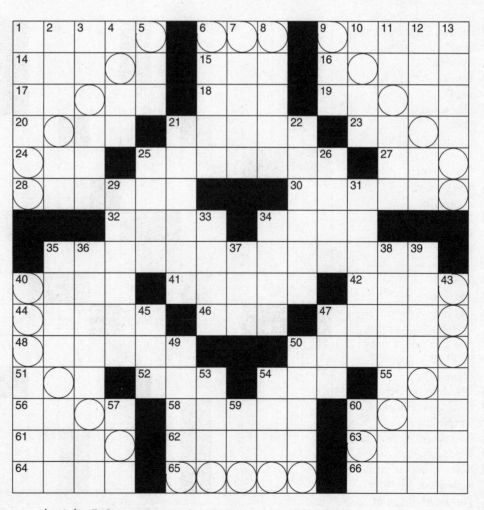

by John E. Bennett

70

ACROSS

1 Twin city of Raleigh
7 Dictionary offering: Abbr.
10 The "m" of $e = mc^2$
14 Italian cheese
15 Tire filler
16 Give off
17 1988 #1 hit for UB40
19 "__ going!"
20 Oak or elm
21 Big feature on a donkey
22 Empty __ (parent whose children have all moved away)
24 1971 hit for Marvin Gaye subtitled "The Ecology"
27 Toy gun pellets
30 Year: Sp.
31 List-ending abbr.
32 Regions
34 "__ Lay Dying"
35 Like some textbooks
39 1920s standard with the lyric "Sugar's sweet, so is she"
43 Woman in "The King and I"
44 12, on a grandfather clock
45 __ bin Laden, 2011 Navy SEALs target
46 Salt, chemically
48 Psychic power, informally
50 June preceder
51 1986 hit for Talking Heads
56 Classical music halls
57 Decay
58 Yawn-inducing
62 Gas in commercial signs
63 1990 hit that samples the bass line from Queen/Bowie's "Under Pressure"
66 1941 film "citizen"
67 Complain, complain, complain
68 Laid down the first card
69 Toboggan, e.g.
70 Route displayer on a dashboard, for short
71 Word with finger or America

DOWN

1 Something thrown at a bull's-eye
2 Pusher's customer
3 Carnival attraction
4 __ pants (baggy wear)
5 See 6-Down
6 With 5-Down, present time
7 Grocery section with milk and yogurt
8 German "a"
9 Crazily fast
10 "Old boys' network" meeting places
11 Friendliness
12 Cry to an attack dog
13 One cubic meter
18 City between Dallas and Austin
23 A pitching ace has a low one, in brief
25 Like a Monday crossword puzzle, relatively speaking
26 Western plateau
27 See 34-Down
28 __ Mawr College
29 Observed
33 Left behind
34 With 27-Down, foe of the Forty Thieves
36 Setting for "The King and I"
37 Funny Bombeck
38 June 6, 1944
40 Removing surgically
41 New York City mayor de Blasio
42 Head: Ger.
47 Barley beard
48 "The Time Machine" race
49 "30 Rock" or "3rd Rock From the Sun"
51 Policy experts
52 Perfect
53 Sierra __ (African country)
54 Bottom-of-the-bottle stuff
55 Flowed back
59 Word that fills both blanks in "This __ is your __"
60 Brother of Cain
61 Jekyll's alter ego
64 Item of apparel often worn backward
65 Commercial lead-in to Pen

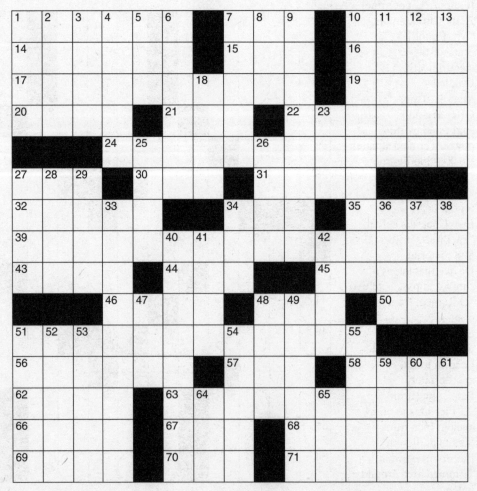

by Peter A. Collins

ACROSS

1 Tailor's unit
5 African virus
10 Ancient Central American
14 "Your majesty"
15 Commercial symbols in Lomé?
17 Source of indigo
18 Reptile at the top of the Jurassic food chain
19 Basis of a refreshing Mideast beverage?
21 Court recorder
22 Speaking up?
26 Cries of dismay
27 Downton Abbey headgear
31 Chill in the air
32 Metonym for Middle America
34 Leader of a group of elves
36 Gavotte, minuet and cancan?
39 Where Theseus slew the Minotaur
40 Tone deafness
41 What a cyclops has in common with a cyclone
42 River in Stephen Foster's "Old Folks at Home"
44 Chomped down on
47 Country completely surrounded by South Africa
50 Ethan Frome's wife
52 Far Eastern mimics?
56 Cry from Juliet
59 Sondheim's "It Takes Two," e.g.
60 Providers of low notes for rumbas?
61 To be, in Toulouse
62 "___ aside . . ."
63 Begins to wake
64 Blond now, say

DOWN

1 Arbitrary non-explanation, after "because"
2 No longer an octogenarian
3 Events in Bonnie and Clyde's biography
4 Her face launched a thousand ships
5 Greek H's
6 ___ weevil
7 Leer
8 Lead-in to land for Willy Wonka's workers
9 Categorize
10 Timid
11 Cabinet dept.
12 The "Y" of TTYL
13 Total jerk
16 Actress Turner
20 Emphatically zero
23 What kindness and graceful aging reveal
24 Quibbles
25 4.0, e.g.
28 Tolkien terror
29 Alternative to cake
30 "___ mañana"
33 Have supper
34 One of the Seven Dwarfs
35 Obama's signature health measure, for short
36 David ___, comic with a famous Richard Nixon impression
37 When repeated, child's term for supper
38 "Wheel of Fortune" buy
39 Cartoon frame
42 Skins' opponent in a pickup game
43 Prevailed
45 Cry after "Psst!"
46 Sampled
48 Indian ___
49 Pres. Jefferson
51 Broke off
53 Prefix with dexterity
54 Burn superficially
55 Rolling stones lack it
56 First U.S. color TV maker
57 Suffix with hazard
58 C.E.O.'s deg.

by Ruth Bloomfield Margolin

72

ACROSS

1 Jazzy James
5 Facing the pitcher
10 Fashion magazine founded in France
14 When doubled, a Hawaiian fish
15 Relative of a cello
16 Who asked "Am I my brother's keeper?"
17 Milky gemstone
18 What might make an adult jump in a pile of leaves
20 Rocker Bon Jovi
21 Defensive spray
22 Greek vowels
23 Home office item that's surprisingly expensive to replace
27 Tokyo-based electronics giant
28 Lose an opportunity
32 Player most likely to shoot a three-pointer
34 Lengthy narrative
36 Genetic code carrier
37 What Ramadan is an annual feature of
41 Sign before Virgo
42 Overly curious
43 Something thrown by a cowboy
44 Painting exhibition
47 Not yielding, as a mattress
48 Obsolescent place to go online
53 Stuffed to the gills
56 Life of Riley
57 Carrier to Seoul, for short
58 West African country whose name is usually rendered in French
61 Actress Polo of "Meet the Parents"
62 Next-to-last element alphabetically
63 Santa __ (California racetrack)
64 Circle segments
65 Fringe
66 Green gemstone
67 "Aha!" . . . or a hint to 18-, 23-, 37-, 48- and 58-Across

DOWN

1 Symbol like "prayer hands" or "heart eyes"
2 Strike lightly
3 "Much appreciated"
4 Suffer
5 Monkey house : monkeys :: __ : birds
6 Hint of color
7 Screw-up
8 India pale __
9 Black goo
10 Repeats word for word
11 Café au __
12 __ Kedrova, Oscar-winning actress for "Zorba the Greek"
13 Wraps up
19 Marlboros, e.g., for short
21 Candy item with plain and peanut varieties
24 "Downton Abbey" countess
25 Coming-out phrase
26 "Don't touch that __!"
29 Bookies
30 Some, in Spain
31 Poi source
32 __ monster (desert lizard)
33 Marketing target
34 Put points on the board
35 Coolers, briefly
38 Participating
39 Privileged few
40 Many a police officer on "The Wire"
45 Ferocious
46 Artist Warhol
47 Celebratory
49 Put on TV again
50 Mean, mean, mean
51 Many a Monty Python skit
52 Beethoven honoree
53 XL or XXL
54 Enthusiastic
55 Half of a fireplace tool
59 Taxi
60 Word repeated in "It takes __ to know __"
61 Mai __

by Bruce Haight

ACROSS

1 First instrument heard in the Beatles' "She's Leaving Home"
5 Marathoner's concern
9 Bulb units
14 Miscellany
15 1982 sci-fi film with a 2010 sequel
16 One who's new on board
17 *Carolina wren, for South Carolina
19 Places to buy furniture to assemble
20 *Turnpike
21 Has control of the wheel
22 Actress Thurman
23 Queen of the Jungle, in comics
25 Pumas and panthers
29 Lawyer: Abbr.
30 Collar
33 Carefree adventure
34 Tale of adventure
36 "__ had enough!"
37 Kipling's "Follow Me __"
38 Asian body of water that's now largely dried up
40 Sallie __
41 Cent gent?
42 Name repeated before "Wherefore art thou"
43 Innocent sort
44 Gift on a 10th anniversary
45 Something worth waiting for?
46 How people with colds may speak
49 Nielsen of "Airplane!"
52 Rice or Curry
53 High spirits
55 *Force from a hiding place
60 __-Saxon
61 Realtor's big day . . . or what each word in the answers to the starred clues can do

62 Surgeon's supply in the old days
63 Wall Street inits.
64 Minuscule div. of a minute
65 Petrol unit
66 Winter Palace resident
67 SFO postings

DOWN

1 Deer, to a tick
2 Member of a mixed quartet
3 Capital of Iran
4 Dinner at which everyone does the dishes?
5 W.W. II naval craft
6 Las Vegas casino with a musical name
7 Ribbed pants, informally
8 Adjourn
9 *Highly antioxidant beverage
10 Pulitzer-winning poet Conrad
11 *Sloth, for one
12 Sign of sadness
13 Meeting of Congress: Abbr.
18 Humorist Bombeck
21 Number of hills in Roma
24 "MMMBop" band
25 Cause to swell
26 "Whose woods these are I think I know" has four
27 *Approve
28 Garlic lover's dish, maybe

31 Be of use
32 Like many bar bouncers
35 "Bravo!"
38 *Place to buy paint
39 Turbulent
43 "Give me an example"
47 Penitent person
48 Many a Punjabi
50 Conger catcher
51 Annual sports prizes
53 Erse speaker
54 Voting against
56 Grand Canyon sight
57 Send packing
58 Like many Craigslist items
59 Private eyes, in slang
61 Neighbor of Mich.

by Michael J. Doran

74

ACROSS

1 Group of tents in the woods
5 San Antonio hoopsters
10 Goofing off
14 Onetime Chevy subcompact
15 Bat mitzvah reading
16 Rodenticide brand with glue traps
17 Goofing off
20 S&P 500, e.g.
21 Rig on the road
22 "Super" game console
23 Jockey's strap
26 Voting against
28 Hack (off)
31 Getting ready to click on, as a link
36 Impress greatly
37 Foreign president with a black belt in judo
38 Heredity transmitter
39 Most's opposite
41 He said "I pity the fool"
42 Mini racing vehicles
43 Gillette razor brand
44 Spooky
46 "Ready, ___, go!"
47 Eating quickly
50 Spots for getting stitches, in brief
51 ___ lily (Utah's state flower)
52 Mamas' boys
54 Browser sub-window
56 Chooses (to)
59 Arab Spring country
63 Storing for future use
67 Trickster in "A Midsummer Night's Dream"
68 Make a grand speech
69 Speak hoarsely
70 Literally, "liquor," in Japanese
71 Archie Bunker, notably
72 Place to store mowers and rakes

DOWN

1 Ladies' undergarment, casually
2 Stratford-upon-___
3 Patch up
4 Game with an annual World Series held in Las Vegas
5 Digs for pigs
6 Luau dish
7 Containers for serving coffee
8 Explosive anger
9 Tribal healer
10 "Don't mind if ___"
11 Where Batman and Superman live
12 ___ Star State (Texas)
13 Pulls the plug on
18 Like nonprofits vis-à-vis taxes
19 What the best man holds for the groom
24 Debtor's note
25 Eggnog spice
27 Attire in old Rome
28 1980s–'90s legal drama that won 15 Emmys
29 Have because of
30 "The Good Earth" author
32 Fathered, as a racehorse
33 Opening remarks
34 Another name for the return key on a Mac
35 Takes a breather
40 ___ and sound
42 Saxophonist with the #1 album "Miracles"
45 ___ Jima
48 Dr. Frankenstein's assistant
49 "Sure thing"
53 Target competitor
54 Sugar and spice amts.
55 Light blue hue
57 Hatcher of "Tomorrow Never Dies"
58 Smelting waste
60 "Love ya!"
61 Freedom from anxiety
62 Manhattan law enforcement grp.
64 "I Like ___" (1950s campaign slogan)
65 "Who am ___ judge?"
66 Tennis court divider

by Zhouqin Burnikel

ACROSS

1 "My Kind of ___ (Chicago Is)"
5 Went 90, say
9 The former Mrs. McCartney
14 What you may think of
15 Concern for beachcombers
16 Tinker to ___ to Chance (Cubs double play combo)
17 Curse of the Billy ___, Cubs "jinx" that ended in 2016
18 Western tribe
19 Things proofreaders look for
20 Hall-of-Famer known as Mr. Cub
23 Racer Yarborough
24 Balls
25 Blog annoyances
27 Backbone-related
30 The year 254
32 Opposite of baja
33 Its inaugural flight was from Geneva to Tel Aviv
35 Kind of blitz
39 2016 award for each Cub
42 Shag or bob
43 English lockup
44 Barely beat
45 Judy Jetson's kid brother
47 Moves like a whirlpool
49 Entertain grandly
52 Trash-toting transport
53 Sleep like ___
54 Wrigley Field events since only 1988
60 Finish pitching in a lopsided game
62 Uncouth one
63 Newswoman Logan
64 Capital in a Cole Porter song
65 Certain tax-free investment, for short
66 Home to French silk makers
67 Bar drink taken in one gulp
68 What many writers write on
69 Cubs slugger with 609 home runs

DOWN

1 Buster Brown's canine sidekick
2 Something whiffed
3 Withdraw gradually
4 Cub, e.g.
5 Targets of close shaves?
6 Some wrap holders
7 First place
8 What many writers write on
9 Allow to
10 Unique feature of Wrigley Field
11 Country whose capital is more than 4,500 feet above sea level
12 Like some humor
13 Burros
21 Stat for Jon Lester
22 Cubs' divisional rivals: Abbr.
26 Hoopsters' hoops
27 Familiar sayings
28 Secret plan
29 Modest reply to a compliment
30 Hall-of-Fame sportscaster Harry who regularly led the Wrigley Field crowd in singing "Take Me Out to the Ball Game"
31 Oscar : films :: ___ : ads
34 Toy block brand
36 "What ___ tell you?"
37 "Picnic" playwright
38 Matures
40 PC brand
41 Thrilling
46 Kylo ___, Adam Driver's role in "Star Wars"
48 Ballpark frank
49 Stadium walkways
50 Internet finance firm
51 Decide to play for pay
52 Glimmered
55 Some early PCs
56 Ascend
57 Chicken salad ingredient
58 Boy with a bow and arrow
59 Mideast capital supposedly founded by a son of Noah
61 Favorite

by David J. Kahn

ACROSS

1 Taste or touch
6 What eyeglass lenses fit in
10 Drug also known as angel dust
13 Ivy League sch. in Philly
14 Furry creature in "Return of the Jedi"
15 W. Hemisphere alliance
16 Driving condition in a blizzard
19 "Man, that smarts!"
20 Lucy's partner
21 Not __ many words
22 Approval from Siskel and Ebert
25 Loosen, as laces
28 Go 4-0 in the Series, e.g.
29 R&B group with the #1 hit "Reach Out I'll Be There"
33 Cockpit info: Abbr.
34 Fairy tale monster
35 Steinbeck's "The Grapes of __"
37 Shirt that might say "I'm with stupid"
40 __ of a gun
41 Plant life
42 Mediterranean fruits
43 __-pitch softball
45 Amusement park with the Nitro roller coaster
47 Elton John's "Candle in the Wind" was rewritten to honor her
49 Rodeo rope
50 1988 film about the Black Sox scandal
54 Tirade
55 __-friendly
56 Western lily
60 How an extreme underdog wins . . . or this puzzle?
63 Note between fa and la
64 Fortuneteller
65 What light bulbs represent in cartoons
66 Naval officer: Abbr.
67 Summer drinks
68 Country music's Tucker

DOWN

1 __ Q's (Hostess brand)
2 Fencing blade
3 Character in "I, Claudius"
4 Michelin winter product
5 Letter holder: Abbr.
6 Bowling alley button
7 "If only!"
8 __ strip (mathematical curiosity)
9 Compete in the Nordic combined, say
10 Traditional Christmas plants
11 Heinz product
12 "Hearts and minds" military maneuver, briefly
17 Words at the altar
18 Printed defamation
23 Rainy
24 Air kiss sound
25 Supernatural tabloid fodder
26 Canceled, as a launch
27 Blinkers
30 Bird that says "Give a hoot! Don't pollute!"
31 Counterparts of amateurs
32 Bollywood dress
36 Word after income, sales or excise
38 Custard base
39 Canadian gas brand
41 Times New Roman, e.g.
42 Pop with no fizz
44 Actress Christine of "Chicago Hope"
46 Focus of a yearly shot
47 __ Alley, shopping area for Harry Potter
48 Made smile
50 Wipe clean, as a blackboard
51 Cosmetician Lauder
52 Approaches
53 N.B.A.'s Magic, on scoreboards
57 The Bible's Garden of __
58 Aussie greeting
59 Greece's Mount __
61 Org. for which Edward Snowden once worked
62 Ignited, as a match

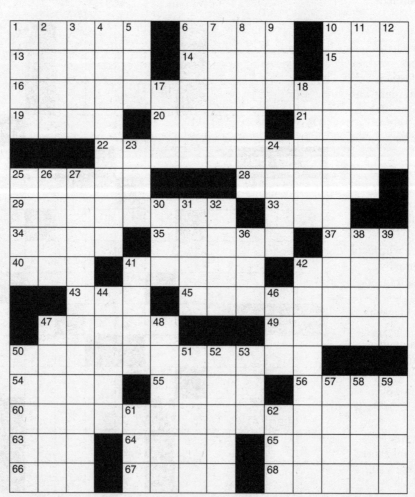

by John Lieb

ACROSS

1 Musical talent, informally
6 Drunkards
10 Quite a ways away
14 Rehearsed a piece through from start to finish, in theater lingo
15 When doubled, a South Seas island
16 Mineral in layers
17 Memorable 2011 hurricane
18 When you get it
20 Like yarn
21 Talking horse of 1960s TV
22 Cock and bull
23 Something might be brought back by this
26 Voodoo spell
27 Ashen
28 Dallas cager, informally
31 In working order
34 Marmalade container
35 Mud
36 "Where the heart is"
37 Versatile eating implement
39 Decorates, as a cake
40 Scent
41 Knot
42 Most sensible
44 Possesses
45 Max's opposite
46 Grace ender
47 Eastern or Western, for hoopsters
53 "Carmen" setting
55 The Canadian loonie or toonie, e.g.
56 Meeting point for tailors?
57 Like the four things named in the circled squares
59 Momma's partner
60 Shoppe descriptor
61 Woes
62 Onetime arcade giant
63 Word before and after "will be"
64 Casual sign-off in a letter
65 Opposite of 57-Across, to Muslims

DOWN

1 Cousin of a cobbler
2 One of the Marx Brothers
3 Outdo
4 What's punched into an A.T.M., redundantly
5 Sault ___ Marie, Ont.
6 Pizza chain found in many food courts
7 Expressed amazement
8 It might involve mutual raising of tariffs
9 Film character who was asked to "Play it"
10 Capital of Jordan
11 Dark brown rodents with long tails and large eyes
12 Proactiv target
13 "Darn!"
19 Mideast's Gulf of ___
21 ___ Theater, venue of "The Phantom of the Opera," the longest-running production in Broadway history
24 "Haha, u r hilarious"
25 Crack shooters
29 Belligerent Greek god
30 Sweater ___
31 "This doesn't look good"
32 Coke or Pepsi
33 Old radio show set in Harlem
34 MSNBC's "Morning ___"
35 Garrison Keillor's home state
38 Trick-taking game with a 48-card deck
43 ___ Lingus
45 Hand, to Javier
46 Something record-breaking
48 Tour de France sights
49 Carolers' repertoire
50 Himalayan land
51 Frank who directed "Mr. Smith Goes to Washington"
52 Kind of client
53 Elitist sort
54 Preppy shirt
58 Bro or sis
59 Musical syllable after "oom"

by Andrew Zhou

ACROSS

1 Taxis
5 Huffed and puffed
9 Wiccan or Druid
14 Fit for the job
15 Demolish
16 Draw out
17 What lions and big engines do
18 Razor brand
19 Zapped with a stun gun
20 "Bowiemania" and "Come Together: America Salutes the Beatles"
23 Be extremely frugal
24 Bill with Hamilton's visage
25 McKellen who played Gandalf
28 1948–94, in South Africa
32 I.S.P. with a butterfly logo
35 What a knife wound might leave
36 Senate staffers
37 "I know! I know!"
39 Makes a blanket, e.g.
42 Common play on fourth down
43 Go __ (no longer follow orders)
45 It may have 40, 60 or 75 watts
47 Shell out
48 Bitter rivals
52 That, in Tabasco
53 Chicken __ king
54 Appear, as problems
58 Children's game . . . or the circled words in 20-, 28- and 48-Across
62 Actress Kirsten of "Spider-Man"
64 Part of an archipelago
65 Letter-shaped metal fastener
66 Chum, in Chihuahua
67 In close proximity
68 "__ goes nothin'!"
69 Senegal's capital
70 Ice cream brand known as Dreyer's west of the Rockies
71 Catch sight of

DOWN

1 Things pushed around a supermarket
2 Multiple-choice options
3 Tony __, 1990s–2000s British P.M.
4 Balkan country once part of Yugoslavia
5 Group that included Demi Moore and Emilio Estevez
6 After curfew
7 Klein of Vox.com
8 What the Forbes 400 measures
9 Flower that's also a girl's name
10 Economist Smith
11 Dressed to the nines
12 Hole in one
13 Homer Simpson's neighbor
21 Diamond officials, informally
22 Buzzer
26 Venue for a rock concert
27 Vile
29 Sprinted
30 Shoshone or Sioux
31 Quick swim
32 Inventor of a "code"
33 Broadway offerings
34 Baddie
38 "Ben-__"
40 T. S. Eliot's Rum __ Tugger
41 Rain jackets
44 Legislator
46 Floating block of ice
49 Majestic Yellowstone creature
50 Literature Nobelist Gordimer
51 Allay, as fears
55 Southern corn breads
56 Take forcibly
57 "Our Gang" dog
59 Links org.
60 Like most consignment shop items
61 Adobe material
62 "Dear old" person
63 "__ Thurman" (Fall Out Boy song)

by Kristian House

ACROSS

1 Croquet needs
5 On
9 Sorority sisters, e.g., in old lingo
14 Skin cream component
15 Bird in a magician's hat
16 Muppet who co-hosted "The Adventures of Elmo in Grouchland"
17 Secure
18 Marmalade ingredient
20 Stack of sheets
22 Historian's Muse
23 Black-and-white swimmer
24 With 53-Across, a sugary treat
26 Blacktop
28 Figured out
29 Snake for a charmer
30 It might end with an early touchdown
32 "Cherry Wine" rapper
35 Purim villain
37 Ones to go pubbing with
40 Classic kitchen volume . . . or a hint to 18-, 24-/53- and 62-Across
43 World capital that celebrated its 1,000th anniversary in 2010
44 Surgeon's insertion
45 Camp bed
46 Areas at rivers' ends
48 Image of Homer, perhaps
50 Bark deeper than a yip
52 ___ Lankan
53 See 24-Across
57 "___ alive!"
59 Color of raw linen
61 Connecticut collegian
62 Sweet and tangy picnic side dish
65 Where Beethoven was born
66 Frequently
67 Voice below soprano
68 Mother ___
69 Poker targets?
70 Sunset's direction
71 Discharge

DOWN

1 Milwaukee brewer
2 Diplomat Root
3 One with zero chance of success
4 Neil who sang "Laughter in the Rain"
5 Stir
6 Commit arson on
7 Like the Kia logo
8 Display of remorse
9 Middling grade
10 Rice-shaped pasta
11 Peppy
12 "Boogie Oogie Oogie" music genre
13 Attacked
19 Egg on
21 They're rich in omega-3 fatty acids
25 Neuter
27 How telecommuters work
30 Large amounts
31 Himalayan grazer
32 To the ___ degree
33 "How brilliant!"
34 Discharge
36 Contents of the Torah
38 Musician Brian
39 York, for one: Abbr.
41 Morning beverage, slangily
42 Fairy tale starter
47 Shade provider
49 Apt (to)
50 Major manufacturer of soda cans
51 Landing spots for Santa
53 Cleans, in a way
54 What a rain cloud over a head may represent, in comics
55 Language in Bollywood films
56 Words to live by
58 Spot hit by a reflex hammer
60 Upset
63 E.R. workers
64 100° or more, say

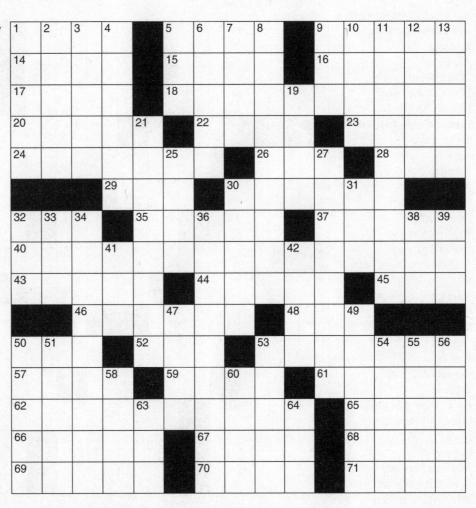

by Jacob Stulberg

ACROSS

1 Sounds like a dog
6 Schism
10 "What have you been ___?"
14 Playwright Edward
15 Spanish "other"
16 Feudal worker
17 Something scary
19 Some Maidenform products
20 Rock band fronted by Michael Stipe
21 Suffix with narc-
23 Words exchanged at the altar
24 "Welcome" thing at the front door
27 It grabs one's attention
30 Like a standard highway
32 ___ wonder (musical artist without a repeated success)
33 Aloe ___
34 "Dagnabbit!"
37 1940s British guns
38 Boastful sort
41 Like some short-lived committees
43 Appear
44 Impulsive
47 Native Israelis
49 Positions higher, as a camera angle
51 Really good joke
54 "Ready, ___, go!"
55 ___ Khan (Islamic title)
56 Vagrant
57 Soccer official, for short
59 "As you ___"
61 Rug rat
66 "Jeopardy!" host Trebek
67 Food, shelter or clothing
68 Source of Peruvian wool
69 Days of old
70 Makes a boo-boo
71 Something it's not mannerly to put on a dinner table

DOWN

1 Cry with "humbug!"
2 Chicken ___ king
3 Baseball hitter's stat
4 Deborah of "The King and I"
5 One of tennis's Williams sisters
6 "Vive le ___!" (old French cry)
7 "No worries"
8 Worries
9 2006 Winter Olympics city
10 Kind of port on a computer
11 Keyboard, monitor, mouse and other devices
12 Exchange, as an older model
13 After a fashion
18 Make ___ (set things right)
22 Are able, biblically
24 "The Real World" cable channel
25 Wonderment
26 Muhammad Ali, for the 1996 Olympics
28 Candy that's "two mints in one"
29 Czar called "the Great"
31 After Karachi, the most populous city in Pakistan
35 Honest ___ (presidential moniker)
36 Get ready for a golf drive
39 Bitcoins, for example
40 Electrical unit
41 Invitation to a questioner
42 One-named R&B singer who won a Grammy for his 2014 album "Black Messiah"
45 Sault ___ Marie, Mich.
46 Successor to F.D.R.
48 "Miss ___" (2016 thriller)
50 Knob next to "bass"
52 "Li'l" guy of old comics
53 Game with straights and flushes
58 Complete, as a crossword grid
60 Program file suffix
62 Mormon Church, for short
63 File folder projection
64 Rock genre
65 Uncooked

by Ned White

ACROSS

1 Parts of a crab that grab
6 Archie Bunker, notably
11 Fig. on an auto sticker
14 Indian prince
15 Hi in HI
16 Wrath
17 Broadcasting sign
18 Away from the office
19 Hither's opposite
20 End of a heated exchange, perhaps
22 H.I.V. drug
23 Endures
24 Kingly
26 Make messy, as a blanket
30 Pedicurist's stone
31 Pedicurist's stick
32 Poise
35 Goose liver spread
36 Game show hire
37 Spring
41 Rapid tempo
43 Dessert that jiggles
44 Heart, essentially
47 Beat the stuffing out of
48 Boxer Patterson
49 It'll take you to another level
52 Addams Family member
53 Following the circled squares, the end to a seasonal song
59 Teen blemish
60 Filmdom's Flynn
61 Witherspoon of "Four Christmases"
62 Fashion look with long 6-Down and eye liner
63 Playing marble
64 Drive ahead
65 Dorm monitors, for short
66 Cartridge filler
67 Criminal evidence, with "the"

DOWN

1 Alfalfa or buckwheat
2 Pop singer __ Del Rey
3 Not completely shut
4 "Hold on a sec!"
5 In a piercing voice
6 Hair over the forehead
7 Admission of defeat
8 Invaders of ancient Rome
9 Home of Wright State University
10 Display of bad temper
11 Mr. __ of "The Karate Kid"
12 Mood-enhancing drug
13 Softhearted
21 Not, to a Scot
25 Maple leaf, for Canada
26 Exercise segment
27 Thurman of "Kill Bill"
28 New York City cultural venue, with "the"
29 Like some boarding schools
30 "The Bells" poet
32 Morning hrs.
33 Sales tax fig.
34 MGM lion
36 Always, in verse
38 Street of film fame
39 Keg contents
40 Capitol Hill sort, for short
42 What's your beef?
43 Assemble in a makeshift way
44 Big pharma company
45 Final syllable of a word
46 Things seen on many state license plates
47 Milne's "Mr. __ Passes By"
49 Wrap brand
50 Historically safe investment, informally
51 Alfred who was a follower of Freud
54 Thus, to Gaius
55 Car in a showroom
56 Car in a tow lot, perhaps
57 Pre-owned
58 Diner on TV's "Alice"

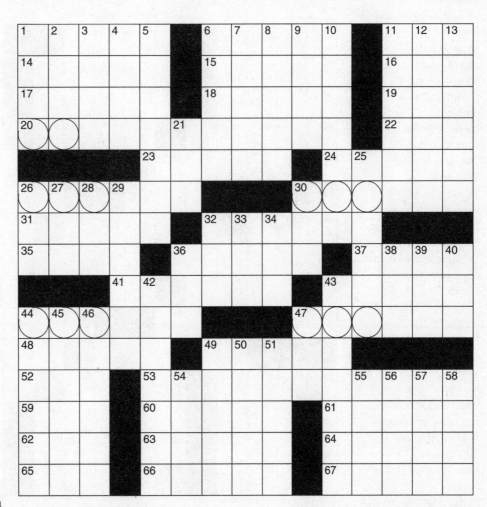

by Ed Sessa

82

ACROSS

1 Lower part of the leg
5 "Mon __!" (French cry)
9 Noted rocker/humanitarian
13 Homeland of 9-Across
14 Omega's opposite, alphabetically
16 Stratford-upon-__
17 Ones taking captain's orders
18 Maestro Kurt __
19 Responsibility
20 Coffee break hour
22 Knight time?
23 Visa alternative
24 Folk singer Pete
26 Frenzied
28 Brother of Donald Trump Jr.
30 "The Star-Spangled Banner," e.g.
34 High/low card
37 Egypt's capital
40 Two-door auto
41 Communication problem . . . illustrated literally by the black squares before 5-, 19-, 26-, 54-, 65- and 73-Across
44 "Have a taste!"
45 Biscuit with English tea
46 Item in a golfer's bag
47 Norway's patron saint
49 Landing approximations, for short
51 Chaim who played Tevye in "Fiddler on the Roof"
54 Formal-sounding commitment
58 Works of Keats
61 Sluggers' stats
63 Great Lakes natives
64 Friends and neighbors
65 Wasn't up to par
67 Slightest bit
68 Late attorney general Janet
69 Mello __ (soft drink)
70 Dart (around)
71 "Make it snappy!"
72 Actress Ward
73 Cookie holders

DOWN

1 Religious offshoots
2 Successful job applicant
3 "Me, Myself & __" (Jim Carrey movie)
4 Music genre for 36-Down
5 Reservoir creator
6 "Now __ me down to sleep"
7 English racing venue
8 "Star Trek" officer with an earpiece
9 Troublemaker
10 It goes down a fallopian tube
11 A sixteenth is a short one
12 Black gemstone
15 Bull-riding venue
21 Friend of Romeo
25 Lobbying org. that fights music piracy
27 Augment
29 "Smokes"
31 Eight, in France
32 Weapon in fencing
33 A __ pittance
34 Choir voice
35 Sagan who hosted "Cosmos"
36 One-named singer from County Donegal
38 __ center (place for a Ping-Pong table)
39 Orchestra reed
42 Moneymaking part of a museum
43 2016 #1 album by Rihanna
48 "__ the Lord my soul to keep"
50 Short __ (quick work)
52 Theater awards
53 City NNE of Paris
55 Garlicky mayo
56 Admit at the door
57 Exams for future J.D.'s
58 Vegetable that becomes gooey when cooked
59 Conks out
60 Sicilian volcano
62 Go along with a bear market
66 __ good deed

by Mark McClain

ACROSS

1 "What a relief!"
5 Pleasant scent
10 Gaelic language
14 Per unit
15 Home on an estate
16 Fail to persevere
17 Legal actions provoked by oversimple jigsaw puzzles?
20 Lead-in to kraut or braten
21 "Well, obviously!"
22 Like some French sauces
23 Ad word suggesting a lack of undesirable moisture
25 Object of early Christian condemnation
27 Mother-of-pearl source
31 Like a short play
35 Law documents concerning pugilists?
38 Tavern
39 Daring
40 See 51-Across
41 Smoke an e-cigarette
42 Paris-to-Berlin dir.
43 Court precedents involving games of hoops?
45 Affirmative to a commanding officer
47 Touchdown pass catchers, e.g.
48 Does a tech job
51 With 40-Across, common deli sandwich
52 Numbskull
55 Animal with an opposable thumb
57 Trace of color
61 Attorneys' fees paid with gold fillings?
64 Departed
65 Company that buried 700,000+ unsold video games in 1983
66 Journey
67 Love god
68 Tatter
69 Conglomerate originally named Tokyo Tsushin Kogyo

DOWN

1 Parrots and ferrets
2 Response to a joke
3 Neutral shade
4 Coaxed
5 Rock-and-roll need
6 Unwelcome cry at the front door
7 Best
8 Chocolaty hot beverage
9 Exist
10 Like most carousel animals
11 Destroy
12 Internet destination
13 Online crafts seller
18 What "oopsy" signals
19 Graceful birds
24 Like some boat motor types
26 Command to a dog after a ball is thrown
27 Monk's home
28 Frontiersman Daniel
29 Wheel connectors
30 Shore birds
32 Humiliate
33 Pickled flower bud
34 Lock of hair
36 Annoy
37 Places for contacts
41 Troublesome critters
43 Flora and fauna
44 South American animal also known as a "hog-nosed coon"
46 Big name in lawn care
49 Google ___
50 Primitive weapon
52 Not working
53 Bambi, e.g.
54 What a help desk provides
56 Ser : Spanish :: ___ : French
58 Fiddling emperor
59 Smile
60 Get a look at
62 ___ Cruces, N.M.
63 Help

by David Alfred Bywaters

ACROSS

1 Monastery leader
6 Everyone working in an office
11 Cousin ___ (Addams Family member)
14 Pixar robot
15 Opposite of black-and-white
16 Gun rights org.
17 Santa player in "The Man in the Santa Claus Suit"
19 Highest roll of a die
20 S.E.C. school near Atlanta, for short
21 Explorer and Escalade, in brief
22 Nutmeg, for one
24 Something sent to Santa
26 Santa player in "The Polar Express"
29 Magnetite and bauxite
31 Temporary break
32 "In that case . . ."
35 Joe of "GoodFellas"
37 Bread box, for short?
39 Cheerleader's cry
40 Santa player in "Elf"
42 Boston ___ Party
43 Environmentalist's prefix
44 Main artery
45 Not more than
46 Moves like water around a drain
48 Big school dance
51 Santa player in "The Santa Clause"
53 Is
57 Resident of Muscat
58 "Yeah, why not!"
60 Mincemeat ___ (Christmas staple)
61 ___ Tin Tin
62 Santa player in "Miracle on 34th Street"
66 R.N.'s special touch
67 River through Paris
68 Les ___-Unis
69 Match, as a bet
70 Past of present
71 Like the settlers of Iceland

DOWN

1 Horrific
2 Flat-bottomed boat
3 Sheep sound
4 Right jolly ___ elf (Santa)
5 Little puzzle
6 Show on which John Candy and Eugene Levy got their starts
7 One of a series at a wedding reception
8 Boxer known as "The Greatest"
9 Gift tag word
10 Terry Gross's NPR program
11 Imply
12 April fool player
13 One of Benjamin Franklin's certainties
18 "Yeah, why not!"
23 Boston footballer, for short
25 Overly
27 Zinger response
28 "Of ___ and Men"
30 Like the population of Wyoming
32 Fury
33 Exact copy
34 Neologism for an on-screen/off-screen relationship
36 Winter hrs. in New York
38 West who said "I used to be Snow White, but I drifted"
40 At one's ___ convenience
41 Barbie or Ken
45 The year 2001
47 Fleming who created James Bond
49 Peruse
50 Astronaut's tankful
51 Legal wrongs
52 Some of them are proper
54 Javelin
55 Some windshields have them
56 Taste or touch
59 Sitting spot for a child visiting Santa
63 "Look at Me, I'm Sandra ___"
64 Max's opposite
65 Intl. group that's the object of many mass protests

by Jason Mueller

ACROSS

1 MacBook __
4 Sounded kittenish
9 Something controlled by rigging
13 Assistance
14 Allergy sufferer's lifesaver
16 Title heroine who says "I would much rather have been merry than wise"
17 Clear adhesive
19 Each
20 Trebly
21 Software fix
23 Pack (down)
25 Backpackers' routes
28 French royal line
32 Mad __
33 Omani money
34 Cardamom or turmeric
35 Ernie in the World Golf Hall of Fame
36 Synagogue singers
38 Something that fits in a lock
39 Add details to, with "out"
41 Marie Antoinette lost hers in la Révolution française
42 Get the ball rolling?
43 1988 crime thriller starring Mel Gibson and Michelle Pfeiffer
46 Sloping water trough
47 Drudge
48 Start of Caesar's boast
50 French cake
54 Surface-dwelling race in "The Time Machine"
56 How this puzzle's three drinks have been served?
59 Booming
60 Like some fancy basketball passes
61 Purge (of)
62 Item in a box in the basement
63 Public squabble
64 A, in Andalusia

DOWN

1 Word repeated in "What's __ is __"
2 Decadent, as cake
3 "Eww!" inducer
4 Pilgrimage destinations
5 Pamphlets, postcards and such
6 Mark Twain, notably
7 Org. concerned with climate change
8 Johnny of "Sleepy Hollow"
9 Bottom-feeding fish known formally as the morwong
10 Like the D-Day assault on Normandy
11 Texter's "As I see it . . ."
12 Trip around the track
15 Cool, quaintly
18 "__ Andronicus"
22 Bridge support
24 Starting place, on a map
26 Find
27 Hägar the Horrible's dog
28 Jewish organization on campus
29 Sycophantic
30 Fortunes
31 Remove, as spilled ink
32 Certain jabs
36 Muchacho's sweetie
37 Back out of
40 "__ Squad" (2016 hit movie)
42 Two-toned horse
44 Bad car to road-trip in
45 Mr. __, host of "Fantasy Island"
49 1961 space chimp
51 Color of unbleached silk
52 Similar (to)
53 Enforcer of the Fed. Meat Inspection Act
54 North Pole worker
55 Reed of the Velvet Underground
57 Spa specialty, briefly
58 Weed out?

by Timothy Polin

ACROSS

1 Go out, as the tide
4 Permit
7 Reply to a captain
10 Brewpub offering, for short
13 Org. that targets traffickers
14 Raised, as a building
16 Partner of neither
17 Mountain on which you might yodel
18 Stockpiling, in a way, as feed
19 Letters in a personals ad
20 Gymnastics floor cover
21 Directive for additional information
22 Cartoon pic
23 Get out of bed
25 TV warrior princess
26 Race loser in an Aesop fable
27 Reflective sorts
29 Fur wraps
31 This: Sp.
32 It's usually behind a viola in an orchestra
36 Flexible Flyers, e.g.
37 December 26 in England? . . . or a hint to each set of circled squares
40 Lispers' banes
43 Scrubbed, as a NASA mission
44 Be __ equal footing
48 Bear witness (to)
50 Soviet premier Khrushchev
52 Caviars
53 Try, as a case
57 Track events
58 Lobster __ diavolo (Italian dish)
59 Hit pay dirt
61 "You __!" ("Absolutely!")
62 On the __ (fleeing)
63 Literary critic Broyard
64 Actress Thurman
65 Get older
66 Bruno Mars or Freddie Mercury

67 Some PCs
68 The "p" in m.p.g.
69 Ram's mate
70 Stockholm's home: Abbr.
71 U.S.P.S. assignment: Abbr.

DOWN

1 Sushi bar finger food
2 Country whose currency, RUBLES, is almost an anagram of its name
3 St. John the __
4 __ Antilles
5 Pennsylvania city or the lake it's on
6 Bygone point-to-point communication
7 Suffix with valid
8 Gossipy sorts
9 Border
10 Proportional to the surroundings
11 Motorized
12 Like the Venus de Milo
15 Summer treat that melts in the sun
24 Naval engineers
26 Massachusetts' Mount __ College
28 Chi-town squad
30 Airport screening grp.
33 Container for dirty clothes
34 Yoko who loved Lennon
35 Common ingredient in pasta
38 C.I.A. precursor
39 Mafia big
40 Batting helmet part

41 Use for an attic or the cloud
42 Ship with smokestacks
45 Theologian Reinhold who wrote the Serenity Prayer
46 Try
47 Ilie who won both the U.S. and French Opens
49 What meditators try to live in
51 Cry upon arriving
54 Tour de France stage
55 Martial __ (judo and others)
56 Violent protests
59 Stare slack-jawed
60 Part of a wolf or a lobster

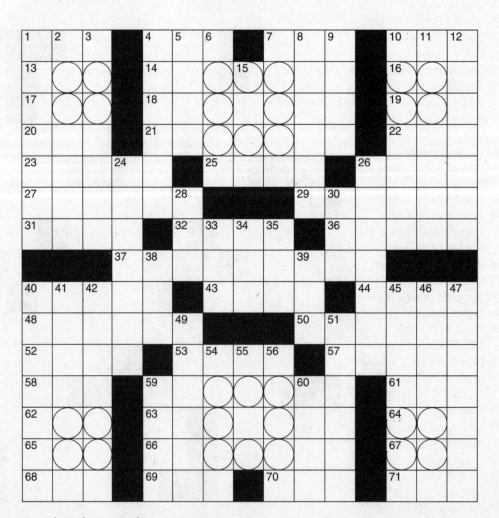

by Jules P. Markey

ACROSS

1 Tease good-naturedly
5 Knock down a notch
10 Old-fashioned outburst
14 ___ Bunt, "On Her Majesty's Secret Service" henchwoman
15 Gently protest
16 Some music in Mumbai
17 *Valentine outline
19 Cry at the start of a poker game
20 Blood line
21 "___ you nuts?"
22 Trail for a dog
23 Summer clock setting: Abbr.
24 *Cost to enter a bar, maybe
27 Dress style
29 "Excusez-___"
30 Controversial novel of 1955
32 *Folksy
37 With: Fr.
38 Nonkosher entree
39 Excited and then some
40 *What to do when coming face to face with a bear
43 Partial rainbow near the horizon
45 What framed Roger Rabbit?
46 Watch a season's worth of episodes in one sitting, say
47 *Delayed consequence
52 "Illmatic" rapper
55 Lose it completely
56 Thor or Loki
57 "All ___ lost"
59 Follower of anything and everything
60 Surprised reaction . . . or a hint to what can precede both halves of the answers to the starred clues
62 "Just do it" sloganeer
63 Doldrums feeling
64 Forthwith, on a memo
65 Throw in the trash
66 Club in a sand trap
67 Actor Ifans of "The Amazing Spider-Man"

DOWN

1 Crusade against "infidels"
2 Stackable cookies
3 Know-it-all
4 N.H.L.'s ___ Memorial Trophy
5 Billboards, e.g.
6 Babysitter's request
7 Verb that's conjugated "amo, amas, amat . . ."
8 Parent who "does it all"
9 Before, poetically
10 ___ Kane, resident of soap TV's Pine Valley
11 Devotee of eSports
12 Ripening, as cheese
13 "Purgatorio" and "Paradiso" poet
18 Silent, as an agreement
22 Clamber up, as a pole
25 Go ___ diet
26 Dairy animal
28 Spank
30 Research site
31 Ingredients in a Caesar salad, to Caesar?
32 New Year's ___
33 Chill (with)
34 Humorist who wrote "Candy / Is dandy / But liquor / Is quicker"
35 Sound from a 26-Down
36 Ingredient in a Caesar salad
38 Suffering from senility, say
41 Pastoral piece?
42 Tiny
43 "___ 'em!" (canine command)
44 Loosen, as a bow
46 One getting a bite at night?
47 007, e.g.
48 Leaf of a book
49 Jobs to do
50 Swords in modern pentathlons
51 Lost's opposite
53 "Good to go"
54 Staircase parts
58 Symbol to the left of a zero on a phone
60 Mountain ___ (soda)
61 More than a fib

by Herre Schouwerwou

88

ACROSS

1 Bouts, as of crying
5 ___ Le Pew (cartoon skunk)
9 Fizzy headache remedy, informally
14 Bra size smaller than a "B"
15 Highway sign next to an off-ramp
16 Extend, as a subscription
17 Not giving up on an argument, say
19 Throat-clearing sounds
20 Words attributed to 41-Across
22 Wyatt of the Old West
23 Hi-___ monitor
24 Apt cry for 41-Across
31 Moving day rental
32 Big laughs, slangily
33 Symbol of busyness
34 Cosmologist Sagan
35 Ninnies
37 Parsley, sage, rosemary or thyme
38 Fleur-de-___
39 Money that needs to be repaid
40 Dresses in Delhi
41 Famous queen, depicted literally
45 Early Beatle ___ Sutcliffe
46 Put into piles, say
47 Something committed by 41-Across . . . or by this puzzle's creator?
54 Attend a funeral, say
55 Merchandise location
56 Keepsake in a cabinet, perhaps
57 Competitor of Wisk
58 First among men
59 Minor fights
60 Cards sometimes hidden up sleeves
61 Blood components

DOWN

1 Monopoly space with the words "Just Visiting"
2 Pimples
3 Wind that might blow one's hat off
4 Malicious
5 Czar called "the Great"
6 Not taxable, e.g.
7 Wood for many a mountain cabin
8 Grammy-winning James
9 Pick-me-up drinks
10 It's nothing new
11 Short race spec
12 Bit of viral web content
13 Cries of pain
18 Article thrown over the shoulders
21 Long, hard journeys
24 Atheist Madalyn Murray ___
25 Persian tongue
26 Prefix relating to sleep
27 Shade of color
28 Fellow film critic of Siskel
29 Eagle's home
30 Belles of the ball
31 The Bruins of the Pac-12
35 Krispy Kreme product
36 Grain used in making Alpha-Bits
37 North Carolina's Cape ___
39 Many Americans whose names end in -ez
40 Feudal workers
42 ___ de corps (fellowship)
43 Tristan's beloved
44 Certain bank policy for A.T.M. withdrawals and wire transfers
47 Brilliant move
48 Ambient quality
49 "The Thin Man" canine
50 Of the flock
51 Point where lines meet
52 Fly high
53 Jane Austen heroine
54 Roast hosts, for short

by Ed Sessa

ACROSS

1 Like some basketball shots and unwanted calls
8 Slangy turndown
11 Law man
14 Woo
15 __ crossroads
16 ". . . fish __ fowl"
17 Markswoman dubbed "Little Sure Shot" [1977]
19 Male swan
20 Site of two French banks
21 Free from
22 Prefix with center
23 High lines
25 Variety of pool [1982]
27 2017 N.C.A.A. basketball champs
30 Opposite of a gulp
32 Rapidly spreading over the internet
33 Mushroom or balloon
35 Group that takes pledges, informally
38 Massage target?
39 Capital city with only about 1,000 residents [2016]
44 Stew morsel
45 "Right away!"
46 Geraint's wife, in Arthurian legend
47 Understand
49 Rallying cry?
51 "Gloria in Excelsis __" (hymn)
52 Landlord's register [1996]
56 Ring on a string
58 Columbia, for one
59 Winds down in a pit?
61 Boise's home
65 President pro __
66 Award won by the starts of 17-, 25-, 39- and 52-Across and 11- and 29-Down
68 __-la-la
69 Get a good look at
70 Country north of Latvia
71 Hankering
72 70-Across, e.g., formerly: Abbr.
73 TV's "Maverick" or "Gunsmoke"

DOWN

1 They may be strapless or padded
2 Solo
3 Luxury hotel chain
4 Oscar winner for "Hannah and Her Sisters"
5 Prepares to be knighted
6 Prefix with tourism
7 Sweetie
8 Nita of silent films
9 Used as the surface for a meal
10 Antihistamine target
11 400 meters, for an Olympic track [2012]
12 Commotion
13 Clay character in old "S.N.L." sketches
18 They're related
24 Search (through)
26 1996 Foo Fighters hit
27 "That's awful!"
28 Hunters' org.
29 Superloyal employee [1971]
31 Crackerjacks
34 Oscar winner for "Hannah and Her Sisters"
36 Caste member
37 Means of avoiding an uphill climb
40 Blankets for open-air travelers
41 Series ender: Abbr.
42 Run out of power
43 Commotion
47 Courageously persistent
48 Noted colonial silversmith
50 Bank jobs
53 Follows orders
54 Deadbeat, e.g.
55 Tennis call
57 Buffoon
60 Eurasian duck
62 Teen woe
63 Wig, e.g.
64 Pearl Buck heroine
67 Helpfulness

by David J. Kahn

90

ACROSS

1 4.0 is a great one
4 Nearsighted cartoon Mr.
9 Garbage-carrying boats
14 Superannuated
15 Denim or linen
16 Ancient land near Lydia
17 Not good
18 "Super 8" actress, 2011
20 Relative who might visit for the holidays
22 Hightail it
23 Secret language
24 "Thanks, Captain Obvious!"
27 Ltr. addition
28 One-named New Age singer
29 Rough, as criticism
31 Industrious little marchers
34 Spring school dance
37 How sardines are often packed
39 "Get the picture?"
40 Flower that attracts pollinating insects
42 Actress Thurman
43 Money in the middle of a poker table
45 Farm tower
46 High point
47 Auto deal for nonbuyers
49 Caltech, e.g.: Abbr.
51 Talk, talk and then talk some more
52 Whistlers in the kitchen
58 Brief letter
59 Dr. Mom's attention, for short
60 Each one in a square is 90°
61 Order to get a soundtrack ready
65 Popular pen
66 Money in the middle of a poker table
67 ___ raving mad
68 Toddler
69 Deal negotiator for athletes
70 State where the Cotton Bowl is held
71 There are four in a gallon: Abbr.

DOWN

1 Not hold back
2 Air Force One, for one
3 Bewilder
4 Ian who wrote "Atonement"
5 Every last bit
6 Fútbol score
7 Onetime "S.N.L." regular Cheri
8 "That sounds good . . . NOT!"
9 Envy or lust
10 Worry
11 Dish in a bowl often served au gratin
12 Tinkler on a porch
13 Wise man
19 Egyptian cross
21 Thumbs-up votes
25 Variety
26 Relatives of rabbits
30 "We ___ to please!"
31 Word before "and ye shall receive"
32 Singer with the 1972 hit "Heart of Gold"
33 One-on-one talk
35 Sash for a kimono
36 Pop singer Zayn formerly of One Direction
38 Opposite of strict
40 Fly-___ (Blue Angels maneuvers)
41 Lacking company
44 Rest for a bit
46 Abbr. before a name on a memo
48 Suffix with cigar
50 Groups of poker chips, typically
53 Locale of a film "nightmare": Abbr.
54 Less than 90°
55 Modern movement initialism . . . or a hint to the starts of 18-, 24-, 40-, 52- and 61-Across
56 "The Waste Land" poet
57 Religious offshoots
58 March Madness org.
62 President before D.D.E.
63 Jazz instrument
64 Savings for the golden years, for short

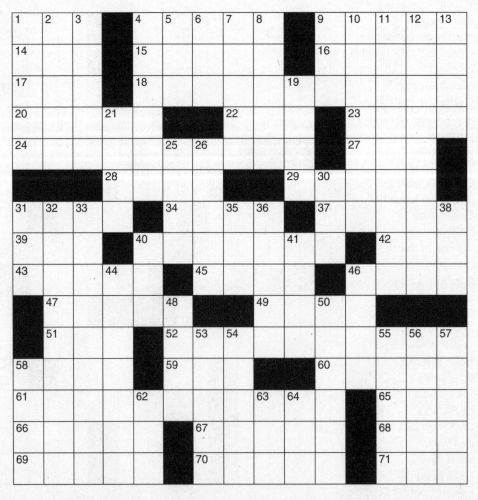

by Zhouqin Burnikel

ACROSS

1 Social adroitness
5 City between Gainesville and Orlando
10 Skateboarder's incline
14 Radar response
15 Mushroom variety
16 Garfield's foil in the comics
17 View furtively
19 Main role
20 Direct, as a collision
21 John of "Saturday Night Fever"
23 Amber Alert, e.g., for short
24 Complete the negotiations
25 Like the number of games in a "best of" series
27 Cut (off)
29 Pitchfork point
30 Secure some urban transportation
33 Rejoice
37 Oscar winner Jared of "Dallas Buyers Club"
38 Buy and sell, as stocks
41 Jacob's biblical twin
42 Decorative pitchers
44 Was vaccinated
46 Pinch in the kitchen
49 Hit with a Taser
50 Terre Haute sch.
51 Prepare for someone's birthday, perhaps
55 Org. for top-notch H.S. students
57 Blue-blooded
58 Hollywood's Diane, Buster or Michael
61 Seed cover
62 Briefly put pen to paper, say
64 "Don't touch that, honey!"
65 Engine capacity unit
66 Increase
67 Poses a poser
68 Relatively cool red giant
69 The second "S" of MS-DOS: Abbr.

DOWN

1 Radio host John
2 Teenage skin malady
3 Takeout food together with a Netflix movie, maybe
4 Garden amphibians
5 Tip of the Arabian Peninsula
6 "Brooklyn Nine-Nine" figure
7 Rocky glacial ridge
8 Look upon with lust
9 High-pH substance
10 Obsolescent desktop accessories
11 "Hello" singer, 2015
12 Sporty Mazda
13 Organ part
18 Qantas Airways symbol
22 Barn topper
24 Practice boxing
25 Look upon with lust
26 Was the clue giver in Pictionary
28 Start of the fourth qtr.
31 Brothels
32 Give up on, in slang
34 Class that covers Reconstruction and Prohibition
35 Neighbor of Vietnam
36 "Swan Lake" article of attire
39 Nod off
40 Letter between zeta and theta
43 Swedish aircraft giant
45 Breathing problem
47 Frowny looks
48 ___ tweed
51 Swahili master
52 Nestlé bars filled with tiny bubbles
53 "Hogan's Heroes" colonel
54 Noted berry farm founder Walter
56 Puts up, as a painting
58 Deborah of "The King and I"
59 Plains tribe members
60 Politico Gingrich
63 Drink with crumpets

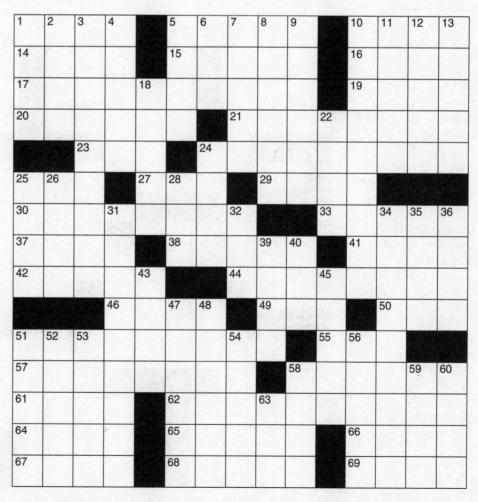

by Peter A. Collins

ACROSS

1 Fruit often seen in still lifes
5 Black wood
10 Fable's message
15 Opera highlight
16 Elaine's last name on "Seinfeld"
17 Flabbergast
18 Historic California route, with "El"
20 Schmoozing gossip
21 Bottoms of high-tops
22 Departs
23 Desirable feature of a rented room
29 Mathematician Turing who was the subject of "The Imitation Game"
30 Genetic copies
31 Forwards, as a misdelivered letter
35 Weaving machine
36 Mani-pedi place
39 2016 film for which Viggo Mortensen earned an Oscar nomination
42 Pig's digs
43 Ancient France
44 Navigation instrument
45 Many Monty Python skits
47 Crumb carriers
48 Common computer peripherals
54 Sigher's words
55 College officials
56 "Here's to the newlyweds!," e.g.
58 Part of a person's psyche . . . or a hidden part of 18-, 23-, 39- or 48-Across?
63 Wonderland girl
64 Division of a play
65 Notion
66 Chill out
67 Played (with)
68 Polo mount

DOWN

1 "Super" group buying campaign ads
2 One-third of pitching's Triple Crown, for short
3 Command between "Ready!" and "Fire!"
4 Chocolate-covered morsel often eaten at the movies
5 Virus in 2014 news
6 Special Forces cap
7 "Gimme a minute"
8 Schoolteacher's org.
9 French designer's monogram
10 With 62-Down, a spring festival
11 Symbols of resistance
12 Talked incessantly
13 Quetzalcoatl worshiper
14 Car deal that's not a purchase
19 Election mo.
23 Skirt fold
24 Hoarse
25 "___ Enchanted" (2004 film)
26 "High" times
27 Govt.-issued security
28 Century 21 rival
29 Paths of pendulums
32 Bother persistently
33 Book with handwritten thoughts
34 Ducked (out) furtively
36 Easel, e.g.
37 Pub purchases
38 Divisions of a play
40 Escape
41 The Enterprise, for example
45 Soft drink in a green bottle
46 2000 Summer Olympics city
48 Smallest OPEC nation
49 Entire
50 Letter that doesn't need an envelope or stamp
51 Designer Geoffrey
52 Got into a row?
53 Nelson Mandela's org.
57 ___-Mex
58 "Was ___ das?" (German question)
59 Cpl., e.g.
60 Altar affirmation
61 Spy novelist Deighton
62 See 10-Down

by Peter Gordon

ACROSS

1 Whole slew
5 Outer protein shell of a virus
11 Verve
14 "Celeste Aida," e.g.
15 Futures analyst?
16 Famous Tokyo-born singer
17 WASHINGTON + R = Intimidation tactic
19 Option words
20 Fusions
21 Smoked marijuana
23 Word repeated in "Ring Around the Rosy" before "We all fall down"
24 MISSOURI + E = "No fooling!"
26 Interpret
27 Martin who wrote "London Fields"
28 Short dance wear
29 Rode the bench
30 Whopper inventor
31 Marching well
33 MARYLAND + O = Period in which nothing special happens
35 Imps are little ones
38 Sacagawea dollar, e.g.
39 __-relief
42 Evelyn Waugh's writer brother
43 Laborious task
44 Salad green
45 NEBRASKA + T = Mortgage specifications
48 Aid for administering an oath of office
49 Segment of a binge-watch
50 Prince William's mom
51 Mule's father
52 CALIFORNIA + N = Majestic beast
55 1920s car
56 Parodied
57 "__ it ironic?"
58 Phishing target: Abbr.
59 Gave an exam
60 "Divergent" actor James

DOWN

1 Places where oysters are served
2 Victim of river diversion in Asia
3 Professional headgear that's stereotypically red
4 Got some sun
5 Fleeces
6 S. Amer. home of the tango
7 Ballet step
8 Straight downhill run on skis
9 "You win," alternatively
10 Put off
11 Get dog-tired
12 Neither here nor there?
13 Prepares to shoot near the basket, say
18 Phishing targets, briefly
22 Scatterbrained
24 Muslim leader
25 One-in-a-million event
27 Affected manner
30 [You crack me up]
31 "Understood, dude"
32 A Bobbsey twin
33 Shaving mishaps
34 English johns
35 Chicago squad in old "S.N.L." skits
36 Passes by
37 Hunter's freezerful, maybe
39 Infantile
40 "Finished!"
41 View, as the future
43 Rears of ships
44 "Curious George" books, e.g.
46 Honor with insults
47 Charge for a plug?
48 Complete block
50 SoCal force
53 Big inits. in the aerospace industry
54 Nod from offstage, maybe

by Bruce Haight

94

ACROSS

1 With 43- and 76-Across, camping aid
6 1950s prez
9 Place to play the slots
15 Veranda
16 They're "Red" in Boston and "White" in Chicago
17 Third-party account
18 "S.N.L." alum Cheri
19 Homie
20 Heroin or Vicodin
21 One function of 1-/43-/76-Across
23 Double curves, as on highways
24 Mournful bell sounds
25 Nuts for squirrels
28 Chop (off)
29 Greek goddess of victory
30 Not fooled by
34 "___ before beauty"
37 Insect in a colony
39 Maple syrup source
40 "Purple ___" (Prince hit)
41 Medicare drug benefit
43 See 1-Across
45 Band that made Justin Timberlake famous
46 Cole ___ (side dish)
47 "___-la-la"
48 Sign of a sellout
50 Sault ___ Marie, Mich.
51 Otherwise
52 Org. advocating pet adoption
54 Like baseball's Pacific Coast League
56 Removed, as chalk
58 Resurrection figure
62 Fad
65 One function of 1-/43-/76-Across
67 "I'd be delighted"
69 12 months, in Tijuana
70 Pong game maker
71 Chef Lagasse
72 ___ de Janeiro
73 Arrested
74 Came clean, with "up"
75 Concorde, for short
76 See 1-Across

DOWN

1 "Mr." on the Enterprise
2 King of the gods in Wagner's "Ring" cycle
3 Memorable 2011 hurricane
4 Form of a papyrus document
5 All a tanker can hold
6 Library ID
7 Cuisine with kimchi
8 Casting out of a demon
9 Corp. head
10 "Quaking" tree
11 One function of 1-/43-/76-Across
12 Nest eggs for later years, in brief
13 Do, re or mi
14 Is in debt
22 Home of "Monday Night Football"
26 Gives the go-ahead
27 Agent, in brief
31 "No" votes
32 Windshield feature
33 Fairy tale's first word
34 Altar area
35 Chutzpah
36 Historical periods
38 Coverings pulled across infields
42 One function of 1-/43-/76-Across
44 Indy vehicles
45 Refuge during the Great Flood
47 Airport screening org.
49 Pool table triangle
53 Handsome man
55 Inverse trig function
57 Fix, as a knot
59 Tehran native
60 Feature lacked by Helvetica type
61 Bale binder
62 Word after bass or treble
63 Where all roads lead, it's said
64 Madison and Fifth in Manhattan: Abbr.
66 Word sung three times before "for the home team" in "Take Me Out to the Ball Game"
68 Not new

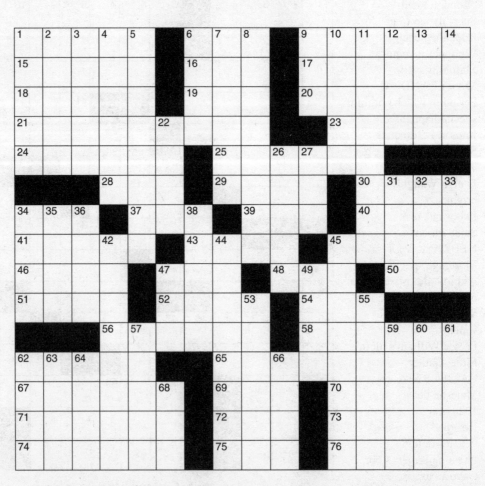

by Gary Kennedy

ACROSS

1 Make a pass at
6 Cousin of lager
9 Deposited soil
13 Dig deeply
14 Baldwin known for his presidential impersonation
15 Village Voice award
16 Dress down
18 TD Garden athlete, informally
19 Gorge oneself, with "out"
20 Smidgen
21 Salmon type
23 Wash. neighbor
24 San ___, Italy
26 "Live Free or Die Hard" director Wiseman
27 Potentially offensive
30 Bread that's often brushed with ghee
31 Early anesthetic
34 Main line from the heart
36 Aquafina competitor
37 "Wow, unbelievable!"
40 Cause of yawns
41 Kitchen cabinet
42 Rainbow ___
43 Others, in Oaxaca
44 "A Dream Within a Dream" writer
45 Big college major, informally
49 Suffix with morph-
50 Onetime giant in consumer electronics
52 Fair-hiring letters
53 Audited, as a class
56 "Be quiet!"
58 X-ray alternative
59 Coveted, as a position
60 Throws a fit
63 Fairy tale meanie
64 Marriott competitor
65 Core belief
66 Lies by the pool, say
67 Penn of "Harold & Kumar" films
68 Figure skating event . . . or what the circled items always come in

DOWN

1 Quaint fashion accessory
2 Enthusiastic assent
3 Friendly Islands native
4 www.wikipedia.___
5 Neither fem. nor masc.
6 Pie ___ mode
7 Future perfect tense in grammar class, e.g.
8 Bounce back
9 Some mechanics' tool collections
10 Informal cry from someone who is duped
11 Bloom on a pad
12 Part lopped off by la guillotine
14 How pasta may be prepared
17 Talent for music
22 Fully explain
25 Nanny goat's cry
28 Plays charades
29 Make rough
32 Brian who composed "Discreet Music"
33 What an air ball misses
35 Train system: Abbr.
36 Scooby-___
37 Big step for a young company, for short
38 Silent "Welcome" giver
39 Reciprocally
40 Cold one
42 You, in Tours
44 Isthmus land
46 Native of Mocha
47 Drugstore location, often
48 Bank jobs
51 Sashimi staple
53 Dalmatian feature
54 Pond organism
55 "Well, all right then"
57 Start of a web address
61 TV show that comes on at 11:29 (not 11:30) p.m.
62 Pekoe, for one

by Zhouqin Burnikel

96

ACROSS

1 TV network whose logo is an eye
4 Singer Mitchell who wrote "Woodstock" (but didn't attend)
8 Whole
14 The "A" of I.P.A.
15 Former Israeli P.M. Ehud
16 __ Tunes (Warner Bros. cartoons)
17 Epoch of rare distinction
19 Tool for the Grim Reaper
20 Opposites of true believers
21 Optima and Cadenza car company
22 "If only __ listened . . ."
23 Archie's wife on "All in the Family"
24 Topic of a happy annual report
27 __ Pieces
29 Celestial Seasonings product
30 Greet with humility
31 Jul. follower
33 Dow Jones stat.
35 Shocked response
36 Something circled on a calendar
40 Second-largest Hawaiian island
42 Aperitif with black currant liqueur
43 __ Paulo, Brazil
44 Darkest part of a shadow
46 Bro, e.g.
48 Concepts not meant to be questioned
53 Period of supreme courage and achievement
56 One-named rap star
57 To and __
58 Fact-gathering org.
59 Do a perfunctory performance
61 Substituted "math" for "mass," say
63 When TV viewership peaks . . . or a hint to 17-, 24-, 36- and 53-Across

64 Timeless, to Shakespeare
65 Houses in Havana
66 TV network whose logo is a peacock
67 Puts back to 0, say
68 X-ray __ (gag gift)
69 "We all __ little mad sometimes": Norman Bates

DOWN

1 More evasive with the truth
2 Marilyn Monroe, notably
3 Something you reach out and take?
4 Author Austen
5 Toothbrush brand
6 Bothers the conscience of
7 Eisenhower, informally
8 Borden milk mascot
9 Like a diet lacking bread or pasta, for short
10 Etch A Sketch or yo-yo
11 Blocking someone's path
12 Puts back in the oven
13 Visine application
15 Tousled look of the recently woken
18 Counterparts of dahs in Morse code
21 Scoundrels
25 In apple-pie order
26 Mind-body exercise
28 Sit and mope
32 Performer with a fan
34 One finally done with finals?
36 Kiss like an Eskimo
37 Land of Blarney
38 Duo plus one
39 Idle drawings
40 Part of a car's exhaust system
41 "You agree with me?," informally
45 Goal for a mountaineer
47 Trumped-up charge
49 Fortitude
50 Beating at chess
51 With hands on hips
52 __ Falls, N.Y.
54 Neap and ebb
55 Uplift
60 Big movie format
62 __-K (early schooling)
63 Mac alternatives

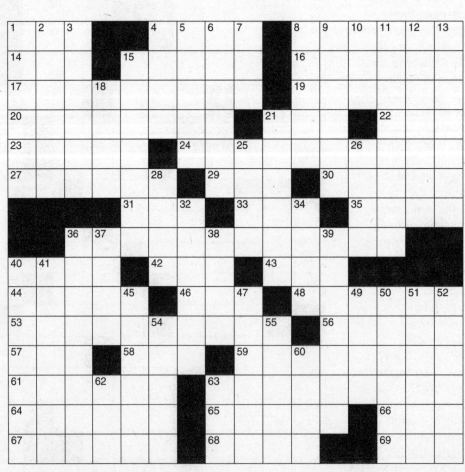

by Jeff Chen and Seth Geltman

ACROSS

1 Peruvian of long ago
5 The end
10 Simoleon
14 Bend to one side
15 "Don't Cry for Me Argentina" musical
16 Where Nepal is
17 Horse breed known for dressage [western writer]
19 Rogen of "Neighbors"
20 It helps you see plays in replays
21 "Finding Dory" fish
22 Genesis garden
23 Raggedy ___
25 Bolt go-with
27 Upset stomach remedy [Brontë governess]
35 Catholic service
36 Dropped a bit
37 Sluggish
38 Modern bookmark
39 Like a silhouette [19th-century U.K. prime minister]
41 Chrysler truck
42 Surface for chalk writing
44 Intend
45 Fortitude
46 Really made the point [TV surgeon played by Ellen Pompeo]
49 Praising poem
50 Pronoun for two or more
51 Tell all
54 "My goodness!"
58 Sprang
62 Its logo consists of four interlocking circles
63 Brains . . . or this puzzle's four shaded names?
65 Public transit option
66 "Storage Wars" network
67 Abate
68 Beach hill
69 One starting a story "Back in my day . . . ," say
70 ___ 360 (game console)

DOWN

1 Pains
2 Justice Gorsuch
3 Guitarist's key-changing aid
4 Zoo collection
5 Tasseled Turkish topper
6 Boxer Drago of "Rocky IV"
7 Highest figure in sudoku
8 List component
9 Island wrap
10 The decimal system
11 Took advantage of
12 Reference
13 Madeline of "Blazing Saddles"
18 Prize you don't want on "Let's Make a Deal"
24 Wine quality
26 Collection of textbook chapters
27 An ex of Donald Trump
28 Religion with the Five Pillars
29 Olympic symbol
30 Bogged down
31 Dwight's opponent in 1952 and '56
32 Liquid hospital supply
33 Furious
34 20 dispensers
35 "Let's go!" to sled dogs
39 Clarinet piece
40 Sondheim's "___ the Woods"
43 Sprint competitor
45 Waterproof fabric
47 Ska relative
48 Dance at a 52-Down
51 Shakespeare, for one
52 Event with 48-Down dancing
53 Pre-service announcement?
55 ___ exam
56 Text message button
57 One side of a Stevenson character
59 Open ___ (start at the bar, maybe)
60 Mexican moolah
61 Fearsome dino
64 Debussy's sea

by Neville Fogarty

ACROSS

1 Doofus
5 Campus bigwig
9 Leave standing at the altar
13 Greek counterpart to Mars
14 "Tickle Me" doll
15 Walks in water up to one's ankles, say
16 Early radio transmitter
18 Download for a Kindle
19 Deep-frying need
20 "The Farmer in the ___"
22 Letter after "ar"
23 Apply gently, as cream
25 Part of "business," phonetically
30 "Raiders of the Lost Ark" star
32 102, in ancient Rome
34 Common Market letters
35 A sensible sort
36 Like a sorry-looking dog
38 Tiny
40 Very thin, as clouds
41 How some ground balls are fielded
43 Longtime news inits.
45 "___ whillikers!"
46 One-cent coin since 1909
49 Ballet footwear
50 Email address ending for a student
51 Busy bee in Apr.
54 Oil cartel
56 Useful item for finding a lost pet
58 Brief brawl
62 Common game in a school gym
64 Soothing succulents
65 U2's lead singer
66 Biblical brother with a birthright
67 Bad thing to blow . . . or what each of the circled letters in this puzzle represents

68 Greek H's
69 Some whistle blowers

DOWN

1 Wash oneself
2 Stackable cookies
3 Citrus peels
4 Norway's capital
5 Announce
6 "Xanadu" band, for short
7 In the thick of
8 At least
9 The "one" in a one-two
10 Vow from a bride or groom
11 Sign between Cancer and Virgo
12 "Shame on you!"
15 "Ver-r-ry interesting!"
17 Elton John/Tim Rice Broadway musical
21 11-Down symbol
24 Prepare, as tea
26 Dummy at a protest march
27 Lasso loop
28 Figure of speech
29 Without purpose
30 Hard-to-hit pitches
31 Freeze
32 Tragic clown in "Pagliacci"
33 Lacking sense
36 Shed old feathers
37 Casual calls
39 Blade in a sporting match
42 Alka-Seltzer sound

44 Blue hues
47 As required, after "if"
48 Classic art subject
51 Pursue, as in tag
52 Rice dish
53 Highest possible grade
55 Geezer
57 Trucker on a radio
58 Never left the bench, say
59 Inventor Whitney
60 Craggy peak
61 Letter after 22-Across
63 Paternity identifier

by Paul Coulter

ACROSS

1 Inner parts of corn
5 Nectar source
10 Turn toward
14 "The __ King"
15 Hayfield worker
16 Airline that flies only six days a week
17 Jessica of filmdom's "Fantastic Four"
18 Duck for cover?
19 Toy block brand
20 Regulation regarding a 2007 #1 Rihanna hit?
23 Jazzy Reese
24 Bagel topper
25 Dallas-to-N.Y.C. direction
26 Jamaican spirits
29 Letters on an N.Y.C.-bound bag
30 Friend's opposite
33 Special observances for a 2014 #1 Pharrell Williams hit?
37 "Damn right!"
39 Cry before "set, go!"
40 Tick off
41 1994 #1 Lisa Loeb hit played at a potluck?
44 Where one might chill
45 The Shangri-__ ("Leader of the Pack" group)
46 Em chasers
47 __-friendly
50 The "O" of S O S, apocryphally
51 Important exam
53 1979 #1 Styx hit played for Little Red Riding Hood?
59 Go out for a while?
60 __ and aahed
61 Sass, in slang
62 Israeli arms
63 Course reversal
64 Feudin' with
65 Radiate, as charm
66 Hit home?
67 Females

DOWN

1 Composer Debussy
2 Some Texas tycoons
3 Toy in a souvenir shop
4 Problem for a comb
5 Adam's family member
6 Olympic track gold medalist Devers
7 "M*A*S*H" man
8 Hit HBO show for Julia Louis-Dreyfus
9 Swashbuckling leading man
10 __ the Cat
11 Trump impersonator Baldwin
12 Hard to fool
13 "Do Ya" rock grp.
21 Wyatt of the Old West
22 Mythical mischief-maker
27 Really funny
28 Mike who played filmdom's Austin Powers
29 Foster child in "Freaky Friday"
30 "Point taken"
31 Olive of cartoons
32 Japan finish?
34 At __ rate
35 "You __ me at 'hello'"
36 Dr. who can't write prescriptions
37 Nile menace
38 N.Y.C. subway overseer
42 Chimney vent
43 Warning letters next to a web link
48 Club attendant
49 Twins Mary-Kate and Ashley
50 Jabba-esque
52 Smidgens
53 Classic TV clown
54 Comic Ansari
55 "The Little Red Hen" refusal
56 Heavy-landing sound
57 Not yonder
58 Bespectacled Dame of comedy
59 Hall & Oates, for example

by Lisa Loeb and Doug Peterson

100

ACROSS

1 Skilled
6 What's more
10 "Once ___ a time . . ."
14 "___ got a deal for you!"
15 Apply, as plaster
16 Repellent
17 First of a series of sci-fi movies starring Sigourney Weaver
18 10:1, for example
19 Computer command for the error-prone
20 Actor who has hosted the Oscars nine times, a number second only to Bob Hope
23 Something stubbed
24 Powerful explosive
28 Baseball's ___ Joe DiMaggio
32 Watchdog org.?
34 Wrath
35 Sound of danger
36 He played Gomez in 1991's "The Addams Family"
38 Prefix with -zoic
39 Tube-shaped pasta
40 Geese formations
41 Comic actor who was an original cast member of SCTV
43 Swiss capital, to French speakers
44 India pale ___
45 Affectedly creative
46 Wild animals
47 Club Med, for one
49 The "f" of fwiw
50 Beginning of a rom-com . . . or a description of 20-, 36- and 41-Across?
57 In fine fettle
60 College in New Rochelle, N.Y.
61 Bert's pal on "Sesame Street"
62 Word of woe
63 Thumbs-down votes
64 Repeated short bits in jazz

65 Agree (with)
66 Itsy-bitsy biter
67 Units of nautical speed

DOWN

1 Melville captain
2 Limp watch painter
3 Satanic
4 Rind
5 Dickens lad who says "God bless us every one!"
6 Worship
7 ___ Gaga
8 Soap bubbles
9 ___ course (part of boot camp)
10 Throat dangler
11 Wrestling win
12 Outdated
13 With 21-Down, military hawk
21 See 13-Down
22 Key of Beethoven's Symphony No. 7: Abbr.
25 Many flooring installers
26 Show the ropes to
27 Alternatives to purchases
28 Preserves preserver
29 World Cup chant
30 Mascara is applied to them
31 1982 Disney film
32 Devastating hurricane of 2012
33 Pint-size
36 $2,000, if you land on Boardwalk with a hotel
37 Iris's place
39 Spring break activity in Miami Beach or Cabo
42 Beloved, in "Rigoletto"
43 Crazy
46 Web crawler
48 Way overweight
49 Thanksgiving meal
51 Haunted house sound
52 New Age singer from Ireland
53 ___ and bear it
54 Help desk offering
55 Fissure
56 What 1 is to 2 and 2 is to 3
57 Journey to Mecca
58 "Aladdin" prince
59 Chemist's workplace

by Dan Margolis

ACROSS

1 Wriggly temptation for a fish
5 To a smaller degree
9 Newswoman Van Susteren
14 Length × width, for a rectangle
15 Rx dosages, e.g.: Abbr.
16 City across the Nile from the Valley of the Kings
17 They might be sealed
18 Apiarist?
20 "Now listen . . ."
22 ___ smasher
23 Trains to Chicago's Loop
24 Flared skirts
26 Org. for some sportswomen
29 Invoice from a souvenir shop?
31 Terse put-down of Sandra's "Gidget" performance?
33 Outrage
34 Toasty
35 King Kong, for one
36 Playlist listing
38 Poorly lit
39 Unsullied
41 ___ Leppard
42 "Paradise Lost" setting
44 Many SAT takers: Abbr.
45 Where to keep divorce papers?
47 Signal Ernie's buddy to step onstage?
51 Blend, as batter
52 Stogies
54 Maiden name preceder
55 Firenze farewell
57 Sitcom segments
59 "Wow, you have violins!"?
62 Influence with higher-ups
63 Long-necked wader
64 Decisive defeat
65 Opera highlight
66 Unlike the proverbial rolling stone
67 ___-serif
68 Microscope part

DOWN

1 Holder for cash and IDs
2 Pro baseball player with an orange-and-black uniform
3 State of rest
4 Lone Ranger accessory
5 Patti in the Grammy Hall of Fame
6 Chef known for "New New Orleans" cuisine
7 17th-century Dutch painter Jan
8 Worrisome org. for a draft dodger
9 Market oversupply
10 Dancer Nureyev
11 Typical specimen
12 Unit of capacity for a bridge
13 17,000-year-old find in France's Lascaux cave
19 Cop's stunner
21 Salon product for a spiky do
25 Dutch cheese
27 Stare open-mouthed
28 Made disappear, in a way
30 Recycling receptacle
32 Title for Maria Theresa of Austria
34 Triumph
36 Quick, suggestive message
37 Badge holders
38 Arnaz of "I Love Lucy"
40 Many a PC cable
41 ___ Plaines, Ill.
43 Look of a room
44 Legal authorities
46 Purple things in several van Gogh paintings
47 Pop-producing toy weapon
48 Continue through time
49 Land, as a fish
50 Electric cars named for an inventor
53 Kind of salami
56 Court fig.
58 Girl's name that's also a 59-Down
59 See 58-Down
60 Maniacal leader?
61 Org. of concern to H&R Block

by Lynn Lempel

ACROSS

1 Doll-making tribe of the Southwest
5 Greatly annoys
10 Long, tedious effort
14 Mathematician Turing
15 Circa
16 Surfer's catch
17 Lively Irish dances
18 Sierra __ (African land)
19 Supermodel from Somalia
20 "From what __ seen . . ."
21 Singers Johnny and Fiona?
23 Good dogs for pheasant hunters
25 Billiard stick
26 Craving
27 Feature of the easily offended
32 2015 climate accord city
34 "Thou __ not . . ."
35 French summer
36 Wildcat with tufted ears
37 Performances by two singers . . . like 21- and 49-Across and 3- and 29-Down?
38 Extinguished, as birthday candles, with "out"
39 Soccer stadium cry
40 Dirt, dust, soot, etc.
41 Soothing ointments
42 Desserts with layered fruit and whipped cream
44 Like fish that are difficult to eat
45 Rap's __ Wayne
46 Salt's partner in potato chip flavoring
49 Singers Keith and John?
54 GPS option: Abbr.
55 "Va-va-__!"
56 Glittery jewelry
57 Negotiator's goal
58 Alleviate
59 Put out, as a statement
60 Ryan of "Boston Public"
61 Parabola shapes

62 Heads of France
63 Huff

DOWN

1 Ones who've traveled to Mecca
2 Martini garnish
3 Singers Patti and Tina?
4 Opposite of outs
5 In abundance
6 Conspires with
7 Stolen stuff
8 Debussy's "Clair de __"
9 Aids in sign-lettering
10 Motions left or right on Tinder
11 Home furnishing product with a shade
12 Like the president's office
13 Trait transmitter
21 Govt. rules
22 May or Polly of fiction
24 Colorful cereal
27 "__ fightin' words!"
28 Despise
29 Singers Tori and Al?
30 See 31-Down
31 With 30-Down, brief article in a paper
32 Sit (down) hard
33 Heroine of Jean Auel's "The Clan of the Cave Bear"
34 Attire not usually seen on casual Friday
37 Tool part used to create holes
38 __ of one's existence
40 Profit
41 James __ (007)
43 Bad thing to go down in
44 Watches episode after episode of a TV series, say
46 Event location
47 Arcade pioneer
48 Ignited again
49 Colored part of the eye
50 Plane engine's sound when taking off
51 Pear variety
52 Otherwise
53 Main point of an idea
57 Dance club bookings, in brief

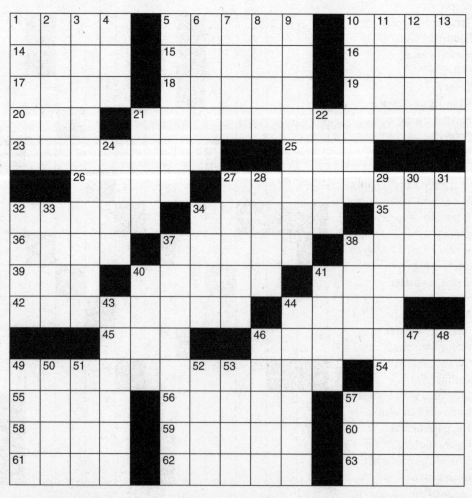

by Susan Gelfand

ACROSS

1 Important consideration for investors
5 Attire that may leave the chest bare
11 Barely lit
14 Demands
16 Concluding musical section
17 One of the premier clubs in the Premier League
19 Native New Zealander
20 A wee hour
21 Southern region where blues developed
28 Swift steeds
29 Words said while running out the door, maybe
30 Comics villain ___ Luthor
31 Applesauce
32 Die
34 "Law & Order: SVU" actor
35 Diamonds are weighed in them
37 Item swiped by Indiana Jones at the start of "Raiders of the Lost Ark"
41 Conversed
43 Gerontologist's subject
44 Crank (up)
47 Hill that's steep on one side and gentle on the other
49 Bush - or an anagram of BUSH plus one letter
50 Annual Austin festival
53 Halved
54 Actress Mazar of "Entourage"
55 Arrival and departure locales hinted at by 17-, 21- and 50-Across
63 CBS show with a "New Orleans" spinoff
64 Treasured possession
65 Pitiful
66 Indigenous people of Singapore
67 Mill devices

DOWN

1 Volcano feature
2 ___ moment (shortly)
3 Phishing target: Abbr.
4 Does awesomely
5 Goulashes, e.g.
6 Pilgrimage site in central Italy
7 Wheel groove
8 Unfold, poetically
9 Negative linking word
10 Roamer of the Serengeti
11 "Pray continue . . ."
12 Conceptualize
13 1979 breakout role for Mel Gibson
15 Dominant faith of Iran
16 French filmdom
18 Places where lines meet
21 When repeated, Hawaiian menu item
22 Classic Camaro
23 Sashimi go-with
24 Wow
25 Accept, as a lesser charge
26 Component
27 "How sweet ___!"
33 Cause of tree damage and downed telephone wires
35 Sandwich usually served with toothpicks
36 Answer to the riddle "What force or strength cannot get through / I, with gentle touch, can do"
38 Dreadful, as circumstances
39 Cross to bear
40 Like the group you're in if you're out, for short
42 Sneeze sound
43 Waste container
44 Dwellers east of the Urals
45 One of the friends on "Friends"
46 Foul-smelling
48 Actress Hepburn
51 County divs.
52 Melodic subjects in music
56 Meas. of engine speed
57 ___-la
58 Up to, informally
59 Author LeShan
60 1977 Steely Dan album
61 Stove setting for simmering
62 ___ admin (IT pro)

by Jason Flinn

ACROSS

1 Explosions
7 Like the posture of humans
12 Person in a detached state?
13 Hit 2017 Jordan Peele thriller
15 With 25-Down, alchemists' quest in a book released on June 26, 1997
17 Office head
18 Money back
19 Evidence for determining paternity
20 Swear (to)
22 Victory
23 Deadly snakes
26 Units in stables
31 Lion in "The Chronicles of Narnia"
35 Coup d'___
37 Enthusiastic
38 Alphabet chunk after D-E-F
39 Column's counterpart
40 Specialist's vocabulary
41 Distinctive atmosphere
42 Jay once seen nightly
43 Fund, as a chair
44 Coming from two speakers
46 Singer Fitzgerald
48 Bill who's a science expert
50 Small program
55 Lawyers' org.
58 "The Descent of Man" author
61 Widespread
62 Star of the film version of the book referenced in 15-Across/25-Down
65 Comparable to a pin, in a phrase
66 Goes "Ah-choo!"
67 Persistently torment
68 Crafty person at a wheel?

DOWN

1 Given benediction, the old-fashioned way
2 Run out, as a subscription
3 ___ Wednesday
4 Evades
5 Shakespeare's "The Winter's ___"
6 Hoity-toity type
7 Self-centered sort
8 Be in a sorry state?
9 Biblical verb ending
10 Like volleyball that's played jointly by men and women
11 Not go straight
12 "Cat on ___ Tin Roof"
14 Passenger-screening org.
15 Letters on a schedule meaning "We'll let you know"
16 Went on dates with
21 What the Titanic did, famously
24 Father: Fr.
25 See 15-Across
27 Of similar character
28 Advance, as money
29 Toy block brand
30 Cold fall
31 Turkish pooh-bahs
32 Open's opposite
33 Abandoned European capital
34 Not quite closed
36 Soldier who's gone missing
40 Jump
42 Allegiance
45 Cause to be cherished
47 Surgical knife
49 Exemplify humanity, say
51 Contest award
52 Subject of a long sentence?
53 Letters before gees
54 Golf peg
55 Palindromic Nabokov title
56 Big party
57 "___ and the King of Siam"
59 Big stinger
60 Nine-digit fig. on a Social Security card
63 Comparative suffix
64 Tennis umpire's call

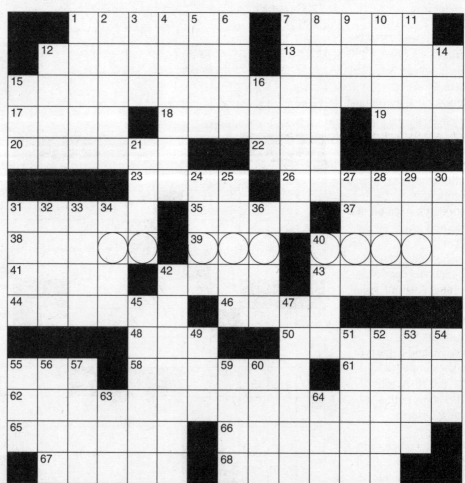

by Brian Greer

ACROSS

1 Exiled leader of 1979
5 Sing smoothly
10 I.R.S. experts
14 Spotted rodent of South America
15 Zoo resident that needs a big tank
16 River of Florence
17 And others, for short
18 Following
19 Word exclaimed with "Get" or "Too"
20 Slight sense that something is seriously shady
23 Minus
24 "Texas tea"
25 Courtroom wear . . . or concern
27 "Just do it" or "I'm lovin' it"
32 One who really brings out the crowds
35 Broody rock genre
36 "Ye" follower on shoppe signs
37 Gene, the singing cowboy
38 Hitters' stats
39 Take advantage of
40 Military unit assembled for sudden attack
42 Generous giving
44 Morales of "Criminal Minds"
45 Jokester
46 Depression-era migrant
48 Fight to the bitter end . . . or a hint to the starts of 20-, 32- and 40-Across
55 "Star Trek: T.N.G." character
56 Stay home for supper
57 "Fine by me"
58 Unwelcome bit of mail
59 Paddle
60 Shakespearean king
61 Artist Warhol
62 Citrusy, e.g.
63 Hamlet, for one

DOWN

1 Eject, as angry words
2 "Thirty days ___ September . . ."
3 Antioxidant-rich berry
4 24,110 years, for plutonium 239
5 Bad state to be in
6 Guitar phrases
7 Chooses
8 Intl. group with two South American members and none in North America
9 "When Harry Met Sally . . ." writer Ephron
10 Exercise on an elliptical machine, informally
11 Middle school math class
12 Annoyingly focused
13 What astronomers call a day on Mars
21 Greek salad topper
22 Florida State athlete, slangily
25 Tortilla chip dip
26 What the River Styx forms the boundary of
27 Bandleader Shaw
28 Quaint dagger
29 Eye woe
30 ___ curiae (friends of the court)
31 Part of the body associated with sneezing, sniffling and snoring
32 Awful-smelling
33 Big mixing containers
34 "___ is not to reason why"
38 Copper alloy used in jewelry
40 State flower of Utah
41 Ireland's Sinn ___
43 Annoying critic
46 In the red
47 Broadway's "___ Boots"
48 Enter
49 Rapper Kanye
50 California's ___ Valley
51 Superhero creator Lee
52 Company that was the first in the U.S. to air a TV ad with a gay couple (1994)
53 Indian flatbread
54 Circular or spiral motion
55 Org. for which Mike Tyson twice held the heavyweight title

by John Guzzetta

106

ACROSS

1 Deals with a problem
6 What X equals in Roman numerals
9 Mature, as wine
12 Polite plea to a parent
13 Yale student, informally
14 Sea, to Debussy
15 *Out-of-vogue hairstyle akin to a mullet
16 What "compares 2 U" in a 1990 #1 Sinead O'Connor hit
18 Ctrl-___-Del
19 When doubled, an African fly
20 Diatribe
21 Thick piece of concrete
23 Like a G.I. cleaning up after a meal, maybe
25 Speak grandly
27 *Condition with feet turned inward
30 Nobel laureate Wiesel
31 Almost vertical, as a slope
32 *How a tot rides on someone's shoulders
34 Nurse, as a drink
36 Gooey road cover
37 *Two ones, in dice
43 Monsoon events
47 Nashville's home: Abbr.
48 Like a centaur or faun . . . or a hint to the answer to each of this puzzle's starred clues
50 Washington's ___ Sound
52 Drug cop
53 Transoceanic alliance since 1949
54 Nike competitor
56 Western tribe member
58 Acorn, for one
59 On the market, as a house
60 *Signs of a much-used book
62 Suffix with nectar or elephant
63 Fib
64 Have the attention of
65 Psychedelic drug, briefly
66 The "L" of L.A.P.D.
67 Sierra ___ (African land)

DOWN

1 Summer vacation lodging
2 Result of three strikes
3 City planner's map
4 Inventor dubbed "The Wizard of Menlo Park"
5 Feature of the word "psalm" or "pterodactyl"
6 Camping stake
7 Race of people in "The Time Machine"
8 The "N" of TNT
9 "Star Wars" queen
10 Hereditary
11 Unit of work
12 "Heads or tails!"
15 Speaks with a hoarse voice
17 *Foolish sort
22 *Really something, with "the"
24 Japanese pond swimmer
26 "There's a mouse!"
28 Andy's boy on "The Andy Griffith Show"
29 Driller in R.O.T.C., maybe: Abbr.
33 Knitting material
35 Dynamism
37 Fuel additive brand
38 Those getting excited when thinking?
39 Made irate
40 Team with the most World Series victories (27)
41 Historical period
42 Layered Austrian pastry
44 Humble response to "How do you do it all?"
45 It is "full of genius, full of the divinity," per Henry David Thoreau
46 Vegas machines
49 Start of a play
51 Kids' batting game
55 Miscellany
57 Frozen waffle brand
59 Chick-___-A
61 Suffix with Caesar

by Max Lauring and Benjamin Lauring

ACROSS
1 Facing difficulty
7 Crow
11 London's ___ Gardens
14 "Hasta ___"
15 Prime rating org.
16 Belief, informally
17 Contributing (to)
18 Neither raise nor fold, in poker
19 Homer's next-door neighbor on "The Simpsons"
20 Rollover problem? [1997]
23 ___ Paulo, Brazil
24 Something a driver may "hang"
25 Jazz pianist Jamal
28 Spectacular disaster [2016]
32 H&R Block staffers
34 Start of the season?
35 Vardalos of "My Big Fat Greek Wedding"
36 Rescue from insolvency [2008]
39 Demoted [2006]
42 Wife of Juan Perón
43 Agency issuance, in brief
45 Get rid of
46 Gender-neutral pronoun [2015]
51 John B, in a Beach Boys hit
52 Particle physics suffix
53 When doubled, a Gabor sister
56 Annual American Dialect Society award given to seven answers in this puzzle
61 Sacha Baron Cohen's "Da ___ G Show"
63 Egg: Fr.
64 Verdi opera based on a Shakespeare play
65 Cent or capita preceder
66 One chain by one furlong
67 "Now wait just one second!"
68 "The Fall of the House of Usher" writer
69 Pink
70 Airing after midnight, say

DOWN
1 Muslim worship leaders
2 Foreign exchange student in "American Pie"
3 "___, the angel of the Lord came upon them": Luke
4 Corner square in Monopoly
5 Either of two wives of Henry VIII
6 ___ opus
7 Like Tokyo's Shinjuku Station, according to Guinness
8 Q-V connection
9 Actor Driver of "Star Wars: The Force Awakens"
10 New York's Stonewall Inn, e.g.
11 Cretan who had the Labyrinth built
12 WNW's opposite
13 Iraq War worry, for short [2002]
21 Puppy's bite
22 Channels 14 and up, for short
26 April fools' sign?
27 Inoperative
28 Lentil dish at an Indian restaurant
29 G.I. tour grp.
30 Money left on the table?
31 Subj. for U.S. citizens-to-be
32 Petty objection
33 Part of a musical instrument made from spring steel
36 Porgy's partner
37 https://www.whitehouse.gov, e.g.
38 Serving from a trolley
40 Western native
41 Play (with)
44 Baseball's Ken Jr. or Sr.
47 When repeated, baby's utterance
48 Furor
49 Explosive in a stick
50 Santa's laugh
53 Video game princess
54 "Skoal!" alternative
55 Soap-on-___
57 Chrysler Building's style, briefly
58 Not just mine
59 Kind of collar
60 Holler
61 Snapchat or Dropbox [2010]
62 One of 13 popes

by Greg Poulos

ACROSS

1 Things kindergartners learn
5 In addition
9 "The Naked ___" (Goya painting)
13 Bit of snow
15 What some bills become
16 Burden
17 Dog-___ (like some old book pages)
18 "Told ya!"
20 With 37- and 52-Across, #11 on the American Film Institute's "100 Years . . . 100 Movie Quotes" list
22 Freezerful
23 Put in a bibliography
24 Have the wheel
26 "Rebecca" author Du Maurier
29 The "Homo" in Homo sapiens
32 In the past
33 Former lovers
37 See 20-Across
41 Accepts begrudgingly, as a minor flaw
42 ___ TV (Time Warner channel)
43 Casting assignments
44 Meryl who portrayed Margaret Thatcher
47 43rd U.S. president, informally
50 One of 18 on an 18-wheeler
51 Bear: Sp.
52 See 20-Across
59 Make over
61 Winter drink
62 Data
63 Plains tribe
64 Drug bust units
65 With 66- and 67-Across, source of this puzzle theme's quote
66 See 65-Across
67 See 65-Across

DOWN

1 Two or three
2 Ho-hum
3 ___ mia (Italian term of endearment)
4 Quick drawing
5 ___ and kicking
6 One poked through the eye?

7 Free goodies at an event
8 Nobel Peace Prize city
9 "The Simpsons" bartender
10 Actress MacDowell of "Four Weddings and a Funeral"
11 Electricity, slangily
12 Fall bloomer
14 Olympic hurdler Moses
19 Shipmate of Capt. Kirk and Mr. Spock
21 Summer in France
25 Peter the Great, e.g.
26 Author Roald
27 Pulitzer Prize-winning author James
28 City with piers
29 Alternatives to mums
30 "The Sopranos" Emmy winner Falco
31 Packers' and Panthers' org.

33 "Make ___ what you will"
34 Portion (out)
35 Raison d'___
36 Campbell's product
38 Athletic achievement award
39 Susan with the 1978 best seller "Compromising Positions"
40 Camera type, for short
44 Something confessed in a confessional
45 Pulling a rabbit out of a hat, e.g.
46 Pull back, as in horror
47 Kind of column in architecture
48 "___ hooks" (shipping caution)
49 Highly successful, in theaterspeak

50 Readied, as a musical instrument
53 Cry of anticipation
54 Big name in photocopiers, once
55 Where the U.S. flag has flown since 1969
56 Anticensorship org.
57 Swiped
58 Abate
60 "You've got mail" co.

by Peter A. Collins

ACROSS

1 No longer a minor
6 Teenager's woe
10 "__ and the Real Girl" (Ryan Gosling film)
14 Video game lover of Princess Peach
15 "Darn it!"
16 Affirm
17 *Sugar craving
19 Whom Dory and Marlin found, in film
20 Niihau neckwear
21 *Carved figurine popular around Christmas
23 *What never goes unpunished, it's said
27 Enroll
28 Iraq War concerns, for short
29 O. J.'s alma mater
31 Son of Aphrodite
32 Bit that might have the heading "About Me"
33 Knight's title
35 Boat in "Jaws"
37 With 39-Across, impressive basketball feat . . . or a feature shared by the answers to the six starred clues
39 See 37-Across
42 Kindle competitor
43 Half of a colon
44 First word of the Lord's Prayer
46 Website subscriber's creation: Abbr.
48 Common place for a sports injury, for short
50 Fantasy beast
51 __ fibrillation (abnormal heart rhythm)
53 *Wheelchair foot strap
56 *Pet cage feature
58 Emceed, e.g.
59 Running behind
60 *Figurehead?
65 P __ psychology (unhelpful spelling clarification)
66 Princess created by L. Frank Baum
67 Garlic unit
68 Small change
69 Witnessed
70 Far from fuzzy, for short

DOWN

1 Baseball execs
2 Kind of food or footage
3 Mined find
4 Brandishes
5 "O.K., understood"
6 Kerfuffle
7 Sights at malls on Black Friday
8 Post-W.W. II alliance
9 Cultural value system
10 Russia's seizure of Crimea, e.g.
11 Big name in skin care
12 Ladies' men
13 Like some enemies or testimonies
18 Scenario before extra innings
22 Like a jigsaw puzzle
23 Prez with the same initials as an N.Y.C. landmark
24 Leave out
25 Stench
26 "I've found it!"
30 Baby
33 Expense item for a political campaign
34 U.N. agcy. headquartered in Geneva
36 Aussie hopper
38 Episode
40 Snapchat's ghost, e.g.
41 Coin of many countries
45 What people know about you, informally
46 Order to relax
47 Dimwit
49 Google's web browser
50 Yale, affectionately
51 "Ask about it at work" sloganeer, once
52 University of New Mexico team
54 Big game
55 Little sucker
57 Seep
61 Manhattan's home: Abbr.
62 Seed case
63 Anticipatory time
64 One crying foul?

by Jerry Miccolis and Jeff Chen

ACROSS

1 Three-syllable foot, as in "bada-bing"
8 Hosp. diagnostic procedure that's noninvasive
11 Cavity filler's deg.
14 German measles
15 Patronizes a restaurant
17 Nickname of Gen. Burgoyne in the American Revolution
19 "Your turn," to a walkie-talkie user
20 Source of fresh water
21 Valentine's Day flower
22 Parts of psyches
24 Skills that no one knows anymore
27 College fund-raiser targets
30 Sound after snap and crackle
31 Law
33 End of a close race
38 Ante matter?
40 Cookie cooker
41 "Drove my Chevy to the __ . . ." ("American Pie" lyric)
42 Bit of turf on a golf course
44 St. Louis landmark
46 High-priced theater section
47 Dish made with romaine lettuce, croutons and Parmesan cheese
50 Busta Rhymes's music
51 __ Lanka
52 Irritable
54 Sombrero-wearing musician
58 Animal docs
60 United __ Emirates
61 Exclamations during eclipses
64 Actress Skye
66 Coiner of the phrase "alternative facts"
70 Taking a sabbatical, e.g.
71 "Le Misanthrope" playwright
72 "You don't __!"
73 Anthem writer Francis Scott __
74 Had the helm

DOWN

1 Jason's ship, in myth
2 Cuatro + cinco
3 Rare blood type
4 Gas sold by the litre
5 Right-angled joint
6 Seattle __ (1977 Triple Crown horse)
7 Domesticated
8 __ Park, N.J.
9 Indian character on "The Big Bang Theory"
10 Midori who lit the torch at the Nagano Olympics
11 Blood drive participant
12 Actress Kirsten
13 Eye woes
16 Henry __, British Army officer who invented the exploding shell
18 What 17-, 33-, 47- and 66-Across exhibit, despite appearances to the contrary
23 "How's it goin'?"
25 Letters before a number on a beach bottle
26 Work like a dog
28 Unit of conductance
29 Suddenly bright stars
31 Electrically flexible
32 __ Pet (kitschy gift)
34 Frère of un père
35 Place sheltered from worldly realities
36 Game company that created Sonic the Hedgehog
37 Dickens's Uriah __
39 Part of A.S.A.P.
43 "Gone With the Wind" plantation
45 Sombrero, e.g.
48 Ocasek of the Cars
49 605, in ancient Rome
53 Keister
54 Powerful sharks
55 Ice show setting
56 Political campaign event
57 Bees' production
59 Small drum
62 Clothes lines?
63 Edinburgh native
65 Observed closely
67 Tibetan ox
68 N.Y.C.'s Madison __
69 Bullring cheer

by Peter Gordon

ACROSS

1 Wound on a dueler
5 Tarnish
8 Dwells (on)
13 Victor who wrote "Les Misérables"
14 "Here, boy!"
15 Benefit
16 Tennis score just before winning a game
17 "This round's —"
18 Like many a smoker's voice
19 "The race has just begun, and it looks like the car from Warsaw will —!"
22 Religious recluse
23 Basic readings for a hospital patient
26 Lungful
27 Hook's henchman
29 In good health
30 "Listen! You can hear the thundering roar as the car from Moscow goes—!"
34 Letters on a wanted poster
35 Supermarket IDs
36 Something kept in reserve?
37 Worry
38 Negative conjunction
39 "We're getting close to the end as the car from Helsinki leads the way to the —!"
43 Animal whose name sounds like a Greek letter
44 Andy's partner in old comedy
45 Luau accessory
46 Wife in Oaxaca
48 Kind of fishing or diving
52 "Wow! The car from Prague ekes out the victory by a nose and takes the —!"
55 World Golf Hall-of-Famer Lorena
57 "On the double!"
58 It "keeps the cold out better than a cloak," per Longfellow
59 Nuisances
60 Bonkers
61 Eclipse, to some
62 Message to one's followers
63 Hearty laugh
64 Online comment

DOWN

1 Diamond, e.g.
2 Old royal house
3 Limber
4 Factor in diagnosing osteoporosis
5 Hustler's game
6 Cartridge contents
7 Shallow water obstacle
8 Tubman of the Underground Railroad
9 Sailor's "Stop!"
10 Person with dreads
11 Circle on a cube
12 Foxy
14 Sandinista's foe
20 Rare grandfather clock numeral
21 Currier's partner in lithography
24 Compare
25 Word in many university names
27 "Wheel of Fortune" turns
28 Timbuktu's land
30 Steps up?
31 Barely ahead
32 Ponytail holder
33 Off-limits activity
37 Switch positions
39 Where China is
40 Desktop computer that runs Safari
41 Like many a new parent
42 Obey
47 Absorber of UV rays
48 Quaffed
49 Instant replay effect
50 Sites for Christmas lights
51 James Bond, e.g.
53 Imprecise, as a memory
54 Son of Rebekah
55 Make a decision
56 Crow's cry

by Brian Thomas

112

ACROSS

1 1997 Nicolas Cage film
7 Took too much of a drug, briefly
11 Biblical symbol of patience
14 St. Francis of ___
15 ___-Hoop (toy)
16 Address beginning "http"
17 1987 Kiefer Sutherland film
19 Item for a T-bar user
20 ___ fly (certain baseball out, informally)
21 Music producer Brian
22 Actor John or his actor son Sean
24 1987 Patrick Swayze film
28 ___ salts (bath supply)
31 Marriage
32 Release
33 Yemeni port
35 Some TVs
38 Lowly worker
39 1982, 1985, 1988 and 2008 Sylvester Stallone film franchise
40 Amazon rodent
41 ". . . ___ saw Elba"
42 Sin associated with the color green
43 Things you put up when you "put 'em up"
44 Vandalized, in a way, as on Halloween
46 Fertile soil
47 1987 Mel Gibson film
52 Things opened at banks: Abbr.
53 35mm camera inits.
54 ___ Beta Kappa
57 The Blue Jays, on scoreboards
58 1994 John Travolta film
63 The Cavaliers, on scoreboards
64 Handmade products website
65 Environmental messes from tankers

66 Concealed
67 Root beer brand
68 Much-derided hairstyle seen in 1-, 17-, 24-, 39-, 47- and 58-Across

DOWN

1 Pets that purr
2 Dept. of Labor arm
3 Tiny amount of time: Abbr.
4 Be laid up in bed
5 Prefix with propyl
6 Early ___ (night owl's opposite)
7 "We're in trouble now!"
8 Hall & Oates, for example
9 Tarzan player Ron
10 Evian competitor

11 Because you never know, it might be needed
12 Big name in pest control
13 Flashy jewelry
18 Stuff that blows up other stuff
23 Zodiac symbol between scales and an archer
24 Pilots' combat
25 Texter's "I believe . . ."
26 Library book words
27 Part of A.D.
28 Otherwise
29 One of 12 on a jury
30 Rep
33 Root beer brand
34 Driver's license issuer, for short
36 Lion taming and tightrope walking, for two

37 Talk back to
39 Rod and ___
43 Woman in Progressive ads
45 Expressed shock
47 Lock fastener
48 Sometimes-bad bacterium
49 Some athletic awards
50 Governor Landon who ran for president in 1936
51 Cover image on Pink Floyd's "The Dark Side of the Moon"
54 Bit of medicine
55 Ozone layer problem
56 The "I" of M.I.T.: Abbr.
59 Actress Hagen
60 Trip inducer, in brief
61 PC "brain"
62 Up to, informally

by Kevin Christian

ACROSS

1 Molded jelly
6 Pitch a tent
10 Snoozes
14 /
15 Dell competitor
16 Spoken
17 Charley ___
18 Actress Taylor of "Mystic Pizza"
19 Tidbit at a Spanish bar
20 Music conglomerate that broke up in 2012
21 Receptacle carried from a crime scene
24 Cosa ___
26 List-ending abbr.
27 Kind of pork on a Chinese menu
30 On fire
34 Appropriate for all audiences, as humor
36 Piano teacher's assignment
38 Fort ___, N.J.
39 Neighbor of an Estonian
40 Coat for a cat
41 "No shoes, no shirt, no service," e.g.
42 Stick in a lake?
43 "Ad ___ per aspera" (motto of Kansas)
45 Light purple
46 Wallace's partner, in claymation
48 Div. that manager Bobby Cox won every year from 1995 to 2005
50 Actor Driver of "The Force Awakens"
52 Crowd chant to an award honoree
55 The Silk Road and others
60 Fish eggs
61 Morning TV co-host
62 Lawn mower brand
63 Mosque V.I.P.s
65 ___ smasher
66 City that's home to the Viking Ship Museum
67 To the ___ (one way to dress)
68 Odorous Le Pew
69 Beginning point for a first flight
70 Singer of the 2012 #1 hit "Somebody That I Used to Know"

DOWN

1 Wan
2 Lovers running to each other may be shown in it
3 Way to get from Gare du Nord to Gare de Lyon
4 Magazine unit: Abbr.
5 Root for
6 Colombian metropolis
7 Tums target
8 Free-for-all
9 Paid part of a magazine
10 Kind of motel
11 Spirited steed
12 "Come to ___!" (gambler's cry)
13 Refinery waste
22 Some military hospitals, for short
23 Establishment with a brunch rush, maybe
25 Precisely
28 Weight
29 Often-forbidden maneuver . . . as hinted at four times in this puzzle
31 Substance that decreases purity
32 Kunis of "Friends With Benefits"
33 One high up on the corporate ladder, informally
34 Pipe problem
35 Shakespearean king
37 River to the Caspian
41 Opposite of set
43 Congressional worker
44 Begin, as a task
45 Running out
47 Title for Tussaud
49 112.5° on a compass: Abbr.
51 Costume that might involve two people
53 Former F.B.I. director James
54 German state or novelist
55 Sand, in golf
56 Having your first shave or buying your first bra, e.g.
57 Each
58 Website links, for short
59 Blow on a horn
64 "O Sole ___"

by Andrew J. Ries

114

ACROSS

1 Falafel holders
6 Piano technician
11 Start of a countdown
14 Food-spoiling bacterium
15 "Remember the __!"
16 Party card game
17 "Tell me the rumors are false!"
19 Kook
20 Revolutionary Guevara
21 Some HDTVs
22 Glowing part of a fire
24 Comprehensive, as a report
27 Put an end to
28 2000 Kevin Spacey/ Helen Hunt film
32 Sounding congested
35 Smash into
36 Leave rolling in the aisles
37 Approximation: Abbr.
38 Oscar-nominated Enya song from 2001's "The Lord of the Rings"
42 Was out to lunch?
43 Apple tablet
45 Dog doc
46 Helped out
48 Offer effusive praise
52 Poe poem that starts "Once upon a midnight dreary," with "The"
53 Long to have
57 Capital of Oregon
58 Sweetie pie
60 "That __ lie!"
61 Get older
62 Improvise
66 California's Big __
67 Sign on a boardinghouse window
68 Cowboys' home
69 D.D.E.'s predecessor
70 Cheese with holes
71 Actress Winona of "Stranger Things"

DOWN

1 Actor Joe of "My Cousin Vinny"
2 Corporate raider Carl
3 Trifled (with)
4 Three-time Frazier foe
5 Take a load off
6 Chinese martial art
7 Neighbor of the radius
8 Yanks : New York :: __ : Washington
9 Letters on an ambulance
10 One whose work is on the house?
11 Popular sandwich order
12 Make a list of
13 Do, re or mi
18 Pretentiously showy
23 Clean Air Act and others
25 Clean Air Act org.
26 It may be read by a psychic
27 Grooming implement
29 Travis of country music
30 Liposuction target
31 Not naturally red-haired, e.g.
32 Singer Diamond or Young
33 Spears at the dinner table
34 "Keep your eyes open!"
39 Stratford-upon-__
40 Hankering
41 Per person
44 Drop precipitously
47 D.D.E., familiarly
49 Lures
50 Bad ones are hard to break
51 Rapper-turned-TV actor
54 Wicked one
55 __ orange
56 Harder to find
57 Pageant wrap
58 Indonesian tourist destination
59 Naval agreements?
63 Like a pitch between the ankles and knees
64 "It's f-f-freezing!"
65 "Yippee!"

by Alan Arbesfeld

ACROSS

1 Kindergarten learning
5 Place with hot rocks
10 Golf shot near a green
14 Cemetery purchase
15 Tells to "Do it!"
16 Long-eared hopper
17 Anchor man?
20 Sacred Egyptian bug
21 Southern drawl, e.g.
22 Snack you might bite or lick
24 "Lovely __" (Beatles song)
25 Sound technician?
32 They come with buds
33 Space ball
34 Star-crossed lover of literature
35 Secretive org.
36 Bare minimum
38 Tennis barrier
39 What dropping off a last child at college is, to many parents
42 Star of "An Inconvenient Truth"
45 Giant in health plans
47 Cancel, as a rocket launch
48 Beat reporter?
51 One not reporting for duty, maybe
52 2017, por ejemplo
53 Cartoon "Ouch!"
55 Suffers from
56 Quaint gestures of gratitude
60 Noshed
61 "Right you __!"
62 Sister brand of Baby Ruth
63 It stains
64 Resting place
65 Executive producer?
66 Blab

DOWN

1 Smartphone downloads
2 Congress's Freedom Caucus, e.g.
3 Nightclub in a Manilow song
4 Olympics no-no
5 Honey brand since 1921
6 "The creation of beauty," per Ralph Waldo Emerson
7 "Yuck!"
8 Maiden name intro
9 Batter, e.g.
10 City said to have big shoulders
11 In great shape
12 Resource in the Mesabi Range
13 Cheeky
18 Hard-to-believe stories
19 One in a cast
23 Instrument with cane blades
24 Steals
25 Hot ones can cause trouble
26 Capital of Samoa
27 Sign akin to "Bridge Out"
28 One of the Gershwins
29 "Hold on, give me a second"
30 Future predictor
31 Many a pledge drive gift
36 Loretta who was the subject of "Coal Miner's Daughter"
37 Word document settings
40 __ pickle
41 5 or 6, for a kindergartner, typically
43 High toss
44 __ Goose (vodka brand)
46 Dame of mystery
47 Consecrate
48 Cognizant
49 Bury
50 Successful prankster's cry
51 Melville monomaniac
54 Span for The New Yorker
56 Know-__
57 Appropriate rhyme for "spa"
58 For
59 Roget's entry: Abbr.

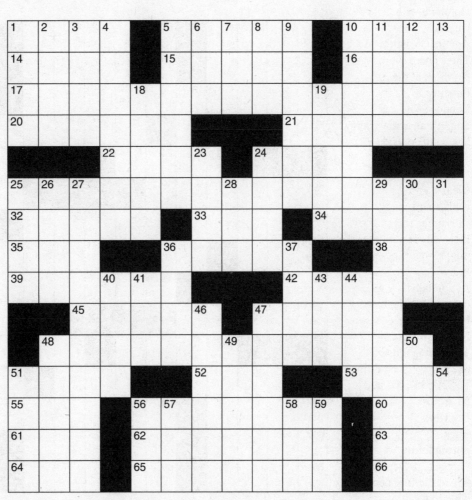

by Harry Smith and Zhouqin Burnikel

ACROSS

1 Georgetown athlete
5 Path left behind by a mower
10 Item on a Native American moccasin
14 Genesis garden
15 Sign after Virgo
16 First word in a fairy tale
17 Service organization with a wheel logo
19 10:1 or 3:2 at a racetrack
20 Get up
21 Prison unit
23 Where Siberia is
25 Connecticut Ivy
26 Wowed
29 Bird of prey's claw
33 Domicile with wheels
38 Agatha Christie's "And Then There Were __"
39 No room at the __
40 Praising
42 London's Old __
43 Something a strawberry has on the outside
45 Wiseass
47 Neighbor of Jordan
49 Cleans, as a chalkboard
50 Christmas trees
53 Place where a mother might sing "Rock-a-Bye Baby"
54 Action taken by a company in distress
58 Breadth
62 Hawaiian feast
63 They bring music to one's ears . . . or a hint to 17-, 21-, 33-, 45- and 54-Across
65 Big vases
66 Rage
67 Surmounting
68 "Let's __ a Deal"
69 Always telling people what to do
70 Broadway award

DOWN

1 Zeus' wife
2 Smell
3 Dubious sighting in the Himalayas
4 Prehistoric Southwest culture
5 Crafty
6 Pagan religious practice
7 Qualified
8 Yours __ (letter sign-off)
9 "Se __ español"
10 Kind of logic in which all values are either true or false
11 Prefix with -plasm
12 "Back in Black" rock band
13 Place for a laptop other than a lap
18 Flip, as a property
22 Diner sandwich, for short
24 Notions
26 Not quite right
27 $$$
28 Li'l __ of the funnies
30 Amours
31 In reserve
32 Long, narrow parts of bottles
34 Good engine sound
35 __ Mae (Whoopi's role in "Ghost")
36 Onetime Russian space station
37 Opposite of exit
41 Obtrusively bright and showy
44 Not concentrated, as light
46 Researcher's wear
48 Televise
51 Program for addicts
52 "__ evil . . ."
53 Gives up, as territory
54 Juicy fruit with a pit
55 Mystique
56 Tug sharply
57 Veers the other way
59 Word after lock or glom
60 Unpaid intern, jocularly
61 Catch sight of
64 Not mind one's own business

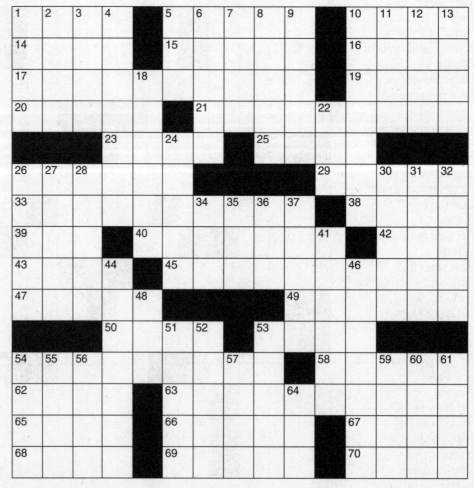

by Brian Thomas

ACROSS

1 Either of the World Series winners of 2004 and '05
4 Pickle variety
8 Talk about ad nauseam
14 James ___, founder of the auction house that sold 38-Across
16 First name in solo flying
17 Gets excited about, e.g.
18 Dietetic restriction
19 Pot thickener?
20 Desires
22 Mucky mess
23 Basketball tactic
25 Jazz Appreciation Mo.
27 Anita of jazz
30 Cartoonist Hoff of The New Yorker
31 Beginning stage
34 Painter Magritte
35 Mountain nymph
36 Morphine, e.g.
38 Renaissance painting that was sold in November 2017 for a record $450.3 million
41 ___ retriever
42 "Nothing ___" (slangy refusal)
43 First name?
44 How some fish are caught
46 Clunky boat
49 Actress Turner
50 "Mazel ___!"
51 Excel
53 Make a request
55 Sagacious
58 Some Shoshonean speakers
59 Shut down
62 100-page stories, say
64 Passionate
65 English king who once owned 38-Across
66 Some may be flying
67 College in Westchester County, N.Y.
68 Colorant

DOWN

1 Leftovers
2 Author known for twist endings
3 Pornographic
4 Observance that begins in March: Abbr.
5 Teeny, for short
6 Lo-cal
7 Creator of 38-Across
8 First name in Solo flying?
9 Author Oz
10 Eliminating the effects of wear and tear on, as was done to 38-Across
11 Lie on one's back and not move, maybe
12 38-Across, for one
13 Met rival from D.C.
15 Finishes, as a cake
21 Someone with intelligence?
24 Do military duty
26 Pad sharer
28 Not with
29 "___-haw!"
32 Make a declaration with a straight face
33 Vampire ___
35 7-Down, for one
37 Boats propelled by poles
38 Mixer at a party
39 "M*A*S*H" actor
40 "Grant" biographer Chernow
41 Gadot of "Justice League"
45 Word said before "then," oxymoronically
46 Like a dame or earl
47 On pins and needles
48 Blues great Smith
52 Main part of a ship
54 Superman without a cape
56 Gallery district in Manhattan
57 Former senator Bayh
59 Is provided with
60 Work of ___ (38-Across, e.g.)
61 Sot's problem
63 The Renaissance, e.g.

by David J. Kahn

118

ACROSS
1 Soothes
6 Aquarium buildup
11 Edmonton's province: Abbr.
14 TV replay technique
15 Hold power, as a monarch
16 Neither's partner
17 "Water Lilies" painter
19 Lab eggs
20 Rock concert blaster
21 Nerve cell part
22 Dust Bowl migrants
24 Beach toy with a handle
26 June, in the L.G.B.T.Q. movement
29 Pacific source of odd weather
31 Like the paths of satellites
32 Impressionist Edgar
33 Muslim pilgrim
35 Snoop (on)
36 Profited
40 Place for salt on a margarita glass
43 Yale students
44 Opposite of losses
48 Simultaneously
51 Negative about
52 Computer programmer, disparagingly
55 Brussels-based defense grp.
56 Revered one in a tribe
57 Indian bread
59 "Fancy that!"
60 Public health org.
61 Personal struggles . . . or, literally, features of 17-, 26-, 36- and 52-Across
65 Sailors' yeses
66 Deliberately hurtful
67 French thanks
68 "Fuhgeddaboutit!"
69 At one's fingertips
70 Poet Nash

DOWN
1 Flew the coop
2 Like Chippendales revues
3 Marking, as windows on Halloween
4 Large egg producer
5 Cream __ (beverage)
6 Knight's wear
7 Téa of "Madam Secretary"
8 Tom Collins ingredient
9 Important datum for Social Security eligibility
10 Place in a crypt
11 Ceremonially names
12 Light, friendly punch
13 With audacity
18 Fair with booths
23 Fish in an ornamental pond
25 Neeson of "Taken"
27 Martial arts centers
28 "__ go bragh!"
30 Covert govt. org.
33 Mythical beauty whose face "launched a thousand ships"
34 French friend
37 Floor model
38 Source of arrogance
39 Jaw-dropping opening?
40 Nascar devotee
41 "Shoulda listened to me . . ."
42 Frantic rush
45 "Briefly . . ."
46 Never ever
47 Strands, as at a ski lodge
49 Wearable souvenir, informally
50 Powerball winner's cry
51 Twosome
53 Attacked from below the hip
54 At the crack of dawn, say
58 Jules Verne captain
62 Gun lover's org.
63 Taker of religious vows
64 Ryan of "Sleepless in Seattle"

by Bruce Haight

ACROSS

1 Soak (up)
4 With 14-Across, weakness for sugar
9 Fix, as a race
12 It's on the waterfront
14 See 4-Across
15 Juno's Greek counterpart
16 Designer Gucci
17 With 25-Down, 2012 British Open winner
18 Those, in Spain
19 What a rolling stone is unlikely to gather
21 Kurt of Nirvana
23 Retro
24 Baby
26 Pile up
27 A little thick
30 Same old, same old
31 Police dept. alert
32 Sharper
35 Cries of disgust
36 Christmas tree decoration . . . or a hint to what the circled letters form
38 Gets underway
41 I'm not buying it!
45 "__ take arms against a sea of troubles": Hamlet
46 Something squirreled away?
50 Like black sheep
51 Tree with smooth bark
53 Long-handled tool
54 Language group that gave us "banjo" and "gumbo"
55 __-chic (hippie-inspired fashion)
56 "But of course!"
57 Popular footwear from Down Under
58 "That would stink"
60 "Gilmore Girls" protagonist
63 Shield
64 Part of a shore dinner
65 Dot-dot-dot, dash-dash-dash, dot-dot-dot
66 "Yahoo!"
67 Put an end to something?
68 Blue Stater, for short

DOWN

1 Baden-Baden, for one
2 "Moby-Dick" light source
3 Human-powered taxi
4 Vermeer and Rembrandt contemporary
5 Tattered
6 Forever and a day
7 Suffix with diet
8 2000s teen drama set in Newport Beach
9 What's left
10 Absolutist's rule
11 Number for a surgeon?
13 Tends to, as a cradle
15 Flip call
20 Show disdain for, in a way
22 Recurring action role for Matt Damon
23 Sound heard from a herd
25 See 17-Across
27 Netflix item
28 "The Holly and the __" (Christmas song)
29 Hearing aid?
33 Archaeological handle
34 Make, as dough
36 Stitch with a hook
37 Fills with fury
38 Loud lament
39 New York City bridge, informally, with "the"
40 Fate who cuts the thread of life
42 2010 Disney film that set a record for the most expensive animated movie ever made
43 Gallery sign
44 Romanian currency
47 Given to talk
48 "Would you look at that!"
49 Worlds
52 Potful for Winnie-the-Pooh
54 Succumb to pressure?
58 Some office printers, for short
59 South American tuber
61 Arles assent
62 Suffix with real or social

by Andrew Kingsley

ACROSS

1 Adhering to old-fashioned modesty
5 Congeal, as blood
9 Gate closer
14 Green precious stone
15 Years and years and years
16 Honolulu hello
17 *Game-quickening timer in basketball
19 Arabian Peninsula nation
20 Charlotte __ (rich dessert)
21 Lyndon Johnson and George W. Bush
22 Food unit counted by a dieter
25 Budgetary excess
26 Golf ball propper-upper
27 Columbus campus, briefly
28 *Snowbirds' destination
30 Cartoondom's Olive __
31 Wealth
33 Tie, as figure skates
35 Clobber in the ring
36 Weirdo
37 Miss America accessory
40 President saying "No!"
43 Utter failure
45 Govt. of the Rebs
47 *Long vegetable with a yellow pod
49 Game of pursuit
50 Take part in 49-Across
51 Mel honored in Cooperstown
52 Ships' direction controllers
54 Mischievous
56 Spunk
57 Small food fish
58 List of popular songs . . . or a hint to the ends of the answers to the starred clues
62 Hairlike projections on cells
63 Wagner's "Liebestod," e.g.
64 Something an arrested person tries to "make"
65 Playful river animal
66 Some "big" burgers
67 Reb's foe

DOWN

1 Nighttime wear, familiarly
2 Cheerleader's cry
3 Words solemnly sworn
4 Subway system
5 Swede who developed a temperature scale
6 Ease up on
7 Without repetition
8 Sound of disapproval
9 Purchase for a newborn
10 "Jeopardy!" host Trebek
11 *Marinara sauce thickener
12 Vice president between Gore and Biden
13 Fairy tale boy who outsmarts a witch
18 Mean witch's pronouncement
21 Soft mineral
22 Bottle stopper
23 Landmass bounded by a mountain chain and three oceans
24 *Dispenser of psychiatric advice to Charlie Brown
25 Notable achievement
29 Book jacket write-up
32 What might turn up dirt on someone?
34 Stars-and-stripes land, for short
36 Call at a deli or barbershop
38 What psychological trauma may leave
39 Swine
41 Like a midlevel general or a so-so movie
42 Hippocratic __
43 Social gaffe
44 "Slumdog Millionaire" setting
45 Cooking oil brand
46 Peak
48 Steamy
53 Churchill Downs event
55 1970s tennis champ Nastase
56 Sorvino of "Mighty Aphrodite"
58 Overly theatrical type
59 Motorists' org.
60 Racket
61 Animal with a rack

by Lynn Lempel

Note: "A couple of years ago I was the answer to number 1-Down in the New York Times crossword puzzle," says best-selling author 1-Across. "At first I was like 'This is the greatest day of my life.' But then my brother-in-law pointed out that it was a Saturday puzzle," which is the hardest of the week. "The clues are so obscure, no one is supposed to know them. He basically told me that until I'm in the Monday or Tuesday puzzle, I'm [24-, 38- and 52-Across]."

ACROSS

1 See blurb
9 Sore spot
16 Convenient to carry
17 Region around San Francisco
18 Strike a chord
19 Check for flaws
20 On the __ (fleeing)
21 Zilch
23 Ja Rule hit that includes the lyric "Wash away your tears"
24 See blurb
29 Falls behind
30 Santa __ winds
31 Playbill listing
32 __-friendly
33 Perform in a play
35 Go bad
38 See blurb
44 Bridal path
45 __ Enterprise
46 "The Catcher in the __"
47 "Later, old chap"
49 Apple apps use it
51 One of the Three Bears
52 See blurb
57 The "A" of U.A.E.
58 Effortlessness
59 Fútbol cheer
60 Threatening person
62 Military vehicle used for reconnaissance
67 Mark never seen in an online crossword
68 Main city in Chile
69 Snow White's sister
70 No-show

DOWN

1 First full month of spring: Abbr.
2 Coffee, slangily
3 Third-year students: Abbr.
4 Islands surrounding lagoons
5 Venice thoroughfare
6 Appointer of Sotomayor and Kagan to the Supreme Court
7 Sandwich that's often stuck with toothpicks
8 Welcomed at the door
9 Tolerate
10 Hackneyed
11 Method: Abbr.
12 Chemical symbol for tungsten
13 Puts up
14 Like some handshakes and formulas
15 Lecherous deity
22 "Halt!," to a sailor
24 Killed, as a dragon
25 Chalupa alternative
26 Dr. Frankenstein's assistant
27 Deadly
28 Vaping devices
33 Burmese or Persian
34 The "75" of $1.75: Abbr.
36 Second-century pope
37 Clip-__ (certain sunglasses)
39 Collection of information
40 Things used on a bridle path
41 Neighbor of Afghanistan
42 Write using a keyboard
43 Get wind of
47 Bullfighter
48 Yoga positions
50 Ukrainian city on the Black Sea
51 Baking container for a cobbler
52 Debussy work whose title is French for "The Sea"
53 Big name in tractors
54 Dog-__ (like some well-read books)
55 Middays
56 Butt muscle
61 Mean dog
63 Hailed vehicle
64 Burmese or Persian
65 Birthday card number
66 __ v. Wade

by Peter Gordon

ACROSS

1 ___ Polo, traveler at the court of Kublai Khan
6 Rings of water around castles
11 Russian fighter jet
14 Come clean
15 Property defacer
16 Signature Obama legislation, for short
17 Jon Bon Jovi torch song?
19 Centerpiece of a frat party
20 Stick in one's ___
21 Province west of Que.
22 Chest muscles, for short
23 J.F.K.'s W.W. II command
26 Tiny battery size
27 Med. school subject
28 Lawyer's charge
29 Elvis Presley torch song?
32 Squid, in Italian cuisine
35 Tough puzzle
36 Bangles torch song?
40 Sudden outpouring
42 Some Canadian petroleum deposits
45 The Doors torch song?
49 "Lower your voice, please"
50 Pale blue hue
51 Horse of a certain color
52 With prudence
55 Fat used in mincemeat
56 Place
57 Match up
58 Sarcastic laugh syllable
59 The Trammps torch song?
64 Opposite of WSW
65 Letter-shaped girders
66 Diplomat
67 Norm: Abbr.
68 Drives the getaway car for, say
69 Grabs some Z's

DOWN

1 Unruly throng
2 Leatherworker's punch
3 Genetic carrier, briefly
4 Ancient Incan capital
5 "Madama Butterfly," for one
6 S.I. or GQ
7 Given out for a time
8 Hebrew for "my Lord"
9 Scottish pattern
10 Crafty
11 Speak gobbledygook
12 Glacial chamber
13 Joke writer
15 Ex-G.I.'s org.
18 Crunchy, healthful snack
22 Pablo Picasso's designer daughter
23 Army E-3: Abbr.
24 Pekoe, for one
25 Under siege
26 "Madama Butterfly" highlight
30 Server with a spigot
31 Transcript figs.
33 To boot
34 Chance upon
37 Pork cut
38 Christmas tree
39 "Inside ___ Davis" (Coen brothers film)
40 Cuts drastically, as prices
41 Pleasingly tangy
43 FedEx competitor
44 Like a wallflower
46 Onetime Dr Pepper rival
47 "Get it?"
48 Wealthy sort, informally
53 Derive via logic
54 Public outburst
57 Kim, to Kourtney or Khloé
59 A day in Spain
60 Yoga chants
61 #vanlife homes, briefly
62 "Let's ___ and say we did"
63 Kvetchers' cries

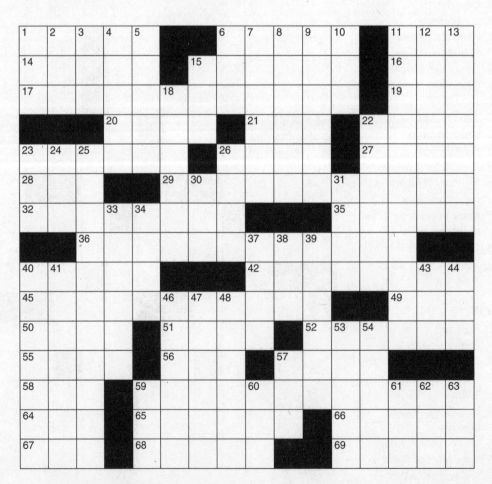

by Matthew Sewell

ACROSS

1 Food ___ (Thanksgiving drowsiness)
5 Ocean predators
10 Get ready, casually
14 Insult
15 Writer Zora ___ Hurston
16 "Follow me!"
17 Disobey a rush order?
19 What prices do during hyperinflation
20 Longest river in Europe
21 Cataract site
23 Word after drum or press
24 How some solve crosswords
26 Vessel for Jack and Jill
28 Red Sea peninsula
31 Disobey a stop order?
35 "Now I get it!"
36 Where Ang Lee was born
38 Singer Lovett
39 Genre for 21 Savage and 50 Cent
40 Frittata ingredient
41 The Mormons, for short
43 Fish with more than 100 vertebrae in its spine
44 First lady's man
46 Author Hemingway
48 Sculptures, e.g.
49 Disobey a standing order?
51 Large artery
53 Cave residents
54 Amazon IDs
56 Nothing but
57 Ukraine's capital
60 Maestro Seiji
63 Like a person who might be called "chrome dome"
65 Disobey a pecking order?
68 Plays with
69 Setting for an outdoor party
70 Vegas hotel with a musical name
71 "Gotta run," in a text
72 Downhill rides
73 Like a half-moon tide

DOWN

1 Winter hrs. in Lake Wobegon
2 Patron saint of Norway
3 Fast-swimming shark
4 2009 aviatrix biopic
5 Alternative to bottled
6 High-___ monitor
7 Exhortation after "Supplies are limited!"
8 Salve ingredient
9 In stitches
10 Some Toshiba products
11 2003, for LeBron James and Dwyane Wade
12 Smartphone notification
13 Jaunty
18 Light
22 Mud wrap site
25 New citizenship seeker
27 Calder Cup org.
28 White House press secretary ___ Huckabee Sanders
29 "Wow, that was fun!"
30 Locale for a West Coast wine tour
32 "Key" hotel personnel
33 Wraps up
34 Airline whose in-flight magazine is Sky
37 A long, long time
42 One of four for "The Star-Spangled Banner"
45 Bumped into
47 Wide-eyedness
50 Make inquiries
52 Native of Japan's "second city"
55 Cowboys' ties
56 Touch
58 AOL and MSN, for two
59 Abbr. after a list
61 Police informant's wear
62 Where most Buddhists reside
64 Broadband letters
66 A helping hand
67 Maple product

by Zhouqin Burnikel

124

ACROSS

1 Pour love (on)
5 Prod
9 Antlered Yellowstone denizens
13 "Vous __ ici" (French for "You are here")
14 Derby entry
15 __ fide (in bad faith)
16 Cries of discovery
17 "Would you mind?"
19 Letter accompanying a college application, informally
20 "This can't be good"
21 N.F.L. team for which Joe Namath was a QB
22 Informal breakfast beverage order
25 Approximately, datewise
26 Cowboy movie setting
27 "Yes," at the altar
29 "Quiet!"
30 "Dumb" bird
31 Botches
33 Hypnotist's command
38 Expensive
39 Actor Jared of "Suicide Squad"
42 College dorm overseers, for short
45 Neckwear for a lobster eater
46 Michigan/Ontario border river
49 Skin care brand
51 "Ulysses" star, 1967
53 Like the first "d" in "Wednesday"
55 Salon job
56 Potentially alarming sight for an ocean bather
57 Cappuccino relative
59 Pizazz
60 Desertlike
61 Skiers' shelter
62 Poker table payment
63 Strong cleansers
64 Like the Amazon rain forest
65 Company heads, in brief

DOWN

1 "Holy Toledo!"
2 Board game named after a Shakespeare play
3 Container for oolong or chai
4 Figure on Superman's chest
5 Stop being strict
6 Branch of dentistry, informally
7 Fireplace residue
8 College person with a "list"
9 Smiley face or frowny face
10 Los Angeles hoopsters
11 Coffee get-together
12 Prepares for a doctor's throat examination
14 Chipper greetings
18 Holder of baseball's highest career batting average (.366)
20 Manipulate
23 In one fell __
24 __ Stein, Green Party candidate for president in 2012 and 2016
28 Twosome
31 Take to the skies
32 Opposite of buys
34 University of Illinois city
35 Nintendo Switch predecessor
36 Cold War weapon inits.
37 "Sure, whatever"
40 Connect with
41 Sunset shades
42 Scamp
43 Where birds of a feather flock together
44 Many a Snapchat pic
46 Santa's vehicle
47 Rich cake
48 Alternative to "net" or "org"
50 Monopoly cards
52 Tablets that run Safari
54 Rock's Jethro __
58 "Skip to My __"
59 Onetime teen heartthrob Efron

by Sam Ezersky

ACROSS

1 Perennial campaign issue
5 Airplane wing feature
9 Cool, giant sun
14 Taken by mouth
15 Sweat spot
16 Remote control button
17 Grinder
18 Totally focused
19 Brooding worry
20 Big part of the New World
23 It's pitched with a pitchfork
24 Present oneself falsely
28 Greek island in the Aegean Sea
31 Common supply for a party
33 One cause for an R rating
34 Wagering venue, briefly
35 Like some missiles
38 Onetime Volvo competitor
39 Compromise . . . or a phonetic hint to this puzzle's shaded squares
43 Bad temper
44 Flashy 1940s men's attire
45 Lead-in to bred or behaved
46 Channel for "Conan"
49 ___-Caps (theater candy)
50 Faux ___
51 Seaside cookout
54 Fast-food chain with a goateed spokesman
56 Flashing light phenomenon
61 Ridiculous
64 Pink
65 Humdinger
66 Arms and legs
67 "The Complete Works of William Shakespeare," e.g.
68 10-Down resident
69 On the nose
70 What's happening and when, informally
71 Recorded message prompt

DOWN

1 Donald ___ Trump
2 ___ Blizzard (Dairy Queen offering)
3 Roseanne of "Roseanne"
4 Animal that hangs upside down in trees
5 Graffiti artist's tool
6 Rich soil
7 Big name in beauty products
8 Game craze of the late 1980s and '90s
9 Falcon rocket launcher
10 Yemen's capital
11 Pull
12 Nativity scene figure
13 Emeritus: Abbr.
21 Country to which Frederick Douglass was a U.S. ambassador
22 Natalie Cole's "___ Got Love on My Mind"
25 Pack, as a car for travel
26 Napoli's nation
27 Field where Jackie Robinson played
28 Like the meter in sonnets
29 Ed of "Modern Family"
30 Popular Belgian beer, for short
32 Fictional tree creature
36 Carmel finish?
37 Letters on an AM dial
38 1960s radical grp.
40 Canon model
41 Tinkered (with)
42 "Knock ___!"
46 Intradermal diagnostic, for short
47 Many a lounge
48 Some tennis wear
52 "___ Live" (daytime news program)
53 Kindle material
55 B equivalent
57 Salinger dedicatee
58 Tip of France?
59 Family
60 Idiot box
61 ___-de-France
62 Put the kibosh on
63 Operator's org.?

by Peter A. Collins

ACROSS

1 Big advertiser at auto races
4 Sunoco competitor
9 Distinctive smell
13 Breakfast restaurant chain
15 Quarter Pounder topper
16 Jay who preceded Jimmy Fallon
17 Singer's latest
19 "What's gotten __ you?"
20 Poems whose titles often start "To a . . ."
21 Con's opposite
22 Alternatives to Nikes
23 Lodge member
24 Like religious institutions vis-à-vis the I.R.S.
26 King Arthur's magician
29 The lion in summer?
30 "Disgusting!"
31 What gigabytes might measure
35 Vexes
39 "We can go safely now"
42 Like food from a West African drive-through?
43 Tire material
44 In the style of
45 Envision
47 Scores two under par
49 "Excuse me?"
55 YouTube posting, casually
56 Praise highly
57 The Diamondbacks, on scoreboards
58 Vicinity
60 __ monster (desert denizen)
61 Final words of Martin Luther King Jr.'s "I Have a Dream" speech . . . or a hint to the endings of 17-, 24-, 39- and 49-Across
64 Wartime friend
65 Actress Christina
66 Chunk of concrete
67 Loch __ monster
68 Approved, as a contract
69 Resting place?

DOWN

1 Covet one's neighbor's wife, e.g.
2 "The Cosby Show" son
3 Volatile situation
4 Mustard in the game Clue, e.g.: Abbr.
5 Bumbling
6 Queen's crown
7 Shout at Fenway Park
8 Final word shouted before "Happy New Year!"
9 Cruet filler at an Italian restaurant
10 Jeans material
11 Not bottled, at a bar
12 Perch in a chicken house
14 Green shampoo
18 __ Pie (frozen treat)
22 Tree toppler
25 French president's palace
26 Catcher's glove
27 Canyon effect
28 More proximate
32 East Lansing sch.
33 Gambling parlor, for short
34 Umbrella part
36 Super bargains
37 Vitamin-rich green vegetable
38 Mmes. of Madrid
40 Dresses up for a comic con, say
41 Fancy tie
46 Grab a bite
48 TV's "2 Broke __"
49 Started
50 Napoleon, on St. Helena
51 Vexes
52 Bobby who sang "Mack the Knife"
53 Big name in vacuum cleaners
54 Sister's daughter, e.g.
59 "Right now!"
61 Payday, often: Abbr.
62 Help
63 Letters on an unfinished sched.

by Agnes Davidson and Zhouqin Burnikel

ACROSS

1 "Later, alligator!"
6 What a divorce may generate for a celeb
11 Cab alternative
14 Pharmaceutical giant that makes Valium
15 Visitor to Roswell, supposedly
16 Post-truth ___
17 Neighborhood where kimchi might be found, informally
18 Its root was once used in root beer
20 Process of aging
22 Minuscule amount
23 Only three-letter astrological sign
24 Yankees great dubbed "The Old Perfessor"
26 What always deserves a good licking?
31 Sushi bar tune
32 Like guyliner, stylistically
33 Word after he or she
35 10th-century Holy Roman emperor
39 Curses . . . or what 18-, 20-, 26-, 48-, 57- and 63-Across are, literally?
43 Schleps
44 Catcher's place
45 Pablo Neruda composition
46 Accessory for a bad hair day
48 Poppycock
51 Chichi Chihuahua accessory
55 Montgomery is its cap.
56 Units of resistance
57 Snitch
63 Exotic
65 English horse-racing venue
66 Informal top
67 Expressways with tolls
68 Dance-based fitness program
69 The "A" of I.P.A.
70 A liquid one is easy to trade
71 Olympic blades

DOWN

1 Torah holders
2 Fawn over, with "on"
3 Blue "W" for Microsoft Word, e.g.
4 "That's a bummer"
5 Martial arts pro
6 Word before metal or instinct
7 Rickman of the Harry Potter films
8 The winks in tiddlywinks, e.g.
9 Old Spanish coin
10 Genetic molecule
11 Weightless state, informally
12 Hopping mad
13 "m" or "n," in phonetics
19 Over and done
21 Thicket
25 Popular D.I.Y. website
26 What "." signifies
27 1847 Melville novel
28 Uncouth fellow
29 ___ of office
30 Climber's spike
34 Show in a showroom, say
36 "___: Legacy" (sci-fi sequel)
37 Bookie's quote
38 "Mm-hmm"
40 Unoriginal piece
41 Exam with logic games, in brief
42 Of the kidneys
47 Video game inspired by pentominoes
49 Slimeball
50 Really, really likes
51 "Ish"
52 A unicycle has one
53 Awards show V.I.P.
54 Pool hall items
58 "Get ___ to a nunnery": Hamlet
59 Word repeated during a mic check
60 Pinnacle
61 Place for a piercing
62 H's, in fraternity names
64 Org. concerned with soil and water

by David Steinberg

ACROSS

1 Ponzi schemes, e.g.
6 Agatha Christie or Maggie Smith
10 Times past noon, informally
14 "Sounds exciting . . ."
15 Iranian currency
16 Applaud
17 Cutting-edge brand?
18 2016 Best Actress Oscar winner for "La La Land"
20 Unwelcome looks
22 Somewhat
23 Encouragement for a matador
24 Half of a half step in music
26 Relieved (of)
27 Biden and Pence, informally
28 Abbr. in an office address
29 Pacific source of unusual weather
31 Stoic politician of ancient Rome
33 Places to get quick cash
36 Chess endings
37 Weight unit equal to about 2,205 pounds
40 Group of eight
43 Gym locker emanation
44 On the briny
48 "Legally ___" (Reese Witherspoon film)
50 Fix, as an election
52 Be nosy
53 "Leaving ___ Vegas"
54 "Puh-LEEZE!"
58 Like the name "Robin Banks" for a criminal
59 Make, as money
60 Grand stories
61 Enthusiastic audience response, informally
64 Bit of clowning around
66 Title of a list of errands
67 ___ Wallace, co-founder of Reader's Digest
68 Fish typically split before cooking
69 Sudden problem in a plan
70 Look for
71 Ariana Grande's fan base, mostly

DOWN

1 "Red" or "White" baseball team
2 Deep-fried Mexican dish
3 Div. for the N.F.L.'s Jets
4 Less talkative
5 Laughs through the nose
6 "Forgot About ___" (2000 rap hit)
7 Put in the cross hairs
8 Caribbean ballroom dance
9 "Seinfeld" character who wrote for the J. Peterman catalog
10 One of two in "Hamilton"
11 Go from 0 to 60, say
12 What sunning in a swimsuit leaves
13 Racer's swimwear
19 Sailor's patron
21 Start to attack
24 Home shopping inits.
25 Back in style
30 Grandmother, affectionately
32 Muscat is its capital
34 Prefix with life or wife
35 Look down on
38 Swirled
39 Jiffy
40 Administrative regions in Russia
41 Eric who sang "Layla"
42 Deep-fried Mexican dish
45 Bond film after "Skyfall"
46 Natural process illustrated by the last words of 18-, 24-, 37-, 54- and 61-Across
47 Novelist Rand
49 Inbox buildup
51 Exceed
55 "Sesame Street" character long rumored to be Bert's lover
56 Something acute or obtuse
57 Chop finely
62 Holiday drink
63 Tree with acorns
65 Successors to LPs

by Paolo Pasco

ACROSS

1 Value of snake eyes in craps
4 Rules as a monarch
10 Difficult endeavor
14 Put on TV
15 87, 89 or 93, on a gas pump
16 With 25-Down, office request
17 Pro at tax time
18 In any place
20 Counterparts of compressions, in physics
22 Wear away
23 ___-X
24 "Get serious!"
25 Member of a Marvel Comics group
29 Divinity school subj.
30 T-X connection
33 Neighbor of the asteroid belt
34 Strip discussed in the Oslo Accords
36 Word with circle or ear
38 Nobel laureate Wiesel
39 Opinion pieces
41 Nashville venue, informally
42 Mork's TV pal
44 Wait for a green light, say
45 Fire and fury
46 Peculiar
47 It doesn't get returned
49 Less sincere, as a promise
51 Make black, in a way
52 El Al hub city
53 "Already?"
56 City straddling Europe and Asia
61 Foreboding
63 Judge Lance of the O.J. trial
64 Book after Chronicles
65 Surface
66 Grazing area
67 Drakes : ducks :: ___ : swans

68 Apt word to follow each row of circled letters
69 Subtext of Jefferson Airplane's "White Rabbit"

DOWN

1 Diplomat's skill
2 Film editor's gradual transition
3 Leftover in a juicer
4 Olympic sport with strokes
5 Repeat
6 Calif.-to-Fla. route
7 Elongated, heavily armored fish
8 U-turn from SSW
9 Opening word?
10 Rear admiral's rear
11 ___ flow
12 Green-lit
13 Richard of "Unfaithful"
19 Coins of ancient Athens
21 Picked up on
24 Place to sing "Rock-a-Bye Baby"
25 See 16-Across
26 Bona fide
27 A narcissist has a big one
28 Relative of an épée
30 Concern for a debt collector
31 Brink
32 More sardonic
35 End of a line on the Underground?
37 Antivirus software brand
40 Divinity sch.
43 Logo with an exclamation mark
48 Annual French film festival site
50 Smoothed out
51 Deep sleeps
53 Particular in a design
54 Ricelike pasta
55 Belgrade denizen
56 Anatomical canal
57 Royal title
58 Outfit in Caesar's senate
59 Pac-12 team
60 Mutual fund consideration
62 Little rascal

by Jim Hilger

130

ACROSS

1 Scuttlebutt
7 ___ Fridays (restaurant chain)
10 Slob's creation
14 Hedy in Hollywood
15 Dessert topper from a can
17 And others, in a bibliography
18 Estrange
19 Org. for Penguins and Ducks
20 Wintry coating
22 Vice president Spiro
23 Cunning
25 Spill the beans
28 Online source for health info
30 Take a stab at
34 "Ye olde" place to browse
36 Up to, as a particular time
37 Govern
38 Goopy roofing material
39 High U.S. Navy rank
42 Farrow in films
43 Building annexes
45 Particle with a charge
46 Thief
48 Students' simulation of global diplomacy, informally
50 Arctic abode
51 "Scram!"
53 Sleepover attire, informally
55 Twisty curves
58 The "P" of PRNDL
60 Scanned lines on a pkg.
62 Diminish the work force . . . or a literal hint to the answers to the four starred clues
65 Deficiency in red blood cells
67 Ship-related
68 Searched thoroughly, with "through"
69 Fighting force
70 Raises
71 Praises highly

DOWN

1 "Galveston" singer Campbell
2 Inauguration Day vows
3 *"Crazy to run into you here!"
4 Erie Canal mule of song
5 Blue or hazel eye part
6 *Newspapers or magazines
7 Fish with a heavy net
8 Form of some shampoo
9 Amin exiled from Uganda
10 One circulating at a party
11 "Trainspotting" actor McGregor
12 Building lot
13 Spurt forcefully
16 Gave a hand
21 Brit. resource for writers
24 "You betcha!"
26 Den
27 *Contest for an areawide seat
29 Controversial chemical in plastics, for short
31 *Nonsense
32 Ballerina's bend
33 Drop running down the cheek
34 Pipe part
35 Angel's band of light
36 Sardine container
40 Like early LPs
41 Response to an online joke
44 Age reached by a septuagenarian
47 1940s–'50s jazz
49 Asian yogurt drink
50 "This ___ test"
52 German cars with a lightning bolt logo
54 Long-winded sales pitch
55 Poet ___ St. Vincent Millay
56 Rise quickly
57 Taken a dip
59 U.S. fort with very tight security
61 Scoundrels
63 Post-O.R. area
64 Stick in the microwave
66 Fire dept. responder, maybe

by Lynn Lempel

ACROSS

1 Sun Devils' sch.
4 Like the Llwynywermod royal estate
9 One free carry-on bag, for many domestic flights
14 Large body of eau
15 Welcome on Waikiki
16 Light-footed
17 Collar
18 Japanese soup tidbit
20 "Frozen" snowman
22 Like the lion's share
23 Pavarotti, for one
25 Part of a barn where hay is stored
26 Ones approving fin. statements
30 Hot and arid
33 Iota preceder
34 Wisconsin city that's home to Lawrence University
36 Coco of couture
37 __ Spiegel (German newsmagazine)
38 Piglet producer
39 Something to shoot for
40 Hip-hop artist with the #1 album "Hip Hop Is Dead"
41 Study, with "on"
43 Large Greek olive
45 Actor Cary of "The Princess Bride"
46 Dictionary
47 Bombard
48 Red Sox archrival, on scoreboards
49 Jazzy James and Jones
52 Historically significant
56 Land celebrated on March 17
57 Like most pet dogs . . . or a hint to this puzzle's circled letters
61 Big fuss
62 Evicts
63 O'Connor's successor on the Supreme Court
64 Company V.I.P.
65 Extract forcefully
66 Title for un hombre
67 Medium power?

DOWN

1 Juvenile retort
2 Bobby who co-founded the Black Panthers
3 Growing problem in cities?
4 "__ is hell"
5 Israeli carrier
6 __ Linda, Calif.
7 General who said the quote at 4-Down
8 "Not so fast!"
9 Vientiane's country
10 "Ha! You fell for my trick!"
11 Central
12 Feeling down
13 Simple top
19 Unfamiliar
21 Stable newborn
24 Monkey often used in research
27 Subject of some September sports reporting
28 Irritated no end
29 Lively Latin dance
31 Riding, say
32 Ticket info
33 Ancient Balkan region
34 "Mad Men" type, informally
35 "Get Out" director Jordan
36 City WSW of Bogotá
39 Opposite of bellum
42 Hates
43 Peeper's vantage point
44 Speck
46 Stretchy materials
48 San Francisco's __ Hill
50 West Wing workers
51 Poke around
53 Annoyance
54 Similar (to)
55 Jared who won an Oscar for "Dallas Buyers Club"
57 Word after show or know
58 Sharer's word
59 "It's no __!"
60 Neither's partner

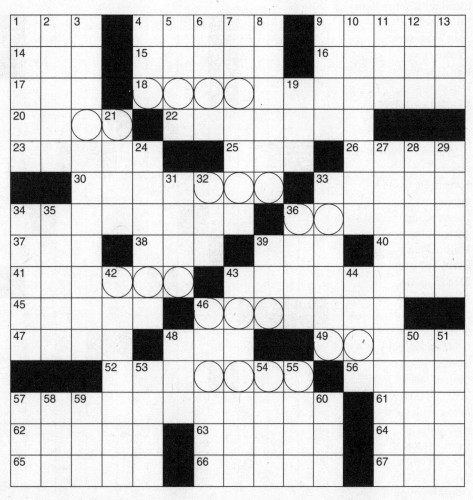

by Emily Carroll

ACROSS

1 Possesses
4 Grape-Nuts or Apple Jacks
10 Ewe's offspring
14 Man's name that's an investment spelled backward
15 Pumpkin color
16 Revered one
17 Pot's cover
18 Traditional night for partying
20 Side of a diamond
22 Thomas ___, "Rule, Britannia" composer
23 Bowling target
24 Texas landmark to "remember"
27 Sampled
29 Curved Pillsbury item
33 Misplace
34 "The Way We ___"
35 "Yeah, right!"
39 Pie ___ mode
40 Detectives
42 Batman portrayer Kilmer
43 Deserve
45 ___-Pacific (geopolitical region)
46 Something to click online
47 Ones calling the plays
50 Teeter-totter
53 Walk with a swagger
54 Every last drop
55 Parade spoiler
58 "Piece of cake" or "easy as pie"
61 40-hour-a-week work
65 Guadalajara gold
66 Actress Falco of "Nurse Jackie"
67 "Hot" Mexican dish
68 Prefix with natal or classical
69 Clarinet or sax
70 Crossed home plate, say
71 One who might follow into a family business

DOWN

1 50%
2 Song for a diva
3 Early TV comic known for "Your Show of Shows"
4 Popular cold and flu medicine
5 "But I heard him exclaim, ___ he drove out of sight . . ."
6 Uncooked
7 One-named Irish singer
8 Ending with golden or teen
9 Makeshift shelter
10 Fleur-de-___
11 Highly capable
12 Multiplex offering
13 Mix
19 Kingdoms
21 "Anything ___?"
25 Whimper like a baby
26 Like most Bluetooth headsets
28 Underhanded
29 Tight-lipped sort
30 Part to play
31 Be confident in
32 Fixes, as shoelaces
36 Forcible removals, as of tenants
37 Pull hard
38 Civic-minded group
40 Fictional mouse ___ Little
41 Male deer
44 Mensa stats
46 Lavish praise on
48 Hangs around for
49 Gave some money under the table
50 More secure
51 Give the slip
52 Actress Kemper of "Unbreakable Kimmy Schmidt"
56 Apple on a desk
57 Pixar's "Finding ___"
59 Nabisco snack since 1912
60 It has phases that are represented by the starts of 18-, 29-, 47- and 61-Across . . . and by 1-Down
62 Was in front
63 Pickle holder
64 Bullfight cheer

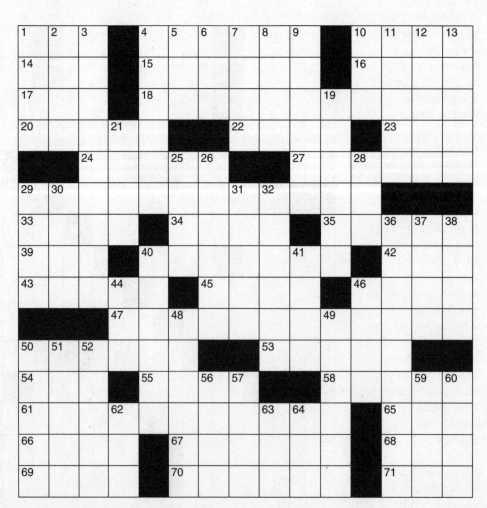

by Alan Arbesfeld

ACROSS

1 Loud commotion
4 Yeshiva leader
9 Films on a grand scale
14 Year, in Spain
15 If a > b and b > c, then a > c, e.g.
16 Kind of lily
17 Winter solstice mo.
18 Lowest point for Americans?
20 Crow
22 Like nylon stockings
23 Audi rival
24 Like the architecture of many cathedrals
27 Visibly blushing
29 American-made sports car with a V-10 engine
32 Plains Indian
33 Posted announcement at a theater entrance
34 Andean capital
35 Southernmost of the Ivies
36 Bass, e.g.
40 Storage tower
43 Mount that has an insurance company named after it
44 Commotion
47 Solvers' cries
48 Film character who says "Give yourself to the dark side"
51 Poll worker's request
53 From the beginning: Lat.
54 Prefix with center
55 Nosy sort
58 ___ room (postdebate area)
59 Prototype, maybe
63 Item in Santa's bag
64 Exhaust
65 Dim with tears
66 Closemouthed
67 Blog entries
68 More or less, informally
69 Letter before tee

DOWN

1 Some schlumpy male physiques
2 Mistakenly
3 "Sorry, Charlie!"
4 Wicked cool
5 Dismiss abruptly
6 Favoritism
7 Not just one or the other
8 Arriver's cry
9 Online greeting
10 Bud
11 "O.K., tell me more"
12 The Tigers of the A.C.C.
13 Pourer's instruction
19 Zig or zag
21 [This tastes awful!]
25 Prefix with commute
26 ___ Wilcox, daughter in E. M. Forster's "Howards End"
28 Amazing, in slang
30 Rapscallion
31 Road worker
36 Rx detail
37 Mel who was the first N.L.'er to hit 500 home runs
38 How many TV shows are shown nowadays
39 Give in
40 Put some money away
41 "Fingers crossed!"
42 SoCal daily
44 Sign on a real or virtual pet
45 Tricky . . . or a tricky description of 18-, 29-, 36-, 48- and 59-Across
46 Words and phrases that sound approximately alike, like "ice cream" and "I scream"
48 Eat stylishly
49 Cute, in modern slang
50 Reply to a ques.
52 Replies to an invitation
56 ___ Accords (1990s peace agreements)
57 Common fishing spot
60 Openly gay
61 ___ bran
62 Org. that sticks to its guns?

by Bruce Haight

134

ACROSS

1 Horror sequel of 2005
6 Reverberation
10 Movers' vehicles
14 Sow, as seeds
15 Clammy
16 Theater award
17 Best-selling autobiography by Priscilla Presley
19 Be the best, in slang
20 Michelle of the L.P.G.A.
21 Any singer of the 1973 #1 hit "Love Train"
22 Actor John of "Problem Child"
24 Neil who sang "Laughter in the Rain"
26 Antiriot spray
27 State capital ESE of Guadalajara
33 Like a porcupine
36 Woods nymph
37 Cartoon "devil," informally
38 Window part
39 Sanders in the Pro Football Hall of Fame
40 Jazzman Stan
41 Onetime competitor of the WB
42 Machine near the end of a car wash
43 ___ Island (amusement park site)
44 Many a 1970s remix
47 Rock's Clapton or Burdon
48 Dressed for a classic fraternity party
52 Fixes, as a photocopier
55 Front's opposite
57 Sch. in Charlottesville
58 Dove calls
59 One with credit . . . or a literal hint to 17-, 27- and 44-Across
62 Queue
63 What separates Nevada from Colorado
64 Barely visible, as a star
65 Rarely getting rain
66 Hang in the balance
67 ___ the bill (pays for something)

DOWN

1 Shoots out
2 "Kate & ___" of 1980s TV
3 Signaled with the hand
4 Singer Kamoze with the 1994 hit "Here Comes the Hotstepper"
5 "There, there"
6 Author Ferber
7 Suffragist Elizabeth ___ Stanton
8 "Lemme think . . ."
9 1990s "Saturday Night Live" character with a cape
10 Whirlpool
11 Touch
12 Stream near the Great Pyramids
13 Crystal ball user
18 Cleanser brand with a name from mythology
23 Like some sprains and tea
25 Primo
26 City hall V.I.P.s
28 High muckety-muck on Madison Avenue
29 Town ___ (colonial figure)
30 Major Calif.-to-Fla. route
31 Oscar-winning actress Blanchett
32 Rocker Osbourne
33 Tater
34 Big ___ (longtime Red Sox nickname)
35 B&Bs
39 Tennis tournament since 1900
40 Percussion in a Buddhist temple
42 Wriggler on a fishhook
43 "Iron Chef" competition
45 Brought to a halt
46 Poison ivy symptom
49 Sound part of a broadcast
50 Happening
51 Pub game
52 Home of the N.C.A.'s Bruins
53 Pinot ___
54 Folk singer Mitchell
55 Muffin material
56 What Ritalin helps treat, for short
60 Had a bite
61 "7 Faces of Dr. ___" (1964 film)

by Michael Black

ACROSS

1 Unwanted email
5 Series of courses?
10 "Buenos días!"
14 Actress Polo
15 Top Trappist, maybe
16 14-time M.L.B. All-Star, to fans
17 Beginning, datewise
18 "Yes, that's my opinion"
20 Like skim milk
22 Takes to the station house
23 Wolf (down)
26 One-named singer with the 2016 #1 hit "Cheap Thrills"
27 The "O" of NATO: Abbr.
30 Physics Nobelist Bohr
32 Big rift
36 Intrinsically
38 Lived like a single guy
40 The "E" of Q.E.D.
41 With 44-Across, Valentine's Day gift . . . or a hint to the shaded squares
42 Regarding
43 The Eternal City
44 See 41-Across
45 Knocks
46 Old school
48 North Africa's ___ Mountains
49 On the down-low
50 Looks to be
52 When to expect someone, for short
53 Airer of "The Bachelor" and "The Catch"
55 Stonehenge priest
57 Dakota tribe that attacked "The Revenant" trappers
61 Enthusiastic
65 Get fouled up, idiomatically
68 Manual reader
69 Father of Phobos
70 Snicker sound
71 "Encore!"
72 Some hard drinks
73 Does some post-shooting film work
74 Reason for a school closing

DOWN

1 Baseball's Musial
2 100 centavos
3 Elvis's middle name
4 Irks
5 Tiki bar drink
6 Flow out
7 Fiver
8 The "her" in the lyric "I met her in a club down in old Soho"
9 Excites
10 Try some Valentine's Day candy?
11 Shipments to smelteries
12 Heading on a poster with a picture of a dog
13 Hubbubs
19 Philosopher Fromm
21 Fashion's Klein
24 PC start-overs
25 Big source of omega-3 fatty acids
27 Schedule at the Met
28 Keep going in Yahtzee
29 One of 22 for U2
31 Pilot
33 Commercial success?
34 Poker advice for Sajak?
35 Greek peak, briefly
37 Try some Valentine's Day candy, sneakily?
39 Investments with fixed rates, for short
41 Item under a blouse
47 "Oops, sorry!"
48 Locale of both the 2018 and 2020 Olympics
51 Bags for guys
54 Home of King Minos
56 Bongos, e.g.
57 Lab medium
58 Actor Calhoun
59 "Hmm . . ."
60 Bedazzled
62 Has the stage
63 Famed "fiddler"
64 Sprouted
66 Sushi fish
67 "Nevertheless . . ."

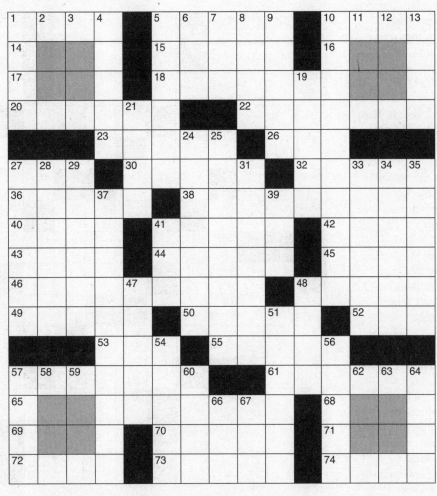

by Bruce Haight

136

ACROSS

1 Skirt bottoms
5 Ticklish Muppet
9 Gets thin on top
14 With: Fr.
15 Banquet
16 Lewis and ___ Expedition
17 GARFIELD + U = Beach V.I.P.
19 "___ at the Bat"
20 City NW of Detroit
21 "Help me, Obi-Wan Kenobi," e.g.
23 Home for Nixon and Reagan: Abbr.
24 "It's a date!"
26 MADISON + A = "Me, too!"
29 Shakespearean cries
30 Bounding main
32 Pathetic group
33 Mysterious sighting in the Himalayas
35 Some rulings on PolitiFact
38 Mortgage, e.g.
39 FILLMORE + V = Movie buff
42 Like racehorses' feet
44 Who asks "What can I help you with?" on an iPhone
45 Author Silverstein
49 Soccer blocker
51 President pro ___
53 Lab eggs
54 HARDING + P = Squeezable exercise tool
57 Actor Snipes of "White Men Can't Jump"
59 Approves
60 Famous ___ cookies
62 River of Cologne
63 Uncle Sam's land, for short
66 COOLIDGE + P = Narc's four-footed helper
68 Humdingers
69 Panache
70 Pistol sound
71 Hybrid picnic utensil
72 Philosophies
73 First half of a Senate vote

DOWN

1 Two-year mark, in a presidential term
2 Wicked look
3 Egoistic demand
4 National Mall, for a presidential inauguration
5 Six-foot bird
6 ___ years (when presidents are elected)
7 Maples formerly married to Donald Trump
8 Like the days of yore
9 Send covertly, as an email
10 Leader in a state roll call: Abbr.
11 Milan opera house
12 "You wish!"
13 Like atria
18 Onetime Pontiac muscle cars
22 What a majority of campaign spending goes toward
25 Dickens's Little ___
27 Store sign on Presidents' Day
28 Aromas
31 Gets ready to shoot
34 "Too rich for my blood"
36 QB Manning
37 Separate, as whites from colors
40 "Got it!," beatnik-style
41 ABC show on weekday mornings, with "The"
42 Absorbs
43 "Star Wars" pilot
46 There's one to honor presidents every February
47 The slightest amount
48 What hens do
49 Grave robbers
50 Word after many presidents' names
52 Bygone Ford make, briefly
55 Celebrated Chinese-born architect
56 Diving venues
58 Queen of ___ (visitor of King Solomon, in the Bible)
61 Poetry competition
64 Mink or sable
65 Query
67 Political connections

by Bruce Haight

ACROSS

1 Something sticking out of Frankenstein's neck
5 Voting coalition
9 Belittle
14 Classic Langston Hughes poem
15 "__ Land" (2016 Best Picture nominee)
16 French author who said "An intellectual is someone whose mind watches itself"
17 Alabama senator Jones
18 Home to Zion National Park
19 Walk with heavy steps
20 adj. under the influence of a drug
23 Long, boring task
24 __-blogging
25 adv. across a barrier or intervening space
30 Singer DiFranco
31 Smoked salmon
32 Bonus
34 "Can I get a hand here?!"
36 Like William Henry Harrison, among U.S. presidents
39 Crowd favorite not getting nominated for an Oscar, e.g.
40 Cough drop brand
42 Apply carelessly, as paint
44 Fresh __ daisy
45 n. spirit, animation
49 Heading with check boxes below it
50 Main part of a selfie
51 Ones who produced the clues for 20-, 25- and 45-Across
57 Sports center
58 Big name in in-flight internet
59 "About __" (2002 movie)
61 Enliven
62 Midmonth date
63 Target of splicing

64 Emails that tell you you've won the lottery, e.g.
65 Fit one inside the other
66 Energy units

DOWN

1 Creation of an Olympic city hopeful
2 "Then again . . . ," in texts
3 Birthplace of Muhammad Ali
4 Switch between windows, e.g.
5 Beat badly
6 Behind schedule
7 "Frozen" snowman
8 U.S. marshal role for John Wayne
9 Brand of probiotic yogurt
10 Makes the rounds?
11 Mine: Fr.
12 Battle of the bulges?
13 FS1 competitor
21 Sound that signifies the end of a basketball game
22 Actress Vardalos
25 When "S.N.L." ends on the East Coast
26 Louis __, French king who was guillotined
27 Consumer giant that makes Bounty, for short
28 "Cimarron" novelist
29 Extinguish
30 "That hits the spot!"

33 LeBron James's org.
35 Credit card designation
37 Confucian path
38 Popular left-leaning news site
41 Nestlé candy popular at movie houses
43 Humdrum
46 Veiled oath?
47 Bean
48 Mammoth time period
51 Delays
52 Viking explorer
53 "Hercules" spinoff
54 Went by motorcycle, say
55 Census data
56 iTunes download
60 "Suh-weet!"

by Joel Fagliano

ACROSS

1 Sound from a pound
4 Discontinued Swedish cars
9 Snapshot
14 ___ Zedong
15 ___ Vanilli, group with three #1 hits in 1989
16 Open the door for
17 Be sick
18 Drip-dry fabric
19 Preferred seat request in an airplane
20 Not dead yet!
23 Substituted (for)
24 Laceless shoe fastener
28 Horror director Craven
29 Warm winter wear
31 Baseball's Gehrig
32 Dilutes
36 ___ ex machina
37 Listens to
38 Sí : Spain :: ___ : France
39 "Fee-fi-fo-fum" sayer
40 Objectives
41 Pick up dry cleaning, go to the post office, etc.
43 ___ v. Wade
44 Author Vonnegut
45 Snakelike fish
46 Avenging spirits of Greek myth
48 With possibly even direr consequences
52 "What is life?," "Why are we here?," etc.
55 Bricklayer, e.g.
58 Slight advantage
59 Soph. and jr.
60 Bathroom unit
61 Be of ___ (avail)
62 Fannie ___ (mortgage company)
63 Full of the latest
64 Glossy finish
65 Midlength records, for short

DOWN

1 Stockpile
2 Bonnie who sang "I Can't Make You Love Me"
3 First ___ (Shakespeare volume)
4 Burns slowly
5 Simulated smooch
6 Like a poker player who's either very confident or really bluffing
7 Like-minded voting group
8 Swim's alternative
9 Mercury or Mars
10 Katherine of "27 Dresses"
11 Settlers of tied games, for short
12 Michael Jackson's "Don't Stop ___ You Get Enough"
13 Tip jar bill
21 Brings to half-mast
22 ___ the Terrible
25 Fresh from the laundry
26 Circular
27 Ejects
29 Go "1, 2, 3, 4 . . ."
30 Injury, in totspeak
32 Where ships dock
33 "Wheel of Fortune" purchases
34 Circus whip-cracker
35 Gloomy
36 Conversation
39 Enjoyed frequently as a child
41 Trick
42 Send on a detour, say
44 With enthusiasm
47 Personal heroes
48 "Well, shucks!"
49 What the first, second and fifth lines in a limerick do
50 Pocketbook part
51 Slalom curves
53 +
54 Pianist/radio host John
55 AOL alternative
56 Breakfasted or lunched
57 Wise old saying . . . like the first words of 20-, 32-, 41- and 52-Across

by Andrea Carla Michaels and Mark Diehl

ACROSS

1 On VHS, say
6 Symbol in the middle of a Scrabble board
10 Nile viper
13 The "S" of NASA
14 Many a summer cottage locale
15 Engagement at 20 paces, maybe
16 Garment that might say "Kiss the cook"
17 Philosopher who said "Man is by nature a political animal"
19 "Montage of a Dream Deferred" poet
21 Pa Clampett of "The Beverly Hillbillies"
22 Ex-G.I.
23 Firebugs' felonies
24 Vicodin, e.g.
27 Fitting
28 Sunshine unit
29 "The Interpretation of Dreams" writer
33 Macho sorts
34 Dictator Amin
35 "HAHAHA!," in texts
39 "Dream Caused by the Flight of a Bee Around a Pomegranate a Second Before Awakening" artist
42 National bird of Australia
45 Singer Carly __ Jepsen
46 Thundered
47 Where Red Square is
49 Fish in a 26-Down
51 Remarks around cute babies
52 "All I Have to Do Is Dream" singers
56 States of emergency
57 Self-evident truth
59 Chow
60 Show deference to an entering judge, say
61 __ Park (Edison's lab site)
62 Special intuition, for short
63 Beans high in protein
64 Early PC platform

DOWN

1 Org. with a 3.4-ounce container rule
2 Food symbolizing America
3 Exemplar
4 Class for a future M.B.A.
5 Mao's successor
6 Roofing material
7 Fortuneteller's deck
8 In the same mold as, with "to"
9 Mold anew
10 Orwell or Wells
11 Singer/actress Gomez
12 __ v. Ferguson (1896 Supreme Court ruling)
15 Feet, slangily
18 John of "Do the Right Thing"
20 "Frozen" reindeer
21 Kid around
25 Iowa college town
26 Common sushi order
27 Superdry
30 Opposite of soar
31 Medicine-approving org.
32 Epitome of stupidity
36 Ingredient in Worcestershire sauce
37 What Lindbergh famously did from New York to Paris
38 Jar tops
40 Many A.C.L.U. staffers
41 News item that its subject never reads
42 Come out
43 Businesses that tend to be busiest at the starts and ends of months
44 Depleted
48 Grouch
49 Bohemian
50 Sprays (down)
53 Pizazz
54 U.S. soccer great Mia
55 Strikes (out)
58 Rapper __ Def

by Ross Trudeau

ACROSS

1 Leatherworker's tool
4 Wrath
7 Sauce often used in a Bloody Mary
14 Port-au-Prince resident
16 "Um-hmm, O.K."
17 Call from a football referee
18 "Please! Anything but!"
19 Onion relative used in soups
20 Little troublemakers
22 Charged particles
23 M.R.I. orderers
24 Versatile bean
25 Texas site of a 1993 siege
27 Itsy-bitsy branch
29 Some DVD players
31 Caustic agent
34 Japan's largest company by revenue
36 Crops used in making cigarettes
38 Ready, willing and __
39 Classic Eric Clapton song about unrequited love
41 Statutes
42 Loses one's hair
44 Hold back, as a yawn
46 Moment, informally
47 World's fair, e.g.
48 Wish
49 Like the water in a baptism
51 Get bent out of shape
53 __ talks (lecture series)
56 Busy time at the drive-thru
58 Nay voter
59 It's made up of DNA
60 Message that might end "R.I.P."
63 Invaded in large numbers
65 17-year insects
66 Standards by which things are measured
67 Follows, as a schedule
68 Monterrey Mrs.
69 Consumed

DOWN

1 Get __ of (grasp)
2 Communion tidbit
3 Vegetarianism or bohemianism
4 Three on a grandfather clock
5 Source of faraway X-rays
6 Foe
7 Pantry containers
8 Long, long __
9 Web crawler, e.g.
10 Web-filled room, often
11 Spot for a food fight
12 Jackie of "Shanghai Knights"
13 Honey Bunches of __
15 "Shameful!"
21 Really revel . . . or a hint to the words formed by the circled letters
24 Take a chair
25 Indiana/Illinois separator
26 White __ sheet
28 Troubles
30 Kurtz's rank in "Apocalypse Now": Abbr.
32 Mournful cry
33 To be, to Tacitus
34 Little things that say "To" and "From"
35 Orchestra reed
37 Scissor cut
40 Swiss mount
43 __ Paese (variety of cheese)
45 Spinning toy
50 Like beer that's not in a bottle
52 Things split in fission
54 Make into 41-Across
55 Not the brightest bulb on the Christmas tree
56 Part bitten by a vampire
57 Mayberry boy
58 "I understand," facetiously
59 Hound's warning
61 Many online banners
62 Bit of butter
64 When a plane is due in, for short

by Chuck Deodene

ACROSS

1 Misgiving
6 Small quarrel
10 Leader from the House of Pahlavi
14 Eating pork, to an observant Jew or Muslim
15 Pac-12 hoops powerhouse
16 ___ Alto, Calif.
17 Not be inert, as two chemical compounds
18 Cognitive scientist Chomsky
19 10-Across's land
20 Puerto Rico clock setting
23 Resealable bag
26 Chair with two hyphens in its name
27 Apple that might be seen on a teacher's desk
28 ___-oriented
32 W.W. II spy org.
33 Genre for Mötley Crüe
35 Incendiary weapon
37 Fitness pro
42 Ohio city on Lake Erie
43 Czech-made auto that's part of the Volkswagen Group
44 "Yes . . . ri-i-i-ight there!"
47 Airplane's direction
49 Like custard
50 Adopted
52 Chain of children's stores founded by the Kaufman brothers (hence its name)
54 Basis of particle physics
58 Nothin'
59 Relative of fake news
60 Ghostly white
64 Fashionable Christian
65 Including all grades, briefly
66 "Bear" that's actually a marsupial
67 Gait faster than a walk
68 Baby's crib part
69 "Bon appétit!"

DOWN

1 Three months: Abbr.
2 Neighbor of Oman, for short
3 Atty.'s org.
4 Neighborhood buzz?
5 "Veritas" for Harvard or "Veritas vos liberabit" for Johns Hopkins
6 Sushi fish
7 Trash bin on a computer screen, e.g.
8 Dead-tired?
9 Acquainted (with)
10 Pointy-eared dog
11 Big maker of gummy bears
12 Los ___ National Laboratory
13 Sweetie pies
21 Like some digital clocks, for short
22 Maria known as "La Divina"
23 Bygone alcopop
24 TV's "How ___ Your Mother"
25 Way
29 "Giant Brain" introduced in 1946
30 Not expressly stated
31 Abbr. in many an urban address
34 Pope said to have died from a heart attack while in bed with his mistress
36 Former heavyweight champion with a tattooed face
38 Soldiers' digs?
39 Canceled, as a mission
40 Tense
41 They may be caught at the beach . . . or out at sea
44 Communications giant . . . or a possible title of this puzzle
45 All talk, no action
46 Bringer of bad luck
48 ___ Pictures (bygone studio)
51 Store known for its Blue Light Specials
53 Stopper
55 Bridge charge
56 "The joke's on you"
57 Off-ramp sign
61 Trek to Mecca
62 Band with the 1977 hit "Telephone Line," in brief
63 Yea's opposite

by Michael Shteyman

142

ACROSS

1 Puts on TV or radio
5 Ending on several central Asian country names
9 Meanie in "Jack and the Beanstalk"
14 U.S. weather agcy.
15 Zeus' wife
16 ___ and wiser
17 1990s TV series about a murder in a town in Washington
19 Film director Kurosawa
20 Made smooth, as wood
21 Part of the conjugation of the French "avoir"
23 And others, for short
24 Bump fists
25 K-K-K-5-5, e.g., in poker
28 Exhibit in an anatomy class
31 Guided
32 Is sick
33 Four-baggers: Abbr.
34 Like favorite stations on a car radio
38 Pie ___ mode
39 Result of failure to comb the hair after sleep, maybe . . . or a feature of 17-, 25-, 49- or 61-Across?
41 School grp.
42 Young male viewed as a sex object
44 Black ___ (covert doings)
45 ___ Ticonderoga
46 Apr. 15 mail addressee
47 Place to pull over on an interstate
49 English monarch with a "lace" named after her
53 ___-rock (music genre)
54 Land between Can. and Mex.
55 Inits. at the start of a memo
56 "You ready?"
59 Drilling tool
61 Hooded snake
64 Thin pancake
65 Place for the banjo in "Oh! Susanna"
66 Exposition

67 N.B.A. star ___ Irving
68 Freezes, with "over"
69 Worry

DOWN

1 Picnic pests
2 State that produces the most corn
3 Weather-related stoppage in baseball
4 Beach footwear
5 Tool building
6 Lipton offering
7 Genesis vessel
8 Word before congestion or spray
9 Job that might involve watching the kids?
10 Variety
11 French farewell
12 "Rats!"
13 Use a stencil on
18 Amorous cartoon skunk
22 "No thanks"
25 President after Nixon
26 Like a sheep with all its wool
27 Praiseful poem
28 Onetime Volvo competitor
29 K, in the NATO alphabet
30 "According to conventional wisdom . . ."
35 Place to drink lined with TVs
36 French "to be"
37 "So long!"
39 Joy Adamson book about Elsa the lioness

40 Fencing sword
43 Coat and ___
45 Decrease
48 Soft mineral
49 Phony doc
50 Unscrupulous moneylending
51 Rarin' to go
52 Republican pol Haley from South Carolina
56 Gets 16-Across
57 Buffalo's lake
58 Sour
60 Prefix with dermis
62 "Monsters, ___" (2001 movie)
63 Word before a maiden name

by Neville Fogarty

ACROSS

1 *One side of a 23-Across piece
6 *Leeway
11 Tolkien's Treebeard, e.g.
14 Switch from plastic to paper, say
15 Hedren of "The Birds"
16 Actress Vardalos
17 Aggregate
18 Buildings in a Washington, D.C., "row"
20 Widespread
21 Julio is part of it
22 *Formation of poker chips
23 Disc-flipping board game hinted at by a word ladder formed by the answers to the nine starred clues
25 Slaps with a court fine
27 Where "Hamlet" opens
29 *Celery unit
33 Largest U.S. univ. system
37 Baltic capital
38 *Hackneyed
40 Not just bite and swallow
41 Haphazard
43 *Sedimentary rock
44 Dollar bill, e.g.
47 Moves heavenward
50 Another name for 23-Across
55 *Pinocchio swallower
56 Part of L.G.B.T.
57 The Panthers of the A.C.C.
58 Twosome in a Shakespeare title
61 Nut jobs
62 Fair-hiring letters
63 Mimic's ability
64 Creator of a logical "razor"
65 Coastal raptor
66 *"___ England Slept" (1938 Churchill book)
67 *Other side of a 23-Across piece

DOWN

1 "Congratulations!"
2 Actor Paul of "American Graffiti"
3 Embarrass
4 Social standing
5 Metric measures: Abbr.
6 Trial figures
7 Prom night rental
8 Police dept. alert
9 H&R Block V.I.P.
10 Mouths, slangily
11 Pioneering computer of the 1940s
12 Eleanor Roosevelt, to Theodore
13 Items on a to-do list
19 Something to do immediately after waking up
21 The whole ball of wax
24 Albanian currency
25 Way too uptight
26 Insider informant
28 Corporate raider Carl
29 H.S. students getting ready for college
30 Up to, informally
31 ___ Khan
32 Airplane seat restraint
34 "Now I get it!"
35 ___ Aviv
36 Farm female
38 Composition of dunes
39 Sounds of disapproval
42 Rules in force in England before the Norman conquest
43 A few: Abbr.
45 Grand Marnier flavor
46 Josephine who wrote "The Daughter of Time"
47 "Shucks!"
48 See-through
49 Big name in cameras and copiers
51 Notable time period
52 Perfumer Nina
53 Brown ermine
54 "Who's there?" response
56 Robt. E. Lee, e.g.
59 Book between Galatians and Philippians: Abbr.
60 The year 1002
61 Setting for simmering

by David Poole

144

ACROSS

1 "Penny Dreadful" channel, for short
4 ___ Longstocking, girl of children's literature
9 Poet Robert who spoke at J.F.K.'s inauguration
14 Highly classified
16 Like four-leaf clovers, supposedly
17 Somehow
19 Nut popular in ice cream
20 Apparatus pulled by oxen
21 Have a mortgage, e.g.
22 Intestinal fortitude, informally
25 "Ah, now it's clear"
27 Play about Capote
30 Walkie-talkie
35 Something that may be hidden behind a framed picture
37 Mixes
38 Ancient Peruvian
39 Stairs
42 Eye part with the iris
43 Odor
45 Table tennis
47 Rare occurrence on "Jeopardy!"
50 Prop for a golf ball
51 Sheet on a mast
52 Co-ops, maybe: Abbr.
54 Abbr. before an alias
57 Pizazz
59 Nut-bearing tree
63 Completely . . . with a summation of 17-, 30- and 47-Across
67 Larsson who wrote "The Girl With the Dragon Tattoo"
68 Sign of a beaver's activity, maybe
69 Exams
70 "Alas . . ."
71 Dove's sound

DOWN

1 "Halt!"
2 Sharpen, as skills
3 Grp. that includes Iraq and Qatar
4 Alternative to bubble wrap
5 Slippery, as winter roads
6 One who gives tips (and gets tips?) at a country club
7 Arrested suspect, informally
8 Roma's country
9 Daisies and dahlias
10 Sign of a well-worn trail
11 Eight: Sp.
12 Polling bias
13 Lebanese city that was once the center of Phoenician civilization
15 Lavish party favors
18 Inquisitive
23 "___ the night before Christmas . . ."
24 Cushiony
26 Readily accept
27 1960s dance craze
28 Cowboy's workplace
29 Stomach woe
31 Given to crying
32 Golfer's gouge
33 "Goodnight" girl of song
34 Missouri river or tribe
36 10 things in an Olympic swimming pool
40 Falafel bread
41 Scissor cut
44 Lipton products
46 "Hop to it!"
48 Thin but strong
49 Most-wanted groups for parties
53 Transmitted
54 Aide: Abbr.
55 Toy on a string
56 W.W. II foe
58 Other: Sp.
60 Common Core dept.
61 Duck-hunting attire, informally
62 Syringe, for short
64 Freshly painted
65 British ref. work
66 French seasoning

by John Wrenholt

ACROSS

1 When Polonius says "Brevity is the soul of wit"
6 Tusked beast
10 Kind of threat
14 Swoon
15 Alan who played Captain Pierce
16 Essential point
17 Agonizes (over)
18 With 61- and 37-Across, famous line by 53-Across in [see circled letters]
20 The "E" in HOMES
21 Nubian heroine of opera
22 Family member who was probably adopted
23 Hairstyle for 53-Across, colloquially
28 Place where trials are conducted
29 Hitting blackjack after blackjack, say
33 Michelangelo masterpiece
36 A few
37 See 18-Across
43 Ambience
44 "Same here!"
45 Is victorious in
48 Swindles
53 Iconic role for 2-/51-Down
56 "What have we here?!"
59 Knock 'em dead
60 Online crafts seller
61 See 18-Across
64 Like old, neglected sweaters, maybe
65 Renaissance Faire instrument
66 Sign of things to come
67 Tree-lined walkway, in France
68 Make slo-o-o-ow progress
69 Concealed mike
70 Entitled sorts?

DOWN

1 Influence
2 With 51-Down, late, beloved actress
3 Certain marketing gimmicks
4 Hell-bent (on)
5 "___ a trap!"
6 "Harrumph!"
7 Brand of artificial fat
8 Deal with a broken teleprompter, say
9 Rae Sremmurd, e.g.
10 Makeup of the planet Hoth
11 Nosedive
12 Squeak stopper
13 Turnoff for drivers
19 "Doctor Faustus" novelist Thomas
24 Mont Blanc, e.g., to locals
25 Cripple
26 Heeds
27 Merit badge displayer
30 Figure on an Aussie Xing sign, perhaps
31 World Series official
32 Formerly named
34 "___ late!"
35 Tennis champ Agassi
37 Deviate during flight, as a rocket
38 Non's opposite
39 Coffee container
40 Speak with a gravelly voice
41 Amy Adams's "Man of Steel" role
42 Puppy sounds
46 British derrière
47 So far, informally
49 Chant after a fútbol goal
50 In fine ___ (healthy)
51 See 2-Down
52 Agree to a proposal
54 Country singer Judd
55 Modern lead-in to space or security
56 Real head-turners?
57 Drag
58 Not deceived by
62 Beer barrel
63 Having four sharps
64 Reference in "Treasure Island"

by Timothy Polin

146

ACROSS

1 "Winnie-the-___"
5 "Kisses, dahling!"
9 Recorded on a cassette
14 Something cleared up by Clearasil
15 Akron's home
16 To whom Butler said "Frankly, my dear, I don't give a damn"
17 Slow-cooked beef entree
19 Used a light beam on in surgery
20 Samuel of the Supreme Court
21 "How do you ___?" (court query)
23 Indenting key
24 Indian tribe that lent its name to two states
26 Fabled city of wealth sought by conquistadors
28 Before, to Byron
29 401(k) relative
31 Versatile piece of furniture
32 Put into law
34 Detroit factory output
35 One with a leg up in the circus business?
39 Trig or calc
41 October birthstones
42 Tel Aviv native
46 Sch. run by the Latter-day Saints
47 Have bills
50 Gambling scam
52 High on pot
54 Bottle alternative
55 Laughs loudly
57 Big name in retail jewelry
58 "Shucks, you shouldn't have!"
60 What the starts of 17-, 26-, 35- and 50-Across are
62 ___ Ste. Marie, Mich.
63 Regarding
64 List-ending abbr.
65 Writers' wrongs?
66 Container for eggs
67 Cincinnati team

DOWN

1 Macy's Thanksgiving event
2 Eye-related
3 Like a live radio announcer
4 Aware of, in cool-cat slang
5 Cow sound
6 Fly swatter sound
7 Passage in a plane
8 Red Monopoly purchases
9 Described, as something in the past
10 "So THAT's the story here!"
11 Carb-heavy buffet area
12 Kindle or Nook
13 Some pudgy, middle-aged physiques, informally
18 Corkscrew-shaped noodles
22 Commotion
25 Asia's ___ Sea
27 Off to the ___ (starting strong)
30 Coll. entrance exam
32 Actor Hawke of "Boyhood"
33 What it takes to tango
35 Hang, Wild West-style
36 Alert to squad cars, for short
37 Big name in potato chips
38 All thumbs
39 Wrong for the role
40 "Go ahead, shoot!"
43 Long-necked waders
44 Language in Vientiane
45 "Your work is wonderful"
47 Airing after midnight, say
48 Little shaver, to a Scot
49 '50s Ford flops
51 Clear the blackboard
53 Many a John Wayne film, informally
56 Takes a chair
59 "Evil Woman" rock grp.
61 "Balderdash!"

by Bruce Haight

ACROSS

1 Harley-Davidson bike, in slang
4 Assume the role of
9 Like Vatican affairs
14 Plains tribe name
15 Emulate Picasso or Pollock
16 "Too rich for my blood"
17 Place to pay the going rate?
19 Skin abnormalities
20 Dummies
21 Dennis the Menace, for one
23 Former G.M. compact
24 Margarine
25 Put at risk
29 Affectedly polite
31 Exactly right
32 Former Nevada senator Harry
34 How Lindbergh crossed the Atlantic
35 Something that might be thrown behind a teacher's back
40 Bowling venue
41 Input for fivethirtyeight .com
42 Like Baroque architecture
44 Purchase payment plan
49 In all probability
52 Add punch to, as the punch
53 ___ pro nobis
54 Cardinal's insignia
55 Florida senator Rubio
56 "O death, where is thy ___?": I Corinthians
58 Masterpiece waiting to be found . . . or a hint to the words in the circled letters
61 Right-hand page of an open book
62 People eaters, maybe
63 Work of Horace
64 Namely, in Latin
65 "Toodles"
66 Room with an easy chair

DOWN

1 "Oh, goody!"
2 Peter with eight Academy Award nominations (and, sadly, zero wins)
3 ___ Globes
4 iPad downloads
5 "Silent" prez
6 ___ Maria
7 W.W. II Allied landing site in Italy
8 Philatelist's buy
9 Polaroid, e.g.
10 Part of the brain believed to control emotion
11 Neptune's Greek counterpart
12 Big name in car parts
13 Capts.' inferiors
18 Booty
22 Rocket launch site
25 Taunt
26 "On the Waterfront" director Kazan
27 "I'm not kidding!"
28 Cincinnati-to-Philadelphia dir.
30 1974 top 10 foreign-language hit
33 Double-___ recession
35 Repeated word for word
36 "The Vampire Chronicles" author
37 The "them" in "Let them eat cake"
38 Restaurant freebie
39 The "thing," to Hamlet
40 Cut (off)
43 Letters on many ambulances
45 King of comedy
46 Mars, for example
47 Give in (to)
48 Guards at Buckingham Palace
50 One of the Three Musketeers
51 Singer Mary J. ___
55 ___ Verde National Park
56 Guru's title
57 Tricked but good
59 "Dr." who co-founded Beats Electronics
60 Actress Susan

by John R. O'Brien

148

ACROSS

1 Views as
6 Place, as a wager
9 Hate with a passion
14 Yank living overseas
15 Gibbon or gorilla
16 Bête ___ (pet peeve)
17 City in upstate New York
18 Got stuck in a rut
20 Time before dinner for socializing
22 Santaland worker
23 Where clouds are
24 Venerable London theater
28 Hero war pilots
31 Source of most of Google's revenue
32 2004 event for Google, for short
33 Polygraphs
36 "Be ___!" ("Help me out here!")
37 Protection for a police officer
40 Heavy burden
41 Repeated parts of songs
42 Sarcastic laugh sound
43 Stand-up comic Schumer
45 Med. school subject
46 Maker of Mashed Potato Bites
48 Colorado winter hrs.
50 Massage
53 Ohio's nickname
57 Certain Hollywood stars . . . or an apt title for this puzzle
60 Companion ship for the Niña and Santa Maria
61 Swell up
62 Locale of Phelps's last five gold medals
63 Like chip shots
64 Targets for a college fund-raising drive, informally
65 Swimming unit
66 Fortunetellers

DOWN

1 Card with two pips
2 Praise enthusiastically
3 Huge blunder
4 "___ the Knife"
5 "Right away!," in the E.R.
6 Vision-correcting procedure
7 In a fitting manner
8 "Woo-hoo!"
9 Declares invalid
10 What chess is played on
11 Top 10 song, say
12 Valuable mine rock
13 Color of beets
19 Well-behaved
21 Something in the plus column
25 Special access for celebs
26 "No bid from me"
27 Stallion-to-be
29 Cartoon frames
30 Summer, in Soissons
31 Starting on
33 Like the Chinese and Hebrew calendars
34 Agile for one's age
35 Uno + due
36 Reebok competitor
37 ___-chic (fashion style)
38 Give out one's address?
39 Whirrer on a muggy day
43 Whom R-rated movies are intended for
44 Spray for self-defense
47 Letter-shaped girder
48 Newspapers, magazines, etc.
49 Online network admin
51 Say
52 Items on an Indian necklace
54 Marx who wasn't one of the Marx Brothers
55 Luxury resort amenities
56 Spare change?
57 Univ. degree for Romney and Bloomberg
58 Every last bit
59 "Skip to My ___"

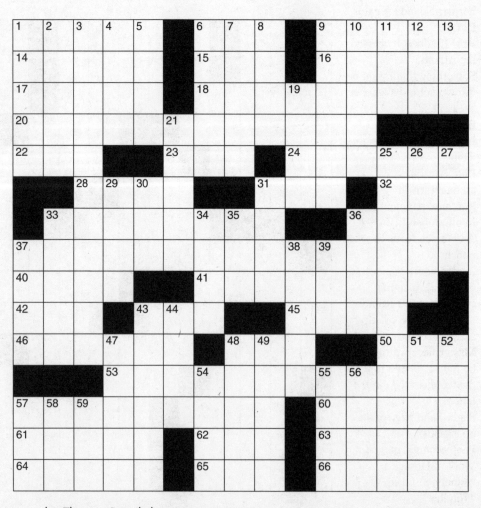

by Zhouqin Burnikel

ACROSS

1 Pulling a rabbit out of a hat, e.g.
6 Kazakhstan's __ Sea
10 Computer company with the slogan "Explore beyond limits"
14 Embarrass
15 Was a passenger
16 It's always getting stepped on
17 Sign of life
18 *Vessel with a large hold
20 Camera part
22 "Seinfeld" stock character?
23 *What a family spends together at the dinner table
26 Competitor of Secret
27 Predecessor of the CW
28 Mauna __
29 Scout's shelter
31 Back on a boat
32 Hilarity, in Internet-speak
34 One side of the Pacific
38 *Branches in a storm?
43 6'11" Channing of the N.B.A.
44 Partridge's tree, in a Christmas song
45 Color TV pioneer
46 Put together, as a team
50 Ham on __
51 Singer Scaggs with the 1976 hit "Lowdown"
52 Front of a boat
55 *Its arrival may be signaled by a ding
58 So-called "house wine of the South"
60 What you might use when you say "Giddyup!"
61 Words that can follow the ends of the answers to the starred clues
63 Sean who played Mikey in "The Goonies"
66 Band with the hit "Whip It"
67 Pope who excommunicated Martin Luther
68 Elbow, maybe
69 Garden of __
70 Puzzlemaker Rubik
71 Strength

DOWN

1 Help at the entrance to a mall
2 Aladdin's monkey
3 Courage in battle
4 Basketball Hall-of-Famer Dan
5 Plush fabric
6 Eyebrow's shape, roughly
7 Criticize severely
8 Skillful
9 Peanut, for one
10 One of the A's in N.A.A.C.P.: Abbr.
11 Roomie
12 Woman who sings "Burn" in "Hamilton"
13 Affix again, as a badge
19 Word before air, fire or water
21 Tolerated
23 Hearty drink
24 Willing to do
25 Everyone, in Dixie
30 Give a lickin'
33 "__ your lip!"
35 First winner of horse racing's Triple Crown, 1919
36 Disguised, briefly
37 Staring
39 Item that might be fervently wanted by a prisoner
40 Start of an idea
41 President after Grant
42 Encroach on someone's land
47 "The Simpsons" bus driver
48 "That's a fine __ of fish!"
49 Devon cathedral city
52 Rod Stewart's "Maggie May," e.g.
53 Had title to
54 Work on a loom
56 Hawk's hook
57 Maki, temaki or uramaki
59 Black, in poetry
62 Prefix with planet
64 "Now __ seen it all!"
65 Just-minted

by Neil Padrick Wilson

150

ACROSS

1 Submissive
5 Heading on a list of errands
9 Moon-related
14 Church recess
15 Iris's place in the eye
16 Make amends (for)
17 Food grown in a paddy
18 Transport for Huck Finn
19 Days of the week in a calendar heading
20 "Keeping my fingers crossed"
23 Chilled jelly dishes
24 Philosopher and social activist West
28 Follow
30 Gabriel García Márquez novel "Love in the Time of ___"
31 Chunk of ice in the ocean
33 Exercise area for convicts
35 Prefix with skeleton
36 Dictator ___ Amin
37 ___ v. Wade
38 First satellite to orbit Earth
43 Swiss capital
44 Attaches by rope, as a ball to a pole
45 Rolling Stones album "Get Yer ___ Out!"
47 Place to wear one's heart, in a phrase
48 Employee at a perfumery
51 Common security device . . . or a feature of 20-, 33- or 38-Across
55 Edible mushroom
58 Out on the ocean
59 Graph line
60 Dentist's tool
61 Book between Matthew and Luke
62 Color shade
63 Recurrent theme
64 Naked
65 "___ small world after all"

DOWN

1 Santa ___ (one of Columbus's ships)
2 "Iliad" and "Odyssey," for two
3 Means of getaway
4 Loudly lamenting
5 Appears after being lost
6 Egg-shaped
7 Challenge
8 Inauguration recitation
9 National ___, bygone humor magazine
10 Downright
11 Immediately
12 Aardvark's morsel
13 Coin flipper at the Super Bowl, informally
21 Mil. training academy
22 Spanish eight
25 Something to look for in an emergency
26 Goof
27 Weighed down (with)
29 Actor Estrada and others
30 TV procedural set in the Big Apple
31 Defeats
32 Kick out of school
34 Words at the altar
39 2011 Oscar-nominated picture set in 1960s Mississippi
40 1930s British P.M. Chamberlain
41 Ticked off
42 What Marie Antoinette supposedly said to "let them" do
43 Indian variety of 17-Across
46 Nay's opposite
49 Brockovich and Burnett
50 Many a reggae musician, informally
52 Send to hell
53 Biblical son of Isaac
54 Jock's antithesis
55 Summer hours in Denver: Abbr.
56 Bobby who played 10 seasons with the Boston Bruins
57 ___ Grande

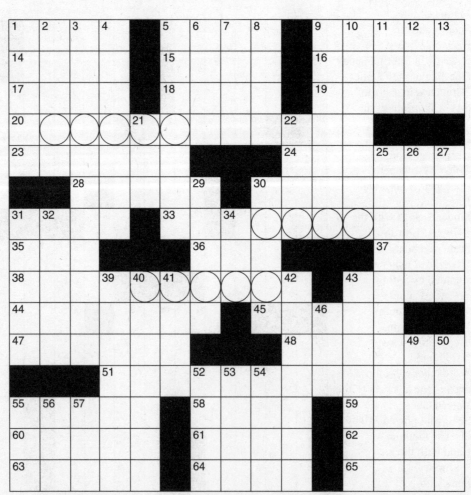

by Andy Hinz

ACROSS

1 Bear whose bed was too hard for Goldilocks
5 With 15-Across, "Don't delay!"
8 First coat for a painter
14 At any point in history
15 See 5-Across
16 Chest of drawers
17 Repeated word before "pants on fire"
18 Queen's place
20 Mexican dish served in a shell
21 Villain's vanquisher
22 On edge
23 Queens' place
26 Loser to the tortoise, in fable
27 Lovey-dovey sound
28 "Let's Get Loud" singer, affectionately
31 People often caution against reinventing it
34 "The ___, the Proud, the Marines"
35 Oafish sort
36 Queens' place
40 In
41 Broadcast
42 Broadcast part
43 Muscle toned from push-ups, informally
44 Comic strip sound from a drunkard
45 Make bread
47 With 57-Across, Queen's place
51 Many a Donald Trump announcement
54 Snowman in "Frozen"
55 Common street name
57 See 47-Across
59 Off-roaders, for short
60 Debonair
61 Fish eggs
62 Place divers explore
63 Hung around
64 Title for two Clue characters
65 Annual Austin festival, for short

DOWN

1 Animal hide
2 Bird-related
3 "See ya"
4 Pointy stone used in early Native American weaponry
5 TV news deliverer
6 Hold together
7 Shake one's booty
8 "Masterpiece Theatre" network
9 In a relaxed rhythm, musically
10 Twisted humor
11 Heart of the matter
12 Prominent Dumbo features
13 1993 football movie starring Sean Astin
19 World Cup sport
24 Asian river whose name is one letter away from an Ivy League college
25 Site of the first-in-the-nation caucuses
28 "The Grapes of Wrath" surname
29 Central points
30 Cookie that's often pulled apart
31 "That's a ___!"
32 David ___, philosopher influenced by Locke
33 Grander than grand
34 Four-term prez
35 2014 Super Bowl performer
37 Secular
38 So done with
39 Teri who played Phoebe's mother on "Friends"
44 Scorcher
45 Inflame with love
46 Charges for some Madison Avenue firms
47 Track-and-field event
48 Bedside buzzer
49 Condom material
50 A cat is said to have nine of them
51 "Ergo . . ."
52 Blemish
53 First place where Napoleon was exiled
56 Warning initials above an Internet link
58 Interest rate setter, with "the"

by Finn Vigeland

152

ACROSS

1 Name of five Norwegian kings
5 Words after work or museum
10 Former Iranian leader
14 How Charles Lindbergh flew across the Atlantic
15 French department capital known in Roman times as Nemausus
16 ___ Nostra (crime group)
17 Rock and roll has one in Cleveland
19 Pro's opposite
20 Org. that monitors gun sales
21 Reached
22 Shop employee
23 Words of greeting
26 Chandon's partner in Champagne
27 Blossom-to-be
28 October birthstone
30 Play, as a guitar
33 Dem.'s counterpart
36 1980s cop show that TV Guide once ranked as the greatest TV drama of all time
40 Dollar bill
41 Robber
42 Singer Fitzgerald
43 Battery for a TV remote
44 Window unit
46 James Earl Jones or Tommy Lee Jones
53 Zones
54 String quartet instrument
55 An evergreen
57 Gentlemen
58 Ruckus
60 Made off with
61 Freezing rain
62 Mexico's ___ California
63 One-named New Age singer
64 Succinctly put
65 What the Ugly Duckling became

DOWN

1 Worker protection org.
2 Reluctant (to)
3 Like the band Josie and the Pussycats
4 Stereo control: Abbr.
5 Walking
6 Saks ___ Avenue
7 Former Italian P.M. whose name means "beloved"
8 Cut again, as grass
9 China's Mao ___-tung
10 Reduced, with "back"
11 Beehive product
12 Houston player
13 Poem like "The swallow flies up / Into a blue evening sky, / Summer's small herald"
18 Devour with the eyes
22 Cookie morsel
24 Laze
25 Share a border with
28 "Well, what have we here!"
29 Brooch
30 ___ Lanka
31 Item in a golfer's pocket
32 B-ball official
33 Alternative to arbitrary governance
34 Wriggly fish
35 Smokey Bear ad, e.g., for short
37 Doesn't leave
38 Deice
39 Gave for a while
43 State that the Arctic Circle passes through
44 Aesthetic taste
45 "Call me ___!" "O.K., you're . . . !"
46 Proverbial waste maker
47 Heavenly hunter
48 "Bad, bad" Brown of song
49 Small egg
50 Houston player, once
51 Metes (out)
52 Spanish wine region, with "La"
56 Horse whose coat is sprinkled with white hairs
58 F.D.R.'s successor
59 "Six-pack" muscles

by Brent Sverdloff and Michael Blake

ACROSS

1 Helps
5 ___-size model
9 Things
14 Licentious man
15 Paying close attention
16 ___ congestion (cold symptom)
17 Small, cute residence?
19 Bygone Toyota sports car
20 Music with conga drums
21 500 sheets of paper
23 Moral toughness
24 Device for killing mosquitoes?
27 Annie who was nicknamed "Little Sure Shot"
31 Like a well-worn dirt road
32 Pouring into a shot glass, e.g.?
36 Come to earth
37 Fair-hiring inits.
38 Stars and ___ (Confederate flag)
42 Relatives of slack jaws?
46 Delilah was his undoing
50 "Stop joshin' me!"
51 What wakes everyone up in the morning at the duck pond?
55 Sch. for future admirals
56 Like books and tea leaves
57 Host at a roast
62 "Ad ___ per aspera" (Kansas' motto)
64 Archenemy of Bugs Bunny . . . who might say things like 17-, 24-, 32-, 42- and 51-Across
66 Wail of an ambulance
67 Den
68 Not ___ deal
69 Having an exhilarating effect
70 Trig function
71 Leave completely filled

DOWN

1 Counterpart of sciences
2 Des Moines's home
3 Fight at 20 paces, say
4 Lays eyes on
5 Expert
6 Advice-giving "Dr." of radio
7 Surprise victory
8 Sauna feature
9 Shoo-___ (overwhelming favorites)
10 Instructed
11 ___ de corps
12 Jarhead
13 On the schedule
18 Goalie Dominik with 16 seasons in the N.H.L.
22 Man's nickname that's just wonderful?
25 Letter before zee
26 Signal from offstage
27 ___ exams (tests at the end of a student's fifth year at Hogwarts)
28 "Eureka!"
29 Family relations
30 "Acid"
33 Wood for archery bows
34 One of the Stooges
35 U.K. lexicon
38 Software problem
39 From ___ Z
40 Letter before sigma
41 Fig. on an application
42 Stir-fry vessel
43 ___ about (approximately)
44 Gaping opening
45 Proprietor
46 Racket sport
47 Sydneysider, for one
48 Words said over and over
49 Chicken
52 Believes
53 ___ Lama
54 PC network overseer
58 Degs. for creative types
59 Country with which the U.S. re-established diplomatic relations in 2015
60 Toolbar heading
61 Narrow advantage
63 "___ last words?"
65 Before, to poets

by Daniel Larsen

154

ACROSS

1 Sunrise
5 Musial in the Baseball Hall of Fame
9 High in the air
14 Soil-related prefix
15 Diva's solo
16 Stubble remover
17 Only president to scale the Matterhorn
19 Love, to Lorenzo
20 Temporary
21 Fine, thin cotton fabric
23 Bill ___, the Science Guy
24 Cheer (for)
26 Women's stockings
27 Only president whose grandfather was also president
29 Move like a bunny
32 Space streakers
35 Moms
36 Had on
37 Only president born outside the continental United States
38 Bo or Checkers
39 Only president to have 15 children
40 Photos, informally
41 Make a quick note of, with "down"
42 Writer Hemingway
43 Airport pickup driver's info
44 Only president to be a lifelong bachelor
46 Mend, as socks
48 Cheerleader's cheer
49 Lead-in to historic
52 Washington's Union ___
55 TV ratings name
57 Former Afghan leader Karzai
58 Only president to be married in the White House
60 Submit a tax return online
61 End in ___ (require overtime)
62 Marc Antony's lover, informally
63 Sports figures?
64 Building annex: Abbr.
65 Eurasian duck

DOWN

1 "Mack the Knife" singer Bobby
2 Excruciating pain
3 Worked on an essay or novel
4 Scent picker-upper
5 Redeemers
6 Sign of an earthquake
7 Be sick
8 Defense alliance since 1949, for short
9 Catherine of ___
10 Tibetan priests
11 Seasonal thinning in the atmosphere over Antarctica
12 Only president to serve as both vice president and president without being elected to either office
13 Card that just beats a deuce
18 Printing mistakes
22 Greek P's
25 Dalton who played 007
27 ___ and haws
28 Give in to gravity
30 Iron and tin sources
31 Saucy
32 Deal (with)
33 Last words?
34 Nut from Hawaii
36 Vegas casino developer Steve
38 Bespectacled Disney dwarf
39 Tourist destination in County Kerry, Ireland
41 Roman goddess, protector of women and marriage
42 Jazz up
44 Wedding figures
45 Epic poem starting with the flight from Troy
47 Slanted
49 Sacred song
50 Soprano Fleming
51 Fund, as a university chair
52 Tom Jones's "___ a Lady"
53 Only president to administer the oath of office to two other presidents
54 March Madness org.
56 Legal entities for partnerships: Abbr.
59 Inc., overseas

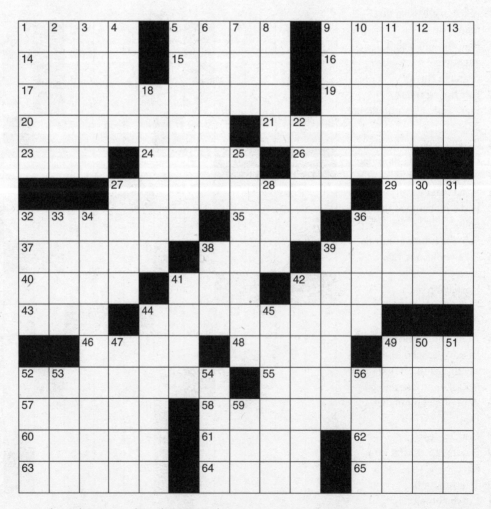

by Ed Stein and Paula Gamache

ACROSS

1 Plants used to make tequila
7 Health resort amenity
10 Penne ___ vodka
14 Flying insect with prominent eyespots
15 University address ender
16 Painful muscle injury
17 Frozen CO_2, familiarly
18 Grooming accessory that may be stuck in the hair
20 Classic American dessert
22 Lays out neatly
23 Granola morsel
24 Tenant
26 "___ already said too much"
28 Smaller cousin of the double bass
30 Would-be attorneys' hurdles, briefly
34 Qatari capital
36 Like some profs.
37 Frame job
38 Cass of the Mamas & the Papas
40 Obi-Wan ___ (Jedi knight)
41 Taking no guff
42 Spitting sound
45 Federal tax agts.
46 Rain delay covers
47 Undergoes oxidation
49 Driver's licenses and such, for short
50 BlackBerry alternative
52 Sans prescription, in brief
54 Washington and environs, informally
57 Material to sketch on
61 Michael Corleone player in "The Godfather"
63 Relating to songbirds
64 Take care of, as the bill
65 Ornamental pond fish
66 Trade associations
67 Genre
68 "www" address
69 Exam for an ambitious H.S. student . . . or what this puzzle has been?

DOWN

1 Opera set in Egypt
2 Trail mix
3 "Parks and Recreation" star
4 "And there it is!"
5 "And so on and so forth"
6 Generic name for a herding dog
7 Congers, e.g.
8 Sharable PC file
9 Invisible emanations
10 Currently
11 ___ Organa ("Star Wars" princess)
12 Having an open, delicate pattern
13 Chests in synagogues
19 Ultimatum's end
21 Societal troubles
25 Barfly
26 Explanatory Latin phrase
27 Physicist Alessandro, inventor of the electric battery
29 Grab a bite
31 Nuclear reactor
32 Went leisurely downriver, perhaps
33 Recasts damaging information in a favorable light, say
35 Plane hijacker
39 How freelance work is typically done
40 Pup : wolf :: ___ : fox
42 Expert
43 Source of healthful fatty acids in a StarKist can
44 Exploiter
48 Absorbs, as gravy
51 5-7-5 verse
53 Wordlessly implied
54 Batty
55 Sicken with sentiment
56 Per person
58 Garment draped over the shoulders
59 Draws to a close
60 Be at leisure
62 Neither here ___ there

by Timothy Polin

156

ACROSS

1 "No problem for me!"
6 Peru's capital
10 Omar of Fox's "House"
14 Dickens's "__ House"
15 Per item
16 Hand lotion ingredient
17 Intimidates, in a way
19 Crime scene barrier
20 Goes to, as a meeting
21 Not as hard
23 Airport up the coast from LAX
24 Flash mobs, once
25 "Science Guy" Bill
26 Jean __, father of Dadaism
29 "Oh, darn!"
32 Fired (up)
34 Period between wars
36 Goat's cry
37 World's fair, for short
38 Circus animals that balance beach balls on their noses
40 "When You Wish __ a Star"
43 Manning who was twice Super Bowl M.V.P.
45 Watch or clock
47 Showed in syndication, say
49 Justice Kagan
50 Numbered hwy.
51 Abbr. before a credit card date
52 Feeling blue
54 __ card (cellphone chip)
56 Exercise in a pool
58 Cross-reference for further information
62 Male deer
63 On a lower floor
66 "__ kleine Nachtmusik"
67 "Ars Amatoria" poet
68 Foe
69 Ones in suits?
70 Big name in pet food
71 Aid in storm-tracking

DOWN

1 "2 Broke Girls" airer
2 Ski area near Salt Lake City
3 "Cool!"
4 Pub game
5 Artist Georgia who is known for her flower canvases
6 Cheryl of "Charlie's Angels"
7 Wall St. debuts
8 Trim the lawn
9 Sleeper's problem
10 Has supper
11 Unlined sheets without any writing
12 Sailor who's smitten by Olive Oyl
13 Get angry
18 Pig noses
22 Name first encountered in Genesis 2
24 "Understand?," slangily
26 Big galoot
27 Tyrannosaurus __
28 Classroom missile
30 Followed a weight-loss plan
31 Alternative to AOL or Yahoo
33 Island ESE of Oahu
35 Pepsi, for one
39 Just knows
41 Month before Nov.
42 Born: Fr.
44 Police dept. figure
46 Van Gogh or Van Dyck
47 Moses parted it
48 Beautifully strange
53 "Me, too"
55 2016 Disney film set in Polynesia
57 10 and 8 for Bart and Lisa Simpson, respectively
58 Do the breaststroke, e.g.
59 Terminals
60 Like the score 7–7
61 Humorous Bombeck
64 Lab eggs
65 Damascus's land: Abbr.

by Zhouqin Burnikel

ACROSS

1 ___ jacket (bit of casualwear)
5 Dish that's sometimes rated in "alarms"
10 Curds and ___
14 Wagon part
15 Like much music
16 In fine fettle
17 Widespread
18 1960s activist Hoffman
19 Has
20 ___ friends (not having to be on one's guard)
22 Quaint inn, informally
24 Cry after "Ready!"
25 Muffed one
27 Bearlike
29 Powerful Renaissance family
32 A book collector might seek a first one
33 Available
34 Spanish girlfriend
35 Italy's shape
36 Setting for much of the movie "Lion"
38 Zippo
42 People encountered by Pizarro
44 Things ghosts lack
46 Riga native
49 Charms
50 In addition
51 What tryptophan is said to induce
52 Place to go for a "me day"
53 Munchkins
55 Nash who wrote "Parsley / Is gharsley"
59 Turner or Fey
61 Bother greatly
63 Tell to "Do it!"
64 Lead-in to a conclusion
65 Movie, informally
66 Class with mats
67 Feature of a late-night show set
68 Words to live by
69 Catch sight of

DOWN

1 Morning joe
2 Start of many a doctor's visit
3 In addition
4 Outcome that's overall unfavorable
5 Windy City "L" overseer
6 Imaginary tiger friend in the comics
7 Not on good terms (with)
8 Done nothing
9 Infamous prison featured in the 1969 best seller "Papillon"
10 "___ knew?"
11 Southernmost U.S. state
12 Weather concern in 11-Down
13 Lackeys
21 Sheepish look
23 Two-masted vessel
26 Socialist Workers Party's ideology
28 Honest sorts . . . or what the circled squares contain?
29 Palindromic boy's name
30 "Be My Yoko ___" (first single by Barenaked Ladies)
31 Pi's follower
32 Former Big Four record co.
34 They're taken out in newspapers
37 Palindromic girl's name
39 Lungful
40 Hollywood ending?
41 Nincompoop
43 River that feeds Lake Nasser
45 Topping in kosher restaurants
46 Didn't run out
47 Have dreams
48 Features of some country singers
49 Region on the Rhine
51 Took effect
54 Area between mountains
56 Plunge
57 Breakfast food with a rhyming slogan
58 In order
60 Totally fine
62 Box office purchase: Abbr.

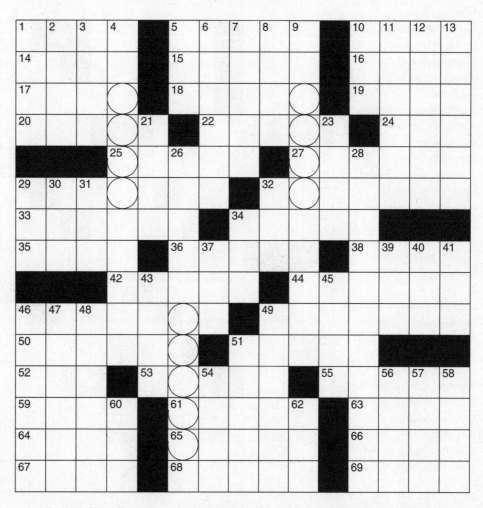

by Jacob Stulberg

158

ACROSS

1 Medicine-approving org.
4 Wine barrel
8 Awards in the ad biz
13 Rainbow shape
14 Opera melody
15 Quick look
16 Paving goo
17 Article of outerwear for an urbanite?
19 Too many of them "spoil the broth"
21 Bunny's movement
22 Component of a science course
23 Article of outerwear for a champagne drinker?
26 Done: Fr.
27 Having a ho-hum attitude
28 Warm greeting
29 Justice Sotomayor
30 Leave full
31 Common weather phenomenon in San Francisco
32 Ankle-high work shoe
33 Article of outerwear for a candy lover?
36 Potato chips, to Brits
39 ___-rock (music genre)
40 Entree that may be slathered in barbecue sauce
44 "Grand" women
45 Classic muscle car
46 Removes the rind from
47 Inlets
48 Article of outerwear for a housekeeper?
50 Lee who directed "Life of Pi"
51 ___ Harbour, Fla.
52 Newspapers, collectively
53 Article of outerwear for a General Motors employee?
57 Bird that gives a hoot
59 Gold standards
60 ___ lily
61 Chinese leader with a Little Red Book

62 Panache
63 Rat or roach
64 No. after a main telephone no.

DOWN

1 What the "Gras" of Mardi Gras means
2 Count with fangs
3 Circus tumbler
4 Witch's laugh
5 Crop up
6 Command to a dog
7 Mary ___ cosmetics
8 Bit from a movie
9 Fond du ___, Wis.
10 Faintest idea
11 Easter Island locale
12 Belgrade native
15 Unappetizing food that might be served with a ladle
18 Carpet variety
20 Thinks, thinks, thinks (about)
23 Small ammo
24 Command spoken while pulling the reins
25 Rambunctious little kids
26 200- or 400-meter run, e.g.
29 Madrid Mrs.
31 N.F.L. three-pointers: Abbr.
32 Droid
34 Alternative to FedEx
35 Thicken, as blood
36 Holders of some music collections
37 Headgear for a drizzly day
38 Descriptive language
41 Annoying
42 Honeycomb product
43 Retired jet, for short
45 Shorebird with a distinctive shriek
46 Caged talker
48 Painters' touches
49 Some computer picture files
51 Memory unit
54 Kilmer of "Top Gun"
55 Nile viper
56 Middle of Arizona?
58 Auction grouping

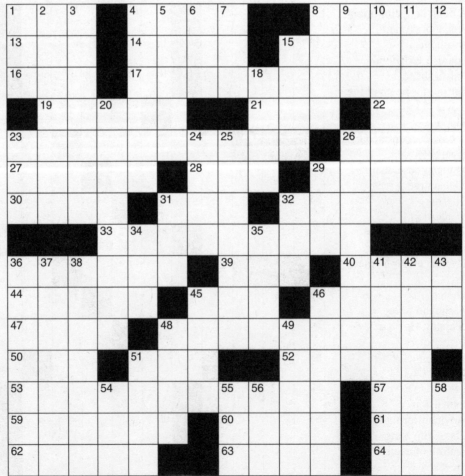

by Susan Gelfand

ACROSS

1 Things that may be displayed on a general's chest
7 "Oh no!," in comics
10 Old Testament prophet
14 "Leave this to me!"
15 West who said "It's better to be looked over than overlooked"
16 Foreign Legion hat
17 Famously unfinished 14th-century literary work, with "The"
20 Hotel name synonymous with poshness
21 Org. whose motto is "We are their voice"
22 Historical period
23 "Happy Days" diner
24 "How cheap!"
27 Exam for the college-bound, for short
29 Reggae relative
30 What one might start over with
35 Arthur Ashe Stadium org.
39 Prevents litter?
40 Beverage that may be 41-Across
41 Alternative to "bottled"
42 "Shame on you!" sounds
43 Losing crunchiness, as chips
45 Ukr., e.g., once
47 Org.'s cousin
48 Historical figure played by David Bowie in "The Prestige"
54 Narcotics-fighting grp.
57 Rapid-fire gun
58 Embellish
59 Uphill aid for skiers
60 "Finally . . ."
64 Cut with a beam
65 Sighs of relief
66 Some family reunion attendees
67 ___ terrier
68 Tennis do-over
69 Like wind chimes

DOWN

1 Millionths of a meter
2 Spam medium
3 "Shhh!"
4 Movie that came out about the same time as "A Bug's Life"
5 Emulate Pinocchio
6 Orch. section
7 Something necessary
8 Gripes
9 It's just for openers
10 Letters on a "Wanted" poster
11 Major scuffle
12 Sydney ___ House
13 Agave fiber used in rugs
18 Sheep sound
19 Job to do
24 Catches some rays
25 Altitudes: Abbr.
26 Gibes
28 States positively
30 Winter hrs. in Texas
31 The Stones' "12 × 5" and "Flowers"
32 Chinese philosopher ___-tzu
33 "___ Baba and the Forty Thieves"
34 Full complement of bowling pins
36 "Give him some space!"
37 Chess champ Mikhail
38 Copy
41 Bones, anatomically
43 Done bit by bit
44 Half of a square dance duo
46 Chunk of concrete
48 Makes void
49 ___ Walton League (conservation group)
50 Given to smooching
51 ___ nth degree
52 Dadaist Max
53 Lead-in to Cat or cone
55 Prop found near a palette
56 ___-craftsy
59 27-Across taker, typically
61 Shape of a three-way intersection
62 Channel with explosive content?
63 52, in old Rome

by Freddie Cheng

ACROSS

1 Lawyer: Abbr.
5 British sports car, briefly
8 What ignorance is, they say
13 One might end "Q.E.D."
15 A pitcher wants a low one, for short
16 "___ One: A Star Wars Story"
17 Atlantic site of strange disappearances
20 Michael who played both Batman and Birdman
21 Aid for a lost driver, for short
22 Big laugh
23 Russian jet
24 Former British P.M. Tony
26 "As is" transaction
30 Frank of the Mothers of Invention
34 WSW's opposite
35 Jazzy Fitzgerald
36 Colorful aquarium swimmers
37 "___ my words"
39 You are here
41 Didn't float
42 Like zombies
44 Cause for being refused a drink at a bar
46 Opposite of bright
47 Four-time M.L.B. All-Star José
48 Excellent service
50 Terse
52 "That feels so-o-o-o nice!"
53 Halloween's mo.
56 Amazement
57 Water down
60 Punny description for 17-, 26- or 48-Across
64 Boredom
65 Sup
66 Florida senator Marco
67 Band with the 2000 hit "Bye Bye Bye"
68 Just for Men offering
69 Treaty

DOWN

1 Alert to squad cars, for short
2 Arduous walk
3 Ripped
4 Start of a playground joke
5 Denim fabric
6 Trump's "The ___ of the Deal"
7 Use Listerine, say
8 Victoria's Secret measurement
9 Chaney of horror
10 Azalea of rap
11 Lieutenant on the original U.S.S. Enterprise
12 "___ and ye shall find"
14 Hopeless
18 Iditarod vehicle
19 Hoppy brew, for short
24 Nonsense, as the Irish might say
25 "Darn!"
26 Leg bone connected to the knee bone
27 Stupid
28 Passionately brainy, say
29 Chicken ___ king
31 Fashion house founded in Milan
32 Emotion causing hyperventilation
33 "___ Another" (NPR game show)
36 It's in the stratosphere
38 Hold on to
40 Weight unit on a bridge sign
43 From east of the Urals
45 One placing a telephone call
48 Organization for Janet Yellen, informally
49 "Button your lip!"
51 Tango requirement
53 Store sign that might be flipped at 9 a.m.
54 Inmates
55 Wee
57 Lavish care (on)
58 Instrument that makes the cheeks puff out
59 Clapton who sang "Layla"
61 Habit wearer
62 "No" vote
63 "Just kidding!"

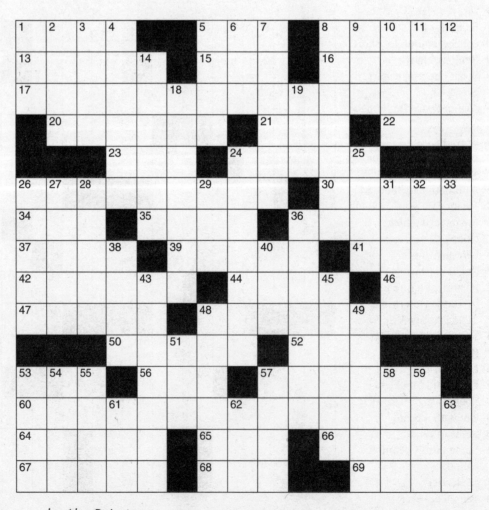

by Alan DeLoriea

ACROSS

1 Pop fan?
4 Numbers to crunch
8 Asian gambling mecca
13 Singer DiFranco
14 Water pitchers
16 Slender woodwinds
17 Asian electronics giant
18 Mystery writer Marsh
19 Sporty car in a Beach Boys song
20 *"It's a Mad, Mad, Mad, Mad World" actor, 1963
22 Year, south of the border
23 A pep talk might boost it
24 *"12 Angry Men" actor, 1957
28 Reduce to particles
30 Online money transfer facilitator
31 Scruff of the neck
32 Made bird noises
35 Pig's digs
36 *"Anatomy of a Murder" actor, 1959
40 "Breaking Bad" network
43 It's a size larger than grande at Starbucks
44 Sounds of satisfaction
48 Like a toasted marshmallow vis-à-vis a non-toasted one
50 Shirt with straps instead of sleeves
53 *"Road Trip" actor, 2000
56 Rice-based Spanish dish
57 PC "brain"
58 Youthful time in one's life . . . which this puzzle might harken solvers back to?
60 Did a smith's job on
62 Prized violin
63 D.C. ballplayer
64 In and of itself
65 Mister, south of the border
66 Prefix with borough
67 Bohemian
68 Puts in stitches
69 Dog breeder's org.

DOWN

1 One admired for his masculinity
2 The tiniest bit
3 Gesture to punctuate a great performance
4 Highest mountain in North America
5 "What a bummer!"
6 Oolong and Earl Grey
7 Popular typeface
8 Bon __ (witticism)
9 Monastic realm
10 Many washers and dryers in apartment buildings
11 Stunt pilot
12 Amer. money
15 Peeved
21 Hitchcock role in almost every Hitchcock film
25 Sporting sword
26 Actress __ Pinkett Smith
27 Journalist Nellie
29 "Micro" and "macro" subject, for short
33 Province west of Que.
34 Passing mention?
37 Winnebago owner, briefly
38 Bone-dry
39 In the buff
40 F.B.I. employee: Abbr.
41 Sponge
42 Behave
45 1996 Olympics site
46 It stores a synagogue's Torah scrolls
47 Moving jerkily
49 "Um . . . O.K."
51 "Superbad" producer Judd
52 Low points
54 Those, to José
55 April, May and June, for example
59 Swimmer's assignment
60 Where you might hear 44-Across
61 Susan of "L.A. Law"

by Damon J. Gulczynski

Note: This collaboration is by the astrophysicist Neil de Grasse Tyson and his Harvard classmate Andrea Carla Michaels (with her 56th puzzle for The Times).

ACROSS

1 Fix, as a cat
5 "Get cracking!"
9 "Jurassic Park" insect casing
14 Pack animal
15 "__ girl!"
16 First lady after Hillary
17 "That's my cue!"
18 Like Dorothy's slippers
19 Boston airport
20 Toe testing the waters?
23 Potentially dangerous bacterium
24 ExxonMobil?
28 "__ Comedy Jam"
29 Command to Rover
32 "Bald-faced" thing
33 "Who goes there, friend or __?"
34 Bowling scoresheet unit
36 Square dance site
37 Oscar nominees' gathering?
41 Vittles
43 Manipulate, as bread dough
44 Bird that hoots
45 Mai __ (cocktail)
48 Admit, with "up to"
49 '50s high school dance
52 Bashful?
55 Inventory items
57 Total hottie?
60 Simple pond life
63 "Me as well"
64 "Voulez-vous coucher __ moi ce soir?"
65 It may be reasonable to a jury
66 Catches forty winks
67 Intertwine
68 New Mexican pueblo builders
69 Exuberance
70 Regarding, in a memo

DOWN

1 Wore an upside-down frown
2 Volcanic rock
3 Many, many
4 1983 film in which Barbra Streisand dresses as a man
5 Suffix with million
6 __ poker
7 Equally large
8 E-commerce site formerly owned by eBay
9 Declare to be true
10 Native New Zealanders
11 Computer program glitch
12 Paleozoic or Mesozoic
13 Sought political office
21 "The Scales" constellation
22 Greek letter before omega
25 Quite a distance off
26 Neither's partner
27 Hamilton's bill
30 Body part to lend or bend
31 Big inits. in trucks
34 1-800-FLOWERS alternative
35 Certain fraternal order member
36 Place to dream
37 Successful auctioneer's last word
38 Commercial game with wild cards
39 Put in stitches
40 Having an aftertaste, as some barbecue sauce
41 Debate position against "against"
42 Have debts
45 140-character messages
46 Drivers' org.
47 John who wrote "The World According to Garp"
49 Reindeer feet
50 Most bizarre
51 1960 Alfred Hitchcock thriller
53 Abu __ (Mideast land)
54 Prebirth
56 President who won the 2009 Nobel Peace Prize
58 "Ain't happening"
59 Finish second
60 Woodworking tool
61 Baseballer Gehrig
62 Rifle or revolver

by Neil deGrasse Tyson and Andrea Carla Michaels

ACROSS

1 Work like Dürer
5 Peter or Paul, but not Mary
9 Bath fixture
14 Lilting melodies
15 Concerning, to a lawyer
16 Musical with the song "Don't Cry for Me Argentina"
17 Trick football play
20 ___ bark beetle
21 One side of a debate
22 Dude, Jamaica-style
23 Office staple since the 1980s
30 Birth control method, for short
31 Peach or plum
32 Descartes's "therefore"
33 Super Bowl-winning QB Bart
36 Bollywood soundtrack instrument
38 ". . . man ___ mouse?"
39 High-ranking British Parliament member
42 Doctors' org.
43 Something one shouldn't make in public
44 Lifesavers for cops and sailors
45 Disposable lighters and pens
47 The mark of Zorro
48 You, abroad
49 Floor warning
55 Good noise from an engine
56 Sarcastic laugh sound
57 Green govt. group
58 Study at a college that doesn't have applications?
64 Seize without legal authority
65 Listening device
66 Ink stain
67 Pool contents?
68 Newspaper essay
69 Old one, in Oldenburg

DOWN

1 Alleviated
2 Duke or dame
3 Pulls an all-nighter, say
4 "The buck stops here" prez
5 Bar on a car
6 Be a busybody
7 Pound sound
8 Family member: Abbr.
9 Genre for Dizzy Gillespie and Charlie Parker
10 Way or means
11 Paul McCartney, for one
12 Onetime telecommunications conglomerate, for short
13 Opposing vote
18 Bullish trends
19 Bully's boast
24 Dame ___ Te Kanawa
25 Entrance for Santa
26 Navel formation?
27 Moves briskly
28 White heron
29 Surf sounds
33 Signs of healing
34 Native of southern India or northern Sri Lanka
35 You can count on them
36 It's no bull
37 Nice location
40 Itchy condition
41 Out in public
46 Baseball or basketball
48 Humiliated
50 Basketball inflaters
51 Invitation heading
52 "Mack the Knife" composer
53 Disney World theme park
54 It's often unaccounted for . . . or a hint to this puzzle's circled letters
58 Short-haired dog
59 Play for a patsy
60 7,485 performances, for Broadway's original "Cats"
61 Noah count?
62 With it
63 [No info yet]

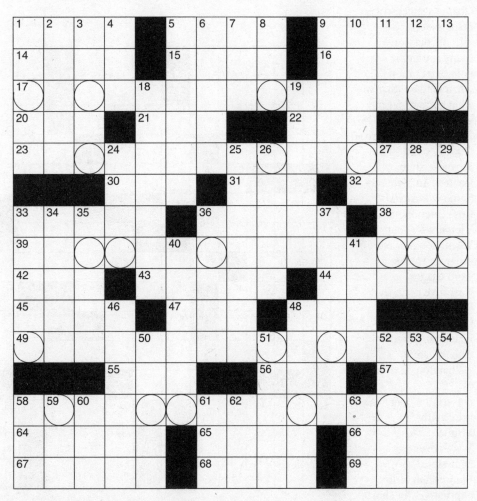

by George Barany and John D. Child

ACROSS

1 Set of pictures at a dentist's
6 Crow's sound
9 Reprieves
15 Event for meeting new people
16 "I love," to Cato
17 Perfect world
18 "The one thing that's clear to me . . ."
20 Picked
21 Appear
22 "Smoking or ___?"
23 Boxing achievements, in brief
24 Distant
29 Narrow water passage
32 "___ day now . . ."
33 Villainous count in the Lemony Snicket books
35 Obama's successor
36 Jason's ship
37 Pull off perfectly
38 Many millennia
39 Police operation . . . or, when read another way, what a grammarian would like to do to 18-, 24-, 52- and 65-Across?
43 Day-___ paint
44 Japanese soup
46 Boaters' implements
47 Some woodwinds
49 Lose traction on the road
50 Vietnamese soup
51 What Google's Ngram program tracks, for word usage
52 Narrative connector
56 Peach pit or walnut
57 Greedy one
58 Peach or walnut
62 Cuba's capital
65 "What do you think of . . . ?"
67 Unscripted comedy, informally
68 Mimic
69 Watch over
70 Blue state?
71 Fluorescent bulb alternative, for short
72 Novices

DOWN

1 Dec. celebration
2 Tick off
3 What car wheels turn on
4 Polite affirmative
5 ___ Lanka
6 Group of books that an educated person is supposed to be familiar with
7 In the company of
8 Blow away
9 Jealous words of congratulations
10 Cultural spirit
11 "You can't joke about that yet"
12 FedEx rival
13 Thanksgiving dessert
14 ___ Juan, Puerto Rico
19 Problem with a shoelace
23 Dance in which one partner might hold a rose between his teeth
25 One might apply gloss to them
26 Things for sale
27 Old-fashioned wine holder
28 Unsuccessful
29 Thorny parts of roses
30 Group of three
31 Enters hurriedly
34 Often-unheeded advice from dentists
36 Ohio city that was once the Rubber Capital of the World
40 Liable to tip over, maybe
41 Expressed amazement
42 Labourite's opponent, in British politics
45 "Most likely . . ."
48 Big electronics chain
51 License plates
53 Choir member
54 "Fingers crossed!"
55 Planted, as discord
59 Sound to fear in the savanna
60 Currency of France or Italy
61 When planes are due to take off, for short
62 That guy
63 "What ___, chopped liver?"
64 Biden and Pence, in brief
65 Actor Holbrook
66 10%-er: Abbr.

by Tom McCoy

ACROSS

1 Even trade
5 Nile predator, briefly
9 Class with masks?
14 Next in line
15 Promise
16 18th-century mathematician who introduced the function
17 Designer Gucci
18 Nick at ___
19 One-named singer who won the 2016 Album of the Year
20 "Sorry I'm in your space, it's an actress thing," said ___
23 Shirt that might have a crew neck, informally
24 Scottish cap
25 "The Raven" writer's monogram
28 "Don't interrupt me on my radio show," said ___
32 "It gets better" spot, e.g., in brief
34 DiCaprio, to fans
35 Prefix with galactic and spatial
36 Works to get
39 Lion's prey
41 Easily fooled
42 Unit of bacon
43 Lennon's widow
45 ___-Mex
46 "Gotta run, pop concert calls," said ___
51 Turn-___
52 Gravestone letters
53 Govt. org. with a drone registry program
54 "Right to the point: You're beautiful, it's true," said ___
60 Advocated
63 Tea type
64 Three, in Berlin
65 Mecca resident
66 Drying oven
67 Harvest, as crops
68 "A man who, when he smells flowers, looks around for a coffin," per H. L. Mencken
69 Rice wine
70 Longings

DOWN

1 Carpet style
2 Word said three times before "What have we here?!"
3 Assistant
4 On the double
5 Hide
6 Inner part of a racetrack
7 Palindromic boy's name
8 Treasure holders
9 Request for a hand
10 Inspiring 1993 movie about a Notre Dame football team walk-on
11 Lager relative
12 Comical Brooks
13 "All we ___ saying is give peace a chance"
21 Just-made
22 Munch on
25 Thing that exists
26 Drug whose generic name is naproxen
27 Measuring cup material
28 Truman and others
29 Rule laid down by a commission: Abbr.
30 "What should I ___?"
31 Material in strands
32 Sauce with pine nuts
33 The Great Tempter
37 Zero, in soccer
38 Occasional
40 Prefix with -versal
44 Not connected to a computer network
47 Pacific ___
48 What stars are in the night sky
49 Letter after sigma
50 Tom who coached the Dallas Cowboys for 29 years
54 Revered "Star Wars" figure
55 Actor LaBeouf
56 Illegal pitching motion
57 Logician's chart
58 Not stand completely straight
59 Nervousness that causes a golfer to miss an easy putt, with "the"
60 Golden State sch.
61 With 62-Down, sci-fi weapon
62 See 61-Down

by Ryan Milligan

ACROSS

1 Inflated senses of self
5 Moisture in the air
10 Flower girl?
14 Muppet with a unibrow
15 Furious
16 The "N" of N.F.L.: Abbr.
17 Coating for fish that you might think would make you tipsy
19 Sound heard in a cave
20 "Cheers!," in Scandinavia
21 Historical periods
23 Derby or fedora
24 Cinderella's carriage
28 Hit the slopes
31 __ v. Wade
32 Cousins of emus
33 Classical paintings
35 Org. that operates the Jupiter orbiter
38 __-C.I.O.
39 Rough estimates . . . or what the ends of 17-, 24-, 52- and 65-Across are?
44 Slangy "sweetie"
45 Pepper's partner
46 California wine valley
47 Popular pain reliever
49 Have a part in a play
51 Talk, talk, talk
52 Waiter's refilling aid
57 Utmost
58 Sport for heavyweights
59 Curses (out)
63 Couple, in a gossip column
65 Overhead cooler
68 Ruler said to have fiddled while Rome burned
69 Superman's birth name
70 Song for a diva
71 Sprouted
72 Underhanded sort
73 Like marathons and maxiskirts

DOWN

1 Recedes, as the tide
2 Sheldon of "The Big Bang Theory," for one
3 Cookie that may be dipped in milk
4 Subway standee's support
5 By way of
6 Works at a museum
7 __ Philippe (Swiss watchmaker)
8 Cheri formerly of "S.N.L"
9 Aired, as old TV shows
10 Suffix with serpent
11 Host of TV's "30 Minute Meals"
12 Cornell University's home
13 Tree huggers?
18 Fuzzy picture
22 One who's all skin and bones
25 Leonardo da Vinci's "__ Lisa"
26 Fruits that are a little grittier than apples
27 "That sounds good - NOT!"
28 Cry big tears
29 Maker of autodom's Optima
30 Words after "Reach Out" in a #1 Four Tops hit
34 Work like a dog
36 Cousin of calypso
37 Quacky insurance giant
40 House of Lords members
41 Scratch target
42 Pollution police, for short
43 Softhead
47 Store window shader
48 __-day Saints (Mormons)
50 Fork-tailed bird
53 Hockey discs
54 "Wait, let me explain . . ."
55 French fabric
56 Majestic
60 Big, round head of hair
61 Street through the middle of town
62 Slight problem
64 Cut the lawn
66 Pasture
67 Kind

by Agnes Davidson and Zhouqin Burnikel

ACROSS

1 Defunct gridiron org.
4 Fireplace holder
9 Rather conservative
14 Chapter in history
15 Race with batons
16 Pink cocktail, informally
17 What zero bars on a cellphone indicates
19 Synthetic fabric
20 Old-fashioned theaters
21 "Memoirs of a Geisha" accessory
22 Bit of dinero
23 Viking tales, e.g.
28 "Shame on you!"
29 Ring decoration
30 Opposite of wane
31 Glowing coal
34 Like advice worth listening to
36 Leg-revealing item of apparel
37 Experts on the brain
40 "Shoot!"
41 Sour milk product
42 "Someone turn on a fan!"
43 Surgery locales, for short
44 Quick hit
45 Notch shape
46 Baseball, in America
53 Cross to bear
54 Puppy's plaint
55 Desktop image
56 Wisecracks
58 Disney character hinted at by the circled letters
60 Apply, as pressure
61 Opening remarks
62 Flood refuge
63 Refugee camp sights
64 Visibly stunned
65 __ chi

DOWN

1 Fifth member in a noble line
2 Tolkien hero
3 Futuristic weapon
4 Canine warning
5 Uprising
6 "I was at the movies - nowhere near the crime," e.g.
7 Understood
8 Look over
9 1996 horror movie with three sequels
10 Done for
11 "Sure, go ahead"
12 Texter's qualifier
13 Mafia V.I.P.
18 Old airline with the slogan "We have to earn our wings every day"
22 Fuss over oneself
24 Modern prefix with skeptic
25 Urged (on)
26 Totaled, as a bill
27 Have life
31 Conclude with
32 Stiller's longtime wife and comedy partner
33 Explode
34 Recreational device that holds 35-Down
35 See 34-Down
36 Imitative
38 Reads carefully
39 Gets even with?
44 Renaissance Faire events
45 Steam and such
47 Sluggish
48 What causes the circled letters to grow?
49 Companion of the Niña and Santa Maria
50 Apple's former instant-messaging program
51 "On the Beach" heroine
52 Gourmet mushroom
56 Boeing product
57 Hacker, but not on a computer
58 __ mater (brain cover)
59 Admit (to)

by Timothy Polin

ACROSS

1 Something to make before blowing out the birthday candles
5 Staple of Greek cuisine
9 All-knowing sort
14 ___ Morita, co-founder of Sony
15 ___ vera
16 Kind of bond in chemistry
17 What Thoreau lived in at Walden Pond
19 Romance or horror
20 Indian Ocean bloc?
22 Hibernation station
23 Measurements of 60-Acrosses
24 Central American bloc?
33 "I'm cool with that"
34 Brother in an order
35 Steel support for concrete
36 Letter insert: Abbr.
37 Non-Jew
39 Bill who popularizes science
40 Many, colloquially
42 Land of Donegal and Dingle Bay
43 Paula of "Paula's Home Cooking"
44 Western European bloc?
47 Multivolume ref.
48 Scottish cap
49 Organization founded in 1945 . . . or a literal description of 20-, 24- and 44-Across?
56 2008 movie with the line "I will find you, and I will kill you"
58 Softening-up words before a request
59 Prevent, as disaster
60 Alkali neutralizer
61 Mishmash
62 ___ profundo (lowest vocal range)
63 Motto for a modern risk-taker, for short
64 Email folder

DOWN

1 Insect with a hanging nest
2 Furnishings retailer with gigantic stores
3 "Awesome!"
4 Office-closing time
5 What phone books are alphabetized by
6 Inter ___
7 Apollo program destination
8 Mercedes-___
9 Words next to a dotted line
10 Cry of lament
11 Elsa's younger sister in "Frozen"
12 Russian space station
13 Diamonds, slangily
18 ___ interface
21 Fitting
24 Christmas carols
25 "You didn't have to tell me"
26 Plants with needles
27 Dead duck
28 "___ next time!"
29 Director Kurosawa
30 Li'l ___
31 Sauce, cheese or noodles, in lasagna
32 Gladiatorial combat site
37 Examine, as a crystal ball
38 Gradually slowing, in music
41 High achievers?
43 Pizza company with a game piece logo
45 Summer setting in D.C.
46 Spreadsheet figures
49 Island instruments, for short
50 Website with the heading "Recently Viewed Items"
51 Style of the Chrysler Building, informally
52 It gets hit on the head
53 Eye amorously
54 Ruhr refusal
55 Opening on a schedule
56 Precursor of Diet Coke
57 Director DuVernay of "Selma"

by Zachary Spitz and Diane Roseman

ACROSS

1 Dict. entries
4 Spinner in a PC drive
9 H.S. class for a future doctor, maybe
14 Good name for a tax adviser?
15 In the know
16 Sound from a hen
17 Big name in athletic wear
19 Underworld, in Greek mythology
20 Mean dog, at times
21 Pines (for)
22 Gumbo vegetable
23 Jellystone Park toon with a bow tie
27 "Girlfriend" boy band
29 __ personality (Dr. Jekyll and Mr. Hyde trait)
30 Bill with Jefferson's portrait
31 Siri runs on it
33 Sac fly result
34 Breather
35 Assortment of appetizers at a Polynesian or Chinese restaurant
38 Stiffly formal
40 Stephen of "The Crying Game"
41 Be under the weather
42 Particle accelerator particle
43 Flight deck guesses about takeoff, for short
45 Loses color
49 Amorous look
53 Bread dipped in hummus
54 Winter neckwear
55 Court jesters, e.g.
57 Set of moral principles
58 Noisemakers at the 2010 World Cup
60 Letter after gamma
61 Former "Saturday Night Live" regular Cheri
62 Horatian creation
63 Gown
64 Some squishy balls
65 Marry

DOWN

1 President during W.W. I
2 Boozehounds
3 $400,000/year, for the U.S. president
4 Telephone
5 Social misfit
6 Implement for a muzzleloader
7 Acapulco gold
8 Three Wise __ (Magi)
9 Sneezing sound
10 Backup strategy
11 Person in charge of fiscal decisions
12 Arctic fishing tools
13 Approvals
18 Radioactive element

21 Novel narrated by Humbert Humbert
24 Title for the Virgin Mary
25 __ ghanouj
26 Decompose
28 Beat patroller
32 Having no doubt about
34 Medical setback
35 Game played with a 48-card deck
36 Tennis great Sampras
37 Gratuity
38 Bacon source
39 One sounding "cock-a-doodle-doo"
44 Pitcher Tom nicknamed "The Franchise"
46 Keep out of sight

47 Investment company whose commercials once had talking babies
48 Mouthed off to
50 Manners of walking
51 Killer whales
52 Blue toon whose enemy is Gargamel
56 Commando weapons
57 TV announcer Hall whose credits include "The Tonight Show"
58 Germany's Otto __ Bismarck
59 Sport-__ (rugged vehicle)

by Peter Gordon

ACROSS

1 Matches, as a bet
5 Suffix with bachelor
9 Miss
13 Pinball game ender
14 Keisters
16 Mozart's "Se vuol ballare," for one
17 Neck of the woods
18 Very, in music
19 "Darn it all!"
20 Practical sort . . . or anagram #1 of the only seven letters used to make this puzzle
22 Ballpark gates
24 Times when the French go en vacances
25 Chasing Moby Dick, say
26 Brightest 1-Down in Aquila
29 Big celeb . . . or anagram #2
32 Bollywood wraps
33 Formal ceremonies
34 One of a pair of map coordinates: Abbr.
36 Awaken
37 Tennis great Monica
38 Meter maid of song
39 Asian new year
40 Animals rounded up in a roundup
41 Foodie, e.g.
42 Sells (for) . . . or anagram #3
44 Standing still
45 The black square chunk in front of 55-, 60- and 63-Across, and others
46 Actor Morales
47 Zionist's homeland
50 More coarse . . . or anagram #4
54 Social reformer Jacob
55 Californie and others
58 "Dies __"
59 Vogue rival
60 U. S. Grant rival
61 "He'd fly through the air with the greatest of __" (old song lyric)
62 Suffix with prank or poll
63 "__ we forget . . ."
64 Concordes, for short

DOWN

1 Sky light
2 Blarney Stone land
3 Zeno's home
4 Result of poor ventilation
5 Pink Pearl, for one
6 Things graded by 7-Down
7 See 6-Down
8 1970s political cause, for short
9 It may be thrown from a horse
10 __ Sea (former fourth-largest lake in the world)
11 Babylon, for the ancient Hanging Gardens
12 Lip
15 Fraidy-cats
21 "That so?"
23 Thomas Hardy heroine
25 Take up or let out
26 Admin. aide
27 "See ya"
28 Like the invitation line "Be there or be square"
29 Roger formerly of Fox News
30 Crème de la crème
31 Deserves V.I.P. treatment
33 Predigital film units
35 Piquant
37 Ben of "Tower Heist"
38 They come along once in a blue moon
40 Store window sign
41 List-ending abbr.
43 Come-on
44 How tableware is often sold
46 __ Park, Colo.
47 Seriously vexes
48 Delta deposit
49 Vex
51 Nest eggs for the golden yrs.
52 Big __ Conference
53 Roger who played a part on "Cheers"
56 Certain util. bill
57 Stein filler

by Bruce Haight

ACROSS

1 Web designer's code
5 One wearing an apron and a puffy white hat
9 One includes "My cup runneth over" in the Bible
14 Has debts
15 Slight amount
16 Like a wolf's howl in the dead of night
17 Gobbledygook
19 Looked open-mouthed
20 Scot's cap
21 "___ is me!"
22 Up in arms
24 Nebraska's capital before Lincoln
26 Grandson of Adam
27 Clock-setting std.
30 Big fat zero
34 Like Jefferson on a list of presidents
35 River through Paris
36 Do laps in a pool
39 Flower that's also a girl's name
42 Spoonful of medicine, say
43 Put forward, as an idea
45 Unlocks
47 Habitual tube watchers
51 Swiss peak
52 Part in a movie
53 Hair that hangs over the forehead
56 Used a lever on
58 "Golly!"
60 Promise-to-pay note
61 Capital of South Korea
63 What a shamed person has to "eat"
66 Stand on three legs?
67 Mideast native
68 On the ___ (recuperating)
69 Lock of hair
70 Metal canisters
71 Hankering

DOWN

1 Book consulted by a do-it-yourselfer
2 Time in Manhattan when it's midnight in Montana
3 Ethel who sang "There's No Business Like Show Business"
4 It was often dropped in the '60s
5 "See ya!"
6 Woodchuck's escape route
7 Airline app datum, for short
8 On the decline
9 Flying horse of Greek myth
10 "Save me a ___!"
11 Notes of a chord played in rapid succession
12 Fib
13 Club ___
18 Path of mowed grass
23 Steal from
25 It might capture an embarrassing comment
26 Bit of appended text
28 Store department selling suits and ties
29 Obstacle for a drone
31 Modern and cool
32 Plan that might include mutual funds, in brief
33 Body of water that separates Africa and Asia
36 Pet safety org.
37 Sheep's coat
38 "It's certainly possible . . ."
40 Hot spring
41 "The best is ___ to come"
44 What amusement parks provide
46 2016 prize for Bob Dylan
48 Who wrote of "sorrow for the lost Lenore"
49 Out-of-date
50 Marksman with an M40
54 Word cried twice before "gone"
55 Napped leather
57 Feels remorse over
58 F.B.I. worker, informally
59 Recedes
61 Ready
62 Place for a bud or a stud
64 Celebrity psychic Geller
65 Down Under bird

by Gary Cee

172

ACROSS

1 Country invaded in 2003
5 H.S. math class
9 Legendary music club in Lower Manhattan, informally
14 Suffix with refresh or replace
15 Parks of Alabama
16 Spartan serf
17 *V.I.P.'s security agent
19 Resort island near Majorca
20 The Rams of the Atlantic 10 Conf.
21 Scholarship money
22 *Nintendo hand-held
24 Disgorges
26 Actress Campbell of "Scream"
27 *Place to plug in a USB cable
33 "Ditto"
36 Utters, informally
37 Does the honors for Thanksgiving dinner
38 Short-sheeting, e.g.
40 Snoring sound
42 Tuscan city
43 Sees eye to eye (with)
45 52, in old Rome
47 Long, single take, in filmmaking
48 *Multiplex, e.g.
51 Stew morsels
52 Exchange vows at the altar
56 *NATO's smallest member, populationwise
60 Stock listings: Abbr.
61 Ariz. neighbor
62 Sacha Baron Cohen character
63 *Where a newspaper's biggest stories go
66 Actress Gaynor of "South Pacific"
67 "E pluribus __"
68 "So __ walks into . . ."
69 Fall of winter
70 What a ponytail partially covers
71 There's no place like it . . . or a word that can precede either half of the answer to each starred clue

DOWN

1 Fill (with)
2 Corporate shuffle, for short
3 Love interest of Pacey on "Dawson's Creek"
4 Amt.
5 "What's right is right" and others
6 Rocky __
7 Haifa's country: Abbr.
8 Doohickey
9 Monstrous creatures
10 French newborn
11 Smooth-talking
12 Schmo
13 "__ With Me" (Sam Smith hit)
18 Purrer in Peru
23 Opposite of sans
25 Act starter
26 Shows some affection
28 Dispenser candy
29 Religious abode
30 Baker's need
31 Artist Magritte
32 Romanov ruler
33 Often-filtered messages
34 Jason's ship
35 __ Levy, Buffalo Bills coach in the Hall of Fame
39 "Don't quit!"
41 1980s Pakistani president
44 W.W. II-era British gun
46 Treater's phrase
49 Enjoyed oneself
50 Wind tile in mah-jongg
53 Insect stage
54 Use Goo Gone on, perhaps
55 Daisy variety
56 Some old PCs
57 Snake's shape
58 Art Deco notable
59 Loaf (around)
60 Government overthrow
64 Single-stranded molecule
65 Part of a tuba's sound

by Gary J. Whitehead

ACROSS

1 Trophies and such
7 Give at no charge, as a hotel room
11 Hypodermic units, for short
14 Magical drink
15 Cousin of a bassoon
16 "Roses __ red . . ."
17 1981 Mel Gibson film, with "The"
19 Fellows
20 Go in
21 Basic beliefs
23 Gorbachev was its last leader: Abbr.
26 404 in old Rome
28 Niagara source
29 __ de mer
30 The Ocean State
33 __ donna
35 They split when they're smashed
36 Motorcycle attachment
39 English pool game
43 Sign up for more issues
45 Scoundrel
46 Arrived like Michael in an old song?
51 Decimal base
52 Spoken
53 Singer Turner
54 Penny
55 Actress Roberts and others
58 Electrical pioneer
60 Explosive initials
61 Had the passenger seat
66 Winning 1-Across can make this grow
67 Blue-green
68 Fancy home
69 Room with an easy chair
70 Master thespians they're not
71 Like a professional haircut

DOWN

1 Mo. before May
2 Court
3 __ disadvantage (handicapped)
4 Equestrian
5 Sad
6 Grab
7 Bullfight
8 Kimono sash
9 Not worth debating
10 French father
11 Kodak, e.g.
12 Lowlife
13 Felt
18 Make a change in the decor
22 "Full" or "half" wrestling hold
23 Diamond V.I.P.'s
24 Delhi dress
25 Moved on ice
27 Dog docs
30 Zoomed
31 Charged particle
32 Cig
34 Just
37 Commercial suffix with Tropic
38 Remainder
40 Smith who sang "God Bless America"
41 Not odd
42 Landlord's due
44 Bleaches
46 Went bad
47 Juice source
48 Malicious
49 Change for a five
50 Epidermal eruptions
54 Feline
56 Part of McDonald's logo
57 Bean type
59 Disoriented
62 Hoover __
63 Lass
64 Western tribe
65 Actor Beatty

by David Pringle

174

ACROSS
1 Nasty habits
6 Homes for hermanos y hermanas
11 "Dracula" creature
14 Blaze of glory
15 African wader
16 Emissions watchdog: Abbr.
17 See 29-Across
19 Dollop
20 Redder, as a tomato
21 Empire State Building style
23 Butcher's cut
25 Bigheads
27 Repeat performance?
28 Semicircle
29 Beginning of a daffy-nition of 17-Across
32 Winter warmer
34 Discover
35 Paid respect to
38 A cheap way to fly
42 Kisses in Castile
44 W.W. II conference site
45 Daffy-nition, part 2
50 For example
51 No in Nuremberg
52 Cambodian currency
53 Eight: Prefix
54 Ballroom dance
57 Chutzpah
59 U.S./Eur. divider
60 End of the daffy-nition
64 Runner Sebastian
65 Old sporty Toyota
66 Pertaining to an arm bone
67 You can get a bang out of it
68 Data processing command
69 __ coil (electrical device)

DOWN
1 American Legion member
2 Rocks at the bar
3 Like much office work
4 Option at a fast-food restaurant
5 "That's enough!"
6 Pay with plastic
7 Feel bad
8 Results of dives
9 Mimic
10 Separate into whites and darks, e.g.
11 Beautify
12 Military helicopter
13 No-nos
18 High-schooler
22 Durbin of Hollywood
23 Young woman
24 Killer whale
26 Barn bird
29 Many a time
30 Cereal grain
31 Area of land
33 Classical Flemish painter
36 Inexact fig.
37 Lintel support
39 Perceives
40 Troublemaker
41 Something to swing on a string
43 __ Lanka
45 Not broken up
46 Formulator of the law of universal gravitation
47 Shrinking __
48 Desire strongly
49 A Baldwin brother
53 Little egg
55 Copy, as a film
56 Former New York City archbishop
58 Drubbing
61 Golf's __ Elder
62 Mule of song
63 Large time piece?

by Sarah Keller

ACROSS

1 Jazz style
6 Reclusive actress Greta
11 Sandwich initials
14 Tehran native
15 Perfect
16 Karel Capek play
17 Rooming house offering
19 Whiz
20 Tints
21 Tasteless
23 Large monkeys
27 Happy-face symbols
29 Peter of "Lawrence of Arabia"
30 Cuban dance music: Var.
31 Make up (for)
32 Rent
33 __ King Cole
36 "__ Lama Ding Dong" (1961 nonsense hit)
37 Nullifies
38 Author Ferber
39 Mrs., in Madrid
40 Like the weather around lighthouses, often
41 Open, as a package
42 Ed of "The Honeymooners"
44 Carve
45 Golf attendants
47 Prayer book
48 Country bumpkins
49 Et __ (and others)
50 Part of a college email address
51 Like a native
58 Bro's sibling
59 Tape deck button
60 Ham it up
61 Asian holiday
62 Cosmetician Lauder
63 Dork

DOWN

1 Baby's mealtime garment
2 Afore
3 Naughty
4 __ case-by-case basis
5 Tiny puncture
6 Scoffs
7 Fusses
8 Stephen of "The Crying Game"
9 Drinker's place
10 Antiquated
11 Drilling tool
12 Like a rabbit's foot, supposedly
13 Deuce toppers
18 Sand hill
22 Priest's robe
23 Wild swine
24 __ of roses
25 Economic cycle
26 Mrs. Chaplin
27 Disreputable
28 Rumple
30 King's time on the throne
32 Apple's apple and Chevron's chevron
34 Win by __
35 Levy imposer
37 Cast a ballot
38 Letter accompanier: Abbr.
40 Toy loved by dogs
41 Without assistance
43 Wordsworth creation
44 "The proof __ the pudding"
45 Toothpaste brand
46 War hero Murphy
47 Dish
49 Suffix with accept
52 Breakfast drinks, briefly
53 No longer working: Abbr.
54 Mercedes competitor
55 Fish eggs
56 Summer on the Seine
57 Belle of a ball

by Alison Donald

176

ACROSS
1 "Qué __?"
5 1970s White House name
11 Revolutionary Guevara
14 Often
15 There are eight in a cup
16 __ Luthor, of "Superman"
17 Evangelist and friend of presidents
19 __ pro nobis
20 1956 Elvis hit that went to #2
21 Sun. talk
22 Mil. weapon that can cross an ocean
23 Some short plays
25 Nosh
27 French composer Erik
29 Turned sharply
32 Diplomat's asset
35 "Tickle me" guy
37 Parenthetical comment
38 Part of H.R.H.
39 Word that can follow the ends of 17- and 62-Across and 11- and 34-Down
41 Break a commandment
42 On __ (winning)
44 Vaccines
45 Understands
46 "Forget about it!"
48 Art supporter
50 Words of agreement
52 German thoroughfare
56 Huck Finn's transport
58 Digital readout, for short
60 Walk nonchalantly
61 __ Baba
62 Takes no chances
64 Word with pool or port
65 Go back to a favorite book
66 Pitcher
67 Language suffix
68 Antsy
69 Some cameras, for short

DOWN
1 Picasso or Casals
2 "March comes in like __ . . ."
3 Figure out
4 As a minimum
5 Energetic one
6 Part of E.U.: Abbr.
7 Genetic molecules
8 Flu symptoms
9 Becomes aware of
10 Mil. award
11 How bidding proceeds in bridge
12 Basil or oregano
13 Midterm, e.g.
18 Gym site, for short
22 Prepares, as Champagne
24 __ Marner
26 Banned apple spray
28 Show host
30 Get to work on Time
31 TV rooms
32 Holier __ thou
33 Prefix with space
34 Dangerous thing to be caught in
36 Gumbo vegetables
39 Dressed
40 First and Second Avenues area, in Manhattan
43 Ransack
45 Spectacles
47 Common allergen
49 Part of Q.E.D.
51 Words of compassion
53 Wrap
54 Morley of "60 Minutes"
55 Observers
56 Preakness, for one
57 "Woe is me!"
59 Not natural
62 In favor of
63 Droop

by Richard Chisholm

ACROSS

1 Ones filling out 1040's, for short
5 Dangers
10 Fed. workplace watchdog
14 Nimble
15 Irish-born actor Milo
16 San __ Obispo, Calif.
17 __ avis
18 Téa of "Hollywood Ending"
19 Greek war god
20 Longtime ABC daytime drama
23 Thought things over
24 "C'est si __"
25 Little white lie
28 Classic children's nursery song
33 BB's and bullets
34 Rowed
35 Lays down the lawn
39 Made a statement on a stack of Bibles?
42 "__ of the D'Urbervilles"
43 Hatred
45 Best buds
47 1970 Jack Nicholson film
53 Folk singer DiFranco
54 Genetic info
55 "It's __ nothing"
57 1952 George Axelord Broadway farce, with "The"
62 Gangster's blade
64 Butcher's offerings
65 Slowish
66 Finish a drive?
67 Capri and Wight
68 City near Provo
69 "You said it, brother!"
70 "This is __ . . ." (radio announcement)
71 Memo

DOWN

1 PC storage accessory
2 Treat for an elephant
3 Once more
4 More hackneyed
5 Massage intensely
6 "Yes, it's clear now"
7 Attempt to score
8 Obi-Wan __ of "Star Wars"
9 Poetic command before "O Ship of State!"
10 Former king of Norway
11 Guaranteed to succeed
12 Hurry
13 Nitwit
21 Bright thought
22 Prefix with European
26 Summer coolers
27 Mattress holders
29 Letters on an ambulance
30 Audi rival
31 Nutso
32 Welcome __
35 Davenport
36 Father of Thor
37 Creating dissension
38 Seek damages
40 Hip-hop
41 Nickname for a 59-Down student
44 __ Griffin, 1960s–'80s talk show host
46 Scorch
48 Deficiency of red blood cells
49 Most reasonable
50 Attachable, as sunglasses
51 Matador charger
52 Bulb holder
56 Moon to June
58 Smooth
59 College where an athlete might wear a "Y"
60 Summers on the Riviera
61 Helper: Abbr.
62 Health resort
63 __ and cheese

by Sarah Keller

178

ACROSS

1 Document burial place
5 Marilyn Monroe mark
9 Full range
14 Like ideal cactus climate
15 E-garbage
16 Degrade
17 Something to play in Kinshasa?
19 Increased, as the score
20 "Come in!"
21 Baby bug
23 Moo goo __ pan
24 Fresh talk
26 From time immemorial
28 Eye part
31 Regained consciousness
33 Like "fuzz" for "police"
34 Rock band equipment
35 High do
38 Beaujolais, e.g.
39 Letters that make you feel important?
42 Unbridged area
43 Cribbage markers
45 Alternative to gin or vodka
46 TV viewer's aid
48 Away, but not completely off-duty
50 Sidestepped
51 French-born satirist Hilaire
53 Author Dinesen
54 Meyers of "Kate & Allie"
55 Live's partner
58 "Phooey!"
62 __ de Mayo
64 Intermediary (or a title for this puzzle)
66 Rivers' destination
67 Cry from the pews
68 Start of a magician's cry
69 Foul
70 Cincinnati team
71 Freeway exit

DOWN

1 Place for a smile
2 Wrinkle remover
3 Buildup on a suit jacket
4 Sidles through a doorway
5 Chow mein additive
6 October birthstones
7 Tibetan priest
8 Reason to call 911: Abbr.
9 Bodywork place
10 Lawyers' org.
11 The Lord's tropical fruit?
12 Run-of-the-mill
13 Not very hot
18 Grove fruit
22 Some Anne Rice characters
25 Bless the food
27 J.F.K. posting, for short
28 Request of an invitee, briefly
29 Nobelist Wiesel
30 Romantic ballroom queues?
31 Bedouin's mount
32 Doctor's org.
36 Hourly charge
37 Guest column
40 Olive __
41 Acerbic pianist Oscar
44 John Belushi was originally on it: Abbr.
47 Start a battle
49 Any of the original 13
51 Breakfast strip
52 Author Jong
53 Laid up
56 Thickening agent
57 Vatican's home
59 __ Hart, sitcom title character
60 Presidential time
61 Go bananas
63 Friskies eater
65 Nav. rank

by Lee Glickstein and Nancy Salomon

ACROSS

1 "Show Boat" author Ferber
5 Sheep cries
9 Sense much used in a bakery
14 Stick-to-itiveness
15 Pac-10 member
16 Shire of "Rocky"
17 Strong wind
18 Metric weight
19 Back street
20 Forecast maker
23 Leader known for his "little red book"
24 Quantity: Abbr.
25 Lucy of "Charlie's Angels," 2000
28 Slugger called the Sultan of Swat
31 Commendation
36 Gaelic tongue
38 Crystal ball user
40 Sea duck
41 "Melrose Place" actress
44 Loos who wrote "Gentlemen Prefer Blondes"
45 Wire screen
46 Fill up
47 Episodes of "Friends" and "Seinfeld," now
49 Within a stone's throw
51 Acid, in the '60s
52 700, on monuments
54 Actor Stephen
56 Motorcyclist's wear, often
63 Final authority
64 Extol
65 Former Baathist state
67 "You're ___ talk!"
68 "Do you come here often?," e.g.
69 Scrabble piece
70 Accelerator or brake
71 Pindar writings
72 Scored 100 on

DOWN

1 Fabergé collectible
2 Shout at a shootout
3 River with Blue and White tributaries
4 Special forces unit
5 Crazy, slangily
6 Farm division
7 Having wings
8 Brazilian dance
9 TV series with Klingons and Romulans
10 Having XY chromosomes
11 Scat queen Fitzgerald
12 Place
13 Place
21 Road topper
22 "Steee-rike!" caller
25 Franz who composed "The Merry Widow"
26 In an old song, the "I'll see you in my dreams" girl
27 Carrier that acquired Piedmont
29 Period in office
30 Beauty of Troy
32 Is sick
33 Perfect
34 Theater reservations
35 Missed the mark
37 "___, Brute?"
39 Switch-hitter known as Charlie Hustle
42 Screwdriver or wrench
43 Pantomime game
48 Educ. site
50 ___ room
53 Yo-Yo Ma's instrument
55 Japanese dog
56 Swim meet division
57 Gazed at
58 "The Thin Man" dog
59 Police action
60 Father's Day month
61 Guitarist Clapton
62 Story
63 Soak (up)
66 Mathematical proof letters

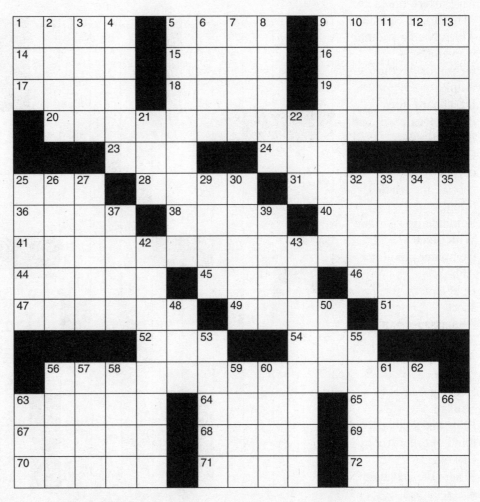

by Randall J. Hartman

ACROSS

1 Morocco's capital
6 "Oh, my stars!"
10 Recipe amt.
14 They're not PC
15 Inner: Prefix
16 Pro __ (one way to divide things)
17 African language family
18 Close
19 They can be refined
20 Ford explorer?
23 Jock: Abbr.
26 Sailor's affirmative
27 Mississippi city where Elvis was born
28 Hospital's __ center
30 Positioned
32 Far Eastern bread
33 "The Hours" role for which Nicole Kidman won an Oscar
36 Genre for Aretha Franklin
37 Dashboard inits.
38 Pupil's locale
41 Billiards great
46 Org. with a complex code
48 ". . . __ the whole thing!"
49 Rejoinder to "Am too!"
50 With grace
52 Computer monitor: Abbr.
53 Bout enders, for short
54 Ambassadors and such, or an appropriate title for this puzzle
58 Ambience
59 Det. Tiger or N.Y. Yankee
60 Blow one's lid
64 Kind of mile: Abbr.
65 Cry out
66 Where the Decalogue was received
67 Shade trees
68 Talk back to
69 Ability

DOWN

1 Josh
2 Physician's org.
3 Roll-on brand
4 When Hamlet sees the ghost
5 Literally, "harbor wave"
6 One often seen in a turban
7 Fit for drafting
8 Ollie's partner
9 Friend of Hamlet
10 Jamboree group
11 Longtime Massachusetts congressman
12 Writer Shelby
13 Give, as a gene
21 Actress Cannon
22 Sport in which Israel won its first Olympic medal
23 Off-roaders, for short
24 ZZ Top, musically
25 Reckless
29 Trademarked fruit name
30 Discontinuance
31 Seuss's "Horton Hears __"
34 "__ a man with seven wives"
35 Popular cereal or magazine
39 Langston Hughes poem
40 Discontinued fliers, quickly
42 River past Luxor
43 Rejects
44 Protective covering
45 Unaffected
46 Demented
47 Initiation, for one
51 French political divisions
52 Marine __
55 Nolo contendere, e.g.
56 Unagi, in a sushi bar
57 Best-selling author Larson
61 Prefix with cycle
62 Chum
63 Up to, informally

by Kevan Choset

ACROSS

1 Jane Austen novel
5 Chopper blade
10 Friend
13 Meat cuts behind the ribs
15 Give the slip
16 Pharmaceutical giant __ Lilly
17 Poker instruction
19 __ v. Wade (1973 Supreme Court decision)
20 Elapsed time
21 Slowly merged (into)
23 Filling maker: Abbr.
24 Saudi export
25 "The final frontier"
27 Slots instruction
31 Burn with hot liquid
34 His and __
35 Cousin of an ostrich
36 "Piece of cake!"
37 Diamond weight
39 Mojave-like
40 Mornings, for short
41 Boot bottom
42 Devoutness
43 Roulette instruction
47 Paris divider
48 Versatile truck, informally
49 __ King Cole
52 Carafe size
54 Step-up
56 Critic __ Louise Huxtable
57 Craps instruction
60 Chess pieces
61 Clear the blackboard
62 Breed of red cattle
63 Mammal that sleeps upside-down
64 Shut out
65 New Jersey five

DOWN

1 Castilian hero
2 Pitcher's place
3 Pitchers' gloves
4 Prelude to a deal
5 Carmaker's woe
6 Racetrack
7 Road goo
8 Strange
9 Closes again, as an envelope
10 Keep working hard
11 __ vera
12 Told a whopper
14 Hide from view
18 Like Darth Vader
22 11-pointer in blackjack
25 Queens ball park
26 Sassy
27 Work at, as a trade
28 Pitched
29 Send forth
30 New York's Giuliani
31 The world has seven of them
32 Where soldiers stay overnight
33 Helper
37 Harry __, Columbia Pictures co-founder
38 Sheltered, nautically
39 Be under the weather
41 How 007 does not like martinis
42 Squinted
44 Formerly known as
45 Orion, with "the"
46 Leave one's mark on
49 Unsophisticated
50 High-class tie
51 Parenting challenges
52 Ewe's baby
53 "I had no __!"
54 Rick's love in "Casablanca"
55 Paradise lost
58 It's north of Calif.
59 Research room

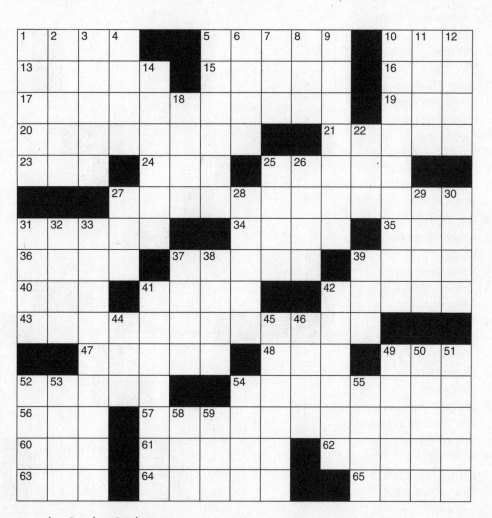

by Gordon Seaberg

182

ACROSS

1 The Beatles or the Stones
5 Penny
9 When repeated, a city in Washington
14 Inter __
15 Penny, maybe, in poker
16 With 3-Down, French-born diarist
17 57-Across song about a request in a gene lab?
20 Not pro
21 Senescence
22 Prefix with dermal
25 Rocky hill
26 Prepare for printing
27 Prefix with gliding
29 Change over at a factory
31 Pulitzer or Tony, as for 57-Across
33 Star of Scorpio
37 57-Across song about a request in the maritime supply store?
40 Varnish ingredient
41 Dye chemical
43 Pouilly-__ (white wine)
46 Individual
47 Board game from India
51 Shade tree
53 Dover's state: Abbr.
54 Slothful
55 Word said twice before "Don't tell me!"
57 Noted Broadway composer
63 With 68-Across, what Fred MacMurray had in a 1960s sitcom
64 007
65 Famed lab assistant
66 Old catalog maker
67 Swear
68 See 63-Across

DOWN

1 __-relief
2 Pint at a pub
3 See 16-Across
4 20th-century art movement
5 Synagogue singer
6 Whole
7 A degree
8 Golf bag item
9 Light switch surrounder
10 Battery end
11 Actress Turner and others
12 Lord or vassal
13 It's a plus in accounting
18 C.D. earnings: Abbr.
19 Howler
22 Mileage rating grp.
23 Manhandle
24 Pitcher Hideki __
26 Honky-__
28 Give __ for one's money
30 Heads' opposite
32 Small sharks
34 Followers of pis
35 Alleviated
36 Fence crossing
38 "Get it?"
39 53, in old Rome
42 Patriots' org.
44 Some patches
45 African antelopes
47 Fence features
48 __ drop of a hat
49 Old Oldsmobile
50 Wishful one
52 Central
56 The one here
58 Brian Williams's employer
59 Old French coin
60 Bigheadedness
61 Charged particle
62 __ Butterworth's

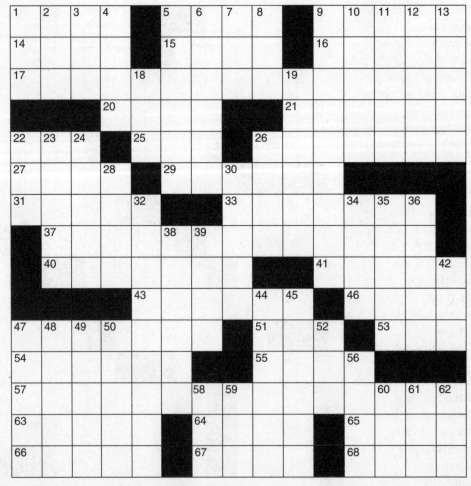

by Stephen Budiansky

ACROSS

1 Lavish entertainment
5 At a distance
9 Russian country house
14 Realtor's unit
15 Exploration org.
16 Actor Hawke
17 Title for Jesus
20 Chi-town team
21 Slimmer's regimen
22 Contents of Bartlett's
23 Peddle
24 Mows
25 Lightest-colored
28 Pre-dye hair shade, often
29 Revolutionary Guevara
32 Champion tennis servers
33 Russia's __ Mountains
34 "Slow down!"
35 1976 Walter Matthau/Tatum O'Neal movie
38 Private investigators, for short
39 Iranian money
40 Africa's Sierra __
41 Suffix with book or freak
42 Baseball glove
43 Expired
44 Smooth, as a drive
45 One of the three H's in a summer weather forecast
46 Gas rating number
49 Coarse fiber
50 "Ugh!"
53 1958 best seller by William J. Lederer and Eugene Burdick
56 Concise
57 Shakespeare's stream
58 Major-__ (bigwig)
59 Name on a deed
60 Store
61 One more time

DOWN

1 Chief parts of adipose tissue
2 Sound in a long hallway
3 Big-mouthed carnivorous dinosaur, for short
4 Hosp. brain readout
5 Make sacred
6 No longer bright
7 Aide: Abbr.
8 The old college cheer
9 Second-in-command
10 One of the Three Musketeers
11 Atkins of country music
12 Big-eared hopper
13 "No ifs, __ or buts"
18 Texas oil city
19 Is, in math
23 Predicate parts
24 Words moving along the bottom of a TV screen
25 Singer Page
26 Suffers after overexercise
27 Bloodsucker
28 Terrific
29 Total confusion
30 Singer Lena or Marilyn
31 Relaxed
33 Come together
34 Tearful
36 Twaddle
37 Sports jacket
42 Christmas display sight
43 Underlying
44 Temporary halt
45 Comedy
46 Director Preminger
47 Prepare to swallow
48 Beach bird
49 Coffee, slangily
50 Universally known figure
51 Arrived
52 "Well, what do you __?!"
54 Thanksgiving side dish
55 Boise's home: Abbr.

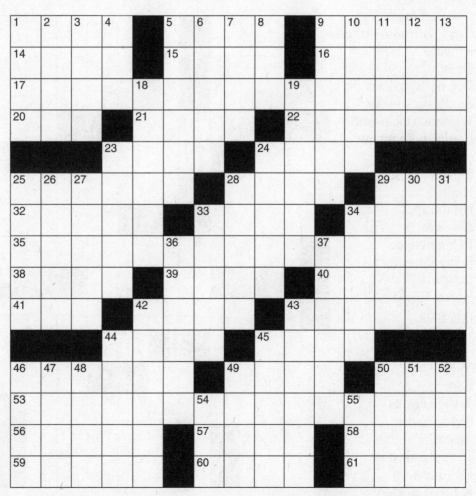

by Janet R. Bender

184

ACROSS
1 Sign at an A.T.M.
5 Smooth
11 Afternoon social
14 Slender instrument
15 Without delay
16 Columnist Buchwald
17 Actress Moore
18 Ringers
20 Freshwater fish with silvery scales
22 For each
23 Cone producer
25 Punch hard
28 Tiny bit
29 Ringers
33 Actress Hatcher
34 Vessel of 1492
35 Ringers
42 Calais concept
43 Ones with war stories
45 Ringers
51 Tater
52 Butcher's, baker's or candlestick maker's
53 Western tribe member
54 Equips with metal plating
57 Indispensable
59 Ringers
62 Hit the spot
65 Air hero
66 In abundance
67 Some investments, for short
68 Noted Turner
69 Aft ends
70 Certain cobras

DOWN
1 Cape __
2 Justice Fortas
3 Shade maker for a siesta
4 __ to the throne
5 Deli meat
6 Kind of clock or number
7 Additionally
8 Voter's finger stainer
9 Scholastic sports grp.
10 Cry of pain
11 Assume responsibility for
12 Raises
13 Confused
19 Late afternoon on a sundial
21 Educated guess: Abbr.
23 Hale
24 Checked a license, informally
26 Trigonometric function
27 Director Kazan
30 Quick drink
31 Old cable TV inits.
32 Jokester
36 Indy 500 locale
37 Summer N.Y. hrs.
38 Hula hoops?
39 A Gabor
40 Habitués
41 Manuscript annotation
44 Copenhagen-to-Prague dir.
45 Evergreen
46 All excited
47 Favorite
48 Rule
49 Showy blooms
50 Encountered
51 Nasser's successor
55 Semis
56 Ella Fitzgerald specialty
58 Largest of seven
60 Barley brew
61 Craggy prominence
63 Utilize
64 Double-180 maneuver

by Gene Newman

ACROSS

1 French cleric
5 Enthusiasm
9 Slightly open
13 "Time __," 1990s sci-fi TV series
14 1950s candidate Stevenson
16 Art __
17 56-Across figure
19 Bushy do
20 Birds' homes
21 Stabbed
23 Job application attachments
24 "Bird on __," 1990 Mel Gibson movie
25 Carrier to Sweden
26 Before: Abbr.
27 Necessary: Abbr.
30 __ Parks, former "Miss America" host
33 Two under par
34 Man's nickname that's an alphabetic run
35 W.C., in England
36 56-Across figure
38 Metal in rocks
39 Popular card game
40 When some TV news comes on
41 Change for a five
42 Superman's symbol
43 Brings into play
44 Singer Sumac
46 Faux pas
48 Fierce one
52 Vance of "I Love Lucy"
54 Place to buy a yacht
55 Mimicked
56 S. Dakota monument
58 __ of Man
59 Happening
60 Johnson who said "Ver-r-r-y interesting!"
61 Loads
62 Puts in extra
63 Spick and span

DOWN

1 Battling
2 Indian who may be 1-Down
3 Foundation
4 Tire out
5 Cutups
6 A sphere lacks them
7 Computer keys: Abbr.
8 Neighbor of a Vietnamese
9 Firefighter Red
10 56-Across figure
11 Farm unit
12 Crucifix
15 Place to dip an old pen
18 "__ la Douce," 1963 film
22 Actor David of "Separate Tables"
24 Laser gas
26 Walks outside the delivery room?
28 To be, in France
29 Opposite of an ans.
30 Ocean-colored
31 Millions of years
32 56-Across figure
33 Set foot in
36 Mrs. Bush
37 "My treat!"
41 One who rows, rows, rows the boat
44 Breadmakers' needs
45 Algebra or trig
47 Disney World attractions
48 Headed (for)
49 Taking out the trash, for one
50 Heart line
51 Chirp
52 Colorado resort
53 __ facto
54 Partner of born
57 Dam project: Abbr.

by Sherry O. Blackard

ACROSS

1 Retreats
7 Dry, as wine
10 It leaves marks on asphalt
14 Triumphant cry
15 Word often said twice before "again"
16 Numbers game
17 She wed George Washington
20 Niagara Falls' prov.
21 Karel Capek play
22 Church nooks
23 Where Washington relaxed
28 Wrath
29 Pi preceder
34 Friend in the Southwest
37 Forsaken
39 Ready for picking
40 State defense organization headed by Washington
43 Its flight attendants' greeting is "Shalom"
44 Magician's start
45 Word prefixed with poly-
46 Edison's New Jersey lab locale
48 "Welcome" site
49 Where Washington's forces wintered
55 Defense aid
59 Writer Fleming
60 Time Warner merger partner of 2001
61 Colonial force headed by Washington
66 __ Stanley Gardner
67 Belfry flier
68 __ corpus
69 Faculty head
70 Not just tear up
71 "Tristram Shandy" author

DOWN

1 Televised sign in football stands
2 Hersey's bell town
3 Love of artistic objects
4 D.C. summer clock setting
5 Fed. biomedical research agcy.
6 Deprive of food
7 Fab Four drummer
8 Directional suffix
9 Dancer Charisse
10 Old record problem
11 Popular sneakers
12 "Picnic" playwright
13 Female deer
18 __ date
19 Rajah's wife
24 Carp
25 "Star Trek: T.N.G." counselor
26 Bellini opera
27 Prefix with potent
30 "The Count of Monte __"
31 Film director Martin
32 Mayberry boy
33 Close
34 Swear to
35 Actor O'Shea
36 Investments usually held for yrs. and yrs.
37 Kind of suit found in a courtroom
38 Sculling need
41 Queen in "The Lion King"
42 Page (through)
47 Chapter 57
48 Avian talkers
50 Needing a good brushing, say
51 Ingest
52 Scarcer
53 Beatnik's encouragement
54 "Family Ties" mom
55 Served past
56 Oral tradition
57 "To Live and Die __"
58 Bingo call
62 Peacock network
63 Musical talent
64 Long.'s opposite
65 Face on a fiver

by Ed Early

ACROSS

1 Livens (up)
5 Snapshot
10 Bedazzles
14 Away from the wind
15 Home run king Hank
16 Retail store
17 Glib responses
19 On the ocean
20 Baffled
21 Canines or bicuspids
23 New Haven collegians
24 Personal bugbear
27 Observer
30 Quattros, e.g.
31 Some sports cars
34 Take into custody
37 Supreme Diana
38 Go bad
39 Indy service break
41 Sport __ (all-purpose vehicle)
42 Med. school subj.
44 Caviar source
45 Price add-on
46 Subway handhold
48 Make into law
50 Kind of stove
53 Smooch
56 Major company in metallic products
57 Drink often served with a lemon twist
60 Skin woe
62 Portfolio hedges
64 Eliot or Frost
65 One of the nine Muses
66 "Lohengrin" soprano
67 Drags
68 Heroic tales
69 Not shallow

DOWN

1 Mama's partner
2 Fill with joy
3 Flower feature
4 Protect, as freshness
5 Free ticket
6 Hems' partners
7 Source of iron or lead
8 Rich pastry
9 Beginning
10 Not an expert
11 Exhausted
12 Before, in verse
13 Depot: Abbr.
18 "Forget it!"
22 Clean air org.
24 "Blue Hawaii" star
25 Far-reaching view
26 "The Private Lives of Elizabeth and __" (1939 film)
28 Common newspaper nickname
29 Art Deco designer
31 Understand
32 Jay Silverheels role
33 Go back to square one
35 Surprise greatly
36 Roman robe
40 Bundle
43 Things held by Moses
47 Chest muscle, for short
49 Neatened
51 Easy strides
52 Designer Ashley
54 Item worn around the shoulders
55 Pick up on
57 Teensy bit
58 Navy noncoms, for short
59 "Rush!" order
60 It may be a walk-up: Abbr.
61 Dove's sound
63 Children's game

by Marjorie Berg

188

ACROSS

1 Film mogul Louis B. (whose company mascot was 26-Across)
6 "Funny!"
10 Hard to fluster
14 Mrs. David O. Selznick, daughter of 1-Across
15 Assist in wrongdoing
16 Hodgepodge
17 One lacking courage
19 On the briny
20 __ Tuesday
21 Take the first step
23 Poland's Walesa
25 Tam sporter
26 Roarer in film intros
29 Sty fare
31 Eucalyptus-loving "bears"
35 Drive-thru dispenser, maybe
36 Gazetteer statistic
38 Sporty Mazda
39 Courage seeker in a 1939 film
43 Top man in the choir?
44 __ proprietor
45 SSW's opposite
46 Fake
48 Crowe's "A Beautiful Mind" role
50 Suffix with chariot
51 Pack and send
53 Reply to "That so?"
55 Deuterium and tritium, to hydrogen
59 Make unreadable, for security
63 Island near Java
64 One feigning courage
66 Tied in score
67 "__ homo"
68 Put __ in one's ear
69 An earth sci.
70 Not fake
71 Cake sections

DOWN

1 Fail to catch
2 Keystone's place
3 Reunion number
4 Sign up
5 Superman player George
6 Barn loft contents
7 Basics
8 Puts on the burner
9 Tear into
10 Formal jacket feature
11 What's more
12 In __ of
13 A drawbridge may span one
18 Render harmless, perhaps, to 26-Across's kin
22 Hardly cramped
24 Round dances
26 Starbucks order
27 Old anesthetic
28 Prophetic signs
30 Argentina's Juan
32 Frankie or Cleo
33 Do penance
34 Less dotty
37 Ike's two-time opponent
40 Exerting little effort
41 Straight: Prefix
42 Former Georgia governor Maddox
47 Sleeping bag closer
49 Suggest subtly
52 Treaty result
54 "Star Wars" genre
55 "__ to differ"
56 Except for
57 Promise product
58 Shelter org.
60 Gape at
61 Whitetail, e.g.
62 Notable times
65 Slithery swimmer

by Gilbert H. Ludwig

ACROSS

1 Look (at), as stars
5 Artist's suffix with land or sea
10 Tortoiselike
14 "__ Around" (#1 Beach Boys hit)
15 Breaking a bad one is good
16 El __, Tex.
17 __-a-brac
18 Big kitchen appliance maker
19 Eight, in Spain
20 Wife of King David
22 Prepare to pop the question
23 Nova Scotia clock setting: Abbr.
24 June 14
26 Hamburger meat
30 Peter who is an eight-time Oscar nominee
32 Last full month of summer
34 Departure's opposite: Abbr.
35 Penny
39 Cheater's aid
40 Yellowish shade
42 Asian nurse
43 President before Wilson
44 Australian hopper, for short
45 Igloo dweller
47 "To be or not to be" soliloquist
50 Woman of "Troy"
51 One taking flight
54 That, in Tijuana
56 Scent
57 "Days of Our Lives," for one
63 "The World According to __"
64 Ne plus __
65 Slightly
66 Feminine suffix
67 Full . . . and happy about it
68 Mideast's __ Strip
69 Active one
70 Cursed
71 School before middle school: Abbr.

DOWN

1 Any of the Bee Gees
2 Taj Mahal site
3 Time, in Mannheim
4 Work on glass, say
5 Former Iranian leaders
6 Awoke
7 Basic rhyme scheme
8 "H.M.S. __"
9 Third letter after delta
10 Light dessert
11 Donned skates, e.g., with "up"
12 Actor Milo
13 Sheeplike
21 Declares
22 __ Kan (pet food)
25 Peter who played Mr. Moto
26 Agreement
27 Atmosphere
28 End-of-week cry
29 Noisy public speaker
31 California/Nevada lake
33 Singer nicknamed the Velvet Fog
36 Oscar winner Jannings
37 Partner of rank and serial number
38 Ending with tele-
41 Side dish at KFC
46 "Scram!"
48 Old Turkish title
49 Ripper
51 Ran amok
52 Poetry Muse
53 Talent
55 Ditchdigger's tool
58 Director Preminger
59 Newspaper unit
60 And others, in footnotes
61 Completely demolish
62 One who raised Cain
64 Inits. in Navy ship names

by Christina Houlihan Kelly

190

ACROSS

1 Actor Damon
5 Great buy, slangily
10 Go yachting
14 Met solo
15 Inventor Nikola
16 Ides of March utterance
17 Timid creature
18 Big name in chips
19 "Hud" Oscar winner
20 Actor Ben with the gang?
23 __-mo
25 Cornhusker State: Abbr.
26 Like good soil
27 Chops to bits
29 Best Actress winner for "Million Dollar Baby"
31 Really enjoyed
32 Democratic honcho Howard
33 Roadside sign
36 Marathoner Frank with candy?
40 Layer?
41 Richly adorn
42 Easy mark
43 Nutty as a fruitcake
45 Motor City hoopster
46 Mel Ott, notably
48 Several eras
49 Unlock, poetically
50 Novelist Evan with a small smooch?
54 Man Friday, e.g.
55 Publicist's concern
56 Workbook segment
59 Puts into play
60 "Our Gang" dog
61 Mower maker
62 Document content
63 Dorm annoyance
64 Cashless deal

DOWN

1 "Spy vs. Spy" magazine
2 "You __ here"
3 Gets soused
4 Pucker-producing
5 Metro entrances
6 Potato sack wt., maybe
7 Renaissance family name
8 K.C. Royal, e.g.
9 Space cadet's place
10 Author/illustrator Maurice
11 First-stringers
12 Europe's "boot"
13 Quiet time
21 Like a stumblebum
22 __ compos mentis
23 Not just a success
24 Like a ballerina
28 Despicable sort
29 Serta competitor
30 Harry Potter accessory
32 Icicle former
33 Become familiar with
34 Fabulous author
35 "Funny Girl" composer Jule
37 Voyages in vain?
38 Place for a title
39 Used to be
43 Up-to-the-minute
44 White Monopoly bill
45 "I yam what I yam" speaker
46 False front
47 Encyclopedia volume
48 Landscaper's tool
50 __ monde
51 "You said it!"
52 Defense grp.
53 Roster removals
57 Lyrical Gershwin
58 Blouse, e.g.

by Deb Amlen

ACROSS

1 Baldwin of the silver screen
5 Recur, as arthritis
10 Father of Seth
14 Actress Hatcher
15 Computer item with a tracking ball
16 Aura being picked up
17 Possibly prompting a reply like 25-, 47- or 62-Across
20 Supersede
21 Immature insects
22 Rink surface
23 Rep.'s opponent
24 Singer Sumac
25 "What?!"
31 Companion of Tarzan
32 It's good only for its waste value
33 T-bone or porterhouse
37 Not so much
39 Noted Tombstone family, once
41 Ancient Roman censor
42 Like beer at a bar
44 River's mouth
46 Sign outside a hit show
47 "What?!"
50 Railroad stop: Abbr.
53 End of a proof
54 Chem. thread
55 Meat-packing pioneer
57 Chosen one
62 "What?!"
64 Slugger Sammy
65 Sailor's "Halt!"
66 "The Thin Man" wife
67 European car
68 Nigeria's largest city
69 Son of Seth

DOWN

1 "__ additional cost!"
2 Pope after Benedict IV
3 Folies Bergère designer
4 Kind of acid
5 Atmosphere, as in a restaurant
6 For both sexes
7 Toothpaste holder
8 "It's no __!"
9 Shotgun shot
10 State unequivocally
11 Split (up)
12 At right angles to a ship
13 Jason's ally and lover, in myth
18 Killer whales
19 Poetic feet
23 Horse with a spotted coat
25 Sign of a saint
26 Unlock
27 Toward sunset
28 Swapped
29 Sheik's bevy
30 And others: Abbr.
34 Facility
35 Gillette brand
36 Wacko
38 Problem with an old sofa
40 Hollywood hopefuls
43 Resentment
45 "Li'l __" (Al Capp strip)
48 Springlike
49 "Phèdre" playwright
50 Final approval
51 Custer cluster
52 Entertain
56 Kind of history
57 For men only
58 Studebaker's fill-up, maybe
59 Daffy Duck or Porky Pig
60 Continental currency
61 Those: Sp.
63 Eggs

by Robert Malinow

192

ACROSS

1 Frisks, with "down"
5 Muhammad's birthplace
10 Elisabeth of "Leaving Las Vegas"
14 Ranch unit
15 Pong maker
16 Hoopster Malone
17 "All I Wanna Do" singer, 1994
19 Toledo's lake
20 Pekoe server
21 Luggage attachment
23 Threw in
24 French article
26 Like woolen underwear?
27 Salsa scooper-uppers
29 Sun. delivery
30 Yeats or Keats
33 Boys' or girls' room, in London
34 Attack by plane
37 Cleansed (of)
38 First U.S. chief justice
40 Hide-hair link
41 No longer in style
43 Press for payment
44 Palm reader, e.g.
45 Hither's partner
46 Rigid bracelet
48 Bill of fare
50 Needle hole
51 Gut course
55 All riled up
57 Rich's partner
58 Say "Uncle!"
59 "Network" star
62 On the ocean
63 No longer in style
64 Add kick to
65 Flat rate?
66 Actor Davis
67 Chapters of history

DOWN

1 Orzo, e.g.
2 Had a yen
3 Radial pattern
4 Eve's tempter
5 Fountain offering
6 Catchall abbr.
7 Cougar or Lynx
8 Hags
9 Sony competitor
10 Summer pest, informally
11 "The Bridge" poet
12 Dickens's — Heep
13 Mournful poem
18 Luke Skywalker's mentor
22 Like the air around Niagara Falls
24 "Looks like trouble!"
25 Lunchtime, for many
28 Congealment
30 Country club figure
31 Mideast export
32 Singer with the 1988 #1 country hit "I'm Gonna Get You"
34 Acted the fink
35 Antagonist
36 Flub
38 Leigh of "Psycho"
39 Month for many Geminis
42 Difficult spot
44 Mariner's measure
46 Guardian Angels toppers
47 Table extension
48 New dad's handout
49 Biscotti flavoring
52 Salvage ship's equipment
53 New Mexico's state flower
54 Cookout leftovers?
56 — facto
57 For the asking
60 Profs' helpers
61 Yalie

by Gail Grabowski

193

ACROSS

1 Brown shade used in old photos
6 Having protected feet
10 Postal delivery
14 Deal maker
15 2:00 or 3:00
16 Skin breakout
17 Head/legs separator
18 Cathedral area
19 Box office take
20 Short-lived success
23 Affirm
26 Congo, formerly
27 Lunch or dinner
28 Hand: Sp.
31 Furthermore
32 Vintage designation
33 Oscar winner for "Scent of a Woman"
35 Short-lived success
40 Octagons, hexagons, etc.
41 The "E" of Q.E.D.
43 Greek cross
46 "__ a man with seven wives"
47 Counterpart of midterms
49 Mary of old films
51 Close of a swimming race
52 Short-lived success
56 10th-grader, for short
57 Skater Lipinski
58 Ballet rail
62 Cleveland's lake
63 Give off
64 Elicit
65 What a detective follows
66 Kind of room
67 Paper size larger than "letter"

DOWN

1 Used a pew
2 Swelled head
3 The "p" of r.p.m.
4 To the degree that
5 Makes amends
6 Former Iranian rulers
7 Mesa dweller
8 Evict
9 Picked from the stack of cards
10 __ cum laude
11 Maine's __ National Park
12 Summer office worker
13 Looked lecherously
21 Founded: Abbr.
22 Atmosphere layer
23 Be inquisitive
24 Atoll protector
25 Iridescent gem
28 "Olympia" painter
29 Deeds
30 Disease research org.
33 Prop for Santa
34 Nafta concept
36 Collar site
37 Lunch meat
38 Asia's shrinking __ Sea
39 "The Lion King" lion
42 Cooking meas.
43 It's on the fringe
44 Toward land
45 Perfect world
47 Blubber
48 Sanford of "The Jeffersons"
50 Marveled aloud
51 Atty.-to-be exams
53 News bit
54 Tattle on
55 Small beam
59 Alternative to a bare floor
60 "His Master's Voice" sloganeer
61 Sushi fish

by Mike Torch

194

ACROSS

1 Hardwood tree
4 Nosed (out)
9 With 69-Across, song from 20-Across
14 Give the umpire grief
15 Mr. Moto player
16 Kid's retort
17 Big inits. in TV comedy
18 1979 musical about a half-mad barber
20 1970 musical about marriage
22 Fury
23 U.S.: Abbr.
24 See 51-Across
29 Container with a screw-top
33 ___ vera
34 Some toy trucks
37 Head of Haiti
38 Broadway composer (of 18-, 20- and 57-Across) born 3/22/1930
43 Rime
44 Oklahoma native
45 "Wishing won't make ___"
46 Encounter, as success
51 With 24-Across, song from 18-Across
55 Height: Prefix
56 Wallach of "The Magnificent Seven"
57 1971 musical about a reunion
60 Song from 57-Across
65 Unforgettable Cole
66 Army inspection?
67 Giant
68 Bell Atlantic merger partner of 2000
69 See 9-Across
70 Refine, as metal
71 One of the Chaplins

DOWN

1 Early '80s political scandal
2 California winemaking county
3 Noted resident of Baker Street
4 "Born Free" lioness
5 Like the answer to this clue
6 Lady Jane ___
7 Before, in verse
8 Jeans material
9 Aspirin maker
10 CPR giver, for short
11 Skater Midori
12 Give the go-ahead
13 The Almighty
19 Noteworthy time
21 Specialist
24 Annoying
25 It's sworn at a swearing-in
26 Peter Fonda title role
27 Reply to the Little Red Hen
28 Consider
30 Utmost
31 Average guys
32 ___ Domini
35 First-rate
36 Old dagger
38 Climb, as a pole
39 Canine from Kansas
40 Bridge hand
41 Ship's front
42 Richard Gere title role
47 ___-Mart
48 Cake toppers
49 Pact
50 Entertained
52 "Die Lorelei" poet
53 Under the weather
54 Light rhythms
57 Party
58 Kind of exam
59 Advanced
60 C.D. holder, maybe
61 Alice's sitcom boss
62 H.S. course
63 "Mazel ___!"
64 Not her

by David J. Kahn

ACROSS

1 Is in a play
5 Layers
11 Tool with teeth
14 Jacket
15 Rang, as bells
16 Swiss canton
17 Famous large deep-blue rock
19 Brooch
20 An hour before midnight
21 Illegally seized
23 Filled with joy
26 Game played on 64 squares
27 Say more
30 Sly maneuver
31 Prophet
32 Make void
34 Money in Mexico
36 Strikebreaker
39 Shows for the first time
41 Yield to desire
43 Similar (to)
44 Cry in court
46 Ordinary
47 Pub projectile
49 Prosperity
51 Maidenform product
52 Hindu social division
54 Admit to wrongdoing
56 Calm down
58 Injuries near beehives
62 Savings for old age, for short
63 Military decoration
66 Get __ of (toss out)
67 Rubs out
68 "Bye"
69 Cheer for a matador
70 Puts trust in, with "on"
71 Site of Napoleon's exile

DOWN

1 Dull hurt
2 Refrigerate
3 Put on reel-to-reel
4 Jobs in the computer field
5 Kind of column
6 Alternative to coffee
7 Male sheep
8 For all to hear
9 Sawbucks
10 Bring forth as evidence
11 Site for eating and entertainment
12 7-Down, astrologically
13 Orchestra section
18 Greek oracle site
22 Kind of monkey
24 __-turvy
25 Hurricane's center
27 Shade of blue
28 Drop, as a doughnut in milk
29 "Just Shoot Me" co-star
31 Daughter's opposite
33 Half of Congress
35 Medium, large and extra-large
37 Ice cream thickening agent
38 Lugosi who played Dracula
40 Hollywood filming locale
42 Minnesota port
45 7-Down's mate
48 Autumn farm worker
50 Estimate the value of
52 Egypt's capital
53 Shower bringer
54 Wild
55 Jigsaw puzzle element
57 Without a doubt
59 Hammer's target
60 Take hold of
61 Portico in Greek architecture
64 Letter before omega
65 __ jeans

by Elizabeth Babikan

196

ACROSS

1 Stared stupidly
6 Light bulb units
11 Sweetums
14 Simple counters
15 Potato growers' home
16 Big galoot
17 Convince a G.I.?
19 Cause to fret
20 Peruvian range
21 Not naked
23 Was dependent
26 Bunt result, maybe
27 Like the Wolfman
28 It goes under a top
30 "The Republic" philosopher
31 Work units
32 Secure position
34 Baseball bat wood
35 Random attack
36 Evidence in a paternity suit
39 No pieces of cake
41 Masterstroke
42 Water balloon sound
44 Wind up or down
45 Tropical lizard
46 "As Good As It Gets" film studio
48 Hit on the noggin
49 Gymnast Mary Lou
50 Go-between
52 Frequently, in verse
53 Refuse to work on the weekend?
58 Actor Billy __ Williams
59 Gives off
60 Hosiery shade
61 Blunder
62 "Belling the Cat" author
63 Casino array

DOWN

1 Burner fuel
2 Justice Fortas
3 Chum
4 Elongated pastries
5 Mickey Mouse operation?
6 Sly trick
7 Tacks on
8 Mai __
9 Bara of old films
10 Touchy subject
11 Dine on some fish?
12 Gift-giver's urging
13 Abutting
18 Uneven?
22 Unit in a terrorist organization
23 Perlman of "Cheers"
24 Corn units
25 Burn trash?
26 Washed
28 Irritate
29 Violinist's application
32 London forecast
33 Sounds from Santa
35 Set sail
37 Microwave, slangily
38 Like two peas in __
40 Hops-drying oven
41 Like some air-conditioning
42 Walked briskly
43 Like better
45 Rant and rave
47 Japanese cartoon art
48 Track action
50 Concerning
51 [You don't mean . . . !]
54 Rejoinder to "'Tain't!"
55 Dynamic __
56 Quick to learn
57 Thumbs-up response

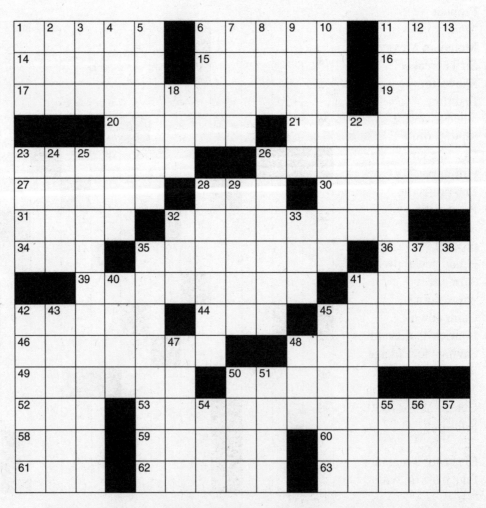

by Victor Fleming and Nelson Hardy

ACROSS

1 Boss
6 Pepsi, for one
10 Not check or charge
14 Event with bucking broncos
15 Banned orchard spray
16 Prefix with suction
17 Woody of "Manhattan"
18 Take a breather
19 Norway's capital
20 "See you later"
21 Check mate?
24 Beyond doubt
25 Some linens
26 Balance beam?
31 "Yow!"
32 Cry heard on a fairway
33 Catch, as a perp
36 Before-test work, informally
37 Simple song
39 Super-duper
40 Brit. word reference
41 Ferris wheel or bumper cars
42 Join
43 Firm offer?
46 Illinois city symbolizing middle America
49 Refusals
50 Vegas spread?
53 Person in a zebra-striped shirt, informally
56 Opposite of gave
57 Whom the cheerleaders cheer
58 Hit musical set in Argentina
60 __ fixe (obsession)
61 Suffix with major
62 Katey of "Married . . . With Children"
63 Loch __ monster
64 Film unit
65 Stable enclosure

DOWN

1 One who complains, complains, complains
2 "__ smokes!"
3 Doing nothing
4 Wide shoe designation
5 Cheese dishes
6 Aladdin's transportation
7 Butter substitute
8 Glasgow gal
9 Beautiful skill
10 Deal finalizer
11 Grocery pathway
12 Leave, slangily
13 B-ball
22 Mess up
23 "How do I love __?"
24 Tread
26 Mispelled, for misspelled, e.g.
27 Irish republic
28 Barely made, with "out"
29 Frequently
30 Kiddie
33 Pinot __ (wine)
34 Voting no
35 When repeated, Road Runner's sound
37 Fiasco
38 Dictator Amin
39 Relatives of termites
41 Completely botch
42 Futile
43 Car stoppers
44 Tooth layer
45 Boar's mate
46 Yeltsin's successor as leader of Russia
47 Eat away at
48 Woodwinds
51 Red Rose
52 $5.15/hour, e.g.
53 Latvia's capital
54 Footnote abbr.
55 Autumn
59 Dyemaker's container

by Christina Houlihan Kelly

ACROSS

1 Throat problem
5 Amorphous movie monster
9 "Quo ___?"
14 Prom night wheels
15 Capital of Italia
16 "No way!"
17 Dermal flare-up
18 Black-bordered news item
19 More up-to-date
20 "Right now!"
23 Gun rights grp.
24 Mandela's org.
25 Rte. recommenders
26 Porker's place
27 Death, to Dylan Thomas
33 Fam. member
34 Morales of "NYPD Blue"
35 Newsman Jim
38 Steams up
40 Where a train pulls in: Abbr.
42 Lamarr of film
43 Hobo's ride, perhaps
46 Ad award
49 Book collector's suffix
50 Part of a love triangle
53 Hole number
55 Friend of Pooh
56 Monument of lexicography, for short
57 Poem of Sappho
58 Hint to the starts of 20-, 27- and 50-Across
64 Innocent ones
66 Mock words of understanding
67 Appear to be
68 Bridge bid, briefly
69 Skirt to twirl in
70 Opposite of "Out!"
71 Rustic

72 Louisiana, e.g., in Orléans
73 "Vissi d'___"

DOWN

1 Pitched too low
2 Rolling in dough
3 Prefix with science
4 Attacks
5 Mile High City team
6 Arcing shots
7 Cut out
8 Philippine peninsula
9 Old, to a car buff
10 Leave speechless
11 Toward the mouth
12 Like krypton
13 Alley cat, perhaps
21 "Bus Stop" playwright
22 Place for some polish
27 "Lou Grant" paper, with "the"
28 One who saves the day
29 His questions are answers
30 Western treaty grp.
31 Deep-six
32 Loser to R.M.N., 1968
36 Author Ferber
37 Meg of "In the Cut"
39 P.T.A. meeting place: Abbr.
41 Inn take
44 Deodorant type

45 Crucifix
47 Resolve, as differences
48 Wasn't in the black
51 So far
52 Black Sea port
53 N'awlins sandwich
54 Hersey's bell town
59 Seal up
60 "The Thin Man" dog
61 Within reach
62 Like a pickpocket's fingers
63 "Peter Pan" pirate
65 Hydrocarbon suffix

by Harvey Estes

ACROSS

1 False god
5 Overly hasty
9 Huge ice chunks
14 Nervously irritable
15 Comic Sandler
16 Mrs. Bush
17 Despot Idi __
18 String tie
19 Houston baseballer
20 Gentle/not gentle
23 Stops from yo-yoing
24 Conqueror of 1066 England
28 The "I" of T.G.I.F.
29 Old what's-__-name
30 Relative of beer
31 1960s radical Hoffman
35 Interval
36 Assert
37 Former pupil/present pupil
41 Stitch's cartoon pal
42 Closemouthed
43 Twinges
44 Serious drug cases, for short
45 "Man's best friend"
46 Fortune 500 listings: Abbr.
48 Firearm, e.g.
50 Loving touches
55 Furious/not furious
57 Fire starter
60 Inch or teaspoon
61 Measure (out)
62 Having a close resemblance
63 Longtime Yugoslav leader
64 Sign to interpret
65 The present
66 Harry Potter's lightning bolt
67 Rome's fifth emperor

DOWN

1 Grins widely
2 Let in
3 Nimble
4 __ Carter, who played Wonder Woman
5 Cottontail
6 Loves to pieces
7 Casa parts
8 Group insurance grps.
9 Taste sensation
10 Light in a light show
11 Not at home
12 Say 2 + 2 = 5, say
13 __ Paulo, Brazil
21 Parisian goodbye
22 Bumbling
25 Expert
26 "I knew it all __!"
27 Bright salamanders
29 Consumes
31 Luminous
32 One who says 34-Down
33 Model builder's wood
34 Wedding declaration
35 Precious stone
36 Org. for cavity fillers
38 In the middle of
39 Harbor boat
40 Unexpected sports outcome
45 Democratic Party symbol
46 Per __ (each)
47 Lincoln, e.g., at Gettysburg
49 Arctic jacket
50 Sour sort
51 __ Says (child's game)
52 "If they could __ now . . ."
53 Start, as school
54 Shorthand taker
56 Boring routines
57 Was in session
58 Mahmoud Abbas's grp.
59 Pitch in for

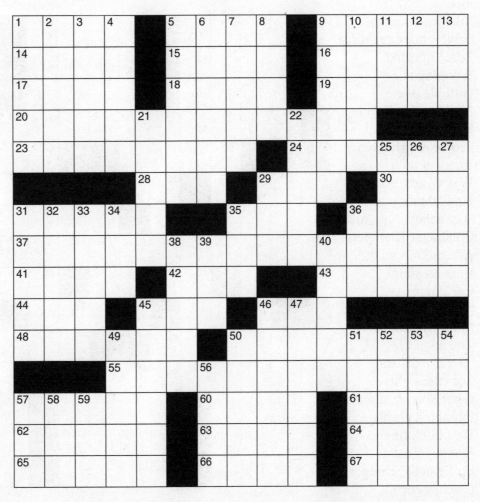

by Norma Steinberg

200

ACROSS
1 Insubstantial stuff
6 "Show Boat" novelist Ferber
10 Regarding
14 Cowpoke competition
15 Wiener schnitzel meat
16 Mix together
17 "That is to say . . ."
18 Eliel Saarinen's son
19 Huff and puff
20 Words following an oath, sometimes
23 Writer Roald
24 Take care of
25 Roman god of love
28 Like Easter eggs
31 Govt. code breakers
32 Peace of mind
34 Womanizer
36 Gullible one
39 Avoid technobabble
42 Something some people return from vacation with
43 WWW addresses
44 Paid attention to
45 "Casablanca" pianist
47 Conductor Klemperer
49 Afternoon socials
50 Russian plain
53 Cashmere, e.g.
55 "I didn't understand a thing you said"
60 The good life
61 "Roseanne" star
62 Sees the sights
64 Grandson of Adam
65 Plumbing problem
66 Blue book filler
67 Flat payment
68 Professional charges
69 Catches one's breath

DOWN
1 Work wk. ender, for most
2 Cakewalk
3 Old music halls
4 Pendant gem shape
5 Accord maker
6 Without highs and lows
7 Consider
8 __ a soul
9 Up in the air
10 Trembling trees
11 Get out of the way
12 Touch of color
13 Garden products brand
21 Words of a worrier
22 Weasel out (on)
25 Unable to move, after "in"
26 City near Phoenix
27 Legal hunting period
29 Dadaism pioneer Max
30 Buck's partner
33 Batting woes
35 Release, as a chain
37 Out of port
38 Highest degrees
40 Worldwide workers' grp.
41 Went wild
46 Most appropriate
48 Pipsqueaks
50 Have the helm
51 Macbeth's title
52 Treble clef lines
54 Aquatic mammal
56 Nearly unique in the world
57 Canal of song
58 Rumple
59 Word after quod
63 Method: Abbr.

by Nancy Salomon

The New York Times

SMART PUZZLES

Presented with Style

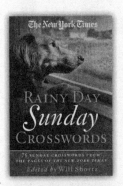 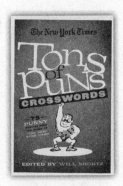  

 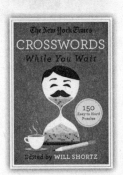  

Available at your local bookstore or online at www.nytimes.com/nytstore

St. Martin's Griffin

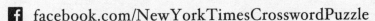
facebook.com/NewYorkTimesCrosswordPuzzle

1

```
E S S O   H A W K   A S P S
T I E R O L E O   G R E E K
H E X A   S E E P   A M A T I
E V E N S T E V E N S   L P S
L E D G E   I C U   Z E E
      E V E L K N I E V E L
U N P C   E O S   A L E V E
K E R O G E N   H A N D L E S
E V E R Y   G O V   A S S T
S E V E N E L E V E N
  R E D E A T   Y I P E S
R M N   A L L A B O U T E V E
H I T O N   A W O L   S T E N
E N E R O   L A R D   M E N S
A D D S     A Y E S   E R T E
```

2

```
O U T E R   F A Q   A B U S E
W H A M O A S U   F U G U E
L U M P S   T H E R A C H E L
S H A R I F   L A R K
    G E N I A L L Y   E T C H
U F O S   V I E   S A Y H E Y
S E T S   E R A   S E E M E
A N C   9 0 S F A D S   M E N
U N H I P   L I E   N A N A
S E I S M S   E W E   A C T S
A L S O   M E T A D A T A
    L O U D   S M U R F S
D R M A R T E N S   B R E A K
A C U T E   N I T   L A N C E
P A G E S   S L Y   E L A T E
```

3

```
I N A T R A P   S T R A N D S
M E S H U G A   T R A V A I L
F U S E B O X   J U N I P E R
I R E N E   S O C A L
N A T   S E T T H E T A B L E
E L S A   L O A N   Y E N
    S E O U L   S U I T E D
  O T T O P R E M I N G E R
S H R I N E   M A M I E
W H O   I A M B   R U N G
M I N U T E S T E A K   P A R
    S H A L E   A O R T A
A S S U A G E   F U R C O A T
H A I R N E T   A R M H O L E
H O P P E R S   B L A S T E R
```

4

```
S C A T   C A T T Y   T B A R
U H U H   A L O H A   H O P I
F E T A   P L A Y W R I G H T
I R O N W O O D   A N G I E
    K A N T   S E N   E D S
S I S S Y   B U T T E D
E D U   S H A R E H O L D E R
R E B A   E L U D E   M O R E
B A T T L E F I E L D   W I N
  L E A D I N   O W N E D
A L E   S S E   B O Z O
L A T K E   F I R E B I R D
G R I N D S T O N E   B L U E
A V E O   L A R G O   L I M B
E A S T   Y I K E S   Y A P S
```

5

```
A M O S   L U N G   J A W E D
L O R E   E T A L   E N A M I
M A C A D A M I A   S I T I N
S T A T E S O F M A T T E R
      B E S   W E A R
P A S H A   T U B E R   T A O
A L T A R S   T A I   M A N N
I C E S K A T I N G R I N K S
N O A H   I O C   H E C K L E
S A M   C L E A R   B E S E T
  B A R E   A P O
  S O L I D L I Q U I D G A S
D I A L S   E B U L L I E N T
O N T O P   D E E S   V E N D
Z E S T Y   A X L E   E K E S
```

6

```
L S D   S O F A   U N T I D Y
O U R   P O O L   N O O G I E
S M A S H H I T   W R O N G S
E M I L E   L A F I T T E
S E N O R A   R U S H H O U R
I R E   E L F   R E S   U S O
T Y R A   B U N T   E S S A Y
    T R A S H H E A P
A D I E U   S L E D   A P B S
R U N   T S P   R E T   R A T
F I S H H O O K   N E W E R A
  P U L L T A B   C A N I T
R E A M E D   H U S H H U S H
U N C A S T   L E A N   P T A
E V E N S O   O N T O   S A M
```

7

```
BOMB ■ ATALL ■ ATMS
ODIE ■ DETOO ■ COOK
BOCA ■ DEFOG ■ HOJO
ONADIET ■ SISENOR
■■ TRIBECA ■■
KOALA ■ MEN ■ PIQUE
AMIE ■ SENSE ■ DULL
TARGET ■■ DASANI
ORS ■ TOV ■ WAX ■ YAZ
■ HOMEGAMES ■
SPCA ■ PSATS ■ AMFM
LEAST ■ PIK ■ FLORA
ALPHABETIZATION
SLEEPER ■ NOWORSE
HARDEES ■ SONNETS
```

8

```
CASH ■ SLAPS ■ POSH
LUTE ■ TORAH ■ ANTE
ADAMSAPPLE ■ IBAR
SIMIAN ■ AMINOR ■
STING ■ HOTPOTATO
ION ■ APACE ■ WIRED
CRAB ■ ART ■ ANDRE
■ APPEALING ■
SPIRE ■ GIN ■ SATE
ARMED ■ ROMAN ■ MAX
TOPBANANA ■ EVENT
VIOLIN ■ EMERGE
FINN ■ GLASSONION
EDGE ■ HOPUP ■ ACED
ZEES ■ TWEEN ■ LADS
```

9

```
SETS ■ UHAUL ■ PSST
IGOT ■ SALSA ■ RITE
LADIESTEES ■ IDOS
ONAPAR ■ STEVENS
■ YET ■ LOU ■ LIBYA
AMOS ■ PANPIPE ■
FAN ■ AONE ■ NASSER
ALL ■ DOGLEGS ■ CRO
RIYADH ■ OSLO ■ OIL
■ LISSOME ■ JUNE
STERN ■ UKE ■ MAN
HALOGEN ■ CARDED
ISAK ■ GOLFCOURSE
ETTE ■ OCEAN ■ LEAK
DEER ■ SOOTY ■ ELIE
```

10

```
GOP ■ ADMITS ■ HIM
ONA ■ ONASSIS ■ ACE
TET ■ WAYNEKNIGHT
■ TRAIL ■ ISWEAR
CLEARSIGN ■ INTO
SURF ■ TASSEL ■
PISTOL ■ HEATLAMP
AGO ■ REF ■ CNN ■ NOR
NINEBALL ■ GASTRO
■ BEFAIR ■ HIED
TODO ■ PLAYBILLS
OHIOAN ■ NUOVA
BACKCOUNTRY ■ BAD
ERE ■ CARPETS ■ ODE
YES ■ THIRDS ■ ROW
```

11

```
PAID ■ EYE ■ MEDAL
DRNO ■ COX ■ DAREME
FENGSHUI ■ RUSSET
■ SHORTWINTERS
AUDIO ■ EPA ■ RIN
WHITEHOPE ■ LETGO
EFS ■ ACE ■ ONPOT
■ CRYSTALBALL ■
CURIE ■ BIO ■ AID
ONEAL ■ ROCKCANDY
MED ■ LAA ■ UNTIE
PAIROFJOKERS ■
OTTAWA ■ WENTWILD
SEEGER ■ NEV ■ EDGE
ENDED ■ SPY ■ ROAN
```

12

```
CARGO ■ EPS ■ PANTS
ABHOR ■ NEO ■ ACURA
SLOPE ■ CRU ■ RODIN
KEMO ■ CHORE ■ RIPE
■ BOWLINGLANE ■
■ FOUL ■ RAPS ■
TSP ■ REALALE ■ PTA
ATOLL ■ DIP ■ SWIRL
MOOED ■ ATE ■ UNTIL
PALACES ■ SKIBAGS
■ THUR ■ ATAB ■
BRA ■ POCKETS ■ RAT
LABS ■ IRISH ■ LENO
UGLY ■ CANTI ■ OATS
RUED ■ AWGEE ■ ODES
```

13

A	T	H	O	L		S	A	S		A	S	L	A	N
S	H	A	M	U		T	U	T		C	H	A	M	P
F	R	Y	E	R		E	R	A		C	R	Y	E	R
O	E	R		E	F	R	O	N		R	E	A	R	
R	E	I	N	D	E	E	R		S	A	W	B	I	T
M	A	D	E		L	O	A	M	Y		D	E	C	K
E	M	E	R	I	L		S	A	N	D		T	A	O
		D	O	F	F		I	D	I	D				
S	T	P		C	L	U	B		R	O	O	T	L	E
S	H	A	M		A	L	A	M	O		W	H	A	M
W	R	Y	E	S	T		H	A	M	O	N	R	Y	E
	O	H	N	O		D	R	Y	E	R		E	E	R
S	W	E	A	R		O	A	T		F	E	A	T	S
P	I	E	C	E		N	I	A		E	N	D	T	O
A	N	D	E	S		A	N	G		O	L	S	E	N

14

G	L	I	B		C	R	I	M	E		F	O	U	R
R	O	M	A		A	E	S	O	P		A	N	N	A
O	N	A	N		S	E	A	B	I	S	C	U	I	T
K	I	C	K	B	A	C	K		P	A	S	T	E	
		R	U	B	E		C	H	A	D				
Z	A	D	O	R	A		G	O	O	D	E	G	G	
E	X	A	L	T		B	E	L	L	E		O	E	R
S	I	L	L		B	R	E	A	D		M	A	N	E
T	O	E		S	E	U	S	S		M	E	T	R	E
	M	Y	S	P	A	C	E		W	E	A	S	E	L
	L	A	K	E		N	A	S	T					
O	A	S	I	S		C	A	P	S	L	O	C	K	
S	T	U	D	M	U	F	F	I	N		O	P	E	N
H	O	M	E		G	R	O	V	E		A	E	R	O
A	M	O	R		H	O	S	E	R		F	L	A	X

15

S	P	A	R		D	R	E		N	E	S	T	S	
O	U	T	E	R	E	A	R		M	I	N	T	E	D
P	R	O	V	I	D	E	R		A	P	R	O	N	S
P	E	L	O	S	I		A	E	S	O	P			
Y	E	L	L		C	A	R	D	S		B	O	S	S
	T	I	A	R	A	S		H	E	R	T	Z		
A	T	T		S	T	E	W		M	I	D	D	I	E
P	A	W		H	E	A	D	S	U	P		E	L	L
P	H	O	B	O	S		E	A	R	P		R	E	L
T	O	B	A	T		S	A	I	D	O	K			
S	E	A	L		T	U	L	L	E		E	L	I	S
	G	L	A	R	E		R	E	N	A	T	A		
F	I	G	A	R	O		E	C	O	N	O	M	I	C
I	C	E	D	I	N		S	A	N	D	B	A	N	K
B	U	R	S	A		E	V	E		I	R	A	S	

16

A	B	A	N	G		K	I	T	E		I	T	I	N
L	E	R	O	I		A	D	I	N		B	O	N	O
L	A	N	T	Z		B	O	T	T	O	M	R	O	W
S	T	E	A	M	R	O	L	L	E	R		E	R	A
E	L	S		O	E	O		E	R	R		O	B	I
T	E	S	S		M	M	L	I		S	P	I	T	
	C	S	I		E	S	T	R	E	E	T			
	M	R	I	N	B	E	T	W	E	E	N			
	F	O	U	N	D	E	R		E	D	Y			
C	L	U	B		H	Y	P	E		A	S	H	E	
O	U	R		A	M	O		O	Z	S		T	O	G
L	M	N		P	A	L	M	R	E	A	D	I	N	G
A	M	F	M	R	A	D	I	O		R	I	L	E	D
D	O	U	R		M	E	N	U		A	N	T	S	Y
A	X	L	E		S	R	I	S		H	A	S	T	E

17

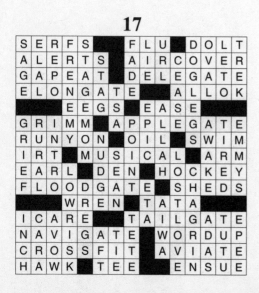

S	E	R	F	S		F	L	U		D	O	L	T	
A	L	E	R	T	S		A	I	R	C	O	V	E	R
G	A	P	E	A	T		D	E	L	E	G	A	T	E
E	L	O	N	G	A	T	E		A	L	L	O	K	
		E	E	G	S		E	A	S	E				
G	R	I	M	M		A	P	P	L	E	G	A	T	E
R	U	N	Y	O	N		O	I	L		S	W	I	M
I	R	T		M	U	S	I	C	A	L		A	R	M
E	A	R	L		D	E	N		H	O	C	K	E	Y
F	L	O	O	D	G	A	T	E		S	H	E	D	S
	W	R	E	N		T	A	T	A					
I	C	A	R	E		T	A	I	L	G	A	T	E	
N	A	V	I	G	A	T	E		W	O	R	D	U	P
C	R	O	S	S	F	I	T		A	V	I	A	T	E
H	A	W	K		T	E	E		E	N	S	U	E	

18

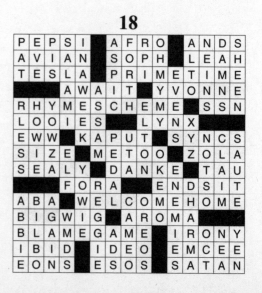

P	E	P	S	I		A	F	R	O		A	N	D	S
A	V	I	A	N		S	O	P	H		L	E	A	H
T	E	S	L	A		P	R	I	M	E	T	I	M	E
	A	W	A	I	T		Y	V	O	N	N	E		
R	H	Y	M	E	S	C	H	E	M	E		S	S	N
L	O	O	I	E	S		L	Y	N	X				
E	W	W		K	A	P	U	T		S	Y	N	C	S
S	I	Z	E		M	E	T	O	O		Z	O	L	A
S	E	A	L	Y		D	A	N	K	E		T	A	U
	F	O	R	A		E	N	D	S	I	T			
A	B	A		W	E	L	C	O	M	E	H	O	M	E
B	I	G	W	I	G		A	R	O	M	A			
B	L	A	M	E	G	A	M	E		I	R	O	N	Y
I	B	I	D		I	D	E	O		E	M	C	E	E
E	O	N	S		E	S	O	S		S	A	T	A	N

19

```
A B E D   A B A F T   A B C S
L E V I   R I D E R   L O U T
B E E S   M O O L A   E Z R A
A B R A H A M S L I N C O L N
    G E N E     N U T
    H A R R I S O N S F O R D
R A Z E D   R E E F   O U T
C I T E   P I C O T   B A B E
A T E   L E D A   C O R A L
  I C H I R O S S U Z U K I
    Y E S     O N A N
F R E D D I E S M E R C U R Y
R E A R   A R U B A   E T A L
O S S O   N I M E S   R A G E
S T Y X   S C O R E   S H A M
```

20

```
S O Y A   C O S T S   P R E K
A S E C   D O N H O   L A C E
A L O H A S H I R T   A S H E
B O W E N   P A R T Y H O P
    F E E D   S U E D
S H O W M E T H E M O N E Y
H O U R   M F A   P H O N E
A D M   B A Y M A R E   I D A
L O O I E   E M O   A C E R
F I R S T R E S P O N D E R
    S T A N   S T U D
S E Q U E N C E   N I N E S
C L U E   G O L D E N C A L F
A L I T   I R K E D   T R I P
R E P O   N E O N S   S C A D
```

21

```
A B C S   C L O W N   I N S O
H A H A   A E G I S   S E E R
S L A V   E A R L W E A V E R
  C T A   S K E D   D I A S
J O H N J A Y     D A D A S
I N A N E R   T O N Y H A W K
M Y M A N   S A A B   N S A
  H A R T C R A N E
E N S   O U I S   O A S E S
T O M S W I F T   M O R A L E
C R E P E     B I R D M A N
  I L E A   M O O G   R A P
P E T E R F I N C H   U R S A
A G E D   E L E C T   M I E N
W A D S   N O S E Y   S A D O
```

22

```
I D I N G   T I M E   K A L B
M A N I A   A N E W   A M I E
B R O K E N B O N E   B E B E
E E N   L E O I   M O N E T
A M I N   V O L L E Y B A L L
T E T O N   A L A   B E E
  T E A P O T S   O L D S
  D I N N E R T A B L E
S P O T   T A K E S T O
P A N   A I R   U R B A N
A L A R M C L O C K   D O P E
M E T O O   R H E A   O P S
M A I A   W E R E A L L S E T
E L O N   A R I A   M E T A L
D E N S   R E N T   A I S L E
```

23

```
B E A D   I P O D   D O G G Y
A X L E   S A R A   A T L A S
R E D L E T T E R   S T O V E
S C O W S   H O T S H O W E R
    E T R E S   H E M
H A S B R O   S O D A P O P
A I R B U B B L E   N A P A
U L T   S E A B E E S   G R R
L E A S   H O R S E M E A T
S Y S T E M S   T R A S H Y
    P D A   S P E E D
B O N E W H I T E   N E R V E
E V I T A   G O O N A H E A D
D E T E R   O R N E   A N N A
S N E R D   R E S T   Y E S M
```

24

```
H A S H   H O L E   R E H A B
E L M O   A M E N   E R O D E
R O U T   L I A M   P I V O T
B U T T O F T H E J O K E
    E L M   S O S   R A T
  H E A D O F T H E T A B L E
S E X   S O A R   S T O O P
P A P A   N A A C P   M A H I
E V E R Y   S H O W   R A D
N E C K O F T H E W O O D S
T N T   D R U   D E N
  E Y E O F T H E S T O R M
P E D A L   F O U R   O R E O
H A L L E   E D G E   U S S R
D R Y E R   T O E D   R O T E
```

25

```
KEGS ▪ RAVED ▪ AJAR
UGLY ▪ ITINA ▪ HOLE
DOOR ▪ PHONELINES
UNWISE ▪ LIDO ▪ AXE
▪ WANNA ▪ SAYWHAT
BOO ▪ OSSO ▪ LAI
ADRAW ▪ SHOULDERS
RIMS ▪ BOGUS ▪ EZEK
RESOURCES ▪ SNIDE
▪ NNE ▪ ETTU ▪ ODD
SIZETWO ▪ SOPUP
UNE ▪ ISPY ▪ SEPIAS
MAPLETREES ▪ SNAP
ALPO ▪ EATIT ▪ EZRA
CLOT ▪ RHINO ▪ TAPS
```

26

```
MARX ▪ ISOLDE ▪ KOA
AVER ▪ DOMAIN ▪ ELL
PINACOLADAS ▪ EDO
SATYR ▪ HEN ▪ OPEN
▪ SALSADANCING
ASL ▪ WOO ▪ OTT
DEADLAST ▪ OVERDO
DAZE ▪ FOALS ▪ TEAT
STYLES ▪ ROADSALT
▪ SUE ▪ UMA ▪ LEO
DOUGLASADAMS
ANNE ▪ TAS ▪ NOBLE
RED ▪ TOSSEDSALAD
KIA ▪ INHERE ▪ ROVE
SLY ▪ MEATAX ▪ SWAN
```

27

```
IMOFF ▪ MTIDA ▪ SMU
CRUDE ▪ OARED ▪ TAR
ESTREETBAND ▪ UGG
▪ TRIO ▪ EDGE
SKYY ▪ IFORMATION
PLEASES ▪ AOSCOTT
HELLO ▪ LGBT
▪ EPLURIBUSUNUM
▪ RELO ▪ TOPIC
MARACAS ▪ MAESTRO
ILOVEPARIS ▪ HOOP
SAME ▪ OCHS
ESC ▪ OHENRYTWIST
RKO ▪ WALDO ▪ YIKES
SAM ▪ NYLON ▪ EIEIO
```

28

```
PBJ ▪ TAMPA ▪ ASFAR
LIE ▪ HASON ▪ UTILE
ENDRESULT ▪ TARSI
ASIAN ▪ LIGHTSON
▪ MERC ▪ LOST ▪
ATH ▪ ROOSTER ▪ BET
TWELVENOON ▪ KERR
BYAGE ▪ MAR ▪ AGGIE
ALDA ▪ REVERTBACK
RAH ▪ MINERVA ▪ NAS
▪ OHIO ▪ OSLO ▪
BANISTER ▪ ALTOS
LUCRE ▪ REDUNDANT
OTHER ▪ INERT ▪ STY
GOODS ▪ KOALA ▪ SOX
```

29

```
RODS ▪ COMFY ▪ ESSO
UTAH ▪ ISERE ▪ TTOP
HOME SWEET HOME
REORG ▪ ACE ▪ LAPEL
▪ NEEDLEPOINT
UTA ▪ NUT ▪ RTE ▪ HAD
PINATA ▪ OLDELI
CEDILLA ▪ PHOEBES
▪ PSY ▪ STE ▪ WFL
IDYL ▪ THREE ▪ IEDS
NITE ▪ STORY ▪ BERT
DOH ▪ HOUSE ▪ DER
IDIAMIN ▪ ALUMINA
REAPERS ▪ TENANCY
ASSENT ▪ THIGHS
```

30

```
SPUR ▪ EDIT ▪ DISH
ALSO ▪ VISAS ▪ EDNA
DOUBLEPARK ▪ ASIS
▪ TREE ▪ AMI ▪ TAFT
UTE ▪ DUNCANPHYFE
FERRARI ▪ CSA ▪ SAN
ORSO ▪ GPA ▪ LOOTS
▪ CHESTBUMP
SANKA ▪ ALP ▪ EASE
UMA ▪ ISR ▪ UTENSIL
MOTORNEURON ▪ ASK
ARIA ▪ USB ▪ GORE
TOOK ▪ FOOLAROUND
RUNE ▪ FLAIL ▪ PLOY
ASSN ▪ ETTE ▪ SERE
```

31

A	T	B	A	T		K	A	T	E		S	O	F	T
W	A	L	L	S		O	L	A	V		A	V	I	A
E	B	O	L	A	Z	A	I	R	E		L	U	N	K
S	L	O	T		O	L	E			F	T	L	E	E
	E	M	I	L	I	A	N	O	Z	A	P	A	T	A
		M	O	C			M	I	X	I	T	U	P	
D	I	C	E	D		I	N	N		T	I	N	A	
A	N	A		E	D	Z	W	I	C	K		O	E	R
N	A	N	S		C	E	O		E	R	N	S	T	
C	R	O	U	T	O	N		I	N	A				
E	R	O	G	E	N	O	U	S	Z	O	N	E	S	
S	E	D	G	E		P	O	O		G	L	E	E	
T	A	L	E		E	A	S	Y	D	O	E	S	I	T
E	R	E	S		S	H	E	A		D	R	A	N	O
P	S	S	T		P	A	T	S		E	S	S	E	N

32

A	W	E		C	I	N	E	M	A		B	I	A	S
L	I	L		I	C	E	M	A	N		R	O	M	E
E	L	I	J	A	H	W	O	O	D		O	W	E	N
C	L	E	O			T	R	E		W	A	N	D	
	W	A	F	F	L	E	I	R	O	N				
S	A	I	D	I	D	O		S	M	I	D	G	E	
A	T	E		G	I	L	D	A		G	E	O	R	G
W	A	S	P		C	L	U	B	S		S	W	A	G
T	R	E	A	D		S	O	N	A	R		N	C	O
O	I	L	R	I	G		E	M	E	R	G	E	S	
			A	D	A	M	D	R	I	V	E	R		
S	O	L	D		B	A	A			N	A	I	L	
T	H	A	I		L	E	M	O	N	W	E	D	G	E
A	I	M	S		E	V	O	K	E	D		E	O	N
R	O	P	E		S	E	N	S	E	S		D	R	S

33

A	R	O	M	A		B	R	O		M	E	C	C	A
S	U	P	E	R	F	O	O	D		A	Q	U	A	S
P	E	T	I	T	I	O	N	S		N	U	R	M	I
		R	E	N	T	A		S	C	A	L	I	A	
A	G	T		M	A	I	N	S	A	I	L			
F	R	A	G	I	L	E		H	U	N		S	L	O
R	A	M	O	S		H	O	L	I	S	T	I	C	
A	B	A	B		S	C	O	O	T		L	E	N	T
I	L	L	I	N	O	I	S			L	A	N	G	E
D	E	E		E	A	T		S	P	A	T	O	U	T
		E	X	P	I	A	T	E	S		S	A	S	
A	D	A	P	T	S		B	A	S	T	A			
V	A	L	I	D		G	U	I	T	A	R	I	S	T
E	R	I	C	A		A	T	R	O	C	I	O	U	S
S	A	S	S	Y		P	S	S		T	A	U	P	E

34

R	I	O	J	A		S	P	U	D	S		D	I	S
A	S	N	E	R		T	E	B	O	W		E	C	O
P	E	E	W	E	E	R	E	E	S	E		V	A	N
T	E	L	E		G	A	R	R		E	W	I	N	G
			L	O	A	F			O	P	A	L		
E	L	L	E	N	D	E	G	E	N	E	R	E	S	
C	A	I	R	O		R	E	M	A	N	D	E	D	
I	T	T		T	R	I	K	E			E	G	O	
G	E	T	A	R	O	O	M			A	R	G	U	E
	R	E	N	E	E	Z	E	L	L	W	E	G	E	R
		R	A	G	S			H	O	L	T			
H	A	B	L	A		A	R	A	B		W	H	A	M
T	H	U		L	I	V	E	S	O	F	E	A	S	E
T	A	G		I	R	E	N	A		Y	E	N	T	A
P	B	S		A	K	R	O	N		I	T	S	O	N

35

G	A	M	E	R		K	G	B		B	R	A	G	G
N	E	U	R	O		L	E	A		E	U	L	E	R
A	R	L	E	S		E	L	L		D	E	L	T	A
S	I	C		I	C	E	L	E	S	S		I	O	C
H	E	H	H	E	H		E	P	I	C	E	N	E	
		A	R	A	C	H	N	I	D	A				
P	L	E	D		R	E	A		N	E	B	U	L	A
G	E	L	D		L	O	R	E	N		O	L	E	G
A	I	K	I	D	O		E	V	E		O	M	O	O
	B	I	T	E	M	A	R	K	S					
B	A	S	S	E	T	T		E	R	E	B	U	S	
E	D	A		D	E	R	A	L	T	E		E	S	T
I	L	L	G	O		A	L	I		S	O	L	T	I
N	E	V	E	U		D	E	M		G	A	L	E	N
G	R	E	E	T		E	G	O		E	K	I	N	G

36

R	A	I	M	I		Z	E	T	A		H	A	L	L
V	R	O	O	M		I	N	O	N		O	B	I	E
S	T	U	M	P		N	Y	U	K		T	O	K	E
			J	E	D	G	A	R	H	O	O	V	E	R
	G	O	E	T	H	E			M	I	E	N	S	
	U	H	A	U	L	R	E	N	T	A	L			
S	I	G	N	S		C	A	I	N		L	I	P	
I	D	O	S		L	D	O	P	A		D	E	C	O
X	E	D		M	A	I	N			T	I	M	E	X
		Y	C	H	R	O	M	O	S	O	M	E		
A	T	S	E	A			A	R	E	N	A	S		
F	O	U	R	T	H	O	F	J	U	L	Y			
T	R	I	O		A	R	L	O		I	S	I	A	H
E	T	T	U		C	Z	A	R		O	U	N	C	E
R	E	S	T		K	O	P	S		T	S	K	E	D

37

```
ETTA ARCING BID
NAAN REINER UKE
EXPOSTFACTO CEL
MEANT LOL VOCAL
YDS ERE IRENA
MARXANDLENIN
BROADS TEA MESA
YOLKS ATS SPELT
RUDE ALI PETREL
DESPOTICALLY
EARLS COL TSA
OHARA TEE EDITS
MUD TREASUREMAP
EGO EARVIN LORE
NOG DJSETS ARRR
```

38

```
STAB ASSN OHGEE
HILL SNEE NOONS
RAGA WAROFWORDS
ERAS ORI LACES
WALTZOFFWITH
ZEN INC CGI
GIJOE MATCHWOOD
ASON BIRCH OVAL
TAKELUNCH SWEDE
EYE ELS OOF
WALKSONWATER
SARGE TRE CAME
WAYOUTWEST TUBE
ARETE AVOW OPED
GASES XENO REDS
```

39

```
LABATT ORCS ANT
ALLPRO ACAI POE
SLIPANDFALL POX
EIS FEES CEMENT
RESTFUL SUNRA
VIP NATTERED
HASAC GOTTI STU
ACAD RUMBA BIAS
LET BALDY DANSK
TRUELIFE GUS
RYANS MURKIER
INDEBT OONA OXO
PEA BROKENBONES
AMY EERO ELVIRA
DOS REEK REACTS
```

40

```
COPCAR STEWPAN
ORIOLE COURAGE
SEADOG HAYRIDES
TON EATON ONSET
OHSTOP MPG
CAPO TEEHEE ORS
ODESSA DOWD PET
MODEL HIP ALEVE
IRA ODEA EYEDUP
CEL PUMMEL ACES
VEE OVERDO
BASED KNAVE LCD
APPROVED ENDURE
ROADWAY NEWMAN
SPRINTS SWINGS
```

41

```
AUDI EDIT ATBAT
BRIM MONO SWAMI
BALLJOINT HELEN
ALLOUT SOY ELSE
VTEN ANTI
NCIS AETNA NAT
NAAN STRIKEBACK
OMNI OUNCE OCHO
RENTSTRIKE DUES
ADO AREEL ZAPS
NANU EPIC
DIBS EAR ANIMUS
ROAST FULLCOUNT
ATLAS RISE USDA
TALIA ONUS SKOR
```

42

```
HAHA CASTS BENT
ERAS OPART ATOM
YALE BELIE DUNE
BOXERREBELLION
UMA LOU
MADAM CAMELCASE
EMILY ALAR KILN
DIS DPLUS DAD
INCA URAL AGAVE
COOLBEANS CANER
LAN ADS
BLOWHOTANDCOLD
LIMO RABID HAJJ
USER TRUCE OREO
RANK HATER LADE
```

43

C	A	B	S		A	L	P	S		S	O	F	A	R
O	M	A	N		D	O	I	T		I	H	O	P	E
S	I	D	E	T	A	B	L	E		T	H	R	O	W
I	D	E	A	S		S	O	N	G	T	I	T	L	E
		K	A	T		T	O	N	I		S	O	D	
S	E	A	T	R	I	P			A	G	S			
I	N	C	H		S	O	R	E	T	H	U	M	B	S
B	O	R	I	S		L	O	X		T	R	O	U	T
S	W	E	E	T	T	O	O	T	H		E	M	L	Y
		F	A	B			S	A	D	T	A	L	E	
E	R	G		R	A	F	T		M	E	H			
S	O	U	L	T	R	A	I	N		V	I	X	E	N
T	A	S	E	R		S	E	A	S	O	N	T	W	O
E	S	T	E	E		T	U	N	E		G	R	O	G
S	T	O	R	K		S	P	O	T		S	A	K	S

44

D	I	P		S	L	O	G		O	T	T	E	R	
O	D	S		H	O	W	E		L	O	A	D	E	D
T	O	Y	D	O	L	L	S		D	O	M	I	N	O
	C	O	O	L	E	S	T		T	E	T	O	N	
A	C	H	E			T	O	U	C	H	D	O	W	N
N	E	O		C	C	S		R	A	P		R	N	A
Y	O	U	T	O	O		A	B	R	A	M			
	T	O	M	M	Y	D	O	R	S	E	Y			
	T	E	P	E	E		O	T	T	A	W	A		
S	N	O		T	E	L		A	T	E		C	O	P
T	O	P	D	O	L	L	A	R		C	H	O	P	
A	T	T	A	R		S	L	I	D	O	U	T		
L	E	S	T	E	R		T	O	D	O	L	I	S	T
L	A	T	E	S	T		A	S	A	P		N	O	W
	T	O	R	T	E		R	O	Y	S		G	L	O

45

H	A	H	A		C	A	P	E	R		P	I	C	T
I	B	E	T		A	L	I	N	E		O	N	O	R
C	O	L	L	A	R	L	E	S	S		O	H	M	Y
	P	U	R	E		R	U	T	H	L	E	S	S	
M	I	L	N	E		F	O	E		E	C	L	A	T
T	H	E	C	A	P	E		F	A	U	L	T	S	
G	O	S	H		A	S	A	R	U	L	E			
E	P	S		A	R	T	L	E	S	S		S	O	B
	G	U	E	S	S	A	T		S	E	G	A		
A	S	P	I	R	E		M	Y	S	T	A	R	S	
L	H	A	S	A		I	O	S		T	I	M	E	S
B	A	S	E	L	E	S	S		C	A	L	L		
E	N	C	L		M	O	T	I	O	N	L	E	S	S
R	I	A	L		A	L	E	R	T		U	S	E	R
T	A	L	E		G	A	R	R	Y		P	S	A	S

46

M	I	A	M	I		A	P	P	S		E	G	G	S
U	R	B	A	N		D	A	R	N		T	R	E	E
G	R	A	N	D	H	O	T	E	L		V	E	N	N
	D	I	S	N	E	Y		H	O	A	R	D		
L	A	S	A	G	N	A		S	U	I	T	E	S	
A	C	U	T	E		I	G	N	O	B	L	E		
R	E	P	E	N	T		I	A	N		A	S	H	Y
V	I	E		T	I	T	A	N	I	C		C	O	E
A	T	R	A		L	E	N		C	A	B	A	L	A
	S	T	R	E	E	T	S		L	O	P	E	S	
O	T	I	T	I	S		T	A	L	L	E	S	T	
D	A	Z	E	D		V	I	O	L	A	S			
O	R	E	M		B	I	G	P	I	C	T	U	R	E
R	O	M	P		B	L	O	B		A	E	S	O	P
S	T	E	T		C	A	R	Y		B	R	A	T	S

47

M	A	C	S		Z	O	O	M		Z	O	O	M	
O	S	H	A		I	T	N	O		I	N	P	U	T
C	H	I	T		L	E	E	R		P	E	R	M	S
K	E	N	O		C	R	A	N	K	S		A	B	A
	A	U	T	H	O	R		A	U	T	H	O	R	
B	A	T	T	Y		T	R	I	P	E				
O	R	O		P	A	S	H	A	S		D	Y	E	S
N	E	W	Y	O	R	K		N	E	W	Y	O	R	K
D	A	N	E		M	E	A	G	R	E		U	N	I
	A	C	I	D	S		A	B	B	O	T			
H	E	A	R	Y	E		H	E	A	R	Y	E		
E	L	L		B	S	H	A	R	P		E	T	C	H
A	L	I	T	O		I	N	R	I		N	C	A	A
T	I	B	E	R		E	T	O	N		O	H	M	S
	S	I	N	G		S	I	N	G		W	A	S	H

48

S	A	G		O	V	A	L		E	F	F	O	R	T
T	E	A		P	A	P	A		M	A	I	D	E	N
E	G	G	H	U	N	T	S		I	M	N	E	X	T
L	E	G	O	S		E	E	N	I	E				
M	A	L	T		B	A	R	R	E	L	R	A	C	E
O	N	E	S	E	L	F		A	M	Y		B	O	X
			E	N	T	E	R		T	R	E	A	T	
	H	E	A	D	S	W	I	L	L	R	O	L	L	
M	O	T	T	O		G	O	T	E	M				
O	U	T		F	A	B		C	R	E	A	T	O	R
D	R	U	M	S	T	I	C	K	S		N	O	N	E
	E	T	H	N	O		A	I	O	L	I			
T	I	P	T	O	E		L	O	G	C	A	B	I	N
I	N	B	O	R	N		T	H	A	I		A	N	I
E	N	J	O	Y	S		S	O	L	D		D	E	N

49

```
A R F S   P A B S T   S D A K
S O U P   A L L A H   T O B E
S U R F E R D U D E   R Y A N
E G O   B E E T   S P O O N
T H R O B   R O G E R M U D D
    U S B   U S O   M O E
A C C T   M I N I   O V I N E
N A R R O W L Y D E F I N E D
G R U E L   I C E S   O D D S
E D S   D I E   L I L
R E A R E N D E D   P A R K S
  A D O R N   S R T A   O I L
A L E X   A R T O O D E T O O
P E R I   T E E N Y   P O S T
E R S E   E P E E S   A R K S
```

50

```
A C U T   P O P O F F   Z I T
L O P E   E N A M E L   E R R
B I T T E R E N E M Y   B R A
A F O R E   B E G   C R E D
    S A L T Y L A N G U A G E
U M P   Y O O   S E E R
R O E G   S N L   A L L W E T
S W E E T H E A R T D E A L S
A N D R E I   P U N   D R I P
    A M B I   S I R   M A S
S O U R P A T C H K I D S
W I N D   S O W   P U P A L
E L I   T A S T E M A K E R S
P E T   S P A T E S   E L L A
T R Y   K O D A K S   S L O T
```

51

```
M A T C H G A M E   B A S H
A L E H O U S E S   C E L L O
N O C O N T E S T   R E B U S
N E H I   V A S S A L A G E
  R E N E   W I Z
S I R   M O R T G A G E D
I N U L I N   W A Y   B U G S
A R M O R   K E Y   L U M E T
M E O W   Z O E   W O B B L Y
  R E M A I N D E R   O S X
  N A P   E T D S
I M P E R F E C T   C A M P
S W I R L   T H A T S A L I E
M A N G O   R E C O I L I N G
S H A Y   E X H I P P I E S
```

52

```
I M A C S   J E N G A   D A M
M E D A L   E C O L I   E R A
O L D F A I T H F U L   V E T
  T I M E O U T   T I N T
T E J A N O   N E B U L A E
I V A N   K F C   N A B S
B I C   S A L A D   D E T E R
I C K   W Y O M I N G   O V A
A T S E A   P E N C E   W E T
  O A R S   L E I   R E N T
M A N S M A N   S P O R T Y
A C H Y   M U S C L E S
R H O   F O R T L A R A M I E
S O L   I S S U E   T R O O P
H O E   T A E B O   H Y E N A
```

53

```
A P P S   S M O R E   D E B S
F R A U   A C R E S   E V E N
C O P P E R C U P S   C O D A
  E L I A   E A R N E R
P U R R S   I R O N F E N C E
S H A M   S N O W   R E E K S
E U R O P E   W N B A
C H E M I C A L S Y M B O L S
  A T R I   R E I N I N
E B S E N   I N H D   G E N E
S I L V E R A G E   A B A T E
C R E A T E   R E N U
O D E D   C A R B O N C O P Y
R I V E   U R B A N   K I T E
T E E D   R A I L S   S L A W
```

54

```
G A R B   S O D S   D R U G S
O B O E   T H R U   D E P O T
B A G G Y E Y E S   S L A T E
I C E   A M E C H E   A N T E
G I R L Y   S K I N N Y D I P
  A S P   S O S A
A S T I   O P A Q U E   T O M
L O W R I S E B U I L D I N G
I W O   S T R E E T   I T E M
  H U L A   E W E
F L A R E G U N S   O U I J A
R A N G   E N E S C O   T E N
E N D I T   C U T O F F S A W
S C E N E   A R A L   L U N A
H E D G E   P O R T   U S S R
```

55

L	A	D	L	E	■	B	A	T	H	■	P	I	P	E
I	C	E	A	X	■	I	S	A	Y	■	I	D	E	A
T	H	E	M	S	■	T	H	E	B	R	E	A	K	S
H	E	R	E	T	O	■	E	B	R	O	■	H	O	E
O	D	S	■	A	N	D	S	O	I	T	G	O	E	S
■	■	K	O	R	E	A	■	■	D	A	H	■	■	■
G	L	I	B	■	P	L	O	W	■	T	O	B	E	Y
W	I	N	S	O	M	E	L	O	S	E	S	O	M	E
B	E	S	E	T	■	Y	E	L	P	■	T	R	O	T
■	■	S	T	P	■	F	A	L	S	E	■	■	■	■
Q	U	E	S	E	R	A	S	E	R	A	■	F	E	D
A	H	L	■	R	E	N	O	■	S	T	A	R	V	E
T	H	A	T	S	L	I	F	E	■	I	Q	U	I	T
A	U	T	O	■	I	T	T	Y	■	S	U	I	T	E
R	H	E	A	■	M	A	G	E	■	H	A	T	E	R

56

A	B	H	O	R	■	B	R	I	T	■	A	H	A	B
L	O	O	I	E	■	L	O	C	I	■	L	E	V	I
P	O	L	L	S	P	O	L	E	S	■	T	A	I	L
O	N	E	P	I	E	C	E	■	F	A	L	S	E	■
■	■	A	N	D	■	■	E	M	I	R	S	■	■	■
A	S	S	N	■	I	M	A	M	A	N	■	H	U	B
F	L	E	S	H	■	I	S	D	U	E	■	E	N	O
T	I	L	■	A	D	D	S	A	D	S	■	E	P	A
E	E	L	■	D	O	L	E	S	■	T	A	L	E	S
R	R	S	■	A	R	E	T	H	A	■	S	S	G	T
■	■	■	C	I	G	A	R	■	M	A	H	■	■	■
S	E	E	T	O	■	I	R	I	S	H	S	E	A	■
I	S	L	E	■	P	A	R	E	S	P	E	A	R	S
C	A	L	M	■	I	C	O	N	■	C	A	C	T	I
K	I	S	S	■	G	E	N	T	■	A	P	S	E	S

57

A	C	T	V	■	C	S	P	A	N	■	S	P	A	M
C	O	R	A	■	O	P	E	R	A	■	I	O	W	A
Q	U	I	N	Q	U	A	G	E	N	A	R	I	A	N
U	P	C	■	V	C	R	■	S	O	D	■	T	I	N
I	L	K	■	C	H	E	R	■	S	P	I	T	E	■
T	E	L	L	■	D	I	B	S	■	L	E	E	R	■
S	T	E	E	P	S	■	C	U	E	C	A	R	D	S
■	■	S	H	A	Q	A	T	T	A	Q	■	■	■	■
M	O	R	T	I	M	E	R	■	S	P	U	R	T	S
A	R	E	A	■	E	D	D	Y	■	E	E	O	C	■
C	O	P	T	O	■	O	A	R	S	■	S	R	I	■
A	T	L	■	L	E	G	■	R	O	C	■	O	P	S
Q	U	E	B	E	C	N	O	R	D	I	Q	U	E	S
U	N	T	O	■	H	A	N	O	I	■	U	N	D	O
E	D	E	N	■	O	T	O	W	N	■	O	D	O	R

58

E	N	D	S	■	M	A	M	B	A	■	S	C	R	A	M
R	O	O	T	■	A	N	D	E	S	■	R	H	O	D	E
N	I	N	E	M	O	N	T	H	S	■	S	I	M	O	N
■	R	U	P	P	■	■	A	I	L	■	N	E	R	D	■
■	T	H	E	F	O	U	R	S	E	A	S	O	N	S	■
B	A	H	■	G	L	E	N	■	T	I	L	T	■	■	■
A	M	O	I	■	A	N	D	■	■	O	R	D	E	R	■
H	O	L	L	Y	W	O	O	D	S	Q	U	A	R	E	S
A	K	E	L	A	■	■	I	C	U	■	P	E	R	V	■
■	■	A	L	S	O	■	N	A	I	F	■	S	O	P	■
S	I	X	T	E	E	N	C	A	N	D	L	E	S	■	■
T	R	E	E	■	T	I	A	■	■	A	L	E	S	■	■
A	U	R	A	L	■	O	N	E	F	I	N	E	D	A	Y
G	L	O	S	S	■	N	I	X	O	N	■	N	U	D	E
S	E	X	E	D	■	S	T	E	R	N	■	A	P	E	S

59

A	C	T	S	■	P	L	A	S	M	■	E	D	G	Y
S	H	I	V	■	R	U	C	H	E	■	V	A	L	E
N	I	N	E	■	U	S	U	A	L	■	I	R	O	N
E	N	G	L	I	S	H	T	R	I	F	L	E	■	■
R	A	S	T	A	S	■	E	D	N	A	■	W	A	S
■	■	E	M	I	T	■	■	D	I	G	E	S	T	■
M	A	Y	■	B	A	K	E	D	A	L	A	S	K	A
A	L	O	T	■	■	O	N	O	■	■	B	A	E	R
P	L	U	M	P	U	D	D	I	N	G	■	Y	D	S
L	E	S	S	O	N	■	■	T	I	O	S	■	■	■
E	Y	E	■	O	H	M	S	■	C	L	U	M	S	Y
■	■	N	O	P	I	E	C	E	O	F	C	A	K	E
U	N	D	O	■	N	A	O	M	I	■	K	R	I	S
S	I	M	P	■	G	L	O	M	S	■	E	I	R	E
E	X	E	S	■	E	S	T	E	E	■	R	A	T	S

60

A	B	A	T	E	S	■	A	R	A	B	■	A	D	S
M	Y	L	O	V	E	■	T	O	F	U	■	N	O	T
P	E	P	P	E	R	P	O	T	T	S	■	I	W	O
■	■	S	N	A	R	L	■	■	H	O	M	E	R	■
C	R	O	P	■	P	I	L	L	O	W	T	A	L	K
R	O	L	O	D	E	X	■	E	M	A	I	L	■	■
A	G	I	T	A	■	I	A	N	■	S	H	O	W	■
S	U	V	■	S	T	U	F	F	I	T	■	O	L	E
S	E	E	S	■	O	N	S	■	A	B	U	S	E	■
■	■	B	A	M	B	I	■	D	E	B	A	S	E	D
T	U	R	K	E	Y	T	R	O	T	■	D	E	N	Y
B	R	A	S	S	■	■	A	R	O	S	E	■	■	■
S	I	N	■	S	T	O	C	K	I	N	G	C	A	P
P	A	C	■	E	A	V	E	■	L	A	G	U	N	A
S	H	H	■	S	P	A	R	■	E	X	S	T	A	R

61

S	I	C	K			T	H	O	S		Y	E	A	R
O	R	E	O	S		S	I	L	K		E	L	L	A
N	O	N	P	C		E	R	I	E		S	I	L	T
A	N	T		O	U	T	T	O	W	I	N			
T	O	R		O	N	S			D	O	D	G	E	
A	N	A	P	P	L	E	A	D	A	Y		O	R	A
		L	E	S	E		Z	I	P	L	I	N	E	S
A	B	B	A		A	M	T	O	O		A	T	W	T
C	O	A	L	E	S	C	E		G	U	N	G		
I	N	N		C	H	I	C	K	E	N	S	O	U	P
D	A	K	A	R			A	E	R		T	S	O	
		S	U	B	M	E	R	S	E		H	M	S	
W	I	L	T		M	O	R	A		A	T	E	A	T
A	C	E	R		W	E	L	T		D	O	R	I	A
X	E	N	O		S	T	E	S		W	E	L	L	

62

O	G	L	E	S		C	S	I		W	R	U	N	G
F	L	O	A	T		R	O	O		E	A	S	Y	A
F	A	N	T	A		A	C	T	I	N	G	O	U	T
E	R	G		N	Y	G	I	A	N	T	S			
D	E	S	A	D	E		A	S	T	O		F	O	X
	T	R	O	W	E	L		R	V	P	A	R	K	
	J	E	A	N		A	L	A		E	L	L	I	E
C	O	M	B	O		S	U	P		R	O	L	O	S
A	D	M	I	N		T	B	S		T	W	I	N	
P	I	E	C	E	D		R	E	D	H	E	N		
T	E	D		S	U	Z	I		H	E	D	G	E	D
	S	H	O	W	C	A	S	E		D	W	I		
S	T	A	T	E	S	E	A	L		D	R	O	O	P
P	O	D	I	A		I	N	S		G	A	W	K	S
A	W	A	R	D		G	T	O		E	E	N	S	Y

63

O	B	A	M	A		C	A	T	T		P	O	S	H
T	A	R	O	T		A	M	O	S		I	T	T	Y
I	N	T	H	E	D	R	I	N	K		T	E	R	P
S	A	S	S		I	O	N	E		M	C	R	A	E
		M	E	M	O	R	Y	C	H	I	P	S		
I	G	O	T	I	T			U	S	E				
N	E	P	A	L		T	U	N	A		S	W	A	T
K	N	U	C	K	L	E	S	A	N	D	W	I	C	H
S	O	S	O		A	D	A	M		Y	O	S	H	I
		T	R	I			S	N	O	P	E	S		
S	M	A	R	T	C	O	O	K	I	E				
H	A	G	U	E		C	R	A	G		B	O	N	A
E	R	I	C		L	U	N	C	H	B	O	X	E	S
M	I	N	K		A	L	O	E		T	W	E	R	K
P	E	G	S		P	I	T	Y		W	E	N	D	S

64

D	O	O	R	S		A	J	A	R		E	T	N	A
I	M	H	I	T		R	A	G	U		A	H	E	M
V	A	M	P	I	R	E	B	A	T		R	A	R	E
A	N	Y	O	N	E		S	T	A	L	L	I	O	N
		P	E	A	S		E	B	A	Y				
F	A	V	E		D	O	E		A	T	O	A	S	T
O	R	O	N	O		D	R	A	G	O	N	F	L	Y
N	I	L		N	O	O	N	D	A	Y		L	A	P
D	E	V	I	L	F	I	S	H		A	B	A	T	E
A	L	O	T	O	F		T	O	W		A	C	E	S
		S	A	N	S		C	H	E	R				
B	E	A	T	N	I	K	S		A	P	O	L	L	O
A	C	T	I		G	I	A	N	T	S	Q	U	I	D
W	H	O	M		H	E	M	I		O	U	T	E	D
L	O	B	E		T	R	E	X		N	E	E	D	S

65

A	L	O	H	A		M	O	S	S		I	K	E	A
L	U	N	A	R		O	H	N	O		P	E	R	U
A	R	T	I	F	I	C	I	A	L	C	H	A	R	T
S	K	O	R		S	H	O	P		H	O	N	O	R
		G	A	L	A		W	I	N	E	R	Y		
C	H	E	E	S	E	S	O	F	I	N	E			
R	O	L	L	S		W	O	K		S	T	O	P	
A	L	L		T	A	B	L	O	I	D		R	O	O
G	E	E	Z		N	Y	E		I	S	U	Z	U	
		I	M	O	U	T	O	F	C	H	E	E	R	
M	U	S	L	I	N		F	L	E	A				
U	N	C	L	E		C	A	F	E		M	Y	R	A
C	H	A	I	N	S	U	N	D	E	R	W	E	A	R
H	I	L	O		A	R	E	A		N	O	T	M	E
O	P	E	N		D	E	W	Y		S	W	I	S	S

66

R	A	T	I	O		C	A	I	T		A	D	A	M
P	L	A	N	K		R	I	D	E		R	E	N	O
M	A	I	N	C	O	U	R	S	E		T	A	G	S
		O	D	E	S			A	D	D	L	E		
L	I	B	E	R	A	L		P	A	G	E	B	O	Y
O	L	E	A	R	Y		S	E	N	E	C	A		
S	A	N	T	A		C	A	A	N		O	T	T	O
E	N	C		L	A	S	T	L	A	P		T	E	X
S	A	H	L		C	P	U	S		I	R	E	N	E
	W	A	L	L	O	P		D	E	F	R	A	Y	
S	W	A	P	O	U	T		L	U	C	K	Y	M	E
T	A	R	T	S		S	A	S	H					
A	T	M	O		N	O	N	S	T	A	R	T	E	R
K	E	E	P		F	L	U	S		R	A	I	N	Y
E	R	R	S		L	E	G	O		T	H	E	S	E

67

```
C L O G   A Q A B A   D E S C
A E R O   V O C A B   R E B A
V I E T N A M E R A   A R A L
      H I S   B A D G I R L
A N T I C   T A R   U S E R S
B A R C E L O N A M E T R O
R I O     A G E   R T E
A R I Z O N A M E M O R I A L
    I N K   O V O   D R E
  C A P T A I N A M E R I C A
W A L D O   O E N   S W O O P
O N E R E E D   I M A
R O T I   M I D D L E N A M E
S L A V   A N N U L   D O U G
T A P E   J E A N S   A L S O
```

68

```
C U S P S   J A I L S   A T M
A T E A M   E N V O I   L O U
N E W P O R T N E W S   G P S
O R E   K A L E     J O S E
N O R I E G A   C H A I R E D
    D R U G T R A F F I C
R I A L   W E L T   T R I
U N D E R T H E W E A T H E R
M A O   B I E R   E M T S
  S P O I L S P O R T S
D E T E S T S   L E A T H E R
A C I D     O D I N   I M O
R O O   M O R N I N G S H O W
C N N   E L I T E   O R A T E
Y D S   L E G O S   S A T E D
```

69

```
D U S T Y   G I N   S E A M S
E N T R E   U N A   S C R A P
A R R O W   L S D   N O O S E
T E A T   C L E A R   L U T E
H A T   L A S T L E G   S I C
S L A T E R   H I T E C H
  H E L D   H A R I
T H E R O U N D S O N M E
C R O W   T E E T H   S A A R
O A T E N   L A V   S E R G E
G I M B A L   J U L I E T
N N E   B A R   T A B   P R E
A C A P   M A C H U   N O E S
T A L C   A P R O N   P S S T
E R S T   S T O U T   R A T S
```

70

```
D U R H A M   D E F   M A S S
A S I A G O   A I R   E M I T
R E D R E D W I N E   N I C E
T R E E   E A R   N E S T E R
  M E R C Y M E R C Y M E
B B S   A N O   E T A L
A R E A S   A S I   U S E D
B Y E B Y E B L A C K B I R D
A N N A   X I I   O S A M A
  N A C L   E S P   M A Y
W I L D W I L D L I F E
O D E O N S   R O T   B L A H
N E O N   I C E I C E B A B Y
K A N E   N A G   O P E N E D
S L E D   G P S   M I D D L E
```

71

```
I N C H   E B O L A   M A Y A
S I R E   T O G O S L O G O S
A N I L   A L L O S A U R U S
Y E M E N S L E M O N S
S T E N O   P R A Y I N G
O Y S   T O P H A T   N I P
  P E O R I A   S A N T A
  F R A N C E S D A N C E S
C R E T E   T I N E A R
E Y E   S W A N E E   B I T
L E S O T H O   Z E E N A
  C H I N A S M Y N A H S
R O M E O R O M E O   D U E T
C U B A S T U B A S   E T R E
A S A N   S T I R S   D Y E D
```

72

```
E T T A   A T B A T   E L L E
M A H I   V I O L A   C A I N
O P A L   I N N E R C H I L D
J O N   M A C E   I O T A S
I N K C A R T R I D G E
  S O N Y   M I S S O U T
G U A R D   S A G A   D N A
I S L A M I C C A L E N D A R
L E O   N O S Y   L A S S O
A R T F A I R   F I R M
  I N T E R N E T C A F E
S A T E D   E A S E   K A L
I V O R Y C O A S T   T E R I
Z I N C   A N I T A   A R C S
E D G E   B E R Y L   I S E E
```

73

```
H A R P . P A C E . W A T T S
O L I O . T R O N . H I R E E
S T A T E B I R D . I K E A S
T O L L R O A D . S T E E R S
. . U M A . S H E E N A . . .
B I G C A T S . A T T . N A B
L A R K . C O N T E . I V E
O M E . A R A L S E A . M A E
A B E . R O M E O . N A I F
T I N . T I P . N A S A L L Y
. L E S L I E . T I M .
G A I E T Y . S M O K E O U T
A N G L O . O P E N H O U S E
E T H E R . N Y S E . N S E C
L I T R E . T S A R . E T D S
```

74

```
C A M P . S P U R S . I D L E
A V E O . T O R A H . D C O N
M O N K E Y I N G A R O U N D
I N D E X . S E M I . N E S
. R E I N . A N T I .
L O P . M O U S I N G O V E R
A W E . P U T I N . G E N E
L E A S T . M R T . K A R T S
A T R A . E E R I E . S E T
W O L F I N G D O W N . E R S
. S E G O . S O N S .
T A B . O P T S . Y E M E N
S Q U I R R E L I N G A W A Y
P U C K . O R A T E . R A S P
S A K E . B I G O T . S H E D
```

75

```
T O W N . S P E D . L I N D A
I D E A . T I D E . E V E R S
G O A T . U T E S . T Y P O S
E R N I E B A N K S . C A L E
. O R B S . T R O L L S
S P I N A L . C C L I V .
A L T A . E L A L . M E D I A
W O R L D S E R I E S R I N G
S T Y L E . G A O L . E D G E
. E L R O Y . E D D I E S
R E G A L E . S C O W .
A L O G . N I G H T G A M E S
M O P U P . B O O R . L A R A
P A R E E . M U N I . L Y O N
S N O R T . S P E C . S O S A
```

76

```
S E N S E . R I M S . P C P
U P E N N . E W O K . O A S
Z E R O V I S I B I L I T Y
Y E O W . D E S I . I N S O
. T W O T H U M B S U P
U N T I E . S W E E P .
F O U R T O P S . A L T
O G R E . W R A T H . T E E
S O N . F L O R A . F I G S
. S L O . S I X F L A G S
. D I A N A . L A S S O
E I G H T M E N O U T .
R A N T . U S E R . S E G O
A G A I N S T A L L O D D S
S O L . S E E R . I D E A S
E N S . A D E S . T A N Y A
```

77

```
C H O P S . S O T S . A F A R
R A N I T . B O R A . M I C A
I R E N E . A H A M O M E N T
S P U N . M R E D . M A L E S
P O P U L A R D E M A N D .
. M O J O . W A N . M A V
U S A B L E . J A R . M I R E
H O M E . S P O R K . I C E S
O D O R . T I E . S A N E S T
H A S . M I N . A M E N .
. N B A C O N F E R E N C E
S P A I N . C O I N . S E A M
N O N K O S H E R . P O P P A
O L D E . I L L S . A T A R I
B O Y S . B E S T . H A L A L
```

78

```
C A B S . B L E W . P A G A N
A B L E . R A Z E . E D U C E
R O A R . A T R A . T A S E D
T R I B U T E A L B U M S .
S C R I M P . T E N . I A N
. A P A R T H E I D E R A
M S N . S C A R . A I D E S
O H O H . K N I T S . P U N T
R O G U E . B U L B . P A Y
S W O R N E N E M I E S .
E S O . A L A . C R O P U P
. D U C K D U C K G O O S E
D U N S T . I S L E . T N U T
A M I G O . N E A R . H E R E
D A K A R . E D Y S . E S P Y
```

79

```
P E G S   A T O P   C O E D S
A L O E   D O V E   E R N I E
B I N D   O R A N G E Z E S T
S H E A F   C L I O   O R C A
T U R K I S H   T A R   G O T
      A S P   R E D E Y E
N A S   H A M A N   M A T E S
T H E J O Y O F C O O K I N G
H A N O I   S T E N T   C O T
    D E L T A S   C E L
A R F   S R I   D E L I G H T
L O O K   E C R U   Y A L I E
C O R N R E L I S H   B O N N
O F T E N   A L T O   L O D E
A S H E S   W E S T   E M I T
```

80

```
B A R K S   R I F T   U P T O
A L B E E   O T R O   S E R F
H A I R R A I S E R   B R A S
      R E M   O T I C   I D O
M A T   N E C K S N A P P E R
T W O L A N E   O N E H I T
V E R A   D R A T   S T E N S
    C H E S T B E A T E R
A D H O C   S E E M   R A S H
S A B R A S   U P T I L T S
K N E E S L A P P E R   S E T
A G A   H O B O   R E F
W E R E   A N K L E B I T E R
A L E X   N E E D   L L A M A
Y O R E   E R R S   E L B O W
```

81

```
C L A W S   B I G O T   M P G
R A J A H   A L O H A   I R E
O N A I R   N O T I N   Y O N
P A R T I N G S H O T   A Z T
      L A S T S   R E G A L
R U M P L E   P U M I C E
E M E R Y   A P L O M B
P A T E   E M C E E   L E A P
    P R E S T O   J E L L O
P U M P E R   P U M M E L
F L O Y D   S T A I R
I T T   M E A N D M Y D R U M
Z I T   E R R O L   R E E S E
E M O   A G A T E   I M P E L
R A S   T O N E R   G O O D S
```

82

```
S H I N   D I E U   B O N O
E I R E   A L P H A   A V O N
C R E W   M A S U R   D U T Y
T E N A M   Y O R E   A M E X
S E E G E R   M A N I C
      E R I C   A N T H E M
A C E   C A I R O   C O U P E
L A N G U A G E B A R R I E R
T R Y I T   S C O N E   T E E
O L A F I I   E T A S
      T O P O L   I S H A L L
O D E S   R B I S   E R I E S
K I T H   A I L E D   I O T A
R E N O   Y E L L O   F L I T
A S A P   S E L A   T I N S
```

83

```
P H E W   A R O M A   E R S E
E A C H   M A N O R   Q U I T
T H R E E P I E C E S U I T S
S A U E R   D U H   W I N E Y
    D R I   P A G A N
A B A L O N E   O N E A C T
B O X E R B R I E F S   B A R
B O L D   O N R Y E   V A P E
E N E   B A S K E T C A S E S
Y E S S I R   S C O R E R S
    C O D E S   H A M
I D I O T   A P E   T I N G E
D E N T A L R E T A I N E R S
L E F T   A T A R I   T R I P
E R O S   S H R E D   S O N Y
```

84

```
A B B O T   S T A F F   I T T
W A L L E   C O L O R   N R A
F R E D A S T A I R E   S I X
U G A   S U V S   S P I C E
L E T T E R   T O M H A N K S
    O R E S   H I A T U S
I F S O   P E S C I   A T M
R A H   E D A S N E R   T E A
E C O   A O R T A   M E R E
    S W I R L S   P R O M
T I M A L L E N   E X I S T S
O M A N I   O K A Y   P I E
R I N   E D M U N D G W E N N
T L C   S E I N E   E T A T S
S E E   T E N S E   N O R S E
```

85

```
P R O . M E W E D . S A I L
A I D . E P I P E N . E M M A
S C O T C H T A P E . A P O P
T H R I C E . P A T C H .
. T A M P . T R A I L S
. H O U S E O F B O U R B O N
L I B S . R I A L . S P I C E
E L S . C A N T O R S . O A R
F L E S H . T E T E . P U T T
T E Q U I L A S U N R I S E .
S L U I C E . P E O N .
. I C A M E . G A T E A U
E L O I . O N T H E R O C K S
L O U D N O L O O K . R I D
F U S E . S C E N E . U N A
```

86

```
E B B . L E T . A Y E . I P A
D E A . E R E C T E D . N O R
A L P . S I L O I N G . S W M
M A T . S E E N O T E . C E L
A R I S E . X E N A . H A R E
M U S E R S . . S T O L E S
E S T A . O B O E . S L E D S
. B O X I N G D A Y .
E S S E S . N O G O . O N A N
A T T E S T . N I K I T A
R O E S . H E A R . M E E T S
F R A . G E T R I C H . B E T
L A M . A N A T O L E . U M A
A G E . P O P S T A R . H P S
P E R . E W E . S W E . R T E
```

87

```
J O S H . A B A S E . E G A D
I R M A . D E M U R . R A G A
H E A R T S H A P E . I M I N
A O R T A . A R E . S C E N T
D S T . C O V E R C H A R G E
. A L I N E . M O I .
L O L I T A . D O W N H O M E
A V E C . H A M . A G O G
B A C K A W A Y . S U N D O G
. C E L . B I N G E .
A F T E R E F F E C T . N A S
G O A P E . G O D . I S N O T
E L S E . D O U B L E T A K E
N I K E . E N N U I . A S A P
T O S S . W E D G E . R H Y S
```

88

```
J A G S . P E P E . B R O M O
A C U P . E X I T . R E N E W
I N S I S T E N T . A H E M S
L E T T H E M E A T C A K E
. E A R P . R E S .
O F F W I T H H E R H E A D
U H A U L . Y U K S . B E E
C A R L . D O P E S . H E R B
L I S . L O A N . S A R I S
A R I E A N T O I N E T T E
. S T U . S O R T .
C A P I T A L O F F E N S E
M O U R N . S A L E S R O O M
C U R I O . T I D E . A D A M
S P A T S . A C E S . S E R A
```

89

```
B L O C K E D . N A H . O H M
R O M A N C E . A T A . N O R
A N N I E O A K L E Y . C O B
S E I N E . R I D O F . E P I
. E L S . N I N E B A L L
U N C . S I P . V I R A L
G R O W . F R A T . E G O
H A M I L T O N B E R M U D A
. P E A . S T A T . E N I D
G R A S P . R A H . D E O
R E N T R O L L . L E I
I V Y . O B O E S . I D A H O
T E M . B E S T M U S I C A L
T R A . E Y E . E S T O N I A
Y E N . S S R . W E S T E R N
```

90

```
G P A . M A G O O . S C O W S
O L D . C L O T H . I O N I A
B A D . E L L E F A N N I N G
I N L A W . R U N . C O D E
G E E Y A T H I N K . E N C
. E N Y A . H A R S H
A N T S . P R O M . I N O I L
S E E . B E E B A L M . U M A
K I T T Y . S I L O . A P E X
. L E A S E . I N S T .
Y A K . T E A K E T T L E S
N O T E . T L C . A N G L E
C U E T H E M U S I C . B I C
A N T E S . S T A R K . T O T
A G E N T T E X A S . Q T S
```

91

```
T A C T   O C A L A   R A M P
E C H O   M O R E L   O D I E
S N E A K A P E E K   L E A D
H E A D O N   T R A V O L T A
    P S A   S E A L A D E A L
O D D   L O P   T I N E
G R A B A C A B     E X U L T
L E T O   T R A D E   E S A U
E W E R S   G O T A S H O T
    D A S H   Z A P   I S U
B A K E A C A K E   N H S
W E L L B O R N   K E A T O N
A R I L   W R O T E A N O T E
N O N O   L I T E R   G R O W
A S K S   S S T A R   S Y S T
```

92

```
P E A R   E B O N Y   M O R A L
A R I A   B E N E S   A M A Z E
C A M I N O R E A L   Y E N T A
      S O L E S       G O E S
P R I V A T E E N T R A N C E
A L A N     C L O N E S
R E S E N D S   L O O M   S P A
C A P T A I N F A N T A S T I C
S T Y   G A U L   S E X T A N T
      F A R C E S     A N T S
Q W E R T Y K E Y B O A R D S
A H M E       D E A N S
T O A S T   I N N E R C H I L D
A L I C E   S C E N E   I D E A
R E L A X   T O Y E D   P O N Y
```

93

```
R A F T   C A P S I D   P E P
A R I A   O R A C L E   O N O
W A R N I N G S H O T   O R S
B L E N D S     U S E D P O T
A S H E S   I M S E R I O U S
R E A D   A M I S   T U T U
S A T   L I A R   I N S T E P
      N O R M A L D A Y
D E V I L S   C O I N   B A S
A L E C   S L O G   K A L E
B A N K R A T E S   B I B L E
E P I S O D E   L A D Y D I
A S S   A F R I C A N L I O N
R E O   S E N T U P   I S N T
S S N   T E S T E D   T H E O
```

94

```
S W I S S   I K E   C A S I N O
P O R C H   S O X   E S C R O W
O T E R I   B R O   O P I A T E
C A N O P E N E R   E S S E S
K N E L L S   A C O R N S
    L O P   N I K E   O N T O
A G E   A N T   S A P   R A I N
P A R T D   A R M Y   N S Y N C
S L A W   T R A   S R O   S T E
E L S E   S P C A   A A A
    E R A S E D   C H R I S T
C R A Z E   C O R K S C R E W
L O V E T O   A N O   A T A R I
E M E R I L   R I O   R A N I N
F E S S E D   S S T   K N I F E
```

95

```
H I T O N   A L E   S I L T
A D O R E   A L E C   O B I E
T O N G U E L A S H   C E L T
P I G   T A D   S O C K E Y E
I D A   R E M O   L E N
N O N P C   N A N   E T H E R
    A O R T A   D A S A N I
I M I N A W E   B O R E D O M
P A N T R Y   T R O U T
O T R O S   P O E   P S Y C H
    E M E   A I W A   E O E
S A T I N O N   S H H   M R I
P L U M   H A S K I T T E N S
O G R E   O M N I   T E N E T
T A N S   K A L   P A I R S
```

96

```
C B S   J O N I   E N T I R E
A L E   B A R A K   L O O N E Y
G O L D E N A G E   S C Y T H E
I N F I D E L S   K I A   H E D
E D I T H   B A N N E R Y E A R
R E E S E S   T E A   B O W T O
    A U G   A V G   G A S P
    R E D L E T T E R D A Y
M A U I   K I R   S A O
U M B R A   S I B   D O G M A S
F I N E S T H O U R   D R A K E
F R O   C I A   M A I L I T I N
L I S P E D   P R I M E T I M E
E T E R N E   C A S A S   N B C
R E S E T S   S P E X   G O A
```

97

I	N	C	A		F	I	N	I	S		B	U	C	K
L	E	A	N		E	V	I	T	A		A	S	I	A
L	I	P	I	Z	Z	A	N	E	R		S	E	T	H
S	L	O	M	O		N	E	M	O		E	D	E	N
			A	N	N				N	U	T			
	M	I	L	K	O	F	M	A	G	N	E	S	I	A
M	A	S	S		S	L	I	D		I	N	E	R	T
U	R	L		R	E	A	R	L	I	T		R	A	M
S	L	A	T	E		M	E	A	N		G	U	T	S
H	A	M	M	E	R	E	D	I	T	H	O	M	E	
		O	D	E				O	U	R				
B	L	A	B		G	O	S	H		L	E	A	P	T
A	U	D	I		G	R	E	Y	M	A	T	T	E	R
R	A	I	L		A	A	N	D	E		E	A	S	E
D	U	N	E		E	L	D	E	R		X	B	O	X

98

B	O	Z	O		D	E	A	N			J	I	L	T
A	R	E	S		E	L	M	O		W	A	D	E	S
T	E	S	L	A	C	O	I	L		E	B	O	O	K
H	O	T	O	I	L		D	E	L	L				
E	S	S		D	A	B		S	I	L	E	N	T	I
			H	A	R	R	I	S	O	N	F	O	R	D
	C	I	I		E	E	C		N	O	F	O	O	L
M	A	N	G	Y		W	E	E		W	I	S	P	Y
O	N	A	H	O	P		U	P	I		G	E	E	
L	I	N	C	O	L	N	P	E	N	N	Y			
T	O	E	S	H	O	E		E	D	U		C	P	A
			O	P	E	C		I	D	C	H	I	P	
S	E	T	T	O		D	O	D	G	E	B	A	L	L
A	L	O	E	S		B	O	N	O		E	S	A	U
T	I	R	E		E	T	A	S		R	E	F	S	

99

C	O	B	S		A	G	A	V	E		F	A	C	E
L	I	O	N		B	A	L	E	R		E	L	A	L
A	L	B	A		E	I	D	E	R		L	E	G	O
U	M	B	R	E	L	L	A	P	O	L	I	C	Y	
D	E	L	L	A			L	O	X					
E	N	E		R	U	M		J	F	K		F	O	E
		H	A	P	P	Y	H	O	L	I	D	A	Y	S
A	M	E	N		R	E	A	D	Y		R	I	L	E
S	T	A	Y	F	O	R	D	I	N	N	E	R		
P	A	D		L	A	S		E	N	S		E	C	O
		O	U	R				F	I	N	A	L		
	B	A	B	E	I	N	T	H	E	W	O	O	D	S
D	O	Z	E		O	O	H	E	D		T	U	D	E
U	Z	I	S		U	T	U	R	N		A	G	I	N
O	O	Z	E		S	I	D	E	A		S	H	E	S

100

A	D	E	P	T		A	L	S	O		U	P	O	N
H	A	V	E	I		D	A	U	B		V	I	L	E
A	L	I	E	N		O	D	D	S		U	N	D	O
B	I	L	L	Y	C	R	Y	S	T	A	L			
			T	O	E			A	M	A	T	O	L	
J	O	L	T	I	N		S	P	C	A		I	R	E
A	L	A	R	M		R	A	U	L	J	U	L	I	A
M	E	S	O		P	E	N	N	E		V	E	E	S
J	O	H	N	C	A	N	D	Y		B	E	R	N	E
A	L	E		A	R	T	Y		B	E	A	S	T	S
R	E	S	O	R	T			F	O	R				
	B	O	Y	M	E	E	T	S	G	I	R	L		
H	A	L	E		I	O	N	A		E	R	N	I	E
A	L	A	S		N	A	Y	S		R	I	F	F	S
J	I	B	E		G	N	A	T		K	N	O	T	S

101

W	O	R	M		L	E	S	S		G	R	E	T	A
A	R	E	A		A	M	T	S		L	U	X	O	R
L	I	P	S		B	E	E	S	T	U	D	E	N	T
L	O	O	K	H	E	R	E		A	T	O	M		
E	L	S		A	L	I	N	E	S		L	P	G	A
T	E	E	B	I	L	L		D	E	E	F	L	A	T
		I	R	E		W	A	R	M		A	P	E	
	S	O	N	G		D	I	M		P	U	R	E	
D	E	F		E	D	E	N		J	R	S			
E	X	F	I	L	E	S		C	U	E	B	E	R	T
S	T	I	R		C	I	G	A	R	S		N	E	E
	C	I	A	O		E	P	I	S	O	D	E	S	
G	E	E	S	T	R	I	N	G	S		P	U	L	L
E	G	R	E	T		R	O	U	T		A	R	I	A
M	O	S	S	Y		S	A	N	S		L	E	N	S

102

H	O	P	I		G	A	L	L	S		S	L	O	G
A	L	A	N		A	B	O	U	T		W	A	V	E
J	I	G	S		L	E	O	N	E		I	M	A	N
I	V	E		R	O	T	T	E	N	A	P	P	L	E
S	E	T	T	E	R	S		C	U	E				
	U	R	G	E		T	H	I	N	S	K	I	N	
P	A	R	I	S		S	H	A	L	T		E	T	E
L	Y	N	X		D	U	E	T	S		B	L	E	W
O	L	E		G	R	I	M	E		B	A	L	M	S
P	A	R	F	A	I	T	S		B	O	N	Y		
		L	I	L			V	I	N	E	G	A	R	
U	R	B	A	N	L	E	G	E	N	D		R	T	E
V	O	O	M		B	L	I	N	G		D	E	A	L
E	A	S	E		I	S	S	U	E		J	E	R	I
A	R	C	S		T	E	T	E	S		S	N	I	T

103

```
R I S K . S A R O N G . . D I M
I N S I S T S U P O N . C O D A
M A N C H E S T E R U N I T E D
. . . K I W I . . . O N E A M .
M I S S I S S I P P I D E L T A
A R A B S . I M L A T E . L E X
H O K U M . P E R I S H . . . .
I C E T . C A R A T S . I D O L
. . . T A L K E D . . A G I N G
A M P . C U E S T A . S H R U B
S O U T H B Y S O U T H W E S T
I N T W O . . . D E B I . . . .
A I R P O R T T E R M I N A L S
N C I S . . P R I D E A N D J O Y
S A D . . M A L A Y S . S A W S
```

104

```
. B L A S T S . E R E C T .
. A L A S K A N . G E T O U T
T H E P H I L O S O P H E R S
B O S S . R E B A T E . D N A
A T T E S T . . W I N . . .
. . . A S P S . S T A L L S
A S L A N . E T A T . K E E N
G H I J K . R O W . L I N G O
A U R A . L E N O . E N D O W
S T E R E O . E L L A . . .
. . . N Y E . . A P P L E T
A B A . D A R W I N . R I F E
D A N I E L R A D C L I F F E
A S N E A T . S N E E Z E S
. H A R R Y . P O T T E R .
```

105

```
S H A H . C R O O N . C P A S
P A C A . H I P P O . A R N O
E T A L . A F T E R . R E A L
W H I F F O F S C A N D A L .
. . . L E S S . . O I L . .
. S U I T . . A D S L O G A N
F A N F A V O R I T E . E M O
O L D E . A U T R Y . R B I S
U S E . S T R I K E F O R C E
L A R G E S S E . E S A I .
. . W A G . . O K I E . . .
. G O D O W N S W I N G I N G
W O R F . E A T I N . O K A Y
B I L L . S P A N K . L E A R
A N D Y . T A N G Y . D A N E
```

106

```
. C O P E S . T E N . A G E
. C O U L D I . E L I . M E R
R A T T A I L . N O T H I N G
A L T . T S E . T I R A D E .
S L A B . O N K P . O R A T E
P I G E O N T O E S . E L I E
S T E E P . P I G G Y B A C K
. . . S I P . . . T A R . .
S N A K E E Y E S . R A I N S
T E N N . P A R T A N I M A L
P U G E T . N A R C . N A T O
. R E E B O K . U T E . N U T
F O R S A L E . D O G E A R S
I N E . L I E . E N G A G E .
L S D . L O S . L E O N E .
```

107

```
I N A J A M . B R A G . K E W
M A N A N A . U S D A . I S M
A D D I N G . S T A Y . N E D
M I L L E N N I U M B U G . .
S A O . U I E . A H M A D .
. . D U M P S T E R F I R E .
. C P A S . T I S . N I A .
B A I L O U T . P L U T O E D
E V A . R E G . T O S S .
S I N G U L A R T H E Y . .
S L O O P . I N O . Z S A
. W O R D O F T H E Y E A R .
A L I . O E U F . O T E L L O
P E R . A C R E . H O L D U P
P O E . R O S Y . O N L A T E
```

108

```
A B C S . A L S O . M A J A
F L A K E . L A W S . O N U S
E A R E D . I C A L L E D I T
W H A T W E V E G O T . I C E
. . . C I T E . . . S T E E R
D A P H N E . G E N U S . .
A G O . O L D F L A M E S
H E R E I S F A I L U R E T O
L E T S S L I D E . T R U
. P A R T S . S T R E E P
D U B Y A . T I R E . .
O S O . C O M M U N I C A T E
R E F A S H I O N . C O C O A
I N F O . O T O E . K I L O S
C O O L . H A N D . L U K E
```

109

G	R	O	W	N		A	C	N	E		L	A	R	S
M	A	R	I	O		D	R	A	T		A	V	O	W
S	W	E	E	T	T	O	O	T	H		N	E	M	O
			L	E	I		W	O	O	D	D	E	E	R
G	O	O	D	D	E	E	D		S	I	G	N	O	N
W	M	D	S			U	S	C		E	R	O	S	
B	I	O		S	I	R		O	R	C	A			
	T	R	I	P	L	E		D	O	U	B	L	E	
	N	O	O	K		D	O	T			O	U	R	
A	C	C	T		A	C	L			O	G	R	E	
A	T	R	I	A	L		H	E	E	L	L	O	O	P
F	E	E	D	D	O	O	R		L	E	D			
L	A	T	E		B	O	O	K	K	E	E	P	E	R
A	S	I	N		O	Z	M	A		C	L	O	V	E
C	E	N	T		S	E	E	N		H	I	D	E	F

110

A	N	A	P	E	S	T		M	R	I		D	D	S
R	U	B	E	L	L	A		E	A	T	S	O	U	T
G	E	N	T	L	E	M	A	N	J	O	H	N	N	Y
O	V	E	R		W	E	L	L			R	O	S	E
	E	G	O	S			L	O	S	T	A	R	T	S
		A	L	U	M	N	I		P	O	P			
A	C	T		P	H	O	T	O	F	I	N	I	S	H
C	H	I	P		O	V	E	N		L	E	V	E	E
D	I	V	O	T		A	R	C	H		L	O	G	E
C	A	E	S	A	R	S	A	L	A	D		R	A	P
			S	R	I		T	E	T	C	H	Y		
M	A	R	I	A	C	H	I		V	E	T	S		
A	R	A	B		O	O	H	S		I	O	N	E	
K	E	L	L	Y	A	N	N	E	C	O	N	W	A	Y
O	N	L	E	A	V	E		M	O	L	I	E	R	E
S	A	Y		K	E	Y		S	T	E	E	R	E	D

111

S	T	A	B		M	A	R		H	A	R	P	S
H	U	G	O		C	O	M	E		A	V	A	I	L
A	D	I	N		O	N	M	E		R	A	S	P	Y
P	O	L	E	I	N	T	O	F	I	R	S	T		
E	R	E	M	I	T	E		V	I	T	A	L	S
		A	I	R		S	M	E	E		F	I	T
R	U	S	S	I	A	N	P	A	S	T		A	K	A
U	P	C	S		O	I	L			F	R	E	T
N	O	R		F	I	N	N	I	S	H	L	I	N	E
G	N	U		A	M	O	S		L	E	I		
S	E	N	O	R	A		D	E	E	P	S	E	A
	C	Z	E	C	H	E	R	E	D	F	L	A	G
O	C	H	O	A		A	S	A	P		L	O	V	E
P	A	I	N	S		Z	A	N	Y		O	M	E	N
T	W	E	E	T		Y	U	K			P	O	S	T

112

C	O	N	A	I	R		O	D	E	D		J	O	B
A	S	S	I	S	I		H	U	L	A		U	R	L
T	H	E	L	O	S	T	B	O	Y	S		S	K	I
S	A	C			E	N	O			A	S	T	I	N
			D	I	R	T	Y	D	A	N	C	I	N	G
E	P	S	O	M			U	N	I	O	N			
L	E	T	G	O		A	D	E	N		R	C	A	S
S	E	R	F		R	A	M	B	O		P	A	C	A
E	R	E	I		E	N	V	Y		F	I	S	T	S
			E	G	G	E	D			L	O	E	S	S
L	E	T	H	A	L	W	E	A	P	O	N			
A	C	C	T	S			S	L	R			P	H	I
T	O	R		P	U	L	P	F	I	C	T	I	O	N
C	L	E		E	T	S	Y		S	P	I	L	L	S
H	I	D		D	A	D	S		M	U	L	L	E	T

113

A	S	P	I	C		C	A	M	P		N	A	P	S
S	L	A	S	H		A	C	E	R		O	R	A	L
H	O	R	S	E		L	I	L	I		T	A	P	A
E	M	I		E	V	I	D	E	N	C	E	B	A	G
N	O	S	T	R	A			E	T	A	L			
		M	O	O	S	H	U		A	F	L	A	M	E
C	L	E	A	N		E	T	U	D	E		D	I	X
L	E	T	T		F	U	R			R	U	L	E	
O	A	R		A	S	T	R	A		L	I	L	A	C
G	R	O	M	I	T		N	L	E	A	S	T		
			A	D	A	M		S	P	E	E	C	H	
T	R	A	D	E	R	O	U	T	E	S		R	O	E
R	I	P	A		T	O	R	O		I	M	A	M	S
A	T	O	M		O	S	L	O		N	I	N	E	S
P	E	P	E		N	E	S	T		G	O	T	Y	E

114

P	I	T	A	S		T	U	N	E	R		T	E	N
E	C	O	L	I		A	L	A	M	O		U	N	O
S	A	Y	I	T	A	I	N	T	S	O		N	U	T
C	H	E			R	C	A	S		F	L	A	M	E
I	N	D	E	P	T	H			C	E	A	S	E	
			P	A	Y	I	T	F	O	R	W	A	R	D
N	A	S	A	L			R	A	M		S	L	A	Y
E	S	T		M	A	Y	I	T	B	E		A	T	E
I	P	A	D		V	E	T			A	I	D	E	D
L	A	Y	I	T	O	N	T	H	I	C	K			
	R	A	V	E	N			A	C	H	E	F	O	R
S	A	L	E	M		B	A	B	E			I	S	A
A	G	E		P	L	A	Y	I	T	B	Y	E	A	R
S	U	R		T	O	L	E	T		R	A	N	G	E
H	S	T		S	W	I	S	S		R	Y	D	E	R

115

A	B	C	S	■	S	A	U	N	A	■	C	H	I	P
P	L	O	T	■	U	R	G	E	S	■	H	A	R	E
P	O	P	E	Y	E	T	H	E	S	A	I	L	O	R
S	C	A	R	A	B	■	■	A	C	C	E	N	T	■
■	■	■	O	R	E	O	■	R	I	T	A	■	■	■
M	A	R	I	N	E	B	I	O	L	O	G	I	S	T
I	P	O	D	S	■	O	R	B	■	R	O	M	E	O
C	I	A	■	L	E	A	S	T	■	N	E	T	■	■
S	A	D	D	A	Y	■	■	A	L	G	O	R	E	■
■	C	I	G	N	A	■	A	B	O	R	T	■	■	■
■	A	L	L	E	N	G	I	N	S	B	E	R	G	■
A	W	O	L	■	A	N	O	■	Y	E	O	W	■	■
H	A	S	■	H	A	T	T	I	P	S	■	A	T	E
A	R	E	■	O	H	H	E	N	R	Y	■	D	Y	E
B	E	D	■	W	H	A	R	T	O	N	■	Y	A	K

116

H	O	Y	A	■	S	W	A	T	H	■	B	E	A	D
E	D	E	N	■	L	I	B	R	A	■	O	N	C	E
R	O	T	A	R	Y	C	L	U	B	■	O	D	D	S
A	R	I	S	E	■	C	E	L	L	B	L	O	C	K
■	■	■	A	S	I	A	■	Y	A	L	E	■	■	■
A	M	A	Z	E	D	■	■	■	T	A	L	O	N	■
M	O	B	I	L	E	H	O	M	E	■	N	O	N	E
I	N	N	■	L	A	U	D	I	N	G	■	V	I	C
S	E	E	D	■	S	M	A	R	T	A	L	E	C	K
S	Y	R	I	A	■	■	■	E	R	A	S	E	S	■
■	■	■	F	I	R	S	■	C	R	I	B	■	■	■
P	A	Y	F	R	E	E	Z	E	■	S	C	O	P	E
L	U	A	U	■	H	E	A	D	P	H	O	N	E	S
U	R	N	S	■	A	N	G	E	R	■	A	T	O	P
M	A	K	E	■	B	O	S	S	Y	■	T	O	N	Y

117

S	O	X	■	D	I	L	L	■	H	A	R	P	O	N
C	H	R	I	S	T	I	E	■	A	M	E	L	I	A
R	E	A	C	T	S	T	O	■	N	O	S	A	L	T
A	N	T	E	■	Y	E	N	S	■	S	T	Y	■	■
P	R	E	S	S	■	■	A	P	R	■	O	D	A	Y
S	Y	D	■	E	M	B	R	Y	O	■	R	E	N	E
■	■	■	O	R	E	A	D	■	O	P	I	A	T	E
■	S	A	L	V	A	T	O	R	M	U	N	D	I	■
G	O	L	D	E	N	■	D	O	I	N	G	■	■	■
A	D	A	M	■	I	N	A	N	E	T	■	T	U	B
L	A	N	A	■	T	O	V	■	■	S	H	I	N	E
■	■	■	A	S	K	■	W	I	S	E	■	U	T	E	S
H	A	L	T	E	D	■	N	O	V	E	L	L	A	S
A	R	D	E	N	T	■	C	H	A	R	L	E	S	I
S	T	A	R	T	S	■	I	O	N	A	■	D	Y	E

118

E	A	S	E	S	■	A	L	G	A	E	■	A	L	B
S	L	O	M	O	■	R	E	I	G	N	■	N	O	R
C	L	A	U	D	E	M	O	N	E	T	■	O	V	A
A	M	P	■	A	X	O	N	■	■	O	K	I	E	S
P	A	I	L	■	P	R	I	D	E	M	O	N	T	H
E	L	N	I	N	O	■	■	O	R	B	I	T	A	L
D	E	G	A	S	■	H	A	J	I	■	S	P	Y	■
■	■	■	M	A	D	E	M	O	N	E	Y	■	■	■
R	I	M	■	■	E	L	I	S	■	G	A	I	N	S
A	T	A	T	I	M	E	■	■	D	O	W	N	O	N
C	O	D	E	M	O	N	K	E	Y	■	N	A	T	O
E	L	D	E	R	■	■	N	A	A	N	■	W	O	W
F	D	A	■	I	N	N	E	R	D	E	M	O	N	S
A	Y	S	■	C	R	U	E	L	■	M	E	R	C	I
N	A	H	■	H	A	N	D	Y	■	O	G	D	E	N

119

S	Ⓞ	P	■	S	W	E	E	T	■	Ⓡ	I	G	■	■
Ⓟ	I	E	R	■	T	O	O	T	H	Ⓗ	E	R	Ⓐ	■
A	L	Ⓓ	O	■	E	R	N	I	E	Ⓔ	S	O	S	■
■	L	I	Ⓒ	H	E	N	■	C	O	B	Ⓐ	I	N	■
B	A	C	Ⓚ	I	N	■	■	C	O	D	D	L	E	■
A	M	A	Ⓢ	S	■	D	I	M	■	U	S	U	A	L
A	P	B	■	S	A	V	V	I	E	R	■	E	W	S
■	■	■	C	A	N	D	Y	C	A	N	E	■	■	■
S	T	A	R	T	S	■	■	R	E	N	T	A	L	■
O	R	T	Ⓞ	■	A	C	O	R	N	■	Ⓡ	A	R	E
B	I	R	Ⓒ	H	■	H	O	E	■	Ⓑ	A	N	T	U
■	Ⓑ	O	H	Ⓞ	■	A	H	A	■	Ⓤ	G	G	S	■
H	O	P	E	N	Ⓞ	T	■	L	O	R	E	L	A	I
P	R	O	T	E	Ⓒ	T	■	M	U	S	S	E	L	S
S	O	S	■	Ⓨ	A	Y	■	S	I	Ⓣ	■	D	E	M

120

P	R	I	M	■	C	L	O	T	■	L	A	T	C	H
J	A	D	E	■	E	O	N	S	■	A	L	O	H	A
S	H	O	T	C	L	O	C	K	■	Y	E	M	E	N
■	■	■	R	U	S	S	E	■	T	E	X	A	N	S
C	A	L	O	R	I	E	■	F	A	T	■	T	E	E
O	S	U	■	S	U	N	B	E	L	T	■	O	Y	L
R	I	C	H	E	S	■	L	A	C	E	U	P	■	■
K	A	Y	O	■	■	N	U	T	■	■	S	A	S	H
■	■	■	V	E	T	O	E	R	■	F	I	A	S	C	O
C	S	A	■	W	A	X	B	E	A	N	■	T	A	G
R	U	N	■	O	T	T	■	R	U	D	D	E	R	S
I	M	P	I	S	H	■	M	O	X	I	E	■	■	■
S	M	E	L	T	■	H	I	T	P	A	R	A	D	E
C	I	L	I	A	■	A	R	I	A	■	B	A	I	L
O	T	T	E	R	■	M	A	C	S	■	Y	A	N	K

121

```
A J J A C O B S ■ A B S C E S S
P O R T A B L E ■ B A Y A R E A
R E S O N A T E ■ I N S P E C T
■ ■ ■ L A M ■ N A D A ■ I C R Y
S T I L L A F I V E L E T T E R
L A G S ■ ■ A N A ■ ■ C A S T ■
E C O ■ A C T ■ S P O I L ■ ■
W O R D S T A R T I N G W I T H
■ ■ A I S L E ■ U S S ■ R Y E
■ T A T A ■ ■ I O S ■ ■ P A P A
L O S A N D E N D I N G I N E R
A R A B ■ E A S E ■ O L E ■ ■
M E N A C E R ■ S C O U T C A R
E R A S U R E ■ S A N T I A G O
R O S E R E D ■ A B S E N T E E
```

122

```
M A R C O ■ M O A T S ■ M I G
O W N U P ■ V A N D A L ■ A C A
B L A Z E O F G L O R Y ■ K E G
■ ■ C R A W ■ O N T ■ P E C S
P T B O A T ■ A A A A ■ A N A T
F E E ■ ■ B U R N I N G L O V E
C A L A M A R I ■ ■ P O S E R
■ ■ E T E R N A L F L A M E ■
S P A T E ■ ■ O I L S A N D S
L I G H T M Y F I R E ■ S H H
A Q U A ■ R O A N ■ W I S E L Y
S U E T ■ P U T ■ S Y N C ■ ■
H A R ■ D I S C O I N F E R N O
E N E ■ I B E A M S ■ E N V O Y
S T D ■ A B E T S ■ R E S T S
```

123

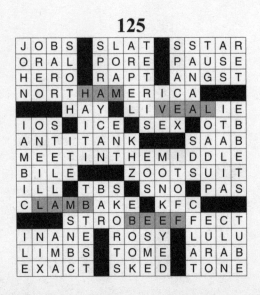

```
C O M A ■ O R C A S ■ P R E P
S L A M ■ N E A L E ■ C O M E
T A K E I T S L O W ■ S O A R
■ V O L G A ■ L E N S ■ K I T
■ I N P E N ■ ■ P A I L ■
S I N A I ■ M O V E A H E A D
A H A ■ T A I W A N ■ L Y L E
R A P ■ E G G ■ L D S ■ E E L
A D A M ■ E R N E S T ■ A R T
H A V E A S E A T ■ A O R T A
■ B A T S ■ ■ I S B N S ■
A L L ■ K I E V ■ O Z A W A
B A L D ■ S T E A L A K I S S
U S E S ■ P A T I O ■ A R I A
T T Y L ■ S L E D S ■ N E A P
```

124

```
D O T E ■ G O A D ■ E L K S
E T E S ■ H O R S E ■ M A L A
A H A S ■ I S T H A T O K A Y
R E C ■ U H O H ■ N Y J E T S
G L A S S O F O J ■ C I R C A
O L D W E S T ■ I D O ■ S H H
D O D O ■ ■ F L U B S ■ ■
■ Y O U W I L L O B E Y ■
■ P R I C Y ■ ■ L E T O
R A S ■ B I B ■ S T C L A I R
A V E D A ■ M I L O O S H E A
S I L E N T ■ P E R M ■ F I N
C A F E A U L A I T ■ Z I N G
A R I D ■ L O D G E ■ A N T E
L Y E S ■ L U S H ■ C E O S
```

125

```
J O B S ■ S L A T ■ S S T A R
O R A L ■ P O R E ■ P A U S E
H E R O ■ R A P T ■ A N G S T
N O R T H A M E R I C A ■
■ ■ H A Y ■ L I V E A L I E
I O S ■ I C E ■ S E X ■ O T B
A N T I T A N K ■ ■ S A A B
M E E T I N T H E M I D D L E
B I L E ■ ■ Z O O T S U I T
I L L ■ T B S ■ S N O ■ P A S
C L A M B A K E ■ K F C ■
■ ■ S T R O B E E F F E C T
I N A N E ■ R O S Y ■ L U L U
L I M B S ■ T O M E ■ A R A B
E X A C T ■ S K E D ■ T O N E
```

126

```
S T P ■ C I T G O ■ O D O R
I H O P ■ O N I O N ■ L E N O
N E W R E L E A S E ■ I N T O
■ O D E S ■ P R O ■ A V I A S
■ E L K ■ T A X E X E M P T
M E R L I N ■ ■ L E O ■ ■
I C K ■ M E M O R Y ■ I R K S
T H E C O A S T I S C L E A R
T O G O ■ R U B B E R ■ A L A
■ ■ S E E ■ ■ E A G L E S
B E G P A R D O N ■ V I D
E X A L T ■ A R I ■ A R E A
G I L A ■ F R E E A T L A S T
A L L Y ■ R I C C I ■ S L A B
N E S S ■ I N K E D ■ S P A
```

127

A D I O S	B A D P R	Z I N
R O C H E	A L I E N	E R A
K T O W N	S A S S A F R A S
S E N E S C E N C E	I O T A
L E O	S T E N G E L
L O L L I P O P	A H I
E M O	S A I D	O T T O I
F O U R L E T T E R W O R D S
T O T E S	H O M E	O D E
H A T	N O N S E N S E
S W E A T E R	A L A
O H M S	T A T T L E T A L E
R E C H E R C H E	A S C O T
T E E	P I K E S	Z U M B A
A L E	A S S E T	E P E E S

128

S C A M S	D A M E	A F T S
O H F U N	R I A L	C L A P
X A C T O	E M M A S T O N E
L E E R S	A B I T	O L E
Q U A R T E R T O N E	R I D
V P S	S T E	E L N I N O
C A T O	A T M S	M A T E S
M E T R I C T O N
O C T A D	O D O R	A S E A
B L O N D E	R I G	P R Y
L A S	I M E A N C O M E O N
A P T	E A R N	E P I C S
S T A N D I N G O	A N T I C
T O D O	L I L A	S C R O D
S N A G	S E E K	T E E N S

129

T W O	R E I G N S	S L O G
A I R	O C T A N E	T A K E
C P A	W H E R E S O E V E R
T E N S I O N S	A B R A D E
G E N	C M O N
A V E N G E R	R E L	U V W
M A R S	G A Z A	I N N E R
E L I E	O P E D S	O P R Y
M I N D Y	I D L E	R A G E
O D D	A C E	E M P T I E R
C H A R	L O D
S O S O O N	I S T A N B U L
P R E M O N I T I O N	I T O
E Z R A	E M E R G E	L E A
C O B S	S P R E A D	L S D

130

G O S S I P	T G I	M E S S
L A M A R R	R E D D I W I P
E T A L I I	A L I E N A T E
N H L	S N O W	A G N E W
S L Y	T E L L A L L
W E B M D	A T T E M P T
S H O P P E	T I L	R U L E
T A R	A D M I R A L	M I A
E L L S	I O N	R O B B E R
M O D E L U N	I G L O O
V A M O O S E	P J S
E S S E S	P A R K	U P C
D O W N S I Z E	A N E M I A
N A U T I C A L	C O M B E D
A R M Y	U P S	E X T O L S

131

A S U	W E L S H	L I M I T
M E R	A L O H A	A G I L E
N A B	R A M E N N O O D L E
O L A F	L A R G E S T
T E N O R	M O W	C P A S
S A H A R A N	T H E T A
A P P L E T O N	C H A N E L
D E R	S O W	P A R	N A S
R E A D U P	K A L A M A T A
E L W E S	L E X I C O N
P E L T	N Y Y	E T T A S
E P O C H A L	E R I N
H O U S E B R O K E N	A D O
O U S T S	A L I T O	C E O
W R E S T	S E N O R	E S P

132

H A S	C E R E A L	L A M B
A R I	O R A N G E	I D O L
L I D	N E W Y E A R S E V E
F A C E T	A R N E	P I N
A L A M O	T A S T E D
C R E S C E N T R O L L
L O S E	W E R E	M Y E Y E
A L A	S L E U T H S	V A L
M E R I T	A S I A	L I N K
Q U A R T E R B A C K S
S E E S A W	S T R U T
A L L	R A I N	I D I O M
F U L L T I M E J O B	O R O
E D I E	T A M A L E	N E O
R E E D	S C O R E D	S O N

133

```
DIN  RABBI  EPICS
ANO  AXIOM  CALLA
DEC  DEATHVALLEY
BRAG  SHEER  BMW
ORNATE  REDDISH
DODGEVIPER  OTOE
SRO  LIMA  PENN
DEEPVOICE
SILO  ETNA  ADO
AHAS  DARTHVADER
VOTERID  DENOVO
EPI  SNOOP  SPIN
DEMOVERSION  TOY
USEUP  BLEAR  MUM
POSTS  SORTA  ESS
```

134

```
SAWII  ECHO  VANS
PLANT  DAMP  OBIE
ELVISANDME  RULE
WIE  OJAY  RITTER
SEDAKA  MACE
OAXACAMEXICO
SPINY  DRYAD  TAZ
PANE  DEION  GETZ
UPN  WAXER  CONEY
DISCOVERSION
ERIC  TOGAED
UNJAMS  BACK  UVA
COOS  CARDHOLDER
LINE  UTAH  FAINT
ARID  PEND  FOOTS
```

135

```
SPAM  MEALS  HOLA
TERI  ABBOT  AROD
ASOF  IBELIEVESO
NONFAT  ARRESTS
SNARF  SIA
ORG  NIELS  CHASM
PERSE  BATCHEDIT
ERAT  BOXED  ASTO
ROME  ROSES  RAPS
ALMAMATER  ATLAS
SLYLY  SEEMS  ETA
ABC  DRUID
ARIKARA  RARING
GOSIDEWAYS  USER
ARES  TEHEE  MORE
RYES  EDITS  SNOW
```

136

```
HEMS  ELMO  BALDS
AVEC  MEAL  CLARK
LIFEGUARD  CASEY
FLINT  PLEA  CAL
WEREON  ANDSOAMI
AYS  SEA  SADLOT
YETI  LIES  LOAN
FILMLOVER
SHOD  SIRI  SHEL
GOALIE  TEM  OVA
HANDGRIP  WESLEY
OKS  AMOS  RHINE
USOFA  POLICEDOG
LULUS  ELAN  BANG
SPORK  ISMS  AYES
```

137

```
BOLT  BLOC  ABASE
ITOO  LALA  CAMUS
DOUG  UTAH  TROMP
HIGHDEFINITION
SLOG  LIVE
OVEREXPLAINED
ANI  NOVA  ADDON
HELP  NINTH  SNUB
HALLS  DAUB  ASA
MEANINGOFLIFE
TODO  FACE
LEXICOGRAPHERS
ARENA  GOGO  ABOY
GINUP  IDES  GENE
SCAMS  NEST  ERGS
```

138

```
ARF  SAABS  PHOTO
MAO  MILLI  LETIN
AIL  ORLON  AISLE
STILLKICKING
STOODIN  VELCRO
WES  COAT  LOU
WATERSDOWN  DEUS
HEARS  OUI  GIANT
AIMS  RUNERRANDS
ROE  KURT  EEL
FURIES  ORWORSE
DEEPTHOUGHTS
MASON  LEGUP  YRS
STALL  USETO  MAE
NEWSY  SHEEN  EPS
```

139

TAPED · STAR · ASP
SPACE LAKE DUEL
APRON ARISTOTLE
LANGSTONHUGHES
JED VET ARSONS
OPIATE APT RAY
SIGMUNDFREUD
HEMEN IDI ROTFL
SALVADORDALI
EMU RAE BOOMED
MOSCOW AHI AWS
EVERLYBROTHERS
REDALERTS AXIOM
GRUB RISE MENLO
ESP SOYS MSDOS

140

AWL IRE TABASCO
HAITIAN IGOTCHA
OFFSIDE NOTTHAT
LEEK IMPS IONS
DRS SOYA WACO
TWIG RCAS LYE
TOYOTA TOBACCOS
ABLE LAYLA LAWS
GOESBALD STIFLE
SEC EXPO HOPE
HOLY WARP TED
NOON ANTI GENE
EPITAPH OVERRAN
CICADAS METRICS
KEEPSTO SRA ATE

141

QUALM TIFF SHAH
TABOO UCLA PALO
REACT NOAM IRAN
ATLANTICTIME
ZIPLOC LAZBOY
IMAC DETAIL OSS
METAL NAPALM
ATHLETICTRAINER
LORAIN SKODA
AHH VECTOR EGGY
TOOKIN KBTOYS
ATOMICTHEORY
NADA HOAX ASHEN
DIOR ELHI KOALA
TROT SLAT ENJOY

142

AIRS STAN GIANT
NOAA HERA OLDER
TWINPEAKS AKIRA
SANDED AIT ETC
DAP FULLHOUSE
SKELETON LED
AILS HRS PRESET
ALA BEDHEAD PTA
BOYTOY OPS FORT
IRS RESTAREA
QUEENANNE ALT
USA FYI ALLSET
AUGER KINGCOBRA
CREPE KNEE FAIR
KYRIE ICES FRET

143

BLACK SLACK ENT
REBAG TIPPI NIA
AMASS EMBASSIES
VAST ANO STACK
OTHELLO AMERCES
ELSINORE
STALE CALSTATE
RIGA STALE CHEW
SLAPDASH SHALE
BANKNOTE
ASCENDS REVERSI
WHALE GAY PITT
GENTLEMEN LOCOS
EEO APING OCCAM
ERN WHILE WHITE

144

SHO PIPPI FROST
TOPSECRET LUCKY
ONEWAYORANOTHER
PECAN PLOW OWE
GUTS ISEE
TRU TWOWAYRADIO
WALLSAFE STIRS
INCA STEPS UVEA
SCENT PINGPONG
THREEWAYTIE TEE
SAIL APTS
AKA BRIO BEECH
SIXWAYSTOSUNDAY
STIEG TREESTUMP
TESTS SADLY COO

145

A	C	T	I	I		B	O	A	R		I	D	L	E
F	A	I	N	T		A	L	D	A		C	R	U	X
F	R	E	T	S		H	E	L	P	M	E	O	B	I
E	R	I	E				A	I	D	A		P	E	T
C	I	N	N	A	M	O	N	B	U	N	S			
T	E	S	T	L	A	B			O	N	A	R	U	N
			P	I	E	T	A				S	O	M	E
Y	O	U	R	E	M	Y	O	N	L	Y	H	O	P	E
A	U	R	A			S	O	D	O	I				
W	I	N	S	A	T			R	I	P	O	F	F	S
		P	R	I	N	C	E	S	S	L	E	I	A	
O	H	O		S	L	A	Y			E	T	S	Y	
W	A	N	K	E	N	O	B	I		M	O	T	H	Y
L	U	T	E			O	M	E	N		A	L	L	E	E
S	L	O	G			W	I	R	E		P	E	E	R	S

146

P	O	O	H		M	W	A	H			T	A	P	E	D
A	C	N	E		O	H	I	O			O	H	A	R	A
R	U	M	P	R	O	A	S	T			L	A	S	E	D
A	L	I	T	O		P	L	E	A	D		T	A	B	
D	A	K	O	T	A		E	L	D	O	R	A	D	O	
E	R	E		I	R	A		S	O	F	A	B	E	D	
		E	N	A	C	T				C	A	R	S		
	S	T	I	L	T	W	A	L	K	E	R			
M	A	T	H			O	P	A	L	S				
I	S	R	A	E	L	I		B	Y	U		O	W	E
S	K	I	N	G	A	M	E		S	T	O	N	E	D
C	A	N		R	O	A	R	S		Z	A	L	E	S
A	W	G	E	E		F	A	I	R	Y	T	A	L	E
S	A	U	L	T		A	S	T	O		E	T	A	L
T	Y	P	O	S		N	E	S	T		R	E	D	S

147

H	O	G		A	C	T	A	S		P	A	P	A	L
O	T	O		P	A	I	N	T		I	M	O	U	T
T	O	L	L	P	L	A	Z	A		C	Y	S	T	S
D	O	D	O	S		I	M	P		G	E	O		
O	L	E	O		J	E	O	P	A	R	D	I	Z	E
G	E	N	T	E	E	L			D	E	A	D	O	N
			R	E	I	D		A	L	O	N	E		
P	A	P	E	R	A	I	R	P	L	A	N	E		
L	A	N	E	S			P	O	L	L				
O	R	N	A	T	E		L	A	Y	A	W	A	Y	
P	R	E	S	U	M	A	B	L	Y		L	A	C	E
	O	R	A		S	T	L			M	A	R	C	O
S	T	I	N	G		H	I	D	D	E	N	G	E	M
R	E	C	T	O		O	G	R	E	S		O	D	E
I	D	E	S	T		S	E	E	Y	A		D	E	N

148

D	E	E	M	S		L	A	Y		A	B	H	O	R
E	X	P	A	T		A	P	E		N	O	I	R	E
U	T	I	C	A		S	T	A	G	N	A	T	E	D
C	O	C	K	T	A	I	L	H	O	U	R			
E	L	F			S	K	Y		O	L	D	V	I	C
		A	C	E	S			A	D	S		I	P	O
	L	I	E	T	E	S	T	S			A	P	A	L
B	U	L	L	E	T	P	R	O	O	F	V	E	S	T
O	N	U	S			R	E	F	R	A	I	N	S	
H	A	R		A	M	Y			A	N	A	T		
O	R	E	I	D	A		M	S	T			R	U	B
			B	U	C	K	E	Y	E	S	T	A	T	E
M	A	L	E	L	E	A	D	S		P	I	N	T	A
B	L	O	A	T		R	I	O		A	R	C	E	D
A	L	U	M	S		L	A	P		S	E	E	R	S

149

M	A	G	I	C		A	R	A	L		A	C	E	R
A	B	A	S	H		R	O	D	E		S	O	L	E
P	U	L	S	E		C	A	R	G	O	S	H	I	P
		L	E	N	S		S	O	U	P	N	A	Z	I
Q	U	A	L	I	T	Y	T	I	M	E		B	A	N
U	P	N		L	O	A		T	E	N	T			
A	F	T		L	O	L	Z			A	S	I	A	
F	O	R	K	E	D	L	I	G	H	T	N	I	N	G
F	R	Y	E			P	E	A	R		R	C	A	
		Y	O	K	E		R	Y	E		B	O	Z	
B	O	W		T	E	X	T	M	E	S	S	A	G	E
S	W	E	E	T	T	E	A			S	P	U	R	
I	N	A	B	O	T	T	L	E		A	S	T	I	N
D	E	V	O		L	E	O	X		S	H	O	V	E
E	D	E	N		E	R	N	O		S	I	N	E	W

150

M	E	E	K		T	O	D	O			L	U	N	A	R
A	P	S	E		U	V	E	A			A	T	O	N	E
R	I	C	E		R	A	F	T			M	T	W	T	F
I	C	A	N	O	N	L	Y	H	O	P	E				
A	S	P	I	C	S				C	O	R	N	E	L	
		E	N	S	U	E		C	H	O	L	E	R	A	
B	E	R	G		P	R	I	S	O	N	Y	A	R	D	
E	X	O			I	D	I			R	O	E			
S	P	U	T	N	I	K	O	N	E		B	E	R	N	
T	E	T	H	E	R	S		Y	A	Y	A	S			
S	L	E	E	V	E				T	E	S	T	E	R	
		H	I	D	D	E	N	C	A	M	E	R	A		
M	O	R	E	L		A	S	E	A		A	X	I	S	
D	R	I	L	L		M	A	R	K		T	I	N	T	
T	R	O	P	E		N	U	D	E		I	T	S	A	

151

P	A	P	A		A	C	T			P	R	I	M	E	R
E	V	E	R		N	O	W			B	U	R	E	A	U
L	I	A	R		C	H	E	S	S	B	O	A	R	D	
T	A	C	O		H	E	R	O		A	N	T	S	Y	
	N	E	W	Y	O	R	K	C	I	T	Y				
	H	A	R	E		C	O	O		J	L	O			
W	H	E	E	L		F	E	W		B	O	O	R		
R	U	P	A	U	L	S	D	R	A	G	R	A	C	E	
A	M	I	D		A	I	R		A	U	D	I	O		
P	E	C		H	I	C		E	A	R	N				
	R	O	C	K	A	N	D	R	O	L	L				
T	W	E	E	T		O	L	A	F		M	A	I	N	
H	A	L	L	O	F	F	A	M	E		A	T	V	S	
U	R	B	A	N	E		R	O	E		R	E	E	F	
S	T	A	Y	E	D		M	R	S		S	X	S	W	

152

O	L	A	V		O	F	A	R	T		S	H	A	H
S	O	L	O		N	I	M	E	S		C	O	S	A
H	A	L	L	O	F	F	A	M	E		A	N	T	I
A	T	F		G	O	T	T	O		C	L	E	R	K
	H	E	L	L	O	H	O	W	A	R	E	Y	O	U
	M	O	E	T			B	U	D					
O	P	A	L		S	T	R	U	M		R	E	P	
H	I	L	L	S	T	R	E	E	T	B	L	U	E	S
O	N	E		T	H	I	E	F			E	L	L	A
	A	A	A			P	A	N	E					
H	O	L	L	Y	W	O	O	D	A	C	T	O	R	
A	R	E	A	S		V	I	O	L	A		F	I	R
S	I	R	S		H	U	L	L	A	B	A	L	O	O
T	O	O	K		S	L	E	E	T		B	A	J	A
E	N	Y	A		T	E	R	S	E		S	W	A	N

153

A	I	D	S		P	L	U	S		I	T	E	M	S
R	O	U	E		R	A	P	T		N	A	S	A	L
T	W	E	E	H	O	U	S	E		S	U	P	R	A
S	A	L	S	A		R	E	A	M		G	R	I	T
	S	W	A	T	M	A	C	H	I	N	E			
O	A	K	L	E	Y			R	U	T	T	E	D	
W	H	I	S	K	E	Y	M	O	V	E				
L	A	N	D		E	O	E		B	A	R	S		
	W	O	W	E	D	M	O	U	T	H	S			
S	A	M	S	O	N		A	W	G	O	O	N		
Q	U	A	C	K	O	F	D	A	W	N				
U	S	N	A		R	E	A	D		E	M	C	E	E
A	S	T	R	A		E	L	M	E	R	F	U	D	D
S	I	R	E	N		L	A	I	R		A	B	I	G
H	E	A	D	Y		S	I	N	E		S	A	T	E

154

D	A	W	N		S	T	A	N		A	L	O	F	T
A	G	R	O		A	R	I	A		R	A	Z	O	R
R	O	O	S	E	V	E	L	T		A	M	O	R	E
I	N	T	E	R	I	M		O	R	G	A	N	D	Y
N	Y	E		R	O	O	T		H	O	S	E		
	H	A	R	R	I	S	O	N		H	O	P		
C	O	M	E	T	S		M	A	S		W	O	R	E
O	B	A	M	A		D	O	G		T	Y	L	E	R
P	I	C	S		J	O	T		E	R	N	E	S	T
E	T	A		B	U	C	H	A	N	A	N			
	D	A	R	N		Y	E	L	L		P	R	E	
S	T	A	T	I	O	N		N	I	E	L	S	E	N
H	A	M	I	D		C	L	E	V	E	L	A	N	D
E	F	I	L	E		A	T	I	E		C	L	E	O
S	T	A	T	S		A	D	D	N		S	M	E	W

155

A	G	A	V	E	S		S	P	A		A	L	L	A
I	O	M	O	T	H		E	D	U		T	E	A	R
D	R	Y	I	C	E		A	F	R	O	P	I	C	K
A	P	P	L	E	P	I	E		A	R	R	A	Y	S
	O	A	T		L	E	S	S	E	E				
I	V	E		C	E	L	L	O		L	S	A	T	S
D	O	H	A		A	S	S	T		S	E	T	U	P
E	L	L	I	O	T		K	E	N	O	B	I		
S	T	E	R	N		P	T	U	I		T	M	E	N
T	A	R	P	S		R	U	S	T	S		I	D	S
	I	P	H	O	N	E		O	T	C				
D	C	A	R	E	A		A	R	T	P	A	P	E	R
A	L	P	A	C	I	N	O		O	S	C	I	N	E
F	O	O	T		K	O	I		G	U	I	L	D	S
T	Y	P	E		U	R	L		A	P	T	E	S	T

156

C	A	N	D	O		L	I	M	A		E	P	P	S
B	L	E	A	K		A	P	O	P		A	L	O	E
S	T	A	R	E	S	D	O	W	N		T	A	P	E
	A	T	T	E	N	D	S		E	A	S	I	E	R
	S	F	O		F	A	D		N	Y	E			
A	R	P		F	U	D	G	E		A	M	P	E	D
P	E	A	C	E	T	I	M	E		M	A	A		
E	X	P	O		S	E	A	L	S		U	P	O	N
	E	L	I		T	I	M	E	P	I	E	C	E	
R	E	R	A	N		E	L	E	N	A		R	T	E
E	X	P		S	A	D		S	I	M				
D	O	L	A	P	S		S	E	E	N	O	T	E	
S	T	A	G		D	O	W	N	S	T	A	I	R	S
E	I	N	E		O	V	I	D		E	N	E	M	Y
A	C	E	S		I	A	M	S		R	A	D	A	R

157

```
J E A N   . C H I L I . W H E Y
A X L E   . T O N A L . H A L E
V A S T (T) A B B I E(E) O W N S
A M O N G(O) B A N D B . A I M
.     . (O) E R R E D . U R S I N E
B O R G I A S   . E D I T I O N
O N H A N D   . A M I G A   .
B O O T   . I N D I A . N A D A
.     I N C A S   . B O D I E S
L A T V I A(N) . A L L U R E S
A S W E L L(L) . S L E E P
S P A   E L V E S . O G D E N
T I N A   E A T A T . U R G E
E R G O   F L I C K   Y O G A
D E S K   . T E N E T . S P O T
```

158

```
F D A   . C A S K . C L I O S
A R C   . A R I A . G L A N C E
T A R   . C I T Y S L I C K E R
.   C O O K S   . H O P . L A B
B U B B L E W R A P . F I N I
B L A S E   . H U G . S O N I A
S A T E   . F O G . B R O G A N
.     S U G A R C O A T   .
C R I S P S   . A L T . R I B S
D A M E S   . G T O . P A R E S
R I A S   . D U S T J A C K E T
A N G   . B A L   . P R E S S
C H E V Y B L A Z E R . O W L
K A R A T S   . S E G O . M A O
S T Y L E   . P E S T . E X T
```

159

```
M E D A L S   . A C K . A M O S
I M O N I T   . M A E . K E P I
C A N T E R B U R Y T A L E S
R I T Z   . A S P C A . E R A
A L S   . T H A T S A S T E A L
.   P S A T   . S K A
C L E A N S L A T E . U S T A
S P A Y S   . A L E . O N T A P
T S K S   . G O I N G S T A L E
.   S S R   . A S S N
N I K O L A T E S L A . D E A
U Z I   . A D O R N . T B A R
L A S T B U T N O T L E A S T
L A S E   . A H S . N I E C E S
S K Y E   . L E T . T I N K L Y
```

160

```
A T T Y   . J A G . B L I S S
P R O O F . E R A . R O G U E
B E R M U D A T R I A N G L E
.   K E A T O N . G P S . Y U K
.     M I G . B L A I R   .
F I N A L S A L E . Z A P P A
E N E   . E L L A . T E T R A S
M A R K   . E A R T H . S A N K
U N D E A D . N O I D . D I M
R E Y E S   . T E N N I S A C E
.     P I T H Y . A A H   .
O C T   . A W E . D I L U T E
P O I N T O F N O R E T U R N
E N N U I . E A T . R U B I O
N S Y N C . D Y E . P A C T
```

161

```
M O M   . D A T A . M A C A U
A N I   . E W E R S . O B O E S
N E C   . N G A I O . T B I R D
S I D C A E S A R   . A N O
M O R A L E   . L E E J C O B B
A T O M I Z E   . P A Y P A L
N A P E   . C O O E D . S T Y
.     O R S O N B E A N
A M C   . V E N T I   . A A H S
G O O I E R   . T A N K T O P
T O M G R E E N . P A E L L A
.   C P U   . S A L A D D A Y S
S H O E D . A M A T I . N A T
P E R S E . S E N O R . T R I
A R T S Y   . S E W S . A K C
```

162

```
S P A Y . A S A P . A M B E R
M U L E . I T S A . L A U R A
I M O N . R U B Y . L O G A N
L I T T L E D I P P E R   .
E C O L I   . G A S G I A N T
D E F . B E G . L I E . F O E
.     F R A M E   . B A R N
.   S T A R C L U S T E R .
F O O D   . K N E A D
O W L . T A I . O W N . H O P
R E D D W A R F   . G O O D S
.   H E A V E N L Y B O D Y
A L G A E . I T O O . A V E C
D O U B T . N A P S . M E S H
Z U N I S . G L E E . A S T O
```

163

```
E T C H █ T S A R █ B A S I N
A I R S █ I N R E █ E V I T A
S T A T U E O F L I B E R T Y
E L M █ P R O █ █ M O N █ █ █
D E S K T O P C O M P U T E R
█ █ I U D █ H U E █ E R G O █
S T A R R █ S I T A R █ O R A
C A B I N E T M I N I S T E R
A M A █ S C E N E █ V E S T S
B I C S █ Z E E █ S I E █ █ █
S L I P P E R Y W H E N W E T
█ █ H U M █ H A R █ E P A █ █
P U R E M A T H E M A T I C S
U S U R P █ W I R E █ B L O T
G E N E S █ O P E D █ A L T E
```

164

```
X R A Y S █ C A W █ L E T U P S
M I X E R █ A M O █ U T O P I A
A L L S I K N O W █ C H O S E N
S E E M █ N O N █ T K O S █ █ █
█ █ █ A L O N G W A Y S O F F █
S T R A I T █ A N Y █ O L A F
T R U M P █ A R G O █ N A I L
E O N █ S T A K E O U T █ G L O
M I S O █ O A R S █ O B O E S
S K I D █ P H O █ T R E N D S
█ █ A N D T H E N I S A Y S █
█ S E E D █ H O G █ T R E E █
H A V A N A █ H O W S A B O U T
I M P R O V █ A P E █ G U A R D
M I S E R Y █ L E D █ T Y R O S
```

165

```
S W A P █ C R O C █ D R A M A
H E I R █ O A T H █ E U L E R
A L D O █ N I T E █ A D E L E
G L E N N C L O S E L Y █ █ █
█ █ T E E █ T A M █ E A P
█ H O W A R D S T E R N L Y
P S A █ L E O █ █ I N T E R
E A R N S █ G N U █ N A I V E
S T R I P █ O N O █ T E X
T A Y L O R S W I F T L Y █
O N S █ R I P █ F A A █
█ J A M E S B L U N T L Y
U R G E D █ C H A I █ D R E I
S A U D I █ K I L N █ R E A P
C Y N I C █ S A K E █ Y E N S
```

166

```
E G O S █ V A P O R █ I R I S
B E R T █ I R A T E █ N A T L
B E E R B A T T E R █ E C H O
S K O A L █ E R A S █ H A T
█ █ P U M P K I N C O A C H
S K I █ R O E █ R H E A S
O I L S █ N A S A █ A F L
B A L L P A R K F I G U R E S
█ B A E █ S A L T █ N A P A
A L E V E █ A C T █ Y A P
W A T E R P I T C H E R █ █
N T H █ S U M O █ R E A M S
I T E M █ C E I L I N G F A N
N E R O █ K A L E L █ A R I A
G R E W █ S N E A K █ L O N G
```

167

```
X F L █ G R A T E █ S T A I D
E R A █ R E L A Y █ C O S M O
N O S E R V I C E █ R A Y O N
O D E A █ O B I █ P E S O █
N O R S E L I T E R A T U R E
█ T U T █ G E M █ W A X
E M B E R █ S A G E █ M I N I
N E U R O S C I E N T I S T S
D A R N █ C U R D █ I M H O T
O R S █ J A B █ V E E █
N A T I O N A L P A S T I M E
█ O N U S █ Y I P █ I C O N
J A P E S █ P I N O C C H I O
E X E R T █ I N T R O █ A R K
T E N T S █ A G A S P █ T A I
```

168

```
W I S H █ L A M B █ S W A M I
A K I O █ A L O E █ I O N I C
S E C L U S I O N █ G E N R E
P A K I S T A N Z A N I A █
█ █ D E N █ █ P H S █
N I C A R A G U A T E M A L A
O K A Y █ M O N K █ R E B A R
E N C █ G E N T I L E █ N Y E
L O T S A █ E I R E █ D E E N
S W I T Z E R L A N D O R R A
█ █ O E D █ █ T A M █ █
█ U N I T E D N A T I O N S
T A K E N █ B E A N A N G E L
A V E R T █ A C I D █ O L I O
B A S S O █ Y O L O █ S E N T
```

169

W	D	S		C	D	R	O	M		A	P	B	I	O
I	R	A		A	W	A	R	E		C	L	U	C	K
L	U	L	U	L	E	M	O	N		H	A	D	E	S
S	N	A	R	L	E	R			L	O	N	G	S	
O	K	R	A		B	O	O	B	O	O	B	E	A	R
N	S	Y	N	C		D	U	A	L			T	W	O
			I	O	S		R	B	I		R	E	S	T
	P	U	P	U	P	L	A	T	T	E	R			
P	R	I	M		R	E	A		A	I	L			
I	O	N			E	T	D	S		P	A	L	E	S
G	O	O	G	O	O	E	Y	E	S		P	I	T	A
	S	C	A	R	F			A	M	U	S	E	R	S
E	T	H	I	C		V	U	V	U	Z	E	L	A	S
D	E	L	T	A		O	T	E	R	I		O	D	E
D	R	E	S	S		N	E	R	F	S		W	E	D

170

S	E	E	S		E	T	T	E			L	A	S	S
T	I	L	T		R	E	A	R	S		A	R	I	A
A	R	E	A		A	S	S	A	I		R	A	T	S
R	E	A	L	I	S	T			S	T	I	L	E	S
			E	T	E	S		A	S	E	A			
A	L	T	A	I	R		A	L	I	S	T	E	R	
S	A	R	I	S		R	I	T	E	S		L	A	T
S	T	I	R		S	E	L	E	S		R	I	T	A
T	E	T		S	T	E	E	R		E	A	T	E	R
	R	E	T	A	I	L	S		A	T	R	E	S	T
			E	L	L	S		E	S	A	I			
I	S	R	A	E	L		S	A	L	T	I	E	R	
R	I	I	S		E	T	A	T	S		I	R	A	E
E	L	L	E		R	E	L	E	E		E	A	S	E
S	T	E	R		L	E	S	T			S	S	T	S

171

H	T	M	L		C	H	E	F		P	S	A	L	M
O	W	E	S		I	O	T	A		E	E	R	I	E
W	O	R	D	S	A	L	A	D		G	A	P	E	D
T	A	M		W	O	E		I	R	A	T	E		
O	M	A	H	A			E	N	O	S		G	M	T
			N	O	T	H	I	N	G	B	U	R	G	E	R
			T	H	I	R	D			S	E	I	N	E
S	W	I	M		P	A	N	S	Y		D	O	S	E
P	O	S	I	T			O	P	E	N	S			
C	O	U	C	H	P	O	T	A	T	O	E	S		
A	L	P		R	O	L	E			B	A	N	G	S
		P	R	I	E	D		G	E	E		I	O	U
S	E	O	U	L		H	U	M	B	L	E	P	I	E
E	A	S	E	L		A	R	A	B		M	E	N	D
T	R	E	S	S		T	I	N	S		U	R	G	E

172

I	R	A	Q		T	R	I	G		C	B	G	B	S
M	E	N	T		R	O	S	A		H	E	L	O	T
B	O	D	Y	G	U	A	R	D		I	B	I	Z	A
U	R	I		A	I	D		G	A	M	E	B	O	Y
E	G	E	S	T	S		N	E	V	E				
			C	O	M	P	U	T	E	R	P	O	R	T
S	A	M	E		S	E	Z		C	A	R	V	E	S
P	R	A	N	K		Z	Z	Z		S	I	E	N	A
A	G	R	E	E	S		L	I	I		O	N	E	R
M	O	V	I	E	T	H	E	A	T	E	R			
				P	E	A	S		S	A	Y	I	D	O
I	C	E	L	A	N	D		C	O	S		M	E	X
B	O	R	A	T		F	R	O	N	T	P	A	G	E
M	I	T	Z	I		U	N	U	M		A	G	U	Y
S	L	E	E	T		N	A	P	E		H	O	M	E

173

A	W	A	R	D	S		C	O	M	P		C	C	S
P	O	T	I	O	N		O	B	O	E		A	R	E
R	O	A	D	W	A	R	R	I	O	R		M	E	N
			E	N	T	E	R		T	E	N	E	T	S
U	S	S	R		C	D	I	V			E	R	I	E
M	A	L		R	H	O	D	E	I	S	L	A	N	D
P	R	I	M	A			A	T	O	M	S			
S	I	D	E	C	A	R		S	N	O	O	K	E	R
		R	E	N	E	W			K	N	A	V	E	
R	O	W	E	D	A	S	H	O	R	E		T	E	N
O	R	A	L			T	I	N	A		C	E	N	T
T	A	N	Y	A	S		T	E	S	L	A			
T	N	T		R	O	D	E	S	H	O	T	G	U	N
E	G	O		C	Y	A	N		E	S	T	A	T	E
D	E	N		H	A	M	S		S	T	Y	L	E	D

174

V	I	C	E	S		C	A	S	A	S		B	A	T
E	C	L	A	T		H	I	P	P	O		E	P	A
T	E	E	T	O	T	A	L	L	E	R		D	A	B
			R	I	P	E	R		A	R	T	D	E	C	O
L	O	I	N		E	G	O	S			E	C	H	O
A	R	C		O	N	E	W	H	O	T	A	K	E	S
S	C	A	R	F			L	E	A	R	N			
S	A	L	U	T	E	D		S	T	A	N	D	B	Y
			B	E	S	O	S		C	A	I	R	O	
I	N	V	E	N	T	O	R	Y	A	T		S	A	Y
N	E	I	N			R	I	E	L		O	C	T	O
T	W	O	S	T	E	P		N	E	R	V	E		
A	T	L		A	G	O	L	F	C	O	U	R	S	E
C	O	E		P	A	S	E	O		U	L	N	A	R
T	N	T		E	N	T	E	R		T	E	S	L	A

175

```
B E B O P   G A R B O   B L T
I R A N I   I D E A L   R U R
B E D A N D B O A R D   A C E
    H U E S       T A C K Y
B A B O O N S   S M I L E Y S
O T O O L E   R H U M B A
A T O N E   L E A S E   N A T
R A M A   V O I D S   E D N A
S R A   F O G G Y   U N B O X
  N O R T O N   I N C I S E
C A D D I E S   P S A L T E R
R U B E S     A L I I
E D U   B O R N A N D B R E D
S I S   E J E C T   E M O T E
T E T   E S T E E   D W E E B
```

176

```
P A S A   G E R A L D   C H E
A L O T   O U N C E S   L E X
B I L L Y G R A H A M   O R A
L O V E M E   S E R   I C B M
O N E A C T S   S N A C K
      S A T I E   S L E W E D
T A C T   E L M O   A S I D E
H E R   C R A C K E R   S I N
A R O L L   S E R A   G E T S
N O S O A P   E A S E L
    S O D O I   S T R A S S E
R A F T   L C D   S A S H A Y
A L I   P L A Y S I T S A F E
C A R   R E R E A D   E W E R
E S E   O N E D G E   S L R S
```

177

```
C P A S   R I S K S   O S H A
D E F T   O S H E A   L U I S
R A R A   L E O N I   A R E S
O N E L I F E T O L I V E
M U S E D     B O N   F I B
  T H R E E B L I N D M I C E
      A M M O   O A R E D
S O D S   S W O R E   T E S S
O D I U M   P A L S
F I V E E A S Y P I E C E S
A N I   R N A   A L L O R
    S E V E N Y E A R I T C H
S H I V   M E A T S   P O K Y
P A V E   I S L E S   O R E M
A M E N   A T E S T   N O T E
```

178

```
F I L E   M O L E   G A M U T
A R I D   S P A M   A B A S E
C O N G O G A M E   R A N U P
E N T E R   L A R V A   G A I
    S A S S     A G E O L D
R E T I N A   C A M E T O
S L A N G Y   A M P   A F R O
V I N   E G O M A I L   G A P
P E G S   R Y E   R E M O T E
  O N C A L L   E V A D E D
B E L L O C     I S A K
A R I   L E A R N   N E R T S
C I N C O   G O B E T W E E N
O C E A N   A M E N   A B R A
N A S T Y   R E D S   R A M P
```

179

```
E D N A   B A A S   S M E L L
G R I T   U C L A   T A L I A
G A L E   G R A M   A L L E Y
  W E A T H E R B U R E A U
    M A O     A M T
L I U   R U T H   P R A I S E
E R S E   S E E R   E I D E R
H E A T H E R L O C K L E A R
A N I T A   M E S H   S A T E
R E R U N S   N E A R   L S D
      D C C     R E A
  L E A T H E R J A C K E T
S A Y S O   L A U D   I R A Q
O N E T O   L I N E   T I L E
P E D A L   O D E S   A C E D
```

180

```
R A B A T   G O S H   T B S P
I M A C S   E N T O   R A T A
B A N T U   N E A R   O R E S
    I N D I A N A J O N E S
A T H   A Y E   T U P E L O
T R A U M A   L A I D   Y E N
V I R G I N I A W O O L F
S O U L   M P H   I R I S
  M I N N E S O T A F A T S
I R S   I A T E   A R E N O T
N I C E L Y   C R T   K O S
S T A T E S P E O P L E
A U R A   A L E R   E R U P T
N A U T   Y E L P   S I N A I
E L M S   S A S S   S K I L L
```

181

E	M	M	A	■	■	R	O	T	O	R	■	P	A	L
L	O	I	N	S	■	E	V	A	D	E	■	E	L	I
C	U	T	T	H	E	C	A	R	D	S	■	R	O	E
I	N	T	E	R	V	A	L	■	■	E	A	S	E	D
D	D	S	■	O	I	L	■	S	P	A	C	E	■	■
■	■	■	P	U	L	L	T	H	E	L	E	V	E	R
S	C	A	L	D	■	■	H	E	R	S	■	E	M	U
E	A	S	Y	■	C	A	R	A	T	■	A	R	I	D
A	M	S	■	S	O	L	E	■	■	P	I	E	T	Y
S	P	I	N	T	H	E	W	H	E	E	L	■	■	■
■	■	S	E	I	N	E	■	U	T	E	■	N	A	T
L	I	T	E	R	■	■	I	N	C	R	E	A	S	E
A	D	A	■	R	O	L	L	T	H	E	D	I	C	E
M	E	N	■	E	R	A	S	E	■	D	E	V	O	N
B	A	T	■	D	E	B	A	R	■	■	N	E	T	S

182

B	A	N	D	■	C	E	N	T	■	W	A	L	L	A
A	L	I	A	■	A	N	T	E	■	A	N	A	I	S
S	E	N	D	I	N	T	H	E	C	L	O	N	E	S
■	■	■	A	N	T	I	■	■	O	L	D	A	G	E
E	P	I	■	T	O	R	■	T	Y	P	E	S	E	T
P	A	R	A	■	R	E	T	O	O	L	■	■	■	■
A	W	A	R	D	■	■	A	N	T	A	R	E	S	■
■	A	B	U	O	Y	L	I	K	E	T	H	A	T	■
■	T	U	N	G	O	I	L	■	■	E	O	S	I	N
■	■	■	■	F	U	I	S	S	E	■	S	E	L	F
P	A	C	H	I	S	I	■	E	L	M	■	D	E	L
O	T	I	O	S	E	■	■	W	A	I	T	■	■	■
S	T	E	P	H	E	N	S	O	N	D	H	E	I	M
T	H	R	E	E	■	B	O	N	D	■	I	G	O	R
S	E	A	R	S	■	■	C	U	S	S	■	S	O	N	S

183

F	E	T	E	■	A	F	A	R	■	D	A	C	H	A
A	C	R	E	■	N	A	S	A	■	E	T	H	A	N
T	H	E	G	O	O	D	S	H	E	P	H	E	R	D
S	O	X	■	D	I	E	T	■	Q	U	O	T	E	S
■	■	■	V	E	N	D	■	C	U	T	S	■	■	■
P	A	L	E	S	T	■	G	R	A	Y	■	C	H	E
A	C	E	R	S	■	U	R	A	L	■	W	H	O	A
T	H	E	B	A	D	N	E	W	S	B	E	A	R	S
T	E	C	S	■	R	I	A	L	■	L	E	O	N	E
I	S	H	■	M	I	T	T	■	L	A	P	S	E	D
■	■	■	P	A	V	E	■	H	A	Z	Y	■	■	■
O	C	T	A	N	E	■	J	U	T	E	■	I	C	K
T	H	E	U	G	L	Y	A	M	E	R	I	C	A	N
T	E	R	S	E	■	A	V	O	N	■	D	O	M	O
O	W	N	E	R	■	M	A	R	T	■	A	N	E	W

184

C	A	S	H	■	S	A	T	I	N	Y	■	T	E	A
O	B	O	E	■	A	T	O	N	C	E	■	A	R	T
D	E	M	I	■	L	O	O	K	A	L	I	K	E	S
■	■	B	R	E	A	M	■	■	A	P	I	E	C	E
F	I	R	■	S	M	I	T	E	■	■	I	O	T	A
I	D	E	N	T	I	C	A	L	T	W	I	N	S	■
T	E	R	I	■	■	■	N	I	N	A	■	■	■	■
■	D	O	P	P	E	L	G	A	N	G	E	R	S	■
■	■	■	■	I	D	E	E	■	■	V	E	T	S	■
■	S	P	I	T	T	I	N	G	I	M	A	G	E	S
S	P	U	D	■	■	S	T	O	R	E	■	U	T	E
A	R	M	O	R	S	■	■	V	I	T	A	L	■	■
D	U	P	L	I	C	A	T	E	S	■	S	A	T	E
A	C	E	■	G	A	L	O	R	E	■	I	R	A	S
T	E	D	■	S	T	E	R	N	S	■	A	S	P	S

185

A	B	B	E	■	Z	E	A	L	■	A	J	A	R
T	R	A	X	■	A	D	L	A	I	■	D	E	C	O
W	A	S	H	I	N	G	T	O	N	■	A	F	R	O
A	V	I	A	R	I	E	S	■	K	N	I	F	E	D
R	E	S	U	M	E	S	■	A	W	I	R	E	■	■
■	■	■	S	A	S	■	P	R	E	V	■	R	E	Q
B	E	R	T	■	■	E	A	G	L	E	■	S	T	U
L	O	O	■	L	I	N	C	O	L	N	■	O	R	E
U	N	O	■	A	T	T	E	N	■	■	O	N	E	S
E	S	S	■	U	S	E	S	■	Y	M	A	■	■	■
■	■	E	R	R	O	R	■	B	E	A	R	C	A	T
V	I	V	I	A	N	■	B	O	A	T	S	H	O	W
A	P	E	D	■	M	T	R	U	S	H	M	O	R	E
I	S	L	E	■	E	V	E	N	T	■	A	R	T	E
L	O	T	S	■	A	D	D	S	■	N	E	A	T

186

H	A	V	E	N	S	■	S	E	C	■	S	K	I	D
I	D	I	D	I	T	■	T	R	Y	■	K	E	N	O
M	A	R	T	H	A	D	A	N	D	R	I	D	G	E
O	N	T	■	■	R	U	R	■	■	A	P	S	E	S
M	O	U	N	T	V	E	R	N	O	N	■	■	■	■
■	■	■	I	R	E	■	■	O	M	I	C	R	O	N
A	M	I	G	O	■	L	O	R	N	■	R	I	P	E
V	I	R	G	I	N	I	A	M	I	L	I	T	I	A
E	L	A	L	■	A	B	R	A	■	E	S	T	E	R
R	O	S	E	L	L	E	■	■	M	A	T	■	■	■
■	■	■	V	A	L	L	E	Y	F	O	R	G	E
A	L	I	B	I	■	■	I	A	N	■	■	A	O	L
C	O	N	T	I	N	E	N	T	A	L	A	R	M	Y
E	R	L	E	■	B	A	T	■	■	H	A	B	E	A	S
D	E	A	N	■	C	R	Y	■	■	S	T	E	R	N	E

187

```
P E P S   P H O T O   A W E S
A L E E   A A R O N   M A R T
P A T A N S W E R S   A S E A
A T A L O S S   T E E T H
      E L I S     P E T P E E V E
        N O T E R     A U D I S
G T S   A R R E S T   R O S S
R O T   P I T S T O P   U T E
A N A T   B E L U G A   T A X
S T R A P     E N A C T
P O T B E L L Y   K I S S
    A L C O A   I C E D T E A
A C N E   P U T O P T I O N S
P O E T   E R A T O   E L S A
T O W S   S A G A S   D E E P
```

188

```
M A Y E R   H A H A   C A L M
I R E N E   A B E T   O L I O
S C A R E D Y C A T   A S E A
S H R O V E   S T A R T O U T
      L E C H   S C O T
L E O   S L O P   K O A L A S
A T M   A R E A   M I A T A
T H E C O W A R D L Y L I O N
T E N O R   S O L E   N N E
E R S A T Z   N A S H   E E R
    S H I P   I T I S
I S O T O P E S   E N C O D E
B A L I   P A P E R T I G E R
E V E N   E C C E   A F L E A
G E O G   R E A L   T I E R S
```

189

```
G A Z E   S C A P E   S L O W
I G E T   H A B I T   P A S O
B R I C   A M A N A   O C H O
B A T H S H E B A   K N E E L
        A S T   F L A G D A Y
P A T T Y   O T O O L E
A U G U S T   A R R   C E N T
C R I B   O C H E R   A M A H
T A F T   R O O   E S K I M O
    H A M L E T   H E L E N
R E F U G E E   E S O
A R O M A   S O A P O P E R A
G A R P   U L T R A   A T A D
E T T E   S A T E D   G A Z A
D O E R   S W O R E   E L E M
```

190

```
M A T T   S T E A L   S A I L
A R I A   T E S L A   E T T U
D E E R   I N T E L   N E A L
    S T I L L E R A N D A L L
S L O   N E B   L O A M Y
M I N C E S   S W A N K
A T E U P   D E A N   G A S
S H O R T E R A N D S W E E T
H E N   G I L D   P A T S Y
    L O O P Y   P I S T O N
  G I A N T   E O N   O P E
H U N T E R A N D P E C K
A I D E   I M A G E   U N I T
U S E S   P E T E Y   T O R O
T E X T   S N O R E   S W A P
```

191

```
A L E C   A C T U P   A D A M
T E R I   M O U S E   V I B E
N O T T O B E B E L I E V E D
O V E R R I D E   L A R V A E
    I C E   D E M   Y M A
H O W C A N T H A T B E
A P E   S C R A P   S T E A K
L E S S   E A R P S   C A T O
O N T A P   D E L T A   S R O
    G I V E M E A B R E A K
S T A   Q E D   R N A
A R M O U R   S E L E C T E E
Y O U R E N O T S E R I O U S
S O S A   A V A S T   N O R A
O P E L   L A G O S   E N O S
```

192

```
P A T S   M E C C A   S H U E
A C R E   A T A R I   K A R L
S H E R Y L C R O W   E R I E
T E A P O T   N A M E T A G
A D D E D   U N E   I T C H Y
    N A C H O S   S E R
P O E T   L O O   S T R A F E
R I D   J O H N J A Y   N O R
O L D H A T   D U N   S E E R
    Y O N   B A N G L E
C A R T E   E Y E   E A S Y A
I N A S T I R   F A M O U S
G I V E   P E T E R F I N C H
A S E A   S T A L E   L A C E
R E N T   O S S I E   E R A S
```

193

```
S E P I A   S H O D   M A I L
A G E N T   H O U R   A C N E
T O R S O   A P S E   G A T E
      O N E H I T W O N D E R
P R O F E S S     Z A I R E
R E P A S T   M A N O   A N D
Y E A R   P A C I N O
  F L A S H I N T H E P A N
    S H A P E S   E R A T
T A U   I M E T   F I N A L S
A S T O R     L A S T L A P
S H O O T I N G S T A R
S O P H   T A R A   B A R R E
E R I E   E M I T   E D U C E
L E A D   M E N S   L E G A L
```

194

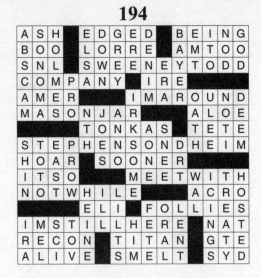

```
A S H   E D G E D   B E I N G
B O O   L O R R E   A M T O O
S N L   S W E E N E Y T O D D
C O M P A N Y   I R E
A M E R     I M A R O U N D
M A S O N J A R     A L O E
    T O N K A S   T E T E
S T E P H E N S O N D H E I M
H O A R   S O O N E R
I T S O     M E E T W I T H
N O T W H I L E     A C R O
    E L I   F O L L I E S
I M S T I L L H E R E   N A T
R E C O N   T I T A N   G T E
A L I V E   S M E L T   S Y D
```

195

```
A C T S   S T R A T A   S A W
C O A T   P E A L E D   U R I
H O P E D I A M O N D   P I N
E L E V E N     U S U R P E D
    E L A T E D   C H E S S
A D D   P L O Y   S E E R
Q U A S H   P E S O   S C A B
U N V E I L S   I N D U L G E
A K I N   O Y E Z   U S U A L
  D A R T   W E A L   B R A
C A S T E   F E S S U P
A P P E A S E   S T I N G S
I R A   P U R P L E H E A R T
R I D   E R A S E S   C I A O
O L E   R E L I E S   E L B A
```

196

```
G A P E D   W A T T S   H O N
A B A C I   I D A H O   A P E
S E L L S O L D I E R   V E X
    A N D E S   D E C E N T
R E L I E D     B A S E H I T
H A I R Y   B R A   P L A T O
E R G S   F O O T H O L D
A S H   P O T S H O T   D N A
    T O U G H I E S   C O U P
S P L A T   E N D   G E C K O
T R I S T A R     B O N K E D
R E T T O N   A G E N T
O F T   S I T S A T U R D A Y
D E E   E M I T S   T A U P E
E R R   A E S O P   S L O T S
```

197

```
C H I E F   C O L A   C A S H
R O D E O   A L A R   L I P O
A L L E N   R E S T   O S L O
B Y E   D E P O S I T S L I P
    S U R E   S H E E T S
T E E T E R T O T T E R
Y I K E S   F O R E   N A B
P R E P   D I T T Y   A O N E
O E D   R I D E   U N I T E
    B U S I N E S S T R I P
P E O R I A   N O E S
U R B A N S P R A W L   R E F
T O O K   T E A M   E V I T A
I D E E   E T T E   S A G A L
N E S S   R E E L   S T A L L
```

198

```
F R O G   B L O B   V A D I S
L I M O   R O M A   I W O N T
A C N E   O B I T   N E W E R
T H I S I N S T A N T   N R A
    A N C   A A A   S T Y
T H A T G O O D N I G H T
R E L   E S A I   L E H R E R
I R E S   S T A   H E D Y
B O X C A R   C L I O   A N A
  T H E O T H E R W O M A N
P A R   R O O   O E D
O D E   O D D S A N D E N D S
B A B E S   A H S O   S E E M
O N E N O   T U T U   S A F E
Y O K E L   E T A T   A R T E
```

199

```
BAAL   RASH   FLOES
EDGY   ADAM   LAURA
AMIN   BOLO   ASTRO
MILDABRASIVE
STEADIES   NORMAN
    ITS   HER   ALE
ABBIE    GAP   AVOW
GRADUATESTUDENT
LILO   MUM    PANGS
ODS   DOG   COS
WEAPON   CARESSES
    ANGRYPATIENT
SPARK   UNIT   METE
ALIKE   TITO   OMEN
TODAY   SCAR   NERO
```

200

```
FROTH   EDNA   ASTO
RODEO   VEAL   STIR
IMEAN   EERO   PANT
   PARDONMYFRENCH
     DAHL   TENDTO
AMOR   DYED   NSA
REPOSE   ROUE   SAP
USEPLAINENGLISH
TAN   URLS   HEEDED
    SAM   OTTO   TEAS
STEPPE   WOOL
  THATSGREEKTOME
EASE   BARR   TOURS
ENOS   DRIP   ESSAY
RENT   FEES   RESTS
```